*THE GUILD*

# Shakespeare

HENRY IV, PART 2
HENRY V

BY
*WILLIAM SHAKESPEARE*

EDITED BY
*JOHN F. ANDREWS*

Forewords by
Patrick Stewart and Christopher Plummer

GuildAmerica Books™
Doubleday Book & Music Clubs, Inc.
Garden City, New York

*Copyright © 1989 by Doubleday Book & Music Clubs, Inc.*
*All Rights Reserved*
*Printed in the United States of America*

*Cover Painting: King Henry V.*
*Painting, frontispiece, endpapers, and book design by Barry Moser.*
*Text is in Baskerville, with display calligraphy by*
*Reassurance Wunder. Binding design by Barry Moser*
*and Hideo Ietaka.*

*Art Director: Diana Klemin, with Rhea Braunstein.*
*Project Editor: Mary Sherwin Jatlow.*

*The Guild Shakespeare™*
*GuildAmerica Books™*
*Trademark registration pending on behalf of Doubleday Book &*
*Music Clubs, Inc.*

# CONTENTS

*FOREWORD*

to

*HENRY IV, PART 2*

by Patrick Stewart

Several years ago, during the filming of a science fiction epic in Mexico City, a group of actors were sitting around killing time, during one of those periods of waiting that movie-making requires. It was a very international group—Americans, British, Germans, Swedes, Italians—and when the subject of Shakespeare arose, each actor listed his favorite plays. The obvious ones were well represented, the ones that put a gleam in a theatre

PATRICK STEWART has played such diverse Shakespearean roles as Henry V, King John, Enobarbus, Oberon, Leontes, Prospero, Touchstone, and King Henry in *Henry IV, Part 2.* He is an Associate Artist of The Royal Shakespeare Company, a Director of Acter Shakespeare Company (U.K.), and an Associate Director of A.C.T.E.R.—A Centre for Theater, Education and Research at the University of California, Santa Barbara.

vii

manager's eye, but of particular interest was the frequency with which the titles of certain "problem" plays appeared: *Coriolanus, Troilus and Cressida* (much loved by actors who have been in it), *Measure for Measure, Pericles,* and, most fondly mentioned, *Henry IV, Part 2.* Not that there is a lack of affection for *Henry IV, Part 1*— on the contrary—but to those who have been in both parts it seems a grand preparation for the major work that is Part 2.

Everyone agreed to its greatness, its richness and diversity of character and language, its complexity of moods and rhythms, and its thrilling structure. There was talk of favorite minor characters (Davy is highly regarded), moments of calm and reflection or of emotional intensity, pieces of stage business. One actor had seen Laurence Olivier's Shallow and vividly described the brilliant physical business of " 'a would manage you his piece thus . . ."

It is a play that actors like to return to again and again, and it can well represent the stages in a career—Prince John, Hal, Henry, Falstaff. It is a great "company" play. Other than the three major characters, I can count fifteen roles that an actor might shine in. It is a play that tests the depths and strengths of a company. No single actor can take the reins of this play and govern each stage of the event. Here the control passes fluidly from actor to actor, restraining indulgence and urging swiftness, lightness, and balance. It demands true ensemble playing, yet bold and vivid interpretations from the principal actors.

Falstaff, Hal, and Henry exist more independently here than in *1 Henry IV*. Although the central issues remain—the morality and responsibility of power, the conflicts between public and private life—we see the three protagonists who are at the center of these issues in a broader series of relationships: Falstaff with the Lord Chief Justice, Doll, Prince John, and Shallow; Hal also with the Lord Chief Justice, with Poins, his brothers, and the Nobles; Henry with his sons and the Earl of Warwick. How different from *1 Henry IV,* where, for example, Falstaff and Hal are on stage together for almost 900 lines; in *2 Henry IV* they share no more than 170. The context of these characters broadens, and with each new encounter a richer life emerges: detailed, idiosyncratic, pulsating with the minutia of city, countryside, and court.

The sense of an English landscape permeates even the most "foreign" of Shakespeare's plays: Warwickshire and London lie like a transparency over the alien worlds of Elsinore, Vienna, Verona, Athens, and Bohemia. But in *2 Henry IV,* Shakespeare moves us across an English countryside whose characteristics impregnate the play and become a tangible part of the audience's experience. "A worm-eaten Hold of rotton Stone," the bleak Northern home of the traitor, Northumberland; the "good Air" of Shallow's orchard arbor; buying a saddle at Pie Corner; dinner at the Lubber's Head in Lumbert Street.

Here is one of the sweetest morsels of dramatic literature, and yet many theatregoers leave it unpicked. Although the two parts of *Henry IV* have been performed in tandem in recent years, the subtitle Part 2 is a curse; box office figures show that though audiences enthusiastically support Part 1, only a percentage will return to see the continuation of the story. And, of course, Part 1 as an entertainment can stand alone, complete and conclusive, the two final couplets confidently reassuring us that, after Shrewsbury, all that is needed is a little tidying up of loose ends. In 1983 when both parts were played in the opening season of the

RSC's new London home at the Barbican, I felt justified at mati-nées in loading those lines with as much uncertainty, doubt, and insecurity as they could bear, while simultaneously firmly in-structing the audience to be back in their seats at 7:30.

This production was not my first encounter with these plays. In 1966 I joined the RSC for the season when Peter Hall revived the *Henry IV*s and *Henry V,* first seen as part of his great Histories Cycle, which included John Barton's reworking of the *Henry VI*s under the title "Wars of the Roses." My contribution was modest, Sir Walter Blunt in Part 1 and Mowbray in Part 2. As Blunt, being given seven of the King's lines in I.i. did not compensate for my having to lie dead for a full fifteen minutes during the battle and being on the receiving end of the biggest putdown in dramatic literature: "this Advertisment is five days old." (This moment comes at the end of the great scene between Hal and his father in III.ii.)

Mowbray has more lines than Blunt, but only two scenes, the second being the wordy, political IV.i–ii, Gaultree Forest. With-out any of the play's major characters, this scene can be tiresome for the audience and is often heavily cut, wrongly in my view. It is a scene of marvelous argument and reason, with sudden bursts of passion fueled by resentment and ancient mistrust. The character of Prince John is most interesting here. Truly his father's son, he acquires real stature, and the contrast with his brother Hal is coolly made. Here is a Prince who seems better fitted to inherit his father's kingdom than does his older brother.

Gaultree Forest is a long scene, for audience and actors alike. In 1966 one of our "spear carriers," John Kane (four years later a wonderful Puck in Peter Brook's *Midsummer Night's Dream*) invented a novel way of keeping the up-stage soldiery amused during those long 350 lines. He fitted a roller-blind device to his tabard which, when operated by a string at the front, revealed colorful and witty notices pinned to the back of his chain-mail. All of this, of course, unseen by the audience and, for a long time, unknown to the principal actors. As the season wore on and his writing inspiration flagged, the notices were replaced by a series of ludicrous and often obscene objects. (I have also recently learned that this same actor for a while fitted a false arm to his shield and was thereby also able to operate a glove puppet to outrageous effect!)

There was another famous practical joker in the scene, Michael Jayston, who played Westmoreland. One matinée, after the truce had been made and the drinking bowl of peace was passing from hand to hand, the seriousness of the moment was somewhat undermined by much spluttering and slopping of "wine" as each actor drank. Only when it reached me did I understand the cause, two frantic goldfish darting about in the bowl.

The placing of the interval is a delicate, contentious matter in Shakespearean productions. It can profoundly affect the impact and rhythm of the central part of a play as well as give prominence and emphasis to one character or theme at the expense of others. At the Barbican in 1983 the Director, Trevor Nunn, insisted that we close the first half with III.i., King Henry's first scene. I was always very uneasy about this: the preceding scene, the Boar's Head with Pistol, Doll Tearsheet, Falstaff, and Hal, was so brilliantly comic and inventive, and moved and excited the audience so, that its conclusion was a natural time for audience respite. The audience often felt this instinctively, so that entering as the King, I would find half of them on their feet, ready to head for the bar. Not the best circumstances in which to begin one's first scene.

The Director's main argument for the positioning of the interval was that the audience must have a knowledge of Henry before the first half ended. He argued that the break would give proper emphasis to Henry's obsession with the Holy Land, his need for release from the consuming guilt of Richard's murder.

This scene opens with the marvelous "sleep" soliloquy. After a few days of rehearsal, Trevor Nunn gave an invaluable note about how to approach it. Henry, he reasoned, is a sick, exhausted, anxiety-ridden insomniac; but to act sickness and exhaustion would have a negative effect on the audience's perception of the man and the scene. Rather, he said, we should play Henry the workaholic, the fighter, whose remaining reserves of energy are being used to capacity. Then the scene becomes active and energised. Instead of being a whine about the cares of Kingship, then, the opening soliloquy becomes an angry argument with "Sleep" and the final, famous line not self-pitying indulgence but amused irony.

To emphasize Henry's bleak, fatalistic view, we included the Quarto lines not found in the Folio:

> O if this were seen,
> The happiest Youth, viewing his Progress through,
> What Peril's past, what Crosses to ensue,
> Would shut the Book and sit him down and die.

It is true that this passage interrupts what seems to be a natural thought progression through to Richard and Northumberland, but the bonus is in the sense of a feverish mind suddenly taking a turning into a bleak and despairing cul-de-sac before returning to the preoccupation with Richard and the justification for the usurpation.

Henry has only one other scene, IV.iv and IV.v being continuous action, and it is, in effect, his death scene. But few death scenes can contain such intricate shifts and changes—and, for Henry, a rollercoaster of emotions.

Following Nunn's principle for III.i, the scene opens confidently and optimistically. But after the loaded cross-questioning of the Princes, Henry is again chewing on the bitter topic of Hal's vicious and dissolute life. Although it is the grim future of his country that seems to fill Henry with such despair, there lies behind this the shadow of a personal and filial betrayal. He feels the "Serpent's Tooth" that Lear would later complain of in his outcry against the ingratitude of his daughters.

Henry asks for music, a surprising and uncharacteristic request. It reveals, however, much more than the poet/playwright at work. It shows us the man of the theatre, the showman/manipulator, the "director," providing the actor playing Hal with a backing, a "music-track" for his speech to his supposed dead father. Without Henry's instruction it would be a brave—or perhaps vulgar—director who would put a music cue here. With it, it becomes a piece of unexpected theatre.

What a painful scene. Family blood-letting as shocking as anything at Shrewsbury. In my experience, no modern playwright, unless it be Edward Albee, can communicate so cruelly, so passionately, so lovingly the anguish of domestic pain and need.

In a moment of intense emotion Shakespeare's audacity in using a simple, sometimes banal phrase has always thrilled me. Lear's "Pray you, undo this Button"; Ophelia's "I hope all will be well"; Leontes' "O, she's warm." In this scene we used the Folio's "O, my Son" at IV.v.183. On the days when we played both parts, the accumulation of feeling released into that line made it necessary for me to apply great restraint.

The master stroke of the scene, however, is Shakespeare's decision to end it with a joke. I never dared hope the audience would laugh at "Which vainly I suppos'd the Holy Land," but often there was the unmistakable sense of an audience smiling.

*Henry IV, Part 2* is richly sprinkled with these heart-stopping one-liners. When the play is only minutes old, Morton's hope-dashing line "I ran from Shrewsbury" always makes my scalp crawl. Hard on that comes Northumberland's "Why, he is dead." This is an unsung scene that always excites me, though never more than in Peter Hall's version, which began with the frantic hammering of steel on the timber of Northumberland's gate. There was once a memorable night during this scene when Northumberland, crying "and hence thou sickly Coif," flung from his head not only coif, but wig. Not only "crafty sick" but crafty bald too.

Falstaff's "I am old, I am old" will cut short the most careless laughter. And when the Lord Chief Justice, the Princes, and the Nobles meet after Henry's death, John of Lancaster's remark "We meet like men that had forgot to speak" is an icy assessment of everyone's apprehension.

Nothing in the play, however, touches me more than Shallow's remark "now comes in the Sweet o' th' Night." I had always assumed that this was the same as Falstaff's "sweetest Morsel of the Night" in II.iv. That is until the summer came to Warwickshire during that season of 1966. On nights off or at weekends I sat in the garden of my cottage, in a small orchard, on the edge of a cornfield; shortly after sunset, while those extraordinary twilights deepened, I often became aware of a delicate and beautiful scent in the air. It was a neighbor, a countryman sitting with us one evening, who at this moment said "Ah, there's the sweet of the night." Later he explained how the night-scented plants release their aroma at a certain moment after sunset.

There have been many times in Stratford—on stage, on the rehearsal floor, in the street, in the fields—when I have felt a presence at my shoulder. But never have I felt it more sharply than when the sixteenth century breathed again in my Warwickshire garden, as potently as it breathes in every corner of this masterpiece, the too often overlooked poor relation of *Henry IV, Part 1*.

*FOREWORD*
to
*HENRY V*
by Christopher Plummer

Let the Lords of Academe cavil if they must; let purists carp; let
critics moan that it is not among the "great" plays, that, in fact, it
is not a play at all, but an outworn allegory; that it has nothing in
it save some fragmented scenes arranged to accompany one or

---

CHRISTOPHER PLUMMER is one of the established classical actors of
his generation in the theatre today. He has performed almost all the
great roles in the Shakespearean canon, ranging from Hamlet, Macbeth,
Richard III, and Iago, to Benedick, Mercutio, and the two Mark Antonys.
Apart from his starring appearances over the years on the stages of
Broadway and London's West End, he has been a leading player at Great
Britain's National Theatre, The Royal Shakespeare Company and, in its
formative years, the Stratford Shakespeare Festival of Canada. Mr. Plummer is a veteran of over forty motion pictures, which have gained him
international renown.

two familiar "arias"; that even before the Empire had decided to crumble, the work had long since served its purpose; that it is merely flag-waving and thoroughly old hat; that it simply out-Herods Herod; and, worst of all sins, that it insists upon glorifying war!

Well! Let 'em grumble if they will, for Shakespeare's *Henry the Fifth* will forever remain one of the glories of literature in the theatre—a masterpiece of epic poetry and uncannily modern prose. A play rich in humanity, it is heroic and romantic, ruthless and profound, crackling with humour and charged with pathos. There is more variety of character within its impassioned sweep than in most of its author's offerings. It is a work for all sizes and ages. And, in spite of what some may think, it can change with the times as swiftly and as easily as the chameleon changes its colours. It has been conceived and executed with a burning energy and a searing imagination that are superhuman in their powers; and it contains, in its opening passage alone, the most eloquent description of the magic of the stage that was ever written by man.

You may have gathered that *Henry V* has long been a favourite of mine! I have known it like a good friend; for at various intervals during my life the old war-horse has quite frequently crossed my path, and each time has not only recaptured my excitement, my respect, and my love, but has brought me nothing but the greatest of good luck!

I had read quite a few Shakespeare plays before I was fourteen, and *Henry V* was one to linger in the mind. My artistic mother, God bless her, had seen to it that from the age of six on, I was taken to every museum, concert hall, and theatre that was remotely possible. From the gallery I watched such actors as Gielgud, Wolfit, Redgrave, Barrault, Vilar, Gerard Phillipe, Edwige Feuillere, Elizabeth Bergner, and that indomitable creature of the thousand faces and voices—the invincible Ruth Draper.

One day at school we were hustled into the assembly hall, and some old actor I didn't know, with long hair, a monocle, and a faded "Director's suit," declaimed Henry's "Once more unto the Breach" speech at us. I was in heaven of course (anything theatrical got me going); but strangely, all the children present, even the most cynical of them, sat spellbound, enthralled, riveted to their seats. The old boy was, to say the least, a bit of a ham, but, by God, those stirring words had found their mark *that* happy morning!

A few weeks later, as part of our English course, the school was given the day off to see Laurence Olivier's newly arrived and highly acclaimed film version of the play. Well, I tell you! Never had I seen Shakespeare presented like that! So modern, so natural, so full of action, and so damned attractive! I was hooked! In those days I fancied myself as a mimic of unusual brilliance (little horror that I was) and, with the help of one other wayward chum, would regale the class during breaks with unflattering imitations of various masters. This time, mightily inspired by the *Henry* film, I committed "Once more unto the Breach" to memory and I waited for the first break the next morning. Then, mixing the vocal style of the old actor with that of Olivier, I hurled at my captive fellow-students a barrage of iambic pentameter I was determined they'd never forget. It must have worked, for they rallied at the end, good little scouts that they were, responding with some pretty convincing war-cries of their own! It was at that moment that I somehow knew what the future held in store—O Fate, thou cruel and irresistible siren—that I, heaven help me, was to be sentenced for life to the theatre! Little did I think that ten years hence I would be the youngest of my country to lead the miraculous new Stratford Shakespearean Festival of Canada, both on home ground and at the Edinburgh Festival, as none other than King Henry the Fifth!

Ours was a unique production. French actors portrayed the French court and invaluably brought to the play a whole other world—a whole other life! Visually stunning, yet extremely intimate and human, our *Henry V* became the story of a rather angry young man reluctant to shed the debauchery of his youth and assume the responsibility of a kingship he did not want, only to discover at the last moment on the battlefield facing those insuperable odds that, without being aware, he at last had grown up: just another soldier, but a King nonetheless. It was a far cry from the rousing piece of Churchillian propaganda of the Forties which England "in its finest hour" had demanded of the film. But it was very raw and very right for the mid-Fifties: the emergence of John Osborne, the growing influence of Brecht, and the birth of the anti-hero. It was like quaffing gallons of champagne to act in that play: I had the best time of my life and I shan't be anything but eternally grateful to Henry and his followers, for they literally gave me my career.

Twenty-five years later I had the audacity to attempt the role again, this time playing the Chorus as well! Can you imagine the arrogance?! Of course the press rightly clobbered me for my aging Henry, but my Chorus was praised. Chorus being an ageless creature, I shall go on playing him, if I can, till I'm ninety. Lately I've been having the most fun of all performing the concert version to William Walton's music with my friend Sir Neville Marriner conducting the symphony orchestras of London, Minneapolis, and Washington. It's a feast! I get to play Henry, Chorus, Falstaff (from *Henry IV*), Duke of Burgundy, and Williams all in a dinner-jacket. Perhaps one day in my dotage, I might even get to play the French Princess as well! Who knows?

There is an afternoon in London in the mid-Seventies I shall never forget. It was the anniversary of the victory at Agincourt, and the Dean of Westminster arranged a celebration in the Abbey, where of course the famous young King is interred. The Dean collected all the best-known living "Henry the Fifths" and huddled us into the narrow choirstalls that form a direct path to the Great Altar.

Filling both sides of the stalls, there we sat, all us "Henrys"— staring at each other. Then the senior "Henry" of us all, Sir Laurence Olivier, walked to the altar, turned, and gave us the "Crispin's Day" speech to honour the occasion. He spoke it beautifully, very quietly, with great dignity and simplicity. The silence was devastating as those words echoed through the vastness of the Abbey. High above our heads, the late afternoon sun shone through stained glass, casting long thin shafts that crossed each other in myriads of coloured lights which spilled upon the ancient stones. It was a haunting moment. One could almost believe that the Shades of Garrick and Irving had stolen away from Poet's Corner and now stood rapt in attention among the dark shadows beside us; and that even Henry of Monmouth himself, tiny Henry, had risen from his effigy in the next room and had come forward, his head pressed against the arches, to listen in the stillness. It seemed for one brief interval that some five hundred years had slipped away and we were suddenly there, all of us, again at Agincourt—and then the moment vanished. Not without leaving me with a deeply thrilling shiver down my spine which anyone, I swear, might have felt at that moment—anyone that is, who is a lover of pageantry, of chivalry, of daring, of the mystery and romance of the old Plantagenet days of the wind in the flags, of the rally of distant trumpets, of the everlasting majesty of language, and of the genius it took to have kept it all—these many centuries—so vividly and so wondrously alive!

Editor's Introduction to

*HENRY IV, PART 2*
and
*HENRY V*

The plays in this volume are among the most intimately related of Shakespeare's works, but it is hard to imagine a pair that have fared more differently in fortune. Critics have usually spoken warmly about *Henry IV, Part 2,* and as Patrick Stewart notes in his delightful foreword to the play, the same has been true of the actors who have had the opportunity to appear in one of its many rewarding roles. Because its title would seem to suggest that *2 Henry IV* is incapable of standing on its own, though, it has rarely enjoyed the kind of success it deserves at the box office. Audiences have ignored it in droves. By contrast, as Christopher Plummer reminds us in his fervent prologue to *Henry V,* it is the critics who have habitually voted against the final installment of Shakespeare's Henriad. Because of its stirring poetry, however, and the potency of its appeal to patriotic sentiment, this historical pageant has long been a favorite with audiences, not only in the theatre but, thanks to Laurence Olivier's vibrant film (1944), in movie houses and on television screens the world over.

Taken together, the two plays complete Shakespeare's triptych on a monarch of epic, if not mythic, stature. *2 Henry IV* picks up where *1 Henry IV* left off, and as it hovers over the waning days of Prince Hal's care-worn father it extends our understanding of what it means to wear an "uneasy" crown in the fallen world of post-medieval England. But of course that is not the play's primary purpose, which is to dramatize the final stages of young Harry's preparation to inherit the throne as the "Star of England." Once the new ruler begins wielding his scepter, *Henry V* sweeps both "Warlike Harry" and us across the Channel to France. Here we see this most dynamic of leaders in a trial by fire that tests his men and his mettle to the utmost. And when he emerges both strengthened and victorious, we are invited to celebrate what Shakespeare and his contemporaries looked back upon as England's finest hour.

Both works display the protagonist against a large and varied backdrop. In *2 Henry IV* we see the Prince in an urban setting that teems with whores and tapsters, swaggerers and thieves. In the play's vignettes of lowlife London we encounter not only the vitality but all the vices and diseases that Elizabethans associated with haunts like Eastcheap, Smithfield, and Lumbert Street. Meanwhile, as we follow the course of the ills that afflict the country at large, we visit the Gloucestershire farm of Justice Shallow, the strongholds of the northern Nobility, and the somber chambers of the King and his Court at Westminster.

In *Henry V* we see England through the eyes of the French,

and France through the eyes of the English. Along the way, through our encounters with soldiers like MacMorrice, Jamy, and Fluellen, we come to appreciate the benefits that accrue when an English monarch is able to enlist the support and win the devotion of his neighbors from Ireland, Scotland, and Wales. And at the end, as we observe the dynastic wooing that will briefly unite the thrones of two traditional enemies, we glimpse a moment of European harmony that is all the more touching for its fragility in a world that will not stand still for happy ever afters.

*2 Henry IV* was probably written in late 1596 or early 1597, shortly after Shakespeare completed *1 Henry IV*. There are signs that it was well along before protests from the powerful Cobham family forced Shakespeare and his company to change the name of the fat knight from Oldcastle to Falstaff (for more on this matter, see the introduction to Volume 3), but whether it was ever performed with Oldcastle in the role is uncertain. If it was not completed by early spring, it may well have been interrupted for the playwright to turn his hand to *The Merry Wives of Windsor,* which seems most likely to have had its first performance in April of 1597. But by the autumn of 1597 at the latest, it was probably in regular repertory with Falstaff firmly installed, and by this point it had no doubt assumed essentially the form it had when it was first published in 1600, in a quarto that may well have been printed from Shakespeare's own draft of the playscript.

For some reason the Quarto originally emerged without the scene (III.i) in which King Henry makes his initial appearance in the drama; shortly thereafter a second issue was published to correct the omission. Not included in either version of the Quarto, however, were eight brief passages (adding up to slightly more than 150 lines) that first saw print in the 1623 Folio text of the play. It is conceivable that at least some of these passages were added later. Most scholars now infer, however, that they were part of the original text but were cut, either to shorten the script for performance or to comply with the orders of a Court censor who insisted on the deletion of material that might be politically sensitive. Four of the passages refer to the deposition of King Richard II, and by 1600 (for reasons outlined in the introduction to Volume 5) that was a very touchy subject.

Like other modern editions of *2 Henry IV,* the Guild text follows the First Quarto except for those passages that are unique to the Folio printing. For the text of *Henry V* (which was probably written and first performed during the spring or early summer of 1599 and which initially appeared in print in a corrupt, unauthorized quarto in 1600) the Guild edition follows the version that appeared for the first time in the 1623 Folio. Here again the authoritative printing seems to have been based on the playwright's own manuscript of the play.

As with *Richard II* and *1 Henry IV,* Shakespeare's primary source for the historical material in *2 Henry IV* and *Henry V* was the 1587 edition of Raphael Holinshed's *Chronicles of England, Scotland, and Ireland.* Once again, though, he seems to have drawn on other sources as well, among them Edward Hall's *Union of the Two Noble and Illustre Houses of Lancaster and York* (1548), Samuel Daniel's *The First Four Books of the Civil Wars Between the Two Houses of Lancaster and York* (1595), and an anonymous play of the mid-1590s on *The Famous Victories of Henry the Fifth.* The playwright also seems to have consulted two books by the historian John Stow, *The Chronicles of England* (1580) and *The Annals of England* (1592), and an influential treatise on *The Governor* (1531) by Sir Thomas Eliot. Meanwhile, as usual, he drew freely on his knowledge of the Bible, the Book of Common Prayer, the writings of Erasmus and other Renaissance humanists, and a broad assortment of legends and folktales about the wild prince who grew up to become the bravest and wisest of England's warrior-kings.

What Shakespeare did with those source materials is, as always, the grand masterpiece to observe. In *2 Henry IV* he redeployed many of the same devices he had put to such brilliant use in *1 Henry IV*. Once again he juxtaposed scenes involving the Court or the Nobility with scenes in the London taverns and scenes in the countryside. Once again he arranged those juxtapositions so that comic situations (normally in prose or in a verse quite different from the stately diction of the more elevated scenes) would echo and thereby comment on more serious situations. And once again he drew on Biblical paradigms and figurative motifs to structure the action and guide the audience's response to its ethical, political, and spiritual implications.

In many instances the episodes in *2 Henry IV* parallel similar episodes in *1 Henry IV*. Thus, for example, we have two scenes in each play where Hal and Poins first plot (II.ii in modern editions) and then execute (II.iv) a trap to catch Falstaff off guard; in both cases the audience is given an opportunity to delight in the resourcefulness with which the play's Father of Lies extricates himself from what would otherwise be a ruinous dilemma. Other parallels include Falstaff's witty catechisms on Honor and on Sack (in V.i of *1 Henry IV* and IV.iii of *2 Henry IV,* respectively), his abuse of the royal commission to conscript soldiers (in IV.ii and III.ii), and his theft of honors in "battle" (in V.iv and IV.iii).

There is, of course, no precedent in *1 Henry IV* for the most painful event in either play, the rejection scene that concludes *2 Henry IV.* But this moment too is anticipated in II.iv.529–30 of *1 Henry IV* when the play-acting Falstaff says "banish plump Jack, and banish all the World" and the Prince replies "I do, I will." In the earlier, comic scene, Falstaff assumes that the "Lion's Whelp" is only kidding. And, true to form, in the final scene of *2 Henry IV* he initially hears no cause for alarm when the new King tells the "Old Man" to begone and "fall to [his] Prayers" (V.v.48).

Part of what makes Falstaff the quintessential "old man" in both plays is what he facetiously calls "the Disease of Not List'ning, the Malady of Not Marking" (I.ii.134–35). To a degree unmatched by any other character in the Henriad, Falstaff is willfully deaf to anything he doesn't wish to heed. Others may be called to account for their debts and their crimes; others may find it necessary to treat the Lord Chief Justice and the younger brother of the Crown Prince with at least a show of respect; others may feel the need to prepare their souls for the Last Judgment. But not Falstaff. With each escape from requital, he becomes more and more confident that he is exempt not only from "the Laws of England" (V.iii.134–35) but from the laws of God. And that, in the final analysis, is why the new King is compelled to turn his back on the holiday jester he describes as the "Tutor and the Feeder of my Riots" (V.v.63).

*2 Henry IV* begins with an exhortation to the audience: "Open your Ears." This advice comes from Rumor, a proverbially unreliable source, to be sure, but in this case a spokesman who proffers wise counsel. Rumor's words echo Matthew 11:15 ("He that hath ears to hear, let him hear"), a passage to which several incidents allude in *1 Henry IV,* and they warn us that "Not List'ning" is the surest way to fall victim to "Slanders," "False Reports," and the other traps (Induction, 6, 8, 16, 40) that lie in wait for the unwary.

A form of this malady proves to be the undoing of the Archbishop and his rebellious allies at Gaultree Forest, and we are reminded that a related malady, "winking" or not seeing, was what led Hotspur to leap "into Destruction" (I.iii.33) at the head of an earlier insurrection against the King. The antidote to both maladies is what the Lord Chief Justice calls "cold Consid'rance" (V.ii.97), and that is the quality the new King manifests at the end of the play when he embraces Falstaff's old Nemesis as the proper "Father" to the new monarch's "Youth."

"Cold Consid'rance" is more or less equivalent to what Duke Theseus calls "cool Reason" in V.i.6 of *A Midsummer Night's Dream,* and, for better or for worse, it epitomizes the "new man" who emerges from the Coronation at Westminster Abbey. It is an aspect of the spiritual "Consideration" (divine wisdom) that Canterbury praises in I.i.28 of *Henry V,* and among other things it refers to the objectivity that prevents a person from being undone by such misleaders as "Imagination" or wishful thinking (I.iii.31), "Surmises" (erroneous inferences), "smooth Comforts false" (flattery), and "Jealousy's Conjectures" (unfounded suspicions).

Ideally, "cold Consid'rance" in a ruler entails temperance (control of his passions), prudence (political sagacity), and justice (sound judgment in the administration of law). But unless it is balanced by such "warm" qualities as love, compassion, and humility, it can turn what would otherwise be virtues into the worst of all vices: a proud aloofness that comes across as unfeeling, calculating, and judgmental.

Prince John exhibits some of the negative aspects of "cold Consid'rance" in the "Christian Care" (IV.ii.115) he shows the rebels (particularly Colevile of the Dale) at Gaultree Forest. For that reason we are less reassured than we might otherwise be when we hear Prince John commend the "Fair Proceeding" he sees in the way his older brother has provided for his "wonted Followers" (V.v.100). By the end of *2 Henry IV* it seems inevitable that Falstaff and the other "good Lads in Eastcheap" must either reform themselves or fall away. But when the newly crowned King banishes Sir John from his presence and announces to all "the World" that "I have turn'd away my former Self" (V.v.58–59), we can't help wondering if in killing "the Heart" of an old man (*Henry V*, II.i.94–95) he hasn't also impaired the heart of the "new man" he is now resolved to be.

That question remains alive in *Henry V*. Because, for all his virtues, the King we see in this play strikes many viewers as much less appealing than the "nimble-footed madcap Prince of Wales" we enjoyed in *1* and *2 Henry IV*.

Critics of Shakespeare's portrayal of Henry V note that the King's French campaign can be construed as a war of aggression. They point out that its primary, though unstated, purpose is "to busy Giddy Minds" at home with "Foreign Quarrels" (*2 Henry IV*, IV.v.209–10) that will keep England's unruly Nobles out of mischief for a while. They note that at the same time that he seizes on the "Salic Law" to justify a claim to the French throne, the King is cleverly diverting our eyes from the flimsiness of his own claim to the English throne (a title that is being implicitly challenged by the Earl of Cambridge in the conspiracy exposed in II.ii). They note that the Archbishop who expounds the desired interpretation of the Salic Law in I.ii has been shown in the preceding scene to have ulterior motives for the reading he provides (he figures that a war with France will busy the minds of those who wish to despoil the Church of its rich land holdings). And they note that in his conduct of the war the King sometimes appears irresponsible (as in his threat to unleash a savage band of rapists and murderers on the besieged Harfleur in III.iii).

It is inconceivable that Shakespeare was unaware of these "problems" with his presentation of "the Mirror of all Christian Kings" (II.Chorus.6). He clearly recognized the craftiness of his Henry V, and he obviously knew that it would be possible to highlight rather than understate the devious aspects of the King's personality. But of course he didn't. What he did instead was to allow those characteristics to be visible in a dark corner of his canvas while the artist focused most of the viewer's attention on those features of the King's reign that offered qualities to admire and deeds to commemorate.

In IV.iii.92–94 of *Macbeth,* Malcolm lists what he identifies as the "King-becoming Graces":

> Justice, Verity, Temp'rance, Stableness,
> Bounty, Perseverance, Mercy, Lowliness,
> Devotion, Patience, Courage, Fortitude.

All of these "graces" are on exhibit in the Henry V of Shakespeare's play. And so are the attributes commended in a simpler scheme that seems to have provided a touchstone for the playwright's contemporaries: a triad comprised of the Lion (a traditional symbol of strength and command), the Fox (a symbol of political acumen and wisdom), and the Pelican (a symbol of piety and self-sacrifice). The Lion and the Fox were most familiar to Elizabethans from Machiavelli's notorious treatise on *The Prince* (published five years after his death in 1532), and their attributes are what we find embodied in "cold Consid'rance." The image of the Pelican derived from medieval bestiaries in which a mother bird was shown offering the blood from her own breast to feed offspring who would otherwise starve.

When Shakespeare gives us "A little touch of Harry in the Night" (IV.Chorus.47), mingling with his men and sharing their discomforts and anxieties on the eve of Agincourt, he makes it clear that this is a King for whom "Ceremony" (IV.i.251–97) is a livery of service rather than a robe of pompous glory. When, shortly thereafter, he has that same Harry inspire his men with his stirring speech on Saint Crispin's Day, he reminds us that this is also a master of Ceremony in its role as the bond that holds a people firm to their most cherished values and traditions.

In some ways, *Henry V* is the most "theatrical" of Shakespeare's works. The Chorus keeps us ever mindful that we are not really in "the vasty Fields of France," that we are actually in the Globe playhouse, a simple "Wooden O," with our eyes glued on what Aristotle defined as nothing more or less than "the imitation of an action." Notwithstanding the Chorus' repeated apologies for the inadequacies of that imitation, the history of *Henry V* in performance would suggest that unless we are gravely deficient in "Imaginary Puissance" indeed, we cannot avoid being carried away by what is arguably the theatre's most eloquent paean to action.

# HENRY IV, PART 2

# NAMES OF THE ACTORS

RUMOR, The Presenter

KING HENRY THE FOURTH
PRINCE HENRY, afterwards crowned King Henry the Fifth

PRINCE JOHN OF LANCASTER
HUMPHREY, DUKE OF
    GLOUCESTER
THOMAS, DUKE OF CLARENCE

Sons to Henry the Fourth
and brethren
to Henry the Fifth

HENRY PERCY, EARL OF
    NORTHUMBERLAND
THE ARCHBISHOP OF YORK
LORD MOWBRAY
LORD HASTINGS
TRAVERS
MORTON
FAUCONBRIDGE
SIR JOHN COLEVILLE

Opposites against
King Henry the Fourth

EARL OF WARWICK
EARL OF WESTMORELAND
EARL OF SURREY
SIR JOHN BLUNT
GOWER
HARCOURT
THE LORD CHIEF JUSTICE
A SERVANT of the LORD
    CHIEF JUSTICE

Of the King's Party

POINS
SIR JOHN FALSTAFF
BARDOLPH
PISTOL

Irregular Humourists

PETO
FALSTAFF'S PAGE       Irregular Humourists

ROBERT SHALLOW
SILENCE       Country Justices

DAVY, Servant to Shallow

FANG and SNARE, Two Sergeants

RALPH MOULDY
SIMON SHADOW
THOMAS WART       Country Soldiers
FRANCIS FEEBLE
PETER BULLCALF

NORTHUMBERLAND'S WIFE
PERCY'S WIDOW, LADY PERCY (Kate)

HOSTESS (Mistress Quickly)
DOLL TEARSHEET
FRANCIS and other DRAWERS

BEADLES and other OFFICERS
GROOMS
PORTER
MESSENGER
SOLDIERS
LORDS
MUSICIANS
ATTENDANTS

Speaker of the EPILOGUE

*Note: With minor modifications, the roster provided here derives from that in the First Folio.*

INDUCTION  *An induction is a speech or dramatic segment that precedes the main action of a play. The best-known example in Shakespeare is the two-scene Induction that introduces* The Taming of the Shrew. *Lines 35–37 indicate that Rumor's induction to* Henry IV, Part 2 *is delivered in front of the decaying castle and fortress (the "Hole" or "Hold") of the Earl of Northumberland. The Castle's inhabitants are anxiously awaiting reliable reports about the just-concluded Battle of Shrewsbury (probably pronounced "Shrowsbury").*

S.D.  Rumor painted full of Tongues.  *The attire of the actor personifying Rumor probably derives ultimately from Book IV of Vergil's* Aeneid, *where* Fama *(Fame or Rumor) is depicted as a monster comprised entirely of eyes, ears, and tongues.*

1  Open your Ears  *This exhortation, addressed to the audience, is an echo of similar admonitions in both parts of the* Henry IV *plays.*

2  The vent of Hearing  *the ear.*

3  the Orient  *the east. Rumor's course to "the drooping West" follows that of the Sun.*

4  still unfold  *constantly disclose.*

5  commenced  *here to be pronounced as a three-syllable word.*

9  covert Enmity  *secret, treacherous malice.*

12  Make fearful Musters  *cause military forces to be summoned in anticipation of rumored attacks.*

4

# Induction

*Enter Rumor painted full of Tongues.*

RUMOR  Open your Ears: for which of you will stop
The vent of Hearing when loud Rumor speaks?
I from the Orient to the drooping West
(Making the Wind my Post-horse) still unfold
The Acts commenced on this Ball of Earth.                    5
Upon my Tongues communal Slanders ride,
The which in ev'ry Language I pronounce,
Stuffing the Ears of Men with False Reports.
I speak of Peace while covert Enmity,
Under the smile of Safety, wounds the World.                 10
And who but Rumor, who but only I,
Make fearful Musters and prepar'd Defense

13 big *both (a) pregnant, and (b) threatening,*

14 Is thought . . . War *Here* child *and* Tyrant *are probably to be treated, respectively, as two- and one-syllable words.*

15 And no such matter *when there is no truth to such suspicions.*

16 Jealousy's Conjectures *the suppositions* (Surmises) *aroused by suspicion* (Jealousy). *Modern editions normally follow the First Folio's punctuation and print "jealousies, conjectures." There is no comma in the Quarto version.*

17 a Stop *a vent-hole to be fingered by a pipe-player to produce a note. Rumor is depicted as a "blunt" instrument (indeed, one with but a single stop), so easy to play that even the many-headed mob can make discordant noise with it.*

21 anathomize *Here the spelling suggests a play on (a)* anatomize, *dissect, and (b)* anathemize (anathematize), *curse.*

22 my Household *Rumor refers to the audience in the theatre.*

23 run before *flee, carrying news of.*

28 Office *function, duty.*

29 Harry Monmouth *Prince Henry (Hal), who was born at Monmouth in Wales.*

31 the Douglas' *the Earl of Douglas'.*

37 crafty sick *Rumor gives us our first clear indication that Northumberland's illness, which kept him home from Shrewsbury, was feigned.*

Whiles the big Year, swol'n with some other
    Grief,
Is thought with child by the stern Tyrant War,
And no such matter? Rumor is a Pipe                     15
Blown by Surmises, Jealousy's Conjectures,
And of so easy and so plain a Stop
That the blunt Monster with uncounted Heads,
The still discordant wav'ring Multitude,
Can play upon it. But what need I thus                  20
My well-known Body to anathomize
Among my Household? Why is Rumor here?
I run before King Harry's Victory,
Who in a bloody Field by Shrewsbury
Hath beaten down young Hotspur and his Troops,         25
Quenching the Flame of bold Rebellion
Ev'n with the Rebels' Blood. But what mean I
To speak so true at first? My Office is
To noise abroad that Harry Monmouth fell
Under the wrath of Noble Hotspur's Sword               30
And that the King before the Douglas' Rage
Stoop'd his anointed Head as low as Death.
This have I rumor'd through the peasant Towns
Between that Royal Field of Shrewsbury
And this worm-eaten Hole of ragged Stone,              35
Where Hotspur's Father, old Northumberland,
Lies crafty sick. The Posts come tiring on,
And not a man of them brings other News
Than they have learnt of me: from Rumor's
    Tongues
They bring smooth Comforts false, worse than
    true Wrongs.                              *Exit.*    40

7

I.i     *The setting remains at Northumberland's castle at Warkworth.*

1       BARDOLPH   *The Lord Bardolph who meets with Northumber-*
        *land here is a very different character from the ruddy-faced*
        *companion of Falstaff and the other Boar's Head Tavern*
        *ne'er-do-wells.*
        keeps   *maintains, guards.*

2       What   *who. Here "what" is used because the Porter's question*
        *has as much to do with the visitor's title and affiliation*
        *(whether friend or enemy) as with his name.*

3       attend   *call on.*

5       knock but at the Gate   *As he speaks this line, the Porter*
        *probably gestures to one of the three doors that would have*
        *been at stage level in the Elizabethan theatre. Lord Bardolph*
        *has probably entered one of the stage's side doors and knocked*
        *at one of the other doors; if so, Northumberland probably*
        *enters from the third door. Whether the Porter speaks from*
        *behind a door at stage level or from a window above is a*
        *matter of conjecture.*

8

# Act One

## Scene 1

*Enter the Lord Bardolph at one Door.*

BARDOLPH   Who keeps the Gate here, ho? Where is
    the Earl?

*Enter Porter*

PORTER   What shall I say you are?
BARDOLPH                     Tell thou the Earl
    That the Lord Bardolph doth attend him here.
PORTER   His Lordship is walk'd forth into the
      Orchard:
    Please it your Honor knock but at the Gate,         5
    And he himself will answer.

*Enter the Earl of Northumberland.*

9

8     **Stratagem**   *Northumberland may mean "piece of strategy," deception; but it is more likely that he refers to the violent clashes that result from such military plotting.*

10    **high Feeding**   *an overly rich diet that causes excessive outbursts of energy.*

11    **bears down**   *knocks down, overwhelms.*

12    **certain**   *trustworthy.*

16    **both the Blunts**   *Shakespeare mentions only one Blunt (Sir Walter) in 1 Henry IV; he is killed by the Earl of Douglas. In all probability, the reference to "both the Blunts" is to be attributed to the same unreliability that characterizes Rumor's other "News."*

19    **Brawn**   *a fatted boar or pig.*
       **Hulk**   *a heavy ship for the carrying of large cargoes.*

21    **follow'd**   *conducted, executed. Lord Bardolph may also be referring to the pursuit of forces in retreat from the front line of battle.*
       **fairly**   *beautifully, triumphantly.*

23    **Fortunes**   *victories, good fortunes.*
       **How is this deriv'd?**   *What is the source of this report?*

26    **good Name**   *both (a) noble birth, and (b) worthy reputation.*

27    **freely**   *both (a) voluntarily, and (b) volubly.*

BARDOLPH                          Here comes the Earl.

*Exit Porter.*

NORTHUMBERLAND   What News, Lord Bardolph?
    Ev'ry minute now
  Should be the Father of some Stratagem.
  The Times are wild; Contention, like a Horse
  Full of high Feeding, madly hath broke loose,       10
  And bears down all before him.

BARDOLPH                          Noble Earl,
  I bring you certain News from Shrewsbury.

NORTHUMBERLAND   Good, and God will.

BARDOLPH                    As good as heart can wish:
  The King is almost wounded to the Death,
  And in the Fortune of my Lord your Son,       15
  Prince Harry slain outright; and both the Blunts
  Kill'd by the hand of Douglas; young Prince John
  And Westmerland and Stafford fled the Field,
  And Harry Monmouth's Brawn, the Hulk Sir John,
  Is Pris'ner to your Son. O such a Day,       20
  So fought, so follow'd, and so fairly won,
  Came not till now to dignify the Times
  Since Caesar's Fortunes!

NORTHUMBERLAND              How is this deriv'd?
  Saw you the Field? Came you from Shrewsbury?

BARDOLPH   I spake with one, my Lord, that came
    from thence,       25
  A Gentleman well bred and of good Name,
  That freely rend'red me these News for true.

*Enter Travers.*

11

30    over-rode    *overtook (riding in the opposite direction, as line 34 makes clear) and then outrode on the trip back.*

32    haply    *by chance (as a result of his fortuitous meeting with me).*
      retale    *retell, repeat. Modern editions normally adapt the Folio spelling and print "retail" here.*

33    Tidings    *Like* News *(line 27), this word can function as either a singular or a plural noun.*

34    Sir John Umfrevile    *It has been plausibly suggested that this was Shakespeare's original name for Lord Bardolph; if so, the name probably survives in the Quarto text because of a lapse in the revision of the printer's manuscript. In the First Quarto "Umfrevile" also appears as the speech designation (emended to Travers in this edition) for line 161.*

37    forspent    *completely spent, exhausted.*

42    Spur was cold    *Travers puns on Harry Percy's nickname; Northumberland will continue the wordplay in lines 49–50.*

44    strook    *struck.*
      armed Heels    *spurs. This reference to the messenger's "hot spurs" is a poignant reminder of how "cold" Hotspur's heels now are.*

45    Jade    *normally a worn-out nag; in this case, a strong horse that is simply "forspent" and "bloodi'd" from battle.*

46    the Rowel-head    *the pointed spur-head.*

53    Silken Point    *a cord or lace that was used to fasten a man's hose (breeches) to his doublet (tight-fitting jacket).*

12

NORTHUMBERLAND    Here comes my servant Travers, who I sent
On Tuesday last to listen after News.

BARDOLPH    My Lord, I over-rode him on the way,    30
And he is furnish'd with no Certainties
More than he haply may retale from me.

NORTHUMBERLAND    Now Travers, what good Tidings comes with you?

TRAVERS    My Lord, Sir John Umfrevile turn'd me back
With joyful Tidings, and, being better hors'd,    35
Outrode me; after him came spurring hard
A Gentleman almost forspent with speed,
That stopp'd by me to breathe his bloodi'd Horse;
He ask'd the way to Chester, and of him
I did demand what News from Shrewsbury.    40
He told me that Rebellion had bad luck,
And that young Harry Percy's Spur was cold.
With that he gave his able Horse the head
And, bending forward, strook his armed Heels
Against the panting sides of his poor Jade    45
Up to the Rowel-head; and, starting so,
He seem'd in running to devour the Way,
Staying no longer Question.

NORTHUMBERLAND                    Ha? Again?
Said he young Harry Percy's Spur was cold?
Of Hotspur Cold-spur? That Rebellion    50
Had met ill luck?

BARDOLPH                My Lord, I'll tell you what:
If my young Lord your Son have not the Day,
Upon mine Honor for a Silken Point

57      hilding   *irresponsible, contemptible.*

59      at a Venter   *at a venture; recklessly, merely venturing a wild guess.*

60      Title-leaf   *title-page. In Shakespeare's time, title-pages were much more descriptive than they are today. For example, the one for this play reads "The Second part of Henrie the fourth, continuing to his death, and coronation of Henrie the fift. With the humours of sir John Falstaff and swaggering Pistol."*

62      Strond   *strand, shore.*

63      a witness'd Usurpation   *evidence of its encroachment.*

69      apter   *prompter, readier.*

71      Woe-begone   *mournful, given over to grief.*

72      Drew   *drew open.*
           Priam   *King of Troy at the time of its fall to the Greeks.*

74      found   *perceived, discovered.*

14

I'll give my Barony. Never talk of it.

NORTHUMBERLAND   Why should that Gentleman
  that rode by Travers          55
  Give then such instances of Loss?

BARDOLPH        Who, he?
  He was some hilding Fellow that had stol'n
  The Horse he rode on, and upon my Life
  Spoke at a Venter. Look, here comes more News.

*Enter Morton.*

NORTHUMBERLAND   Yea, this man's Brow, like to a
  Title-leaf,            60
  Foretells the nature of a tragic Volume:
  So looks the Strond whereon th' imperious Flood
  Hath left a witness'd Usurpation.
  —Say Morton, didst thou come from Shrewsbury?

MORTON   I ran from Shrewsbury, my Noble Lord,  65
  Where hateful Death put on his ugliest Mask
  To fright our Party.

NORTHUMBERLAND  How doth my Son and Brother?
  Thou tremblest, and the whiteness in thy Cheek
  Is apter than thy Tongue to tell thy Errand.
  Ev'n such a Man, so faint, so spiritless,    70
  So dull, so dead in look, so Woe-begone,
  Drew Priam's Curtain in the dead of Night
  And would have told him half his Troy was
    burnt,
  But Priam found the Fire ere he his Tongue,
  And I my Percy's Death ere thou report'st it.  75

78    Stopping  *stuffing full. The verb* stop *has the same meaning in I.ii.48.*

83    But . . . Son  *Both here and in line 192 the phrase "my Lord" is interpreted in this edition as a reference to Hotspur rather than to Northumberland. Since the early texts do not normally set off parenthetical phrases with commas, expressions such as this can often be interpreted in more than one way. In line 104, by contrast, "my Lord" is set off by commas in the Quarto and parentheses in the Folio.*

84    Suspicion  *apprehension, fear. The reference to Suspicion's "ready Tongue" recalls the description of Rumor in the Induction.*

87    is chanced  *has occurred. Here* chanced *is disyllabic.*

88    Tell . . . lies  *Here Northumberland is encouraging Morton, a mere retainer, to be so bold as to tell an Earl his prophesying spirit has misled him.*

91    gainsaid  *contradicted.*

95    Fear or Sin  *fearful (threatening) or sinful.*

98    belie  *lie about.*

This thou would'st say, "Your Son did thus and
  thus,
Your Brother thus, so fought the Noble
  Douglas,"
Stopping my greedy Ear with their bold Deeds;
But in the end, to stop my Ear indeed,
Thou hast a Sigh to blow away this Praise,                    80
Ending with "Brother, Son, and All are dead."
MORTON    Douglas is living, and your Brother yet;
  But for my Lord your Son—
NORTHUMBERLAND                Why, he is dead!
  See what a ready Tongue Suspicion hath!
  He that but fears the thing he would not know        85
  Hath by Instinct knowledge from others' Eyes,
  That what he fear'd is chanced. Yet speak,
    Morton:
  Tell thou an Earl his Divination lies,
  And I will take it as a sweet Disgrace,
  And make thee rich for doing me such Wrong.          90
MORTON    You are too Great to be by me gainsaid;
  Your Spirit is too true, your Fears too certain.
NORTHUMBERLAND    Yet for all this, say not that
    Percy's dead.
  I see a strange Confession in thine Eye:
  Thou shak'st thy Head and hold'st it Fear or
    Sin                                                95
  To speak a Truth. If he be slain, say so:
  The Tongue offends not that reports his Death,
  And he doth sin that doth belie the Dead,
  Not he which says the Dead is not alive.

101    a Losing Office   *a responsibility that can only serve to his disadvantage.*

108    Faint Quittance   *weak responses.*

110    never-daunted   *never intimidated.*

112    In few   *in brief, in a few words.*

114    Being bruited once   *once it became known.*

115    temper'd   *having the strength and resiliency of well-treated steel. Modern editions normally place a hyphen before this word to create a compound adjective. But unlike "never-daunted" (line 110), it is not hyphenated in either of the original texts.*

116    Metal   *The two spellings of this word in the original texts capture its double meaning in this context:* mettal *(Quarto) and* Mettle *(Folio). Both senses refer to Hotspur's valor;* Metal *is the spelling adopted here because it fits with "steeled" and reinforces the imagery of the "Fire and Heat" (line 114) used to temper steel (lines 115–16).*

117    abated   *both (a) made dull (a sense developed in line 118), and (b) beaten down.*

119    it Self   *its self. Like* my self, your self, *and* thy self, it self *is normally rendered as two words in Shakespeare's text.* It and his *are the usual Elizabethan forms for what we now render as* its.

120    Upon Enforcement   *when propelled.*

122    Lightness   *both (a) swiftness (in retreat), and (b) lack of substance (in this case valor) and manliness.*

18

Yet the first Bringer of Unwelcome News          100
Hath but a Losing Office, and his Tongue
Sounds ever after as a sullen Bell
Rememb'red tolling a departing Friend.
BARDOLPH   I cannot think, my Lord, your Son is dead.
MORTON   I'm sorry I should force you to believe          105
That which I would to God I had not seen;
But these mine Eyes saw him in Bloody State,
Rend'ring Faint Quittance, weari'd and
    out-breath'd,
To Harry Monmouth, whose swift Wrath beat down
The never-daunted Percy to the Earth,          110
From whence with Life he never more sprung up.
In few, his Death, whose Spirit lent a Fire
Ev'n to the dullest Peasant in his Camp,
Being bruited once, took Fire and Heat away
From the best temper'd Courage in his Troops;          115
For from his Metal was his Party steeled,
Which, once in him abated, all the rest
Turn'd on themselves, like dull and heavy Lead.
And as the Thing that's Heavy in it Self
Upon Enforcement flies with greatest Speed,          120
So did our Men, heavy in Hotspur's Loss,
Lend to this Weight such Lightness with their
    Fear
That Arrows fled not swifter toward their Aim
Than did our Soldiers, aiming at their Safety,
Fly from the Field. Then was that Noble
    Worcester          125
So soon ta'en Pris'ner, and that furious Scot,
The bloody Douglas, whose well-lab'ring Sword

19

128    th' Appearance of the King    *In V.iii and V.iv of* 1 Henry IV *there are several references to decoys of the King.*

129    'Gan    *began to.*
       vail his Stomach    *lose his intestinal fortitude.*
       grace    *countenance, approve by example.*

131    Stumbling in Fear    *Douglas' capture is described somewhat less flatteringly in V.v of* 1 Henry IV. *According to Shakespeare's principal source, Holinshed's* Chronicles of England, Scotland, and Ireland *(1587), "the Earl of Douglas, for haste, falling from the crag of an high mountain, brake one of his cullions [testicles], and was taken"* captive.

133    Pow'r t'    *army to. Both words are elided metrically.*

136    I . . . mourn    *Northumberland means that he does not have time to mourn now: he will grieve properly hereafter.*

137    Physic    *medicine, healing power.*

138    Having . . . Sick    *which would have made me sick had they been well (good).*

140    weak'ned    *The Quarto spelling suggests a play on* weak-kneed.

141    buckle under Life    *give way under the sheer weight of living.*

142    Impatient of his Fit    *rebelling against his affliction.*

145    nice    *delicate, lacking in manliness.*

146    scaly Gauntlet    *a glove covered with metal plates.*

147    Coif    *the head-cap worn by an invalid.*

149    flesh'd    *having tasted bloody flesh, and now eager for the hunt.*

150    bind . . . Iron    *put a helmet on my head.*

Had three times slain th' Appearance of the
   King,
'Gan vail his Stomach and did grace the Shame
Of those that turn'd their Backs, and in his
   Flight,                                    130
Stumbling in Fear, was took. The Sum of all
Is that the King hath won, and hath sent out
A speedy Pow'r t' encounter you, my Lord,
Under the conduct of young Lancaster
And Westmerland. This is the News at full.    135
NORTHUMBERLAND    For this I shall have Time enough
   to mourn:
In Poison there is Physic, and these News,
Having been Well, that would have made me Sick,
Being Sick, have in some measure made me Well.
And as the Wretch whose Fever-weak'ned Joints,    140
Like strengthless Hinges, buckle under Life,
Impatient of his Fit, breaks like a Fire
Out of his Keeper's Arms, ev'n so my Limbs,
Weak'ned with Grief, being now enrag'd with
   Grief,
Are thrice themselves. Hence therefore, thou
   nice Crutch:                                145
A scaly Gauntlet now with joints of Steel
Must glove this Hand. And hence, thou sickly
   Coif:
Thou art a Guard too wanton for the Head
Which Princes, flesh'd with Conquest, aim to
   hit.
Now bind my Brows with Iron, and approach    150

151     ragged'st   *ruggedest.*
            Spight   *spite, malice.*

153     Let Heav'n kiss Earth   *Let the clouds and the earth merge in a torrential downpour.*

156     To feed . . . Act   *Northumberland's theatrical metaphor is a call for immediate violence.*

157     one Spirit . . . Cain   *Northumberland invokes Cain, not as the cursed wanderer (an image that occurs several times in* Richard II*), but as the archetype of all murderers. Cain's envy of his younger brother, Abel, led him to slay him (Genesis 4).*

161     strained   *both (a) overwrought, and (b) constrained, enforced (by your griefs).*

163     Complices   *accomplices (but with the positive sense of "colleagues").*

166     cast th' Event   *calculated the consequences.*

167     Accompt   *account.*

168     make Head   *raise a head (army) in rebellion.*

169     Dole   *dealing out.*

170–71     walk'd . . . o'er   *This image recalls* 1 Henry IV, *I.iii. 189–91.*

172     advis'd   *aware.*

172–73     capable / Of   *subject to.*

173     forward   *bold, ambitious.*

The ragged'st Hour that Time and Spight dare
    bring
To frown upon th' enrag'd Northumberland.
Let Heav'n kiss Earth; now let not Nature's
    Hand
Keep the wild Flood confin'd; let Order die,
And let this World no longer be a Stage                    155
To feed Contention in a ling'ring Act.
But let one Spirit of the first-born Cain
Reign in all Bosoms, that, each Heart being set
On Bloody Courses, the rude Scene may end,
And Darkness be the burier of the Dead.                    160

TRAVERS   This strained Passion doth you wrong,
    my Lord.

BARDOLPH   Sweet Earl, divorce not Wisdom from
    your Honor.

MORTON   The Lives of all your loving Complices
    Lean on your Health, the which, if you give
        o'er
    To stormy Passion, must perforce decay.                165
    You cast th' Event of War, my Noble Lord,
    And summ'd th' Accompt of Chance before you
        said
    "Let us make Head." It was your pre-surmise
    That in the Dole of Blows your Son might drop.
    You knew he walk'd o'er Perils, on an Edge             170
    More likely to fall in than to get o'er.
    You were advis'd his Flesh was capable
    Of Wounds and Scars, and that his forward
        Spirit

174    where . . . rang'd  *a commercial metaphor comparing "Danger" to a free-ranging fleet of trading ships.*

177    stiff-borne  *resolutely pursued. But this phrase could also apply to a more fleshly kind of uprising.*

178    bring  *Many editors follow the Second Folio and emend to "brought." Others emend "hath" to "doth."*

180    engaged to  *committed or pledged to make good on (like merchants who have risked borrowed capital).*

182    wrought out Life  *emerged with our lives.*

184    Chok'd the Respect  *suffocated all consideration.*

185    o'erset  *both (a) capsized, and (b) wagered so far beyond our means (as a result of what we have already lost) that our only option is to go for broke.*

190    well-appointed Pow'rs  *well-equipped forces.*

191    with a double Surety  *Morton means that, as a prelate, the Archbishop is able to command allegiance from both the bodies and the spirits of the troops pledged to him.* Surety *often means "security," unwarranted self-assurance.*

192    My Lord . . . Corpse  *Unlike the Archbishop, Hotspur was only able to command the spiritless bodies of his soldiers.*

201    Turns Insurrection to Religion  *Morton's point is that, by invoking a higher spiritual authority, the Archbishop is able to persuade his troops that they are fighting, not as sinful rebels against God's anointed Deputy, but as sanctified ministers of Divine justice.*

24

Would lift him where most trade of Danger
    rang'd;
Yet did you say "Go forth." And none of this,                    175
Though strongly apprehended, could restrain
The stiff-borne Action. What hath then befall'n?
Or what hath this bold Enterprise bring forth,
More than that Being which was Like to Be?
BARDOLPH   We all that are engaged to this Loss           180
Knew that we ventur'd on such dang'rous Seas
That if we wrought out Life 'twas ten to one,
And yet we ventur'd for the Gain propos'd,
Chok'd the Respect of likely Peril fear'd,
And since we are o'erset, venture again.                         185
Come, we will all put forth Body and Goods.
MORTON   'Tis more than Time, and my most Noble
    Lord
I hear for certain, and dare speak the Truth:
The gentle Archbishop of York is up
With well-appointed Pow'rs; he is a man                           190
Who with a double Surety binds his Foll'wers.
My Lord your Son had only but the Corpse,
But Shadows and the Shows of Men, to fight.
For that same word Rebellion did divide
The Action of their Bodies from their Souls,                     195
And they did fight with Queasiness, constrain'd
As men drink Potions, that their Weapons only
Seem'd on our side: but for their Spir'ts and
    Souls,
This word Rebellion, it had froze them up
As Fish are in a Pond. But now the Bishop                        200
Turns Insurrection to Religion,

25

202      **Suppos'd**   *assumed to be.*

204      **enlarge his Rising**   *enhance the credibility of his uprising. The unintended suggestiveness of this phrase gives a reminder that the Archbishop is acting more like a man of the flesh than of the spirit (Galatians 5:17).*

204–5      **with . . . Stones**   *Not only is the Archbishop claiming to derive "his Quarrel and his Cause" from Heaven (line 206); he is parading as a religious relic the blood he has scraped from the cell where the late King was martyred.*

207–8      **a bleeding . . . Bullingbrook**   *According to Morton, the Archbishop is depicting England itself as a wounded victim, "Gasping for Life" under the tyrannical hand of a Cain-like Bullingbrook.*

209      **More and Less**   *people of both high and low estate.*
          **flock**   *Morton's verb is aptly chosen. Not only does it depict the Archbishop as a shepherd (a traditional image for Christ and his "pastors," shepherds); it also suggests that the people are following him like obedient sheep.*

I.ii      *This scene takes place on a street in London.*

S.D.      **with . . . Buckler**   *The sword and buckler (a small round shield) the Page bears may be his own rather than Falstaff's (by Shakespeare's time these weapons were associated with the servant classes). It is probably the Page's armor that prompts Falstaff to refer to the tiny young man as a "Giant" in line 1.*

2      **Water**   *urine sample. Falstaff has just had a medical check-up.*

4      **ow'd**   *owned.*

Suppos'd Sincere and Holy in his Thoughts.
He's follow'd both with Body and with Mind,
And doth enlarge his Rising with the Blood
Of fair King Richard, scrap'd from Pomfret
    Stones;                                     205
Derives from Heav'n his Quarrel and his Cause,
Tells them he doth bestride a bleeding Land,
Gasping for Life under great Bullingbrook,
And More and Less do flock to follow him.

NORTHUMBERLAND   I knew of this before, but to
    speak truth,                                 210
This present Grief had wip'd it from my Mind.
Go in with me, and counsel ev'ry man
The aptest way for Safety and Revenge.
Get Posts and Letters, and make Friends with
    Speed:
Never so Few, and never yet more Need.    *Exeunt.*  215

# Scene 2

*Enter Sir John Falstaff, with his Page
bearing his Sword and Buckler.*

FALSTAFF   Sirrah, you Giant, what says the Doctor to
    my Water?
PAGE   He said, Sir, the Water itself was a good
    healthy Water; but for the Party that ow'd it,

27

5      moe   *more in number.*

         knew for   *knew how to cure. The Doctor's comment is similar to that of the Physician who tells Macbeth that there are some illnesses wherein "the Patient must minister to himself" (Macbeth, V.iii).*

6      gird   *jeer, gibe.*

7–8    Clay-Man   *Falstaff refers to mankind in general, as a foolish species composed ("compounded") of earth ("Clay").*

9      intends to   *tends to, prompts.*

16     Mandrake   *a plant whose long, forked root seemed man-like in shape.*

18     Agot   *agate. Falstaff probably alludes to the tiny figures carved on agate-stones and worn as jewels.*

21     Juvenal   *juvenile, youth.*

23     fledge   *fledged; down-covered, like a young chick.*

25     stick   *hesitate.*

26     Face Royal   *Falstaff alludes to the Royal, a ten-shilling coin stamped with the head of the monarch.*

27–29  He may . . . it.   *If the Prince went to a barber for a shave, his meager beard would cost him so little that he could hold on to his Royal.*

33     Dommelton   *dumbhead.*

35     Slops   *baggy breeches.*

he might have moe Diseases than he knew for. 5

FALSTAFF    Men of all sorts take a pride to gird at
me: the Brain of this foolish compounded Clay-
Man is not able to invent any thing that
intends to Laughter more than I invent or is
invented on me. I am not only Witty in my Self, 10
but the cause that Wit is in other Men. I do
here walk before thee like a Sow that hath
overwhelm'd all her Litter but one; if the
Prince put thee into my Service for any other
reason than to set me off, why then I have no 15
Judgment. Thou whoreson Mandrake, thou art
fitter to be worn in my Cap than to wait at my
Heels. I was never mann'd with an Agot till
now; but I will inset you neither in Gold nor
Silver but in Vile Apparel, and send you back 20
again to your Master for a Jewel. The Juvenal,
the Prince your Master, whose Chin is not yet
fledge: I will sooner have a Beard grow in the
Palm of my Hand then he shall get one off his
Cheek; and yet he will not stick to say his 25
Face is a Face Royal. God may finish it when
he will: 'tis not a Hair amiss yet. He may
keep it still at a Face Royal, for a Barber
shall never earn Sixpence out of it. And yet
he'll be crowing as if he had writ Man ever 30
since his Father was a Bachelor. He may keep
his own Grace, but he's almost out of mine, I
can assure him. What said Master Dommelton
about the Satin for my Short Cloak and my
Slops? 35

29

38    Band    *bond, agreement to pay for services rendered.*

39    the Glutton    *Falstaff refers to the rich man (often referred to as Dives) in Luke 16:19–31; after refusing alms to Lazarus while alive, Dives eventually begs to have Lazarus put a drop of water on his burning tongue in Hell.*

41    Achitophel    *the treacherous counselor who deserted King David and joined Absalom's conspiracy against him (2 Samuel 15–17).*

41–42    to bear . . . Hand    *to lead a gentleman on with encouragement.*

43–45    Smoothy-pates . . . Girdles    *Falstaff satirizes the close-cropped hairstyles and pretentious apparel of London's Puritan "Citizens."*

46    taking up    *assuming obligations by ordering on credit.*

47    I had as live    *I had as lief (I would just as soon).*

52–53    Horn of Aboundance    *Horn of Plenty. Falstaff's image combines (a) a symbol of great wealth (the Cornucopia), and (b) a symbol of misplaced security (the horned brows of a foolish cuckold who doesn't notice his wife's infidelity). In line 55* Lanthorn *(a common spelling of "lantern") continues the play on horns.*

59–60    I bought . . . Smithfield.    *I hired him in St. Paul's Cathedral (where unemployed laborers sought work), and he is now buying me a horse in Smithfield (a livestock market north of the Cathedral).*

61    Stews    *brothels.*

PAGE    He said, Sir, you should procure him better
        Assurance than Bardolph. He would not take his
        Band and yours: he liked not the Security.
FALSTAFF · Let him be damn'd like the Glutton! Pray
        God his Tongue be hotter! A whoreson                    40
        Achitophel! A Rascal, "Yea forsooth" Knave, to
        bear a Gentleman in Hand, and then stand upon
        Security! The whoreson Smoothy-pates do now
        wear nothing but high Shoes and bunches of Keys
        at their Girdles, and if a man is through with          45
        them in honest taking up, then they must stand
        upon Security. I had as live they would put
        Ratsbane in my Mouth as offer to stop it with
        Security! I look'd 'a should have sent me two
        and twenty Yards of Satin, as I am a true               50
        Knight, and he sends me Security! Well he may
        sleep in Security, for he hath the Horn of
        Aboundance; and the Lightness of his Wife
        shines through it—where's Bardolph?—and yet
        can not he see though he have his own Lanthorn          55
        to light him.
PAGE    He's gone in Smithfield to buy your Worship a
        Horse.
FALSTAFF    I bought him in Paul's, and he'll buy me
        a Horse in Smithfield. And I could get me but          60
        a Wife in the Stews, I were mann'd, hors'd,
        and wiv'd.

        *Enter the Lord Chief Justice and Servant.*

PAGE    Sir, here comes the Noble Man that committed

31

64      for . . . Bardolph   *According to Sir Thomas Elyot's* The Governor *(1531), the Prince struck the Lord Chief Justice "for sending one of his minions (upon desert) to prison." In response, the Justice ordered the Prince to jail, and the King replaced the Prince on the Privy Council with his younger brother (Thomas, Duke of Clarence), an action the King alludes to in III.ii.32–33 of* 1 Henry IV.

65      Wait close   *Stay near. What Falstaff probably means is "let's hold back," but by now the Lord Chief Justice has already seen him.*

68      in question   *under investigation. The Justice refers to the Gadshill Robbery, which took place in II.ii of* 1 Henry IV.

71      Charge   *military command.*

75      I am deaf   *Falstaff plans to pretend deafness. But in the process he illustrates the spiritual deafness proverbially associated with what the New Testament referred to as the "old man" (man in his unregenerate state, refusing to hear warnings of the damnation he would suffer if he didn't repent). See Matthew 11:13–19 and Ephesians 5:22–29. Falstaff describes his "Disease" in lines 134–35.*

81      What? . . . begging?   *As the Servant plucks Falstaff by the elbow, Falstaff brazenly pretends to interpret his gesture as a request for alms.*

84–85    on any side but one   *on any side but the King's.*

90      Setting . . . aside   *assuming that my honor as a Knight and Soldier would allow me to do anything so dishonorable as lie.*

the Prince for striking him about Bardolph.

FALSTAFF   Wait close, I will not see him.                    65

JUSTICE   What's he that goes there?

SERVANT   Falstaff, and 't please your Lordship.

JUSTICE   He that was in question for the Robb'ry?

SERVANT   He, my Lord, but he hath since done good
Service at Shrewsbury, and, as I hear, is now        70
going with some Charge to the Lord John of
Lancaster.

JUSTICE   What, to York? Call him back again.

SERVANT   —Sir John Falstaff!

FALSTAFF   —Boy, tell him I am deaf.                           75

PAGE   —You must speak louder: my Master is deaf.

JUSTICE   I am sure he is to the hearing of any
thing good. —Go pluck him by the Elbow, I must
speak with him.

SERVANT   Sir John!                                            80

FALSTAFF   What? A young Knave and begging? Is there
not Wars? Is there not Employment? Doth not
the King lack Subjects? Do not the Rebels need
Soldiers? Though it be a Shame to be on any
side but one, it is worse Shame to beg then        85
to be on the worst side, were it worse than
the name of Rebellion can tell how to make it.

SERVANT   You mistake me, Sir.

FALSTAFF   Why Sir, did I say you were an Honest Man?
Setting my Knighthood and my Soldiership aside,    90
I had lied in my Throat if I had said so.

SERVANT   I pray you Sir, then set your Knighthood
and your Soldiership aside, and give me leave
to tell you, you lie in your Throat if you say

96      **leave**   *permission. So also in line 93. But in line 98, Falstaff uses the word to mean "pardon" and "liberty," respectively.*

96–97   **I lay . . . to me?**   *I forgive (set to one side and fail to avenge) that which touches my honor?*

98      **If thou tak'st leave**   *if you take the liberty of doing what I refuse to permit you to do.*

99      **You hunt counter**   *You are like a hunting dog pursuing the scent backwards (running in the wrong direction from the quarry). Falstaff is probably punning on* Counter *(the name of a London prison), and he may also be alluding to the female genitalia (and thus suggesting that the Justice and his servant would be better advised to go chasing after prostitutes).*

100     **avaunt!**   *be gone!*

105     **abroad**   *up and about.*

106     **by advice**   *with the approval of your doctor.*

107     **clean**   *completely.*

108     **an Ague**   *a fever or other malady.*

109     **Saltness of Time**   *Falstaff probably refers to the use of salt as a preservative for meat that would otherwise rot with age.*

111     **reverend**   *respectful.*

120     **Apoplexy**   *stiffness or paralysis, as from a stroke or seizure.*

I am any other than an Honest Man. 95

FALSTAFF   I give thee leave to tell me so? I lay
aside that which grows to me? If thou get'st
any leave of me, hang me. If thou tak'st leave,
thou wert better be hang'd. You hunt counter:
hence, avaunt! 100

SERVANT   Sir, my Lord would speak with you.

JUSTICE   Sir John Falstaff, a word with you.

FALSTAFF   My good Lord, God give your Lordship good
Time of Day! I am glad to see your Lordship
abroad. I heard say your Lordship was sick: I 105
hope your Lordship goes abroad by advice. Your
Lordship, though not clean past your Youth,
have yet some smack of an Ague in you, some
relish of the Saltness of Time in you; and I
most humbly beseech your Lordship to have a 110
reverend Care of your Health.

JUSTICE   Sir John, I sent for you before your
Expedition to Shrewsbury.

FALSTAFF   And 't please your Lordship, I hear his
Majesty is return'd with some Discomfort from 115
Wales.

JUSTICE   I talk not of his Majesty. You would not
come when I sent for you.

FALSTAFF   And I hear, moreover, his Highness is
fall'n into this same whoreson Apoplexy. 120

JUSTICE   Well, God mend him. I pray you let me
speak with you.

FALSTAFF   This Apoplexy, as I take it, is a kind of
Lethargy, and 't please your Lordship, a kind
of Sleeping in the Blood, a whoreson Tingling. 125

35

126     What   *why.*

127     it Original   *its origin, cause.*

128     Study   *worry, excessive contemplation.*

129     Galen   *Greek physician (129–199 A.D.), still revered as a medical authority in Shakespeare's time.*

130     Deafness   *It is characteristic of Falstaff to attribute to others the same defects and vices to be found in himself.*

136     withal   *with.*

137     punish you by the Heels   *put your heels in the irons worn by prisoners.*

140     Job   *Falstaff alludes to the Old Testament figure proverbial for his long-suffering patience in affliction. Falstaff puns on two senses of "patient" (line 141): (a) enduring suffering without complaint, and (b) submitting to medical treatment as a patient.*

142     in respect of Poverty   *Falstaff alludes to debtor's prison; but his image is also a facetious reminder of the vows of poverty taken by saints.*

145     Dram of a Scruple   *Falstaff continues the medical metaphor with a reference to two measurements of "Potions." An apothecary's dram was an eighth of an ounce; a scruple was a third of a dram. Here* Scruple *also means doubt or hesitancy.*

150     the Laws . . . Land-service   *the laws providing immunity from civil prosecution for those engaged in military service.*

JUSTICE    What tell you me of it? Be it as it is.

FALSTAFF    It hath it Original from much Grief, from
    Study, from Perturbation of the Brain. I have
    read the Cause of his Effects in Galen; it is a
    kind of Deafness.                                        130

JUSTICE    I think you are fall'n into the Disease,
    for you hear not what I say to you.

FALSTAFF    Very well, my Lord, very well; rather,
    and 't please you, it is the Disease of Not
    List'ning, the Malady of Not Marking, that I    135
    am troubled withal.

JUSTICE    To punish you by the Heels would amend the
    attention of your Ears, and I care not if I
    do become your Physician!

FALSTAFF    I am as poor as Job, my Lord, but not so    140
    patient. Your Lordship may minister the Potion
    of Imprisonment to me in respect of Poverty;
    but how I should be your Patient to follow
    your Prescriptions, the Wise may make some
    Dram of a Scruple, or indeed a Scruple itself.    145

JUSTICE    I sent for you, when there were Matters
    against you for your Life, to come speak with
    me.

FALSTAFF    As I was then advis'd by my learned
    Counsel in the Laws of this Land-service, I    150
    did not come.

JUSTICE    Well, the truth is, Sir John, you live in
    great Infamy.

FALSTAFF    He that buckles himself in my Belt cannot
    live in less.                                        155

JUSTICE    Your Means are very slender, and your

37

161–   **I am . . . Dog.**   *Falstaff appears to be comparing himself to*
62      *a blind man whose seeing-eye dog has led him to food and*
     *forced him to get fat.*

163   **gall**   *rub and irritate. The Lord Chief Justice compares Fal-*
     *staff's earlier crime to a "Wound" that has now been "heal'd"*
     *by his "Day's Service" at Shrewsbury (his "killing" of Hot-*
     *spur).*

167   **your quiet o'erposting**   *your offense having been quietly*
     *passed over.*

171   **smell a Fox**   *be suspicious (as with a man smelling a fox in his*
     *hen-house). Falstaff implies that he is being falsely accused.*

174   **Wassel Candle**   *a large, fat candle used for feasts (such as*
     *Christmas) when wassails (healths) were drunk with spiced*
     *wines and ales.*

175   **Wax**   *Falstaff puns on* wax *as a verb meaning "grow."*

175–   **approve the Truth**   *prove the truth of my words.*
76

182   **your . . . Light**   *Falstaff alludes to 2 Corinthians 11:14,*
     *where Satan is described as "an angel of light." But he also*
     *alludes to the coin known as the* angel, *which he hopes will*
     *"go" (pass as acceptable currency) even though it is "Ill"*
     *(cracked and thus lighter than normal).*

186   **Coster-mongers' Times**   *times dominated by fruit and vege-*
     *table vendors.*

187   **Bearod**   *bear-ward, one who keeps and displays bears.*
     **Pregnancy**   *intellectual quickness, gravity of mind.*

Waste is great.

FALSTAFF   I would it were otherwise; I would my
Means were greater and my Waste slender.

JUSTICE   You have misled the youthful Prince.    160

FALSTAFF   The young Prince hath misled me. I am the
Fellow with the Great Belly, and he my Dog.

JUSTICE   Well, I am loath to gall a new-heal'd
Wound. Your Day's Service at Shrewsbury hath
a little gilded over your Night's Exploit on    165
Gadshill. You may thank the Unquiet Time for
your quiet o'erposting that Action.

FALSTAFF   My Lord.

JUSTICE   But since all is well, keep it so: wake
not a sleeping Wolf.    170

FALSTAFF   To wake a Wolf is as bad as smell a Fox.

JUSTICE   What, you are as a Candle: the better part
burnt out.

FALSTAFF   A Wassel Candle, my Lord: all Tallow. If
I did say of Wax, my Growth would approve the    175
Truth.

JUSTICE   There is not a White Hair in your Face but
should have his effect of Gravity.

FALSTAFF   His effect of Gravy, Gravy, Gravy!

JUSTICE   You follow the young Prince up and down,    180
like his Ill Angel.

FALSTAFF   Not so, my Lord: your Ill Angel is Light,
but I hope he that looks upon me will take me
without weighing. And yet in some respects I
grant I cannot go. I cannot tell: Virtue is of    185
so little regard in these Coster-mongers' Times
that true Valor is turned Bearod, Pregnancy is

39

188    Tapster    *bartender, one who drew beverages from the tap.*

189    giving Reckonings    *telling customers how much they owe for their drinks.*

190    appertinent    *pertinent, pertaining.*

193–    you do . . . Galls    *you evaluate the intensity of our passions*
94    *by the maliciousness of your envy.*

195    Vaward    *vanguard, forefront.*

196    Wags    *lively wits.*

199    Characters    *signs (such as letters of the alphabet).*

203    Single    *insignificant.*

204    blasted with Antiquity    *blighted with age.*

209    hallowing    *shouting halloo to hunting dogs.*
Anthems    *psalms and hymns.*

210    approve    *prove, demonstrate.*

212    Caper with me    *try to out-dance me.*

213    Marks    *pieces of currency worth thirteen shillings, fourpence.*

215    Year    *ear (a common spelling and pronunciation).*

216    Sensible    *both (a) feeling pain, and (b) acting prudent.*

217    check'd    *reproved, scolded.*

made a Tapster and his quick Wit wasted in
giving Reckonings. All the other Gifts
appertinent to Man, as the Malice of this Age                    190
shapes them, are not worth a Gooseberry. You
that are Old consider not the capacities of us
that are Young: you do measure the Heat of our
Livers with the Bitterness of your Galls. And
we that are in the Vaward of our Youth, I must            195
confess, are Wags too.

JUSTICE  Do you set down your Name in the Scroll of
Youth, that are written down Old with all the
Characters of Age? Have you not a Moist Eye, a
Dry Hand, a Yellow Cheek, a White Beard, a              200
Decreasing Leg, an Increasing Belly? Is not
your Voice Broken, your Wind Short, your Chin
Double, your Wit Single, and ev'ry part about
you blasted with Antiquity? And will you yet
call your self Young? Fie, fie, fie, Sir John!              205

FALSTAFF  My Lord, I was born about three of the
Clock in the afternoon with a White Head, and
something a Round Belly. For my Voice, I have
lost it with hallowing and singing of Anthems.
To approve my Youth further I will not. The               210
truth is, I am only Old in Judgment and
Understanding; and he that will Caper with me
for a thousand Marks, let him lend me the
Money, and have at him! For the Box of the
Year that the Prince gave you, he gave it like            215
a Rude Prince, and you took it like a Sensible
Lord. I have check'd him for it, and the Young
Lion repents: marry not in Ashes and Sackcloth,

219   in New Silk and Old Sack   *Falstaff implies that the Prince's "repentance" has been the very opposite of the "sackcloth and ashes" (Matthew 11:21, Luke 10:13) normally associated with true penance or remorse.*

221   Companion   *Here, as is usually the case in Shakespeare, the word has negative connotations.*

234   spit white   *Falstaff probably means "spit like a healthy man."*

236   thrust upon it   *sent to put it down.*
       ever   *forever.*

237   alway   *always.*
       trick   *trait, habit.*

241   terrible   *terrifying.*

243   a Rust   *inactivity.*
       scour'd   *scrubbed, polished.*

245   honest   *virtuous, properly behaved.*

but in New Silk and Old Sack.

JUSTICE   Well, God send the Prince a better                 220
    Companion.

FALSTAFF   God send the Companion a better Prince:
    I cannot rid my Hands of him.

JUSTICE   Well, the King hath sever'd you: I hear you
    are going with Lord John of Lancaster against        225
    the Archbishop and the Earl of Northumberland.

FALSTAFF   Yea, I thank your pretty sweet Wit for it.
    But look you pray, all you that kiss my Lady
    Peace at Home, that our Armies join not in a
    Hot Day: for by the Lord, I take but two Shirts     230
    out with me, and I mean not to sweat
    extraordinarily. If it be a Hot Day, and I
    brandish any thing but a Bottle, I would I
    might never spit white again. There is not a
    dangerous Action can peep out his Head but I        235
    am thrust upon it. Well, I cannot last ever,
    but it was alway yet the trick of our English
    nation, if they have a good thing, to make it
    too common. If ye will needs say I am an Old
    Man, you should give me Rest: I would to God       240
    my Name were not so terrible to the Enemy as
    it is. I were better to be eaten to Death with
    a Rust than to be scour'd to Nothing with
    Perpetual Motion.

JUSTICE   Well, be honest, be honest, and God bless       245
    your Expedition.

FALSTAFF   Will your Lordship lend me a thousand
    Pound to furnish me forth?

JUSTICE   Not a Penny, not a Penny: you are too

43

250     impatient to bear Crosses   *The Justice puns on three mean-
        ings: (a) eager to line your pockets with silver coins (which
        were stamped with crosses), (b) eager to carry extra burdens
        and subject yourself to afflictions, and (c) quick to retaliate
        rather than to suffer insults and injuries patiently. In view of
        Falstaff's cowardice, the last implication is ironic, and may be
        spoken by the Justice with a note of sarcasm.*

252–    fillip . . . Beetle   *flip me into the air with a pile-driving
53      mallet so big that three men are required to wield it.*

253–    Age and Covetousness   *Old men were proverbial for their
54      miserly acquisitiveness: Falstaff accuses the Lord Chief Justice
        of being too stingy to lend him money.*

255     Gout   *a swelling of the joints (especially of the big toe) owing to
        an excess of uric acid in the blood. The affliction was associated
        primarily with old men.*

256     Pox   *syphilis.*

256–    both . . . Curses   *both ages of man anticipate my curses (by
57      falling ill of their own excesses).*

260     Groats   *four-pence coins.*

262     Consumption   *wasting away, as from tuberculosis.*

273     Color   *pretext. The term is associated with chameleon-like be-
        havior.*

276     Commodity   *profit. Falstaff will use his military service
        (which may mask his dissolute life) as the basis for a disability
        pension.*

44

impatient to bear Crosses. Fare you well. 250
Commend me to my Cousin Westmerland.

*Exeunt Chief Justice and Servant.*

FALSTAFF  If I do, fillip me with a three-man
Beetle! A man can no more separate Age and
Covetousness than 'a can part Young Limbs and
Lechery: but the Gout galls the one, and the 255
Pox pinches the other, and so both the Degrees
prevent my Curses. —Boy!

PAGE  Sir?

FALSTAFF  What Money is in my Purse?

PAGE  Seven Groats and Two Pence. 260

FALSTAFF  I can get no Remedy against this
Consumption of the Purse. Borrowing only
lingers and lingers it out, but the Disease is
incurable. Go bear this Letter to my Lord of
Lancaster, this to the Prince, this to the Earl 265
of Westmerland, and this to Old Mistress
Ursula, whom I have weekly sworn to marry
since I perceiv'd the first White Hair of my
Chin. About it, you know where to find me.

*Exit Page.*

A Pox of this Gout, or a Gout of this Pox: for 270
the one or the other plays the Rogue with my
Great Toe. 'Tis no matter if I do halt: I have
the Wars for my Color, and my Pension shall
seem the more reasonable: a good Wit will make
use of any thing. I will turn Diseases to 275
Commodity.                                        *Exit.*

45

I.iii     *This scene takes place at the palace of the Archbishop of York.*

S.D.    Fauconbridge   *This nobleman is mentioned only here; he has no lines to speak, either here or elsewhere in the play. In all likelihood, Shakespeare drew his name from Holinshed's account of the meeting depicted in this scene. Other "mutes" (characters who are given entrances but have nothing to say in a scene) appear elsewhere in the Quarto text.*

1       our Cause   *both (a) our case against the King, and (b) the reason for our taking up arms.*

5       allow th' Occasion of   *accept the justification for.*

7       in our Means   *given our resources.*

8       big   *brave, intimidating.*

9       Puissance   *might.*

10–11   Our . . . File / To   *the forces we have gathered to date approach the number of.*

12      Supplies   *reinforcements.*
        Hope   *expectation.*

14      incensed   *kindled.*

17      hold up Head   *hold their own.*

18      marry   *indeed, truly. This expression probably originated as an oath referring to the Virgin Mary.*

# Scene 3

*Enter the Archbishop, Thomas Mowbray (the Earl Marshal),*
*the Lord Hastings, Fauconbridge, and Lord Bardolph.*

BISHOP   Thus have you heard our Cause and known
    our Means;
    And my most Noble Friends, I pray you all
    Speak plainly your Opinions of our Hopes.
    —And first Lord Marshal, what say you to it?

MOWBRAY   I well allow th' Occasion of our Arms,     5
    But gladly would be better satisfied
    How in our Means we should advance our selves
    To look with Forehead bold and big enough
    Upon the Pow'r and Puissance of the King.

HASTINGS   Our present Musters grow upon the File    10
    To five and twenty thousand Men of Choice,
    And our Supplies live largely in the Hope
    Of great Northumberland, whose Bosom burns
    With an incensed Fire of Injuries.

BARDOLPH   The Question, then, Lord Hastings,
    standeth thus:     15
    Whether our present five and twenty thousand
    May hold up Head without Northumberland.

HASTINGS   With him we may.

BARDOLPH              Yea marry, there's the Point:

47

21      by the Hand     *in hand, firmly committed.*

22      Theme     *matter, issue.*

24      Incertain     *uncertain.*
        admitted     *included in our calculations.*

26      Cause     *case, situation; cause of defeat.*

27      lin'd     *fortified, as one does when sewing lining into a garment.*

28      Eating the Air     *feeding himself on nothing. The chameleon was thought capable of sustaining itself on nothing but air.*

29      in Project of     *in the projection of, based on the expectation of.*

31      with great Imagination     *on the basis of nothing more substantial than his uncontrolled imaginings.*

33      winking     *his eyes closed.*

36      Yes     *yes it will hurt.*
        this . . . War     *the kind of war we are now discussing.*

37      the instant Action     *the action under immediate review.*

38      so     *thus.*

40      Warrant     *assurance, encouragement.*

43      Figure     *the full scope of the completed design.*

44      Erection     *construction. But this word also serves as an ironic reminder that the Rebels' cause resembles other kinds of uprising erected on nothing more substantial than a man's "great Imagination" (line 31). The situation Bardolph describes is comically echoed in II.iv 283–84.*

48

But if without him we be thought too feeble,
My Judgment is we should not step too far                    20
Till we had his Assistance by the Hand.
For in a Theme so Bloody-fac'd as this,
Conjecture, Expectation, and Surmise
Of Aids Incertain should not be admitted.
ARCHBISHOP    'Tis very true, Lord Bardolph: for
        indeed                                               25
    It was young Hotspur's Cause at Shrewsbury.
BARDOLPH    It was, my Lord, who lin'd himself with
        Hope,
    Eating the Air, and Promise of Supply,
    Flatt'ring himself in Project of a Power
    Much smaller than the smallest of his Thoughts;          30
    And so with great Imagination,
    Proper to Madmen, led his Pow'rs to Death
    And, winking, leapt into Destruction.
HASTINGS    But by your leave, it never yet did hurt
    To lay down Likelihoods and Forms of Hope.               35
BARDOLPH    Yes, if this present Quality of War,
    Indeed the instant Action, a Cause on Foot,
    Lives so in Hope: as in an early Spring
    We see th' appearing Buds, which to prove
        Fruit
    Hope gives not so much Warrant as Despair                40
    That Frosts will bite them. When we mean to
        build,
    We first survey the Plot, then draw the Model;
    And when we see the Figure of the House
    Then must we rate the Cost of the Erection,
    Which if we find outweighs Ability                       45

49

47    In fewer Offices   *with a smaller number of functions and quarters.*
    at least   *in the worst case.*
    desist   *decline.*

52    Consent . . . Foundation   *come to an agreement about what constitutes a firm basis for proceeding.*

53    Estate   *means.*

56    Figures   *mere calculations.*

60    Cost   *investment; here a partly completed structure.*

61    weeping Clouds   *Lord Bardolph's image suggests that the raining clouds will be weeping in pity for the folly of the foolish builder. Lord Bardolph's architectural metaphor would probably have reminded the audience of Jesus' parable about the two foundations (Matthew 7:24–27 and Luke 6:47–49). In Matthew, Jesus says that the person "that heareth these sayings of mine, and doeth them not, shall be likened unto a foolish man, which built his house upon the sand: And the rain descended, and the floods came, and the winds blew, and beat upon that house; and it fell: and great was the fall of it."*

62    churlish   *harsh, disagreeable.*
    Tyranny   *cruel exploitation.*

66    so   *even so.*

69    To us   *as far as it affects us.*

70    as the Times do brawl   *in view of the number of conflicts the times now force upon the King's attention.*

What do we then but draw anew the Model
In fewer Offices, or, at least, desist
To build at all? Much more, in this great Work
(Which is, almost, to pluck a Kingdom down
And set another up) should we survey                    50
The Plot of Situation and the Model,
Consent upon a sure Foundation,
Question Surveyors, know our own Estate,
How able such a Work to undergo,
To weigh against his Opposite. Or else               55
We fortify in Paper and in Figures,
Using the Names of Men instead of Men,
Like one that draws the Model of an House
Beyond his Pow'r to build it, who, half
      through,
Gives o'er and leaves his part-created Cost           60
A naked Subject to the weeping Clouds
And Waste for churlish Winter's Tyranny.
HASTINGS   Grant that our Hopes, yet likely of
      fair Birth,
Should be Still-born, and that we now
      possess'd
The Utmost Man of Expectation: I                      65
Think we are so a Body strong enough,
Ev'n as we are, to equal with the King.
BARDOLPH   What, is the King but five and twenty
      thousand?
HASTINGS   To us no more, nay not so much, Lord
      Bardolph,
For his Divisions, as the Times do brawl,            70

72 perforce *of necessity.*
  a third *no more than a third.*

74 sound *echo, as with an empty chamber.*

76 sev'ral *various.*

80 baying *here to be treated as a one-syllable word.*

81 like *likely.*

85 on *proceed.*

86 publish *make public.*

88 surfeited *become overfed, thus causing a revulsion of the appetite.*

89–90 An Habitation . . . Heart. *Like Lord Bardolph's earlier analogy (lines 41–62), the Archbishop's image recalls Jesus' parable about the two foundations in Matthew 7:24–27. What the Archbishop says is that anyone who tries to construct a political state on "the Vulgar Heart" (the affections of the common people) is like the foolish man of the parable who tried to "build his house upon the sand."*
  giddy *teetering dizzily.*

91 fond Many *foolish multitude.* Many *is a literal translation of the Greek phrase* hoi polloi, *"the many."*

92 beat Heav'n *both (a) made the sky reverberate with the sound of applause, and (b) anticipated or outdid Heaven in bestowing favor ("blessing").*

94 trimm'd . . . Desires *dressed in the attire you prayed for.*

Are in three Heads: one Pow'r against the
   French
And one against Glendow'r, perforce a third
Must take up us. So is the unfirm King
In three divided, and his Coffers sound
With hollow Poverty and Emptiness.             75
ARCHBISHOP   That he should draw his sev'ral
   Strengths together
And come against us in full Puissance
Need not to be dreaded.
HASTINGS            If he should do so,
To French and Welch he leaves his Back unarm'd,
They baying him at the Heels. Never fear that.    80
BARDOLPH   Who is it like should lead his Forces
   hither?
HASTINGS   The Duke of Lancaster and Westmerland;
Against the Welsh, himself and Harry Monmouth;
But who is substitut'd against the French
I have no certain Notice.
ARCHBISHOP          Let us on,       85
And publish the Occasion of our Arms.
The Commonwealth is sick of their own Choice:
Their over-greedy Love hath surfeited.
An Habitation giddy and unsure
Hath he that buildeth on the Vulgar Heart.    90
O thou fond Many, with what loud Applause
Did'st thou beat Heav'n with blessing
   Bullingbrook
Before he was what thou wouldst have him be!
And being now trimm'd in thine own Desires,
Thou, beastly Feeder, art so full of him    95

53

96    thou provok'st thy self to cast him up    *you are trying to induce vomiting in order to rid yourself of him.*

102    enamor'd on his Grave    *in love with his grave. In the light of what Morton has said in I.i.200–206, the Archbishop's contempt for the populace sounds a bit disingenuous. If the people now revere Richard's grave, after all, they have been encouraged to do so by the reliquary blood the Archbishop himself has "scrap'd from Pomfret Stones." On the one hand, the Archbishop says that only a fool would build his "Habitation" on the "Vulgar Heart"; on the other hand, despite his contempt for and distrust of the "fond Many," he is founding his rebellion on the support he has actively solicited from precisely that political base. It doesn't seem to occur to him that he is building on sand.*

105    admired    *worshipped, marveled at.*

107    Man Accurs'd    *fallen man, man cursed with the consequences of Adam's disobedience in the Garden of Eden. The image derives from Genesis 3:17–19.*

108    Past . . . worst.    *Ironically, the Archbishop here describes his own "Thoughts" (line 107), which thereby become defined as those of a "Man Accurs'd."*

109    draw our Numbers    *gather our troops.*

110    Time's Subjects    *at the mercy of Time for the success of our enterprise.*

54

That thou provok'st thy self to cast him up.
So, so, thou common Dog, didst thou disgorge
Thy Glutton-bosom of the Royal Richard,
And now thou wouldst eat thy dead Vomit up
And howl'st to find it. What Trust is in these
   Times?                                                    100
They that when Richard liv'd would have him
   die
Are now become enamor'd on his Grave.
Thou that threw'st Dust upon his goodly Head
When through proud London he came sighing on
After th' admired Heels of Bullingbrook,           105
Cri'st now "O Earth, yield us that King again
And take thou this!" O Thoughts of Man
   Accurs'd:
Past and to come seems best; things present worst.

MOWBRAY   Shall we go draw our Numbers and set on?

HASTINGS   We are Time's Subjects, and Time bids be
   gone.                                *Exeunt.*   110

II.i    *This scene takes place on a street in London, probably near the Boar's Head Tavern.*

S.D.    and an Officer or two    *The imprecision of this stage direction is one of many indications that the manuscript used to print the First Quarto was close to, if not identical with, Shakespeare's own draft script for the play. "Permissive" stage directions (those that allow the company a good deal of latitude in staging a scene, depending on available resources) are usually taken to be a sign that the manuscript used was in a pre-rehearsal state, at a time when the playwright was still imagining how, say, an entrance might be managed, but was doing so without actually having tried out the script on the stage.*

1    ent'red the Action    *initiated the legal proceedings. The Hostess is suing Falstaff for debt. Master Fang is the Sheriff's Sergeant.*

3    Yeoman    *Snare, the Sergeant's assistant.*
lusty    *vigorous, strong.*

4    'a    *he.*
stand to 't    *stand up and fight like a real man. But this phrase could also refer to another way for a "lusty Yeoman" to enter an "Action." In similar fashion* stabb'd *in line 13 reminds us of the kind of "House" (line 14) the Hostess maintains.*

# Act Two

## Scene 1

*Enter the Hostess of the Tavern and an Officer
or two.*

HOSTESS   Master Fang, have you ent'red the Action?
FANG   It is ent'red.
HOSTESS   Where's your Yeoman? Is't a lusty Yeoman?
   Will 'a stand to 't?
FANG   Sirrah, where's Snare?                                   5
HOSTESS   O Lord ay, good Master Snare!
SNARE   Here, here.
FANG   Snare, we must arrest Sir John Falstaff.
HOSTESS   Yea, good Master Snare, I have ent'red him
   and all.                                                     10
SNARE   It may chance cost some of us our Lives, for
   he will stab.
HOSTESS   Alas the Day, take heed of him: he stabb'd
   me in mine own House, most beastly, in good

57

16    foin   *thrust. Like "stab" and "Weapon" (lines 12, 13, 16),* foin *was often used with sexual implications.*

18    close   *Fang means "grapple" or engage in hand-to-hand combat; but another meaning of* close *is "embrace" sexually.*

22    Vice   *vise (grip). This Folio reading seems better than the Quarto's "view."*

23    going   *The Hostess probably refers to Falstaff's going off to battle without paying his bills. But* going *could also mean "foining."*

24    thing upon my Score   *item on my accounts. But since a "score" was literally a notch or slit cut with a knife (to tally a drink), the Hostess' phrase carries an unintended sexual meaning as well.*

27    Pie-Corner   *an intersection in the West Smithfield district of London; many cooks had shops there.*

29    Lubbers-head   *The Hostess probably means "Leopard's Head."* Lubber *means "bumpkin."*
    Lumbert   *Lombard.*

31    Exion   *action.*
    Case   *the Hostess' complaint against Falstaff. As a term for the female genitalia, however,* Case *continues the Hostess' unintended sexual equivocation. So do "long one," "borne," "fubb'd," "bear," and "Offices" in the lines that follow.*

41    Malmsy-nose   *The Hostess compares Bardolph's nose to a sweet red wine.*

faith! 'A cares not what Mischief he does, if            15
his Weapon be out; he will foin like any Divel;
he will spare neither Man, Woman, nor Child.
FANG    If I can close with him, I care not for his
Thrust.
HOSTESS    No, nor I neither, I'll be at your Elbow.       20
FANG    And I but fist him once; and 'a come but
within my Vice!
HOSTESS    I am undone by his going, I warrant you;
he's an infinitive thing upon my Score. Good
Maister Fang, hold him sure. —Good Master      25
Snare, let him not scape; 'a comes continually
to Pie-Corner (saving your Manhoods) to buy a
Saddle, and he is indited to Dinner to the
Lubbers-head in Lumbert Street to Master
Smooth's the Silk Man. I pray you, since my    30
Exion is ent'red, and my Case so openly known
to the World, let him be brought in to his
Answer. A hundred Mark is a long one for a
poor lone woman to bear, and I have borne and
borne and borne, and have been fubb'd off and   35
fubb'd off and fubb'd off, from this day to
that day, that it is a Shame to be thought on.
There is no Honesty in such dealing, unless a
Woman should be made an Ass and a Beast, to
bear ev'ry Knave's Wrong.                       40

*Enter Sir John and Bardolph and the Boy.*

Yonder he comes, and that arrant Malmsy-nose
Knave Bardolph with him. Do your Offices, do

59

49     Quean   *bawd, whore.*

50     Channel   *drainage ditch, gutter (which frequently contained raw sewage).*

54     honeysuckle   *The Hostess probably means "homicidal."*

55     Honey-seed   *The Hostess means "homicide" (whose last syllable was probably pronounced* -seed*).*

56     queller   *killer.*

59     Rescue   *a call for help.*

61     wo't   *wilt.*
       ta   *thou.*

62     Hempseed   *The Hostess may mean "homicide" again; but it is equally likely that she is referring to one who is destined for the gallows (with "Hemp" alluding to the Hangman's rope).*

63     Scullian   *kitchen wench.*
       Rampallian   *ruffian.*

64     Fustilarian   *probably an ad hoc word derived from "fustilugs" (a contemptuous term for a fat woman).*
       tickle your Catastrophe   *make your posterior smart. The Page has learned a great deal about creative swearing from his master.*

67     stand to me   *defend me. But "stand to" could also refer to another way for a man to "be good" (line 66) to a woman.*

60

your Offices, Master Fang and Master Snare;
do me, do me, do me your Offices.

FALSTAFF   How now, whose Mare's dead? What's the    45
matter?

FANG   I arrest you at the Suit of Mistress Quickly.

FALSTAFF   Away, Varlets! Draw, Bardolph! Cut me off
the Villain's Head! Throw the Quean in the
Channel.    50

HOSTESS   Throw me in the Channel? I'll throw thee
in the Channel! Wilt thou, wilt thou, thou
bastardly Rogue? Murder, murder! Ah, thou
honeysuckle Villain, wilt thou kill God's
Officers and the King's? Ah, thou Honey-seed    55
Rogue, thou art a Honey-seed, a Man-queller,
and a Woman-queller.

FALSTAFF   Keep them off, Bardolph!

OFFICER   A Rescue! A Rescue!

HOSTESS   —Good People, bring a Rescue or two!    60

*Falstaff's Page attacks her.*

Thou wo't, wo't thou? Thou wo't, wo't ta? Do
do, thou Rogue! Do, thou Hempseed!

PAGE   Away, you Scullian, you Rampallian, you
Fustilarian: I'll tickle your Catastrophe!

*Enter the Lord Chief Justice and his Men.*

JUSTICE   What is the matter? Keep the Peace here,
ho!    65

HOSTESS   Good my Lord, be good to me! I beseech
you, stand to me.

71     —Stand from him, Fellow!    *The Justice probably addresses this line either to Bardolph or to the Page.*

80–81   Or I . . . Mare.    *The Hostess means that she will haunt Falstaff every night like a nightmare. Once again, however, her words convey an unintended sexual meaning. Falstaff picks up on it in his reply (lines 82–83).*

82     ride the Mare    *By "Mare" Falstaff probably means the Hostess herself; his implication is that if the Hostess tried to give him a hard time, he would quickly put her in her place and charm her back into submission to him. His imagery is sexual, but what he describes is a pattern of exploitation that goes well beyond an occasional "ride."*

83     vantage of Ground    *elevated position from which to mount.*
       get up    *both (a) mount a mare, and (b) "stand to" (as in line 67).*

85     Good Temper    *self-discipline, proper disposition.*

92     parcel-gilt    *partially gilded (with gold on the inside of the goblet).*
       Dolphin    *the name of one of the Hostess' tavern rooms.*

93     Seacoal    *mineral coal, normally transported by sea from Newcastle.*

94     Wheeson    *Whitsun (Pentecost, seven weeks after Easter).*

95     liking    *likening, comparing.*

JUSTICE   How now, Sir John, what are you brawling
    here?
    Doth this become your Place, your Time, and
        Business?
    You should have been well on your way to York.     70
    —Stand from him, Fellow! Wherefore hang'st
        thou upon him?
HOSTESS   O my most worshipful Lord, and 't please
    your Grace, I am a poor Widow of Eastcheap,
    and he is arrested at my Suit.
JUSTICE   For what Sum?                                75
HOSTESS   It is more than for some, my Lord; it is
    for all I have. He hath eaten me out of House
    and Home; he hath put all my Substance into
    that fat Belly of his; but I will have some of
    it out again. —Or I will ride thee a' Nights      80
    like the Mare.
FALSTAFF   I think I am as like to ride the Mare if
    I have any vantage of Ground to get up.
JUSTICE   How comes this, Sir John? What Man of
    Good Temper would endure this Tempest of         85
    Exclamation? Are you not asham'd to enforce a
    poor Widow to so rough a course to come by her
    own?
FALSTAFF   What is the gross Sum that I owe thee?
HOSTESS   Marry if thou wert an Honest Man, thy Self   90
    and the Money too. Thou didst swear to me upon
    a parcel-gilt Goblet, sitting in my Dolphin
    Chamber, at the Round Table by a Seacoal Fire,
    upon Wednesday in Wheeson Week, when the
    Prince broke thy Head for liking his Father to a   95

96    Winsor    *Windsor.*

99    Keech    *The Butcher's name derives from the name for the tallow (animal fat) he rolled up for delivery to the candlemaker.*

100    Gossip    *a familiar term of address, roughly equivalent to "neighbor," and here carrying the implication "fellow Goodwife."*

101    mess    *supply.*

102    Prawns    *shrimp.*
       whereby    *The Hostess means "whereupon."*

104    green    *fresh, raw.*

106    familiarity    *familiar, friendly, equal.*

109    and . . . Shillings    *This detail says everything about both Falstaff and the pliable, generous Hostess he misuses so outrageously.*

110    Book Oath    *oath on the Bible.*

113–   that . . . you    *Falstaff's implication is that if what the Host-*
14     *ess says about him is true, then what she says about the Justice is just as likely to be true.*

114    in Good Case    *better off.*

115    distracted her    *driven her mad.*

120    confident Brow    *self-assured manner.*

123    a level Consideration    *a just weighing of the evidence in the case.*

124    practic'd upon    *tricked, deceived, taken advantage of.*

singing man of Winsor; thou didst swear to me
then, as I was washing thy Wound, to marry me,
and make me My Lady thy Wife. Canst thou deny
it? Did not Goodwife Keech, the Butcher's Wife,
come in then and call me Gossip Quickly;          100
coming in to borrow a mess of Vinegar, telling
us she had a good dish of Prawns, whereby thou
didst desire to eat some, whereby I told thee
they were ill for a green Wound? And didst
thou not, when she was gone down stairs,          105
desire me to be no more so familiarity with
such Poor People, saying that ere long they
should call me Madam? And didst thou not kiss
me, and bid me fetch thee thirty Shillings? I
put thee now thy Book Oath, deny it if thou       110
canst!

FALSTAFF  My Lord, this is a poor Mad Soul, and she
says up and down the Town that her eldest Son
is like you. She hath been in Good Case, and
the truth is Poverty hath distracted her. But     115
for these foolish Officers, I beseech you I
may have Redress against them.

JUSTICE  Sir John, Sir John, I am well acquainted
with your manner of wrenching the True Cause
the False Way. It is not a confident Brow, nor    120
the throng of Words that come with such more
than impudent Sauciness from you, can thrust
me from a level Consideration. You have, as it
appears to me, practic'd upon the easy Yielding
Spirit of this Woman and made her serve your      125
uses both in Purse and in Person.

131    current   *both (a) immediate, and (b) genuine (like true currency, "sterling").*

132    Sneap   *rebuke (a Yorkshire word related to "snub").*

133    honorable Boldness   *an outspoken defense of my honor.*

136    my humble Duty rememb'red   *though bearing in mind my humble duty to you.*

138–
39    being . . . Affairs   *Falstaff reminds the Justice that he is under orders to lead a charge of troops to York. Since the Lord Chief Justice has already asked Falstaff why he is still in London (line 70), Falstaff's opportunistic resort to the cover of military immunity at this point is ever so slightly lacking in credibility.*

140    You . . . wrong   *You speak as one whose military prerogatives permit you to do wrong with impunity.*

141    in th' effect of your Reputation   *in a manner compatible with the reputation a knighthood implies.*

143    Come hither, Hostess.   *While the Lord Chief Justice talks with the Messenger (lines 144–46), Falstaff speaks privately with the Hostess.*

152    fain   *willing, content. But the Hostess probably means "forced."*
       Plate   *silver serving utensils.*

HOSTESS    Yea in truth, my Lord.

JUSTICE    Pray thee peace. —Pay here the Debt you
     owe her, and unpay the Villainy you have done
     with her. The one you may do with sterling          130
     Money, and the other with current Repentance.

FALSTAFF    My Lord, I will not undergo this Sneap
     without Reply. You call honorable Boldness
     impudent Sauciness. If a Man will make curtsy
     and say nothing, he is Virtuous. No my Lord,        135
     my humble Duty rememb'red, I will not be your
     Suitor. I say to you I do desire Deliverance
     from these Officers, being upon hasty
     Employment in the King's Affairs.

JUSTICE    You speak as having power to do wrong;        140
     but answer in th' effect of your Reputation, and
     satisfy the poor Woman.

FALSTAFF    Come hither, Hostess.

*Enter a Messenger (Master Gower).*

JUSTICE    Now Master Gower, what News?

GOWER    The King, my Lord, and Harry, Prince of
     Wales,                                              145
     Are near at hand; the rest the Paper tells.

FALSTAFF    As I am a Gentleman.

HOSTESS    Faith, you said so before.

FALSTAFF    As I am a Gentleman. Come, no more
     words of it.                                        150

HOSTESS    By this Heav'nly Ground I tread on, I must
     be fain to pawn both my Plate and the Tapestry
     of my Dining Chambers.

154     Glasses . . . drinking    *Glass vessels, rather than metal tankards and goblets, are now the only fashion.*

155     sleight Drollery    *a clever comic scene. Editors normally adopt the Folio spelling,* slight *(of which* sleight *could be a variant). Both words were used in reference to artistic craft.*

156–    Story . . . Waterwork    *Renderings of the Prodigal Son and*
57      *of German hunting scenes were popular in England.*

162     draw the Action    *withdraw the charges.*

163     Humour    *seizure of irrationality.*

164     set on    *incited by someone else. Falstaff is now addressing the Hostess condescendingly as if she were not really responsible for the "injury" she has done him.*

166     Nobles    *gold coins valued at six shillings, eight pence. The amount the Hostess requests is ten percent of what Falstaff owes her.*

168     Let . . . shift.    *"Forget it, I'll make other arrangements for my leisure."*

170     you shall have it    *you shall have your way (and further credit).*

173     Will I live?    *Falstaff's implication is "My life upon it!"*

173–    hook on    *stick close to her. Falstaff probably addresses this*
74      *order to Bardolph, with the implication that he should make sure that the Hostess suffers no more "humours."*

181     Basingstoke    *a town forty-five miles southwest of London.*

FALSTAFF   Glasses, Glasses is the only drinking;
         and for thy Walls, a pretty sleight Drollery,          155
         or the Story of the Prodigal, or the Garman
         Hunting in Waterwork, is worth a thousand of
         these Bed-hangers, and these Fly-bitten
         Tapestries. Let it be ten Pound if thou canst.
         Come, and 'twere not for thy Humours, there's    160
         not a better Wench in England. Go wash thy
         Face and draw the Action. Come, thou must not
         be in this Humour with me. Dost not know me?
         Come, come, I know thou wast set on to this.
HOSTESS   Pray thee, Sir John, let it be but twenty       165
         Nobles; i' faith I am loath to pawn my Plate,
         so God save me, law.
FALSTAFF   Let it alone, I'll make other shift. You'll
         be a Fool still.
HOSTESS   Well, you shall have it, though I pawn my        170
         Gown. I hope you'll come to Supper. You'll pay
         me all together?
FALSTAFF   Will I live? —Go with her, with her, hook
         on, hook on.
HOSTESS   Will you have Doll Tearsheet meet you at        175
         Supper?
FALSTAFF   No more words, let's have her.
                              *Exit Hostess with Sergeant.*
JUSTICE   I have heard better News.
FALSTAFF   What's the News, my Lord?
JUSTICE   Where lay the King tonight?                      180
GOWER   At Basingstoke, my Lord.
FALSTAFF   I hope, my Lord, all's well. What is the
         News, my Lord?

69

185     Horse    *cavalry (as opposed to the foot soldiers mentioned earlier).*

194     Dinner    *the midday meal. Falstaff probably wants to request some more money for his "military requirements."*

195     wait upon    *attend to the needs of. The Lord Chief Justice has just told Gower to "go [come] along with me."*

198     take Soldiers up    *enlist troops.*

201–2    What . . . John?    *The Lord Chief Justice is reminding Falstaff once again that he appears to be hard of hearing. Since line 191, Falstaff has been ignoring the Justice, addressing all his remarks to Gower.*

204–6    This . . . fair.    *As he speaks these lines Falstaff probably dons his fencing "Manners," contemptuously mocking the Justice with a "tap" of his sword as he parts. Once again Falstaff has effected a clever escape, and he cannot resist a small gesture of triumph as he savors yet another victory over his stern antagonist.*

207     lighten    *The Justice probably means "enlighten" (by removing your spiritual blindness and letting you see yourself as the foolish reprobate you are). But* lighten *could also mean "strike with lightning." In addition, there is wordplay on "light" with reference to (a) Falstaff's "great" weight, and (b) Falstaff's "light" (frivolous) character, his lack of gravity.*

JUSTICE   Come all his Forces back?

GOWER   No, fifteen hundred Foot, five hundred Horse                                                                      185
    Are march'd up to my Lord of Lancaster,
    Against Northumberland and the Archbishop.

FALSTAFF   Comes the King back from Wales, my
    noble Lord?

JUSTICE   You shall have Letters of me presently.
    —Come, go along with me, good Master Gower.                                    190

FALSTAFF   My Lord—

JUSTICE   What's the matter?

FALSTAFF   Maister Gower, shall I entreat you with
    me to Dinner?

GOWER   I must wait upon my good Lord here, I thank                                 195
    you, good Sir John.

JUSTICE   Sir John, you loiter here too long, being
    you are to take Soldiers up in Counties as you
    go.

FALSTAFF   Will you sup with me, Maister Gower?                                          200

JUSTICE   What foolish Maister taught you these
    Manners, Sir John?

FALSTAFF   Maister Gower, if they become me not,
    he was a Fool that taught them me. —This is the
    right Fencing-grace, my Lord: tap for tap, and                                        205
    so part fair.

JUSTICE   Now the Lord lighten thee: thou art a
    great Fool.                                                                    *Exeunt.*

II.ii     *This scene probably takes place at the Prince's residence in London. This is the first time we have seen him since his victory at the battle of Shrewsbury in* 1 Henry IV.

3     attach'd to   *affected, taken hold of.*

5     discolors   *both (a) causes to blush, and (b) casts in a bad light.*

6     Complexion   *both (a) physical countenance, and (b) character (with particular reference to the balance of the Prince's humours).*

7     show vildly in me   *make me seem vile, disreputable.*

7–8     Small Beer   *weak beer; here a metaphor for the Prince's taste for companions who are lacking in substance and gravity.*

9–10     loosely studied   *lacking in sober consideration.*

10     remember   *be mindful of, take note of.*
        Composition   *mixture, substance.*

11     Belike   *perhaps, probably.*

12     got   *begotten, conceived.*

18     with these   *in addition to these.*

19     once   *This is the Quarto reading. Many editors follow the Folio and print* ones.
        bear   *bear in mind.*

20–21     one for Superfluity   *one for use as a spare.*

# Scene 2

*Enter the Prince and Poins, with another.*

PRINCE   Before God, I am exceeding weary.

POINS   Is't come to that? I had thought Weariness
durst not have attach'd to one of so High
Blood.

PRINCE   Faith it does me, though it discolors the          5
Complexion of my Greatness to acknowledge it.
Doth it not show vildly in me to desire Small
Beer?

POINS   Why a Prince should not be so loosely
studied as to remember so weak a Composition.     10

PRINCE   Belike then my Appetite was not Princely
got: for by my troth, I do now remember the
poor creature Small Beer. But indeed these
humble considerations make me out of love with
my Greatness. What a Disgrace is it to me to     15
remember thy Name? Or to know thy Face
tomorrow? Or to take note how many pair of
Silk Stockings thou hast with these, and those
that were thy Peach-color'd once? Or to bear
the Inventory of thy Shirts, as one for     20
Superfluity and another for Use. But that the
Tennis Court Keeper knows better than I, for

73

21–31 **But . . . strengthened.** *These lines involve multiple puns, but their general sense is that Poins is an extravagant young gallant whose expensive stockings and shirts (many of them imported from Holland) are being consumed by his leisure activities, particularly those involving "Low Countries" (whores), who are "shifting" (contriving) to "shift" (transfer) Poins's "Ruins" (castoff "shifts" or shirts) from his back to those of their bawling bastard children.*

26 **Low Countries** *a pun on (a) Holland, (b) the nether regions of the body, (c) low haunts, and (d) prostitutes.*

27 **Holland** *fine linen imported from Holland.*

30 **not in the fault** *not to be blamed for how they came into the world. Indeed, the Prince notes, even Poins's bastards shall inherit the kingdom of God (Luke 18:16–17).*

31 **Kinreds** *Kindreds.*

41 **stand the push** *stand up to the thrust, with bawdy wordplay on* Wits *and* thing.

43 **it is not meet** *it is not appropriate, or to be expected.*

45–46 **for fault of** *for lack of.*

48 **Very hardly** *only with great difficulty. Poins assumes, along with everyone else in the world, that a young man in the Prince's position would be happy, rather than sad, at the prospect of inheriting a rich kingdom.*

50 **Divel's Book** *the Devil's list of those marked for Hell.*

51 **Obduracy and Persistency** *refusal to turn from evil ways.*

74

it is a Low Ebb of Linen with thee when thou
keepest not Racket there, as thou hast not
done a great while, because the rest of the                    25
Low Countries have made a Shift to eat up thy
Holland. And God knows whether those that bawl
out the Ruins of thy Linen shall inherit His
Kingdom. But the Midwives say the Children are
not in the fault, whereupon the World increases,             30
and Kinreds are mightily strengthen'd.

POINS    How ill it follows, after you have labor'd
so hard, you should talk so idly! Tell me how
many good young Princes would do so, their
Fathers being so sick as yours at this time is.              35

PRINCE    Shall I tell thee one thing, Poins?

POINS    Yes faith, and let it be an excellent good
thing.

PRINCE    It shall serve among Wits of no higher
breeding than thine.                                         40

POINS    Go to, I stand the push of your one thing
that you will tell.

PRINCE    Marry I tell thee it is not meet that I
should be sad now my Father is sick, albeit I
could tell to thee, as to one it please me for              45
fault of a better to call my Friend, I could
be sad, and sad indeed too.

POINS    Very hardly, upon such a Subject.

PRINCE    By this Hand, thou thinkest me as far in
the Divel's Book as thou and Falstaff for                    50
Obduracy and Persistency. Let the End try the
Man. But I tell thee, my Heart bleeds inwardly

55   Ostentation   *open display.*

63   keeps the Road-way   *takes the common course. Although the Prince appears to be complimenting Poins here, the context would suggest that he is also remembering that "wide is the gate, and broad is the way, that leadeth to destruction, and many there be which go in thereat" (Matthew 7:13). At this point in his life the Prince is struggling to prepare himself to "enter . . . in at the strait gate." What he is coming to terms with in the process is his painful awareness that many of his companions will be unable to "lighten" themselves enough to join the Prince on the "narrow . . . way" (Matthew 7:14) his "Greatness" (line 15) requires him to take.*

65   accites   *summons, leads.*

67   Lewd   *given over to loose and base behavior.*

68   engraffed   *affixed, grafted.*

70   well spoke on   *well spoken of, of a good reputation.*

72   Second Brother   *Younger brothers, lacking in inheritance because of the laws of primogeniture, were often left to shift for themselves. As a result, they frequently became dissolute and engaged in shifty, if not criminal, behavior.*

73   Proper Fellow of my Hands   *a good fighter, good with my hands.*

76   'a had   *he received.*

78   Ape   *The Page is aping the behavior of his reprobate master.*

that my Father is so sick; and, keeping such
Vile Company as thou art hath in Reason taken
from me all Ostentation of Sorrow.                              55

POINS   The Reason?

PRINCE   What wouldst thou think of me if I should
weep?

POINS   I would think thee a most Princely Hypocrite.

PRINCE   It would be Every Man's Thought; and thou          60
art a blessed Fellow to think as Every Man
thinks; never a Man's Thought in the World
keeps the Road-way better than thine. Every
Man would think me an Hypocrite indeed. And
what accites your most worshipful Thought to           65
think so?

POINS   Why because you have been so Lewd, and so
much engraffed to Falstaff.

PRINCE   And to thee.

POINS   By this Light I am well spoke on, I can hear        70
with mine own Ears: the worst that they can
say of me is that I am a Second Brother, and
that I am a Proper Fellow of my Hands, and
those two things I confess I cannot help. By
the Mass, here comes Bardolph.                             75

*Enter Bardolph and Boy.*

PRINCE   And the Boy that I gave Falstaff; 'a had
him from me Christian, and look if the fat
Villain have not transform'd him Ape.

BARDOLPH   God save your Grace.

PRINCE   And yours, most noble Bardolph.                    80

77

84       **Pottle-pot**  *a two-quart tankard of ale. Poins attributes Bardolph's complexion to his shame at having taken a tankard's virginity.*

90       **Alewive's Petticoat**  *Like prostitutes, alewives often wore red taffeta petticoats; alehouses often had red-latticed windows.*

93       **Althaea's Dream**  *As lines 95–97 make clear, the Page is comparing Bardolph's face to a firebrand, a piece of burning wood. Althaea was a Calydonian Queen whose son Meleager was destined to live for as long as a firebrand the Fates had placed on her fire remained unburnt. The "Dream" the Page refers to is probably that of Hecuba, the fateful Queen of Troy who learned in her sleep that she would give birth to a "firebrand" (Paris) whose raging lust would eventually result in the burning of Troy.*

100–2    **O that . . . thee.**  *Poins gives the Page sixpence to help "preserve" the young "Blossom" from the deadly cankerworm (the corrupting influence of Falstaff).*

103–4    **And . . . wrong.**  *If the three of you don't do enough among you to turn him into a hanged criminal, the gallows will have been cheated.*

109      **Martlemas**  *Martinmas (November 11), the Feast of Saint Martin's, was a traditional harvest festival. Poins is probably comparing Falstaff to the fatted oxen and boars (see line 157) that were roasted and eaten on that occasion.*

111      **the Immortal . . . Physician**  *This line recalls the Lord Chief Justice's remarks at I.ii.5 and elsewhere. It also echoes Matthew 9:12.*

POINS   Come, you virtuous Ass, you bashful Fool:
must you be blushing? Wherefore blush you now?
What a maidenly Man at Arms are you become?
Is't such a matter to get a Pottle-pot's
Maidenhead?                                                      85
PAGE   'A calls me e'en now, my Lord, through a red
Lattice, and I could discern no part of his
Face from the Window. At last I spied his Eyes,
and methought he had made two Holes in the
Alewive's Petticoat and so peep'd through.      90
PRINCE   Has not the Boy profited?
BARDOLPH   Away, you whoreson upright Rabble, away!
PAGE   Away, you rascally Althaea's Dream, away!
PRINCE   Instruct us, Boy: what Dream, Boy?
PAGE   Marry, my Lord, Althaear dreamt she was      95
deliver'd of a Firebrand, and therefore I call
him her Dream.
PRINCE   A Crown's worth of good Interpretation!
There 'tis, Boy.
POINS   O that the Blossom could be kept from      100
Cankers! Well, there is Sixpence to preserve
thee.
BARDOLPH   And you do not make him hang'd among
you, the Gallows shall have wrong.
PRINCE   And how doth thy Master, Bardolph?      105
BARDOLPH   Well, my Lord; he heard of your Grace's
coming to Town. There's a Letter for you.
POINS   Deliver'd with good respect, and how doth
the Martlemas, your Master?
BARDOLPH   In Bodily Health, Sir.                          110
POINS   Marry, the Immortal Part needs a Physician,

79

114    Wen   *a swollen tumor.*

115    holds his Place   *maintains (merits) his position of honor.*

117–    Every . . . King.   *Poins notes that Falstaff parades his title*
19      *every time he mentions his name, like those who claim kinship*
       *with the King.*

122–    takes . . . conceive   *acts as if he doesn't understand.*
23

127    fetch it   *derive their ancestry.*
       Japhet   *one of Noah's sons.*

131    a Certificate   *a legal document, not a letter.*

132–    "I will imitate . . . Brevity"   *Falstaff is probably thinking*
33      *of Caesar's famous "Veni, vidi, vici" (I came, I saw, I con-*
       *quered).*

134    sure   *surely.*

140    at idle times   *at your leisure.*

but that moves not him; though that be sick,
it dies not.

PRINCE  I do allow this Wen to be as familiar with
me as my Dog, and he holds his Place: for                    115
look you how he writes.

*He hands Poins Falstaff's Letter.*

POINS  "John Falstaff, Knight." Every man must know
that as oft as he has occasion to name himself,
even like those that are kin to the King. For
they never prick their Finger but they say                   120
"There's some of the King's Blood spilt." "How
comes that?" says he that takes upon him not
to conceive. The Answer is as ready as a
borrowed Cap: "I am the King's poor Cousin,
Sir."                                                         125

PRINCE  Nay they will be kin to us, or they will
fetch it from Japhet. But the Letter: "Sir
John Falstaff, Knight, to the Son of the King
nearest his Father, Harry, Prince of Wales,
greeting."                                                    130

POINS  Why this is a Certificate.

PRINCE  Peace. "I will imitate the Honorable Romans
in Brevity."

POINS  He sure means Brevity in breath: short-
winded.                                                       135

PRINCE  "I commend me to thee. I commend thee,
and I leave thee. Be not too familiar with
Poins, for he misuses thy Favors so much that
he swears thou art to marry his sister Nell.
Repent at idle times, as thou may'st, and so                 140
farewell.

81

142      by yea and no    *This, the mildest of oaths, was associated with Puritans who wished to eschew all swearing. It derived from the Sermon on the Mount, where Jesus says "let your communication be, Yea, yea; Nay, nay: for whatsoever is more than these cometh of evil" (Matthew 5:37).*

144      with my Familiars    *to those who are my intimate friends.*

148      That's . . . Words.    *That would be tantamount to making him eat his words twenty times over (because of Falstaff's great love of Sack, a white Spanish wine).*

153      thus . . . Time    *in this kind of folly we waste our precious time (and it in turn wastes us away).*

154      the Wise    *departed saints.*

158      Frank    *sty. The Prince refers to the Boar's Head Tavern.*

161      Ephesians . . . Church.    *Like "Corinthians," "Ephesians" was a term for reprobate, loose-living characters such as the Boar's Head idlers. "Old Church" was a designation for Falstaff's kind of congregation, "corrupt according to the deceitful lusts" (Ephesians 4:24).*

164      Doll Tearsheet    *"Doll" was a common name for prostitutes, and the hyphenated form of "Tear-sheet" (which is how the name is normally rendered in the early texts) makes it graphically clear that this "Doll" lives up to her name.*

166      proper    *respectable.*

168      Heicfors    *heifers, young cows.*

Thine by yea and no, which is as much as
to say 'as thou usest him,' Jack Falstaff
with my Familiars; John with my Brothers
and Sisters, and Sir John with all Europe."                 145

POINS    My Lord, I'll steep this Letter in Sack and
make him eat it.

PRINCE    That's to make him eat twenty of his Words.
But do you use me thus, Ned? Must I marry your
Sister?                                                      150

POINS    God send the Wench no worse Fortune, but I
never said so.

PRINCE    Well, thus we play the Fools with the Time,
and the Spirits of the Wise sit in the Clouds
and mock us. Is your Master here in London?                  155

BARDOLPH    Yea my Lord.

PRINCE    Where sups he? Doth the Old Boar feed in
the Old Frank?

BARDOLPH    At the Old Place, my Lord, in Eastcheap.

PRINCE    What Company?                                      160

PAGE    Ephesians, my Lord, of the Old Church.

PRINCE    Sup any Women with him?

PAGE    None, my Lord, but old Mistress Quickly and
Mistress Doll Tearsheet.

PRINCE    What Pagan may that be?                            165

PAGE    A proper Gentlewoman, Sir, and a Kinswoman
of my Master's.

PRINCE    Even such kin as the Parish Heicfors are to
the Town Bull. Shall we steal upon them, Ned,
at Supper?                                                   170

POINS    I am your Shadow, my Lord; I'll follow you.

PRINCE    Sirrah, you Boy, and Bardolph: no word to

174    There's for your Silence. *As he speaks these words, the Prince gives money to both Bardolph and the Page.*

178    Road  *a common term for prostitutes. This line suggests an additional implication for "Road-way" in line 63.*

180    Saint Albons  *a town about twenty miles north on the Great North Road.*

181    bestow  *conduct.*

184    Jerkins  *jackets.*

185    Drawers  *tavern waiters.*

186–87    From . . . Case.  *When Zeus (Jove) decided to seduce Europa, he took the form of a bull and carried the maiden across the Mediterranean to Crete.*
Decension  *descent in station.*

188    Prentice  *apprentice. The Prince is probably thinking of Francis the Drawer, with whom he and Poins had had some fun in II.iv of 1 Henry IV.*

190    weigh with  *be equal in weight to. Here the implication is "justify," provide a good reason for.*

II.iii    *This scene takes place at Warkworth, the castle of the Earl of Northumberland.*

2    Give Even Way  *provide a smooth ride. Northumberland is saying "please don't give me a hard time."*

your Master that I am yet come to Town.
There's for your Silence.

BARDOLPH   I have no Tongue, Sir.                           175

PAGE   And for mine, Sir, I will govern it.

PRINCE   Fare you well: go.        *Exeunt Bardolph and Page.*
This Doll Tearsheet should be some Road.

POINS   I warrant you, as common as the Way between
Saint Albons and London. .                                  180

PRINCE   How might we see Falstaff bestow himself
tonight in his true Colors, and not our selves
be seen?

POINS   Put on two Leathern Jerkins and Aprons, and
wait upon him at his Table as Drawers.                      185

PRINCE   From a God to a Bull, a heavy Decension:
it was Jove's Case. From a Prince to a
Prentice: a low Transformation, that shall be
mine. For in every thing the Purpose must
weigh with the Folly. Follow me, Ned.        *Exeunt.*   190

# Scene 3

*Enter Northumberland, his Wife, and the Wife
to Harry Percy (Kate).*

NORTHUMBERLAND   I pray thee, loving Wife and
gentle Daughter,
Give Even Way unto my Rough Affairs.

3    Visage   *countenance, expression, here depicted as a mask to be put on to match that of "the Times."*

7    at Pawn   *at stake, at risk.*

8    but   *except for.*
     redeem it   *make good on it, reclaim it.*

9    yet   *nevertheless.*

11   more endear'd to it   *both (a) more heavily staked (wagered) on it, and (b) more tied to the venture by your love of one dear to you (Hotspur).*

15   Who then persuaded you to stay at home?   *According to IV.i.16 of* 1 Henry IV, *Northumberland was "grievous Sick."*

18   stuck   *fixed, like the Sun in its sphere ("gray Vault").*

20   Chevalry   *chivalry, knightly warriors.*

21   Glass   *both (a) mirror, and (b) example.*

24   thick   *rapidly, the words coming thickly upon one another. This adverb has often been interpreted as a reference to a speech impediment (a stutter or stammer), but line 26 makes it clear that it refers instead to Hotspur's impetuosity, and perhaps to a tendency for him to speak too loudly (not "low," soft).*

27   Would turn . . . Abuse   *would alter their normally perfect diction.*

29   Affections of Delight   *their preferred pleasures and pastimes.*

Put not you on the Visage of the Times,
And be, like them, to Percy troublesome.

WIFE  I've given over; I will speak no more:                    5
Do what you will, your Wisdom be your Guide.

NORTHUMBERLAND  Alas, sweet Wife, my Honor is at
    Pawn,
And, but my going, nothing can redeem it.

KATE  O yet for God's sake go not to these Wars!
The Time was, Father, that you broke your Word           10
When you were more endear'd to it than now,
When your own Percy, when my Heart's dear
    Harry,
Threw many a Northward Look to see his Father
Bring up his Pow'rs; but he did long in vain.
Who then persuaded you to stay at home?                      15
There were two Honors lost, Yours and your
    Son's.
For Yours, the God of Heaven brighten it;
For His, it stuck upon him as the Sun
In the gray Vault of Heav'n, and by his Light
Did all the Chevalry of England move                          20
To do brave Acts. He was indeed the Glass
Wherein the Noble Youth did dress themselves.
He had no Legs that practic'd not his Gait;
And speaking thick, which Nature made his
    Blemish,
Became the Accents of the Valiant.                           25
For those that could speak low and tardily
Would turn their own Perfection to Abuse
To seem like him. So that in Speech, in Gait,
In Diet, in Affections of Delight,

30    Humours of Blood   *quirks resulting from their valorous temperaments.*

31    Mark   *guidepost.*
Copy and Book   *model and manual.*

34    unseconded   *unsupported.*

36    abide a Field   *stand up in a field of battle.*

38    defensible   *capable of sustaining a defense.*

40    To hold . . . nice   *to be more exacting and meticulous about the demands of honor.*

41    Let them alone.   *Let them manage without you.*

45    Monmouth   *Prince Henry (Hal), so called because he was born at Monmouth in Wales.*
Beshrew your Heart   *May your heart be cursed, shamed.*

46    Sp'rites   *spirits (spelled* spirites *in the Quarto).*

47    With . . . Oversights   *by lamenting anew my past errors.*

50    worse provided   *less prepared to meet it.*

52    Puissance   *strength.*
Taste   *test.*

53    get Ground and Vantage   *gain some ground and obtain an advantage.*

56    So   *thus.*

57    suff'red   *allowed.*

In Military Rules, Humours of Blood,                    30
He was the Mark and Glass, Copy and Book,
That fashion'd others. And him (O wondrous Him,
O Miracle of Men!), him did you leave,
Second to none, unseconded by you,
To look upon the hideous God of War                     35
In Disadvantage, to abide a Field
Where nothing but the sound of Hotspur's Name
Did seem defensible: so you left him.
Never, O never do his Ghost the wrong
To hold your Honor more precise and nice               40
With others than with him. Let them alone.
The Marshal and the Archbishop are strong;
Had my sweet Harry had but half their Numbers,
Today might I, hanging on Hotspur's Neck,
Have talk'd of Monmouth's Grave.
NORTHUMBERLAND                    Beshrew your Heart,    45
Fair Daughter, you do draw my Sp'rites from me
With new lamenting ancient Oversights;
But I must go and meet with Danger there,
Or it will seek me in another place
And find me worse provided.
WIFE                              O fly to Scotland      50
Till that the Nobles and the armed Commons
Have of their Puissance made a little Taste.
KATE   If they get Ground and Vantage of the King,
Then join you with them like a Rib of Steel
To make Strength stronger. But for all our
    Loves,                                              55
First let them try themselves. So did your Son;
He was so suff'red; so came I a Widow,

61      Recordation   *a memorial.*

63      his   *its. In Shakespeare's time the neuter possessive pronoun was usually rendered either as* his *or as* it.

64      Still-stand   *standstill. Northumberland's image is similar to several that occur in* Julius Caesar *and* Antony and Cleopatra. *It suggests that this is a critical moment, both for England and for the individuals and forces contending to mount the "Tide" of history. If the tide is indeed at "his Height," the implication is that it will soon be receding for one side or the other.*

65      Fain would I go   *I would like to go.*

II.iv   *With this scene we move to the Boar's Head Tavern for the Supper encounter arranged in II.i and II.ii.*

S.D.   Drawer   *waiter.*

2      Apple-johns   *apples that were kept for as long as two years before being eaten and were thought to be at their best when old and wrinkled. They were often compared to old, impotent men, and in some cases to men who had degenerated into pimps.*

8      wither'd Knights   *Falstaff does not like to be reminded that he is old and withered. Like the "latter Spring" referred to in* 1 Henry IV, *I.ii.174, he prefers to believe that he has drunk the elixir of perpetual youth.*

And never shall have length of Life enough
To rain upon Remembrance with mine Eyes
That it may grow and sprout as high as Heaven          60
For Recordation to my Noble Husband.
NORTHUMBERLAND   Come, come, go in with me,
    'tis with my Mind
As with the Tide swell'd up unto his Height,
That makes a Still-stand, running neither way.
Fain would I go to meet the Archbishop,          65
But many thousand Reasons hold me back.
I will resolve for Scotland. There am I
Till Time and Vantage crave my Company.   *Exeunt.*


# Scene 4

*Enter Francis and a second Drawer.*

FRANCIS   What the Divel hast thou brought there,
    Apple-johns? Thou knowest Sir John cannot
    endure an Apple-john.
DRAWER   Mass, thou say'st true: the Prince once set
    a Dish of Apple-johns before him, and told him          5
    there were five more Sir Johns, and, putting
    off his Hat, said "I will now take my leave of
    these six dry, round, old, wither'd Knights."
    It ang'red him to the Heart, but he hath forgot
    that.          10

11     cover   *cover the table with a cloth.*

12     Sneak's Noise   *Sneak's musicians.*

13     would fain   *would like to.*

15     straight   *right away.*

17     anon   *soon.*

20     Old Utis   *a grand old time.* Utis *(normally spelled "utas") can mean either "noise" or "jollity." Its literal meaning is "octave," and it refers to an eight-day period of festivity.*

21     Stratagem   *trick, practical joke.*

24     Temperality   *the Hostess' word for "temper," mood.* Pulsidge   *a Quicklyism for "pulse."*

27     law   *la, a meaningless interjection.*

28     Canaries   *canary, a sweet wine imported from the Canary Islands. But "canaries" can also refer to a vigorous dance, and the Hostess' imagery suggests that Doll's pulse is dancing.*

29     perfumes   *permeates (searches) and stimulates.*

32     hem!   *Down with it! Let's go! Compare Shallow's expression in III.ii.232.*

FRANCIS   Why then cover and set them down, and
    see if thou canst find out Sneak's Noise. Mistress
    Tearsheet would fain hear some Music.

*Enter Will (a third Drawer).*

WILL   Dispatch! The Room where they supp'd is too
    hot: they'll come in straight.                    *Exit.*   15
FRANCIS   Sirrah, here will be the Prince and Master
    Poins anon, and they will put on two of our
    Jerkins and Aprons, and Sir John must not know
    of it; Bardolph hath brought word.
DRAWER   By the Mass, here will be Old Utis: it will          20
    be an excellent Stratagem.
FRANCIS   I'll see if I can find out Sneak.        *Exeunt.*

*Enter Mistress Quickly and Doll Tearsheet.*

HOSTESS   I' faith Sweet-heart, methinks now you are
    in an excellent good Temperality. Your Pulsidge
    beats as extraordinarily as Heart would desire,          25
    and your Color, I warrant you, is as red as
    any Rose, in good truth, law. But i' faith you
    have drunk too much Canaries, and that's a
    marvelous searching Wine, and it perfumes the
    Blood ere one can say "What's this?" How do             30
    you now?
DOLL   Better than I was: hem!
HOSTESS   Why that's well said: a good Heart's worth
    Gold. Lo here comes Sir John.

93

35    When . . . Court    *a snatch from the ballad "Sir Launcelot du Lake."*

36    Jordan    *chamber-pot.*

39–40    and . . . sick    *both (a) being women, they get seasick even in calm waters, and (b) being prostitutes, they are unhappy when business is slack.*

43    You make fat Rascals    *Taking "muddy Rascal" in the sense of sluggish, lean deer, Falstaff implies that Doll's "Sect" turns them into bloated, diseased ones.*

50    our Chains and our Jewels    *Doll interprets "catch" (line 48) as "steal."*

51    Brooches . . . Ouches    *names for both (a) jewels, and (b) sores.*

52    come halting off    *to emerge impaired from (a) battle, and (b) intercourse.*

53    Breach    *an opening, in both a military and a sexual sense.*
      Pike    *both (a) a bladed spear, and (b) the male "weapon."*

55    charg'd Chambers    *both (a) loaded cannons, and (b) tubs in which victims of syphilis were bathed in medicinal powders.*

56    Cunger    *conger, a type of eel (and a phallic symbol).*

60    Rheumatic    *The Hostess probably means "choleric" (a hot and dry humour); a cold, "rheumatic" (phlegmatic) condition resulted from excess moisture.*

62    Confirmities    *The Hostess means "infirmities" (here confirmed ones).*

*Enter Sir John, singing.*

FALSTAFF  "When Arthur first in Court"—empty the          35
    Jordan—"and was a worthy King"— —How now,
    Mistress Doll?

HOSTESS  Sick of a Calm, yea good faith.

FALSTAFF  So is all her Sect; and they be once in a
    Calm, they are sick.                                    40

DOLL  A Pox damn you, you muddy Rascal: is that all
    the Comfort you give me?

FALSTAFF  You make fat Rascals, Mistress Doll.

DOLL  I make them? Gluttony and Diseases make;
    I make them not.                                        45

FALSTAFF  If the Cook help to make the Gluttony,
    you help to make the Diseases, Doll. We catch
    of you, Doll, we catch of you. Grant that, my
    poor Virtue, grant that.

DOLL  Yea Joy, our Chains and our Jewels.                  50

FALSTAFF  Your Brooches, Pearls, and Ouches: for to
    serve bravely is to come halting off; you know,
    to come off the Breach, with his Pike bent
    bravely, and to Surgery bravely; to venture
    upon the charg'd Chambers bravely.                      55

DOLL  Hang your self, you muddy Cunger, hang your
    self!

HOSTESS  By my troth, this is the Old Fashion! You
    two never meet but you fall to some Discord.
    You are both, i' good truth, as Rheumatic as        60
    two Dry Toasts; you cannot one bear with
    another's Confirmities. —What the Good-year,
    one must bear, and that must be you; you are

95

64–65    Weaker . . . Vessel   *Quickly gives an amusing sexual twist to 1 Peter 3:7.*

67    Hogshead   *a large cask of wine or ale.*

67–68    a whole . . . Stuff   *a whole merchant's shipment of Bordeaux wine.*

69    Hulk   *a large cargo ship.*
        Hold   *storage compartment below deck; here a reference to Falstaff's belly.*

74    Ancient   *ensign (the officer who bore the colors).*

76    swaggering   *blustering, swearing threateningly.*

90    Tilly-fally   *a mild oath, roughly equivalent to "fiddlesticks."*
        ne'er tell me   *don't try to tell me [he's not a swaggerer].*

96

the Weaker Vessel, as they say, the Emptier
Vessel. 65

DOLL   Can a weak, empty Vessel bear such a huge,
full Hogshead? There's a whole Marchant's
Venture of Burdeaux Stuff in him: you have
not seen a Hulk better stuff'd in the Hold.
—Come, I'll be Friends with thee, Jack. Thou 70
art going to the Wars, and whether I shall
ever see thee again or no there is no body
cares.

*Enter Drawer.*

DRAWER   Sir, Ancient Pistol's below, and would
speak with you. 75

DOLL   Hang him, swaggering Rascal! Let him not
come hither: it is the foul-mouth'd'st Rogue in
England.

HOSTESS   If he swagger, let him not come here. No,
by my faith I must live among my Neighbors. 80
I'll no Swaggerers; I am in good Name and Fame
with the very best. Shut the Door, there comes
no Swaggerers here. I have not liv'd all this
while to have Swaggering now. Shut the Door, I
pray you. 85

FALSTAFF   Dost thou hear, Hostess?

HOSTESS   Pray ye pacify your self, Sir John; there
comes no Swaggerers here.

FALSTAFF   Dost thou hear? It is mine Ancient.

HOSTESS   Tilly-fally, Sir John, ne'er tell me; and 90
your ancient Swagg'rer comes not in my Doors.

97

92      before   *summoned to appear before.*
          Tisick   *The good Master's name echoes "phthisic," a tubercular cough.*
          Debuty   *the Deputy of the Ward, a citizen responsible for good government in a jurisdiction.*

96      was by   *had stopped in.*

97      Civil   *properly behaved.*

98      'a   *he.*

99      whereupon   *for what reason.*

105–6    tame Cheater   *Falstaff probably means a petty hustler or sharpster, one who lives by his wits and does no great harm. But* Cheater *could also mean "escheator," an officer who handled property that reverted to the realm either because it had no designated heir or because it was confiscated on legal grounds.*

108     Barbary Hen   *Guinea hen. The term was often applied to prostitutes.*

114     Maisters   *Here as elsewhere, Shakespeare employs a spelling (and probably a pronunciation) that remains close to the original Latin word,* magister.

117     and 'twere   *as if I were.*

118     abide   *stand, tolerate.*

I was before Master Tisick the Debuty t' other
day, and as he said to me, 'twas no longer ago
than Wed'sday last, "Ay, good faith, Neighbor
Quickly," says he (Maister Dumbe our Minister          95
was by then), "Neighbor Quickly," says he;
"receive those that are Civil, for," said he,
"you are in an Ill Name." Now 'a said so, I
can tell whereupon. "For," says he, "you are
an Honest Woman, and well thought on; therefore        100
take heed what Guests you receive; receive,"
says he, "no Swaggering Companions." There
comes none here: you would bless you to hear
what he said. No, I'll no Swagg'rers.

FALSTAFF   He's no Swagg'rer, Hostess: a tame          105
Cheater, i' faith; you may stroke him as
gently as a Puppy Greyhound. He'll not swagger
with a Barbary Hen if her Feathers turn back
in any show of resistance. —Call him up,
Drawer.                                    *Exit Drawer.*   110

HOSTESS   Cheater call you him? I will bar no Honest
Man my House, nor no Cheater; but I do not
love Swaggering, by my troth; I am the worse
when one says "Swagger." Feel, Maisters, how I
shake; look you, I warrant you.                        115

DOLL   So you do, Hostess.

HOSTESS   Do I? Yea in very truth do I, and 'twere
an Aspen Leaf; I cannot abide Swagg'rers.

*Enter Ancient Pistol and Bardolph and Page.*

PISTOL   God save you, Sir John.

99

121    charge    *toast, salute.*

121–   discharge upon    *both (a) toast in reply, and (b) "fire."*
22

125    Pistol-proof    *Falstaff implies that the Hostess is well-proven
       (armored) and long past the point where she can be impreg-
       nated.*

127    drink no Proofs    *reciprocate no toasts or pledges.*

134–   I am . . . Maister.    *I am pledged to Falstaff. "Meat" was a
35     term for whore. Here Doll may be trying to say something more
       dignified: "I am only meet (suitable) for your betters."*

136    I know you    *Pistol's implication is "I know you too well to
       believe that you are exclusively devoted to Falstaff."*

137    Bung    *both (a) bung-nipper (pickpocket), and (b) bung-hole
       (a term for both the opening in a cask and the anus).*

139    Chaps    *cheeks.*
       Cuttle    *(a) cutpurse, pickpocket, and (b) cutthroat.*

141    Basket-hilt    *the curved strip on a sword to protect the hand.*
       stale Juggler    *worn-out impostor.*

142–   with . . . Shoulder    *Points were laces or tags for attaching
43     the cuirass (breastplate) to the shoulders. Doll's implication is
       either (a) that Pistol has no shoulders to which to attach
       armor, or (b) that his armor is worn out and lace-less.*

147    Discharge . . . Company    *both (a) remove yourself from
       our presence, and (b) "go off" (lines 146–47) elsewhere.*

FALSTAFF    Welcome, Ancient Pistol. Here, Pistol, I    120
    charge you with a Cup of Sack. Do you discharge
    upon my Hostess.
PISTOL    I will discharge upon her, Sir John, with
    two Bullets.
FALSTAFF    She is Pistol-proof: Sir, you shall not    125
    hardly offend her.
HOSTESS    Come, I'll drink no Proofs, nor no Bullets.
    I'll drink no more than will do me good for no
    man's pleasure, I.
PISTOL    Then to you, Mistress Dorothy, I will charge    130
    you.
DOLL    Charge me? I scorn you, scurvy Companion!
    What, you poor, base, rascally, cheating, lack-Linen
    Mate! Away, you mouldy Rogue! Away! I am Meat
    for your Maister.    135
PISTOL    I know you, Mistress Dorothy.
DOLL    Away, you cutpurse Rascal, you filthy Bung,
    away! By this Wine, I'll thrust my Knife in your
    mouldy Chaps and you play the saucy Cuttle
    with me. Away, your Bottle-ale Rascal, you    140
    Basket-hilt stale Juggler you! Since when, I
    pray you, Sir? God's Light, with two Points on
    your Shoulder? Much!
PISTOL    God let me not live but I will murther your
    Ruff for this.    145
FALSTAFF    No more, Pistol: I would not have you go
    off here. Discharge your self of our Company,
    Pistol!
HOSTESS    No, good Captain Pistol, not here, sweet
    Captain!    150

101

151    abhominable   *inhuman. Elizabethans thought that this word derived from* ab *(away from) and* homine *(man).*

152    And   *if.*

158    Stew'd Pruins   *Stewed prunes were proverbially associated with brothels. Prunes were thought to be an aphrodisiac.*

161    "Occupy"   *This word had become "ill sorted" (abused) to mean copulate, possess sexually.*

165    Heark thee hither   *Come here and listen.*

169–70    Pluto's damn'd Lake   *Hell. Pluto was God of the classical Hades; the "Lake" Pistol refers to is probably Phlegethon, the River of Fire.*

171    Erebus   *another name for Hell.*

173    Faitors   *swindlers.*
        Hiren   *Pistol's name for his sword. When he mentions it in line 189, the Hostess thinks that he is calling for a whore. From line 173 on in this scene, most of Pistol's lines parody works of popular literature and drama that would have been familiar to the audience.*

174    Peesel   *Pistol.*

175    beseek   *beseech.*
        aggravate   *increase. The Hostess probably means "moderate."*

177–81    Shall . . . Greeks?   *Pistol garbles a passage from Christopher Marlowe's* Tamburlane.

180    Troiant   *Trojan, probably with a play on "truant."*

DOLL    Captain, thou abhominable, damn'd Cheater,
art thou not asham'd to be call'd Captain? And
Captains were of my mind, they would truncheon
you out for taking their Names upon you before
you have earn'd them. You a Captain? You Slave,        155
for what? For tearing a poor Whore's Ruff in a
Bawdy House! —He a Captain? Hang him, Rogue!
He lives upon mouldy Stew'd Pruins and Dried
Cakes. A Captain? God's Light, these Villains
will make the word as odious as the word            160
"Occupy," which was an excellent good word
before it was ill sorted. Therefore Captains
had need look to 't.

BARDOLPH    Pray thee go down, good Ancient.

FALSTAFF    Heark thee hither, Mistress Doll.        165

PISTOL    Not I! I tell thee what, Corporal Bardolph:
I could tear her! I'll be reveng'd of her!

PAGE    Pray thee go down.

PISTOL    I'll see her damn'd first, to Pluto's
damn'd Lake, by this Hand, to th' Infernal         170
Deep, with Erebus and Tortures vile also!
Hold Hook and Line, say I. Down, down, Dogs!
Down Faitors! Have we not Hiren here?

HOSTESS    Good Captain Peesel, be quiet! 'Tis very
late i' faith. I beseek you now aggravate your       175
Choler.

PISTOL    These be good Humours indeed! Shall Pack-
horses and hollow, pamper'd Jades of Asia
which cannot go but thirty Mile a day compare
with Caesars and with Cannibals and Troiant         180
Greeks? Nay rather damn them with King

182    **Cerberus**   *the three-headed dog who guarded the entrance to Hades.*

       the Welkin   *the heavens.*

183    **fall foul for Toys**   *quarrel over trivial matters.*

193    **Calipolis**   *Mully Mahamet's wife in George Peele's* Battle of Alcazar.

194–95    **Si . . . contento.**   *"If Fortune torments me, Hope contents me."*

195    **Broadsides**   *all the guns firing at once from one side of a warship.*

197    **Sweet-heart**   *Pistol addresses his sword as he puts it down.*

198    **And are Et Ceteras no things?**   *Pistol is using two terms for the female genitalia (*Et Ceteras, *a common euphemism, and* no things, *referring to an anatomical "deficiency"). The answer to his rhetorical question, then, is yes.*

200    **Neaf**   *fist. Pistol is offering a sign of peace and farewell.*

200–1    **we have . . . Stars**   *we have had great times together. The "Seven Stars" are probably a constellation.*

203    **Fustian**   *bombastic, ranting.*

205    **Galloway Nags**   *inferior Irish horses, normally used as hackneys.*

206    **Quait**   *quoit, throw (as one tosses a quoit or ring at a peg).*

206–7    **Shove-groat Shilling**   *a coin used in a miniature version of shuffleboard.*

211    **imbrue**   *bleed.*

Cerberus, and let the Welkin roar! Shall we
fall foul for Toys?

HOSTESS   By my troth, Captain, these are very
bitter words. 185

BARDOLPH   Be gone, good Ancient, this will grow to
a Brawl anon.

PISTOL   Men like Dogs give Crowns like Pins. Have
we not Hiren here?

HOSTESS   A' my word, Captain, there's none such 190
here. What the Good-year, do you think I would
deny her? For God's sake, be quiet.

PISTOL   Then feed and be fat, my fair Calipolis.
Come give 's some Sack! *Si fortune me tormente,
sperato me contento.* Fear we Broadsides? No, 195
let the Fiend give Fire! Give me some Sack,
and Sweet-heart, lie thou there. Come we to
full points here? And are Et Ceteras no things?

FALSTAFF   Pistol, I would be quiet.

PISTOL   Sweet Knight, I kiss thy Neaf. What, we 200
have seen the Seven Stars.

DOLL   For God's sake, thrust him down stairs! I
cannot endure such a Fustian Rascal.

PISTOL   Thrust him down stairs! Know we not
Galloway Nags? 205

FALSTAFF   Quait him down, Bardolph, like a Shove-
groat Shilling: nay, and 'a do nothing but
speak nothing, 'a shall be nothing here.

BARDOLPH   Come, get you down stairs!

PISTOL   What, shall we have Incision? Shall we 210
imbrue? Then Death rock me asleep, abridge my
doleful Days. Why then let grievous, ghastly,

105

213    untwind   *untwine.*
        the Sisters Three   *the three Fates (Clotho, Lachesis, and Atropos); one held the spindle on which the thread of a person's life was spun, one pulled the thread, and the third cut it.*

220    Tirrits   *tantrums.*

228    'a   *he.*
        shrewd   *fierce, sharp.*

229    a'   *of.*

232    brave   *defy.*

235    Chops   *fat cheeks.*

236    Hector   *the chief defender of Troy in the war with the Greeks.*

237    woorth   *worth.*
        Agamemnon   *the chief general of the Greeks in the Trojan War.*

238    Nine Worthies   *the renowned champions of antiquity. Three were pagan (Hector, Alexander, and Julius Caesar); three were Hebrew (Joshua, David, and Judas Maccabeus); and three were Christian (Arthur, Charlemagne, and Godfrey of Boullion).*

taping Wounds untwind the Sisters Three. Come
Atropos, I say.

HOSTESS  Here's goodly Stuff toward!                                    215

FALSTAFF  Give me my Rapier, Boy.

DOLL  I pray thee, Jack, I pray thee do not draw!

FALSTAFF  Get you down stairs!

*He draws and fights with Pistol.*

HOSTESS  Here's a goodly Tumult! I'll forswear
keeping House afore I'll be in these Tirrits                             220
and Frights so. Murder, I warrant now! Alas,
alas, put up your naked Weapons; put up your
naked Weapons!          *Exeunt Pistol and Bardolph.*

DOLL  I pray thee, Jack, be quiet; the Rascal's
gone. Ah, you whoreson little valiant Villain,                          225
you!

HOSTESS  Are you not hurt i' th' Groin? Methought
'a made a shrewd Thrust at your Belly.


*Re-enter Bardolph.*


FALSTAFF  Have you turn'd him out a' doors?

BARDOLPH  Yea Sir, the Rascal's drunk. You have                        230
hurt him, Sir, i' th' Shoulder.

FALSTAFF  A Rascal to brave me!

DOLL  Ah you sweet little Rogue you! Alas poor Ape,
how thou sweat'st! Come let me wipe thy Face.
Come on, you whoreson Chops. Ah Rogue, i' faith                        235
I love thee: thou art as valorous as Hector of
Troy, woorth five of Agamemnon, and ten times
better than the Nine Worthies. Ah Villain!

239–40    toss the Rogue in a Blanket    *What Falstaff threatens is a traditional punishment for cowards (and something like what he himself receives in* The Merry Wives of Windsor*).*

241    and . . . and    *if . . . if.*

242–43    I'll . . . Sheets    *Doll will reward Falstaff's valor with another kind of tossing. Here* canvas *means "cover with canvas" (sheets).*

247    like Quicksilver    *as quickly as mercury.*

248–49    like a Church    *Doll is probably enjoying an amiable joke at the expense of Falstaff's size and lumbering movements.*

249–50    Bartholomew Boar-pig    *a roast pig of the type to be eaten on Saint Bartholomew's Day (August 24) in London's Smithfield district.*

251    Foining    *"thrusting," here used as a sexual euphemism. Compare II.i.16.*

254    Death's-head    *skull, a* memento mori *emblem (a reminder of the inevitability of death). As usual, Falstaff does not wish to be reminded of the need to prepare his soul for the Day of Judgment.*

257    Pantler    *pantry-servant.*
chipp'd    *removed the crust from.*

261    thick    *lacking in mobility, dull.*
Tewksbury Mustard    *Tewksbury, a town in Gloucestershire, was celebrated for its mustard.*

262    Conceit    *intelligence, ability to conceive intellectually.*

FALSTAFF   A rascally Slave! I will toss the Rogue
     in a Blanket.                                                    240
DOLL   Do, and thou dar'st for thy Heart; and thou
     dost, I'll canvas thee between a pair of
     Sheets.

*Enter Music.*

PAGE   The Music is come, Sir.
FALSTAFF   Let them play. —Play, Sirs! —Sit on my           245
     Knee, Doll. A rascal bragging Slave! The Rogue
     fled from me like Quicksilver.
DOLL   I' faith, and thou follow'dst him like a
     Church, thou whoreson little tidy Bartholomew
     Boar-pig. When wilt thou leave Fighting a' Days       250
     and Foining a' Nights, and begin to patch up
     thine old Body for Heaven?

*Enter Prince and Poins, disguised.*

FALSTAFF   Peace, good Doll, do not speak like a
     Death's-head. Do not bid me remember mine End.
DOLL   Sirrah, what Humour's the Prince of?               255
FALSTAFF   A good shallow young Fellow: 'a would
     have made a good Pantler; 'a would 'a chipp'd
     Bread well.
DOLL   They say Poins has a good Wit.
FALSTAFF   He a good Wit? Hang him, Baboon! His          260
     Wit's as thick as Tewksbury Mustard; there's
     no more Conceit in him than is in a Mallet.
DOLL   Why does the Prince love him so then?

109

265–66    **Cunger and Fennel**    *conger eels seasoned with fennel (an herb).*

266–67    **drinks . . . Flapdragons**    *Falstaff refers to a game in which candle-ends were floated on liquor as flapdragons (the name for such floating objects). In one form of the game the candle-ends were lit, and one either had to drink off the liquor, avoiding them, or gulp them down flaming.*

271    **breeds no Bate**    *starts no quarrels.*

272    **gambol**    *sportive, "gamboling."*

277    **Haber-de-poiz**    *avoirdupois (weight in pounds and ounces).*

278    **Nave of a Wheel**    *(a) hub, and (b) "wheel-shaped knave."*

279    **Ears cut off**    *a punishment for slander and perjury.*

281    **where**    *whether.*

281–82    **his Poll claw'd**    *his head scratched. Doll is caressing Falstaff.*

286    **Saturn and Venus**    *Saturn was associated with old age, Venus with love. The two planets are rarely conjoined.*

288    **fiery Trigon**    *Bardolph. The Zodiac was composed of four "trigons" (triads) of three signs each, with each trigon corresponding to one of the four elements. Bardolph is called the "fiery Trigon" because of his ruddy, choleric nature.*

289    **Old Tables**    *account books. Poins is courting Quickly.*

290    **Counsel-keeper**    *confidante, go-between for assignations.*

FALSTAFF    Because their Legs are both of a bigness, 265
and 'a plays at Quoits well, and eats Cunger
and Fennel, and drinks off Candle's-ends for
Flapdragons, and rides the Wild Mare with the
Boys, and jumps upon Join'd-stools, and swears
with a good Grace, and wears his Boots very
smooth, like unto the Sign of the Leg, and 270
breeds no Bate with telling of discreet
Stories, and such other gambol Faculties 'a
has that show a Weak Mind and an Able Body,
for which the Prince admits him. For the
Prince himself is such another: the Weight of 275
a Hair will turn Scales between their
*Haber-de-poiz.*

PRINCE    Would not this Nave of a Wheel have his
Ears cut off?

POINS    Let's beat him before his Whore. 280

PRINCE    Look where the wither'd Elder hath not his
Poll claw'd like a Parrot.

POINS    Is it not strange that Desire should so many
years outlive Performance?

FALSTAFF    Kiss me, Doll. 285

PRINCE    Saturn and Venus this year in Conjunction?
What says th' Almanac to that?

POINS    And look whether the fiery Trigon his Man be
not lisping to his Master's Old Tables: his
Note-book, his Counsel-keeper! 290

FALSTAFF    Thou dost give me flattering Busses.

DOLL    By my troth, I kiss thee with a most constant
Heart.

FALSTAFF    I am old, I am old.

111

297    Stuff   *material.*
         Kirtle   *skirt.*

300    Thou 't   *thou wilt.*

301    and   *if*

303–4    hearken a' th' End   *wait till the end, and you'll see.*

309    Continents   *both (a) the continents of the world, and (b) that which is contained in Falstaff's globular belly.*

313    draw you out   *apprehend you.*

317    Iesu   *Jesus. Here as elsewhere in Shakespeare, an* i *appears where modern spelling would call for a* j *(a letter not yet in common use). The word was probably pronounced "Yesu" rather than "Jesu" in Elizabethan England.*

319    Compound   *mass, quantity.*

322    How . . . you!   *Doll is not pleased by Falstaff's acquiescence to the interruption.*

325    take not the Heat   *fail to act while you are angry.*

DOLL   I love thee better than I love e'er a scurvy                    295
    young Boy of them all.

FALSTAFF   What Stuff wilt have a Kirtle of? I shall
    receive Money a' Thursday; shalt have a Cap
    tomorrow. A merry Song! Come, it grows late.
    We'll to Bed. Thou 't forget me when I am gone.      300

DOLL   By my troth, thou 't set me a-weeping and
    thou say'st so. Prove that ever I dress my self
    handsome till thy return. Well, hearken a' th'
    End.

FALSTAFF   —Some Sack, Francis.                             305

PRINCE, POINS   Anon, anon, Sir.

FALSTAFF   Ha? A bastard Son of the King's? And art
    thou not Poins his Brother?

PRINCE   Why thou Globe of sinful Continents: what a
    Life dost thou lead?                                     310

FALSTAFF   A better than thou: I am a Gentleman,
    thou art a Drawer.

PRINCE   Very true Sir, and I come to draw you out
    by the Ears.

HOSTESS   O the Lord preserve thy Grace! By my troth,      315
    welcome to London! Now the Lord bless that
    sweet Face of thine. O Iesu, are you come from
    Wales?

FALSTAFF   Thou whoreson mad Compound of Majesty!
    By this light Flesh and corrupt Blood, thou art       320
    welcome!

DOLL   How? You fat Fool, I scorn you!

POINS   My Lord, he will drive you out of your
    Revenge and turn all to a Merriment if you
    take not the Heat.                                       325

113

326      Candle-mine   *Candles were made of tallow (animal fat), a substance Falstaff represents in quantities large enough to mine.*

          vildly   *vilely.*

327      now   *just a moment ago.*

332      and   *if. In II.iv of 1 Henry IV, Falstaff maintained that he knew that the Prince was one of the robbers who stole his booty; it was because of this (and Falstaff's "instinct" against harming "the True Prince"), he said, that he and his companions fled rather than fight back. If so, the Prince says now, Falstaff also knew that the Prince was in the room while Falstaff was disparaging him just a moment ago.*

338–   drive . . . Abuse   *force you into a corner where all you can*
39       *do is confess that you abused my name knowingly and willfully.*

350      careful   *caring, concerned.*

354      entire   *total.*

356      close   *be reconciled.*

PRINCE   You whoreson Candle-mine, you! How vildly
did you speak of me now, before this honest,
virtuous, civil Gentlewoman?

HOSTESS   God's blessing of your good Heart! And so
she is, by my troth.                                         330

FALSTAFF   Didst thou hear me?

PRINCE   Yea, and you knew me as you did when you
ran away by Gadshill; you knew I was at your
back, and spoke it on purpose to try my
Patience.                                                      335

FALSTAFF   No, no, no, not so: I did not think thou
wast within hearing.

PRINCE   I shall drive you then to confess the
willful Abuse, and then I know how to handle
you.                                                           340

FALSTAFF   No Abuse, Hal; a' mine Honor, no Abuse.

PRINCE   Not to dispraise me, and call me Pantler
and Bread-chipper, and I know not what?

FALSTAFF   No Abuse, Hal.

POINS   No Abuse?                                             345

FALSTAFF   No Abuse, Ned, i' th' World, honest Ned,
none. I disprais'd him before the Wicked . . .
—that the Wicked might not fall in love with
thee: in which doing I have done the part of a
careful Friend and a true Subject, and thy           350
Father is to give me thanks for it. No Abuse,
Hal. —None, Ned, none. —No, faith, Boys,
none.

PRINCE   See now whether pure Fear and entire
Cowardice doth not make thee wrong this               355
virtuous Gentlewoman to close with us. Is she

115

359  Zeal  *fervent loyalty.*

362  prick'd down  *marked with a prick (a tiny check) in his account book of those to be damned.*

363  irrecoverable  *beyond redemption.*
    Privy  *private, personal.*

365  Maltworms  *habitual beer-drinkers. Beer is made from fermented malt (barley).*

374  quit  *forgiven (probably because Falstaff is willing to "relieve" her of the debt by wiping the slate clean so that the books show him owing her nothing).*

375–  for . . . howl  *for allowing meat to be served during Lent.*
77

378  Vitlars  *victuallers, food-servers.*

382–  His Grace . . . against.  *Falstaff's words probably have at*
83    *least two implications: (a) by calling you "Gentlewoman," the Prince is bestowing "Grace" (favor) and dignity on a woman his "Flesh" knows to be a whore in reality; and (b) by acting so sanctimonious with me and pretending to disapprove of all I represent, "his Grace" is trying to be something his "Flesh" tells him he cannot be (a Puritan and a dignified Monarch, above the vices of the Tavern-world in which he is most truly at home). In other words, Falstaff appears to be saying about the Prince almost precisely what the Prince was saying about himself at the beginning of II.ii: namely that, in the words of Galatians 5:17, "the flesh lusteth against the Spirit, and the Spirit against the flesh."*

116

of the Wicked? Is thine Hostess here of the Wicked? Or is thy Boy of the Wicked? Or honest Bardolph, whose Zeal burns in his Nose, of the Wicked? 360

POINS Answer, thou Dead Elm, answer.

FALSTAFF The Fiend hath prick'd down Bardolph irrecoverable, and his Face is Lucifer's Privy-Kitchen, where he doth nothing but roast Maltworms. For the Boy, there is a Good Angel 365 about him, but the Divel blinds him too.

PRINCE For the Women?

FALSTAFF For one of them, she's in Hell already, and burns poor Souls; for the other, I owe her Money, and whether she be damn'd for that I 370 know not.

HOSTESS No, I warrant you.

FALSTAFF No, I think thou art not; I think thou art quit for that. Marry there is another Indictment upon thee, for suffering Flesh to 375 be eaten in thy House contrary to the Law, for the which I think thou wilt howl.

HOSTESS All Vitlars do so: what's a Joint of Mutton or two in a whole Lent?

PRINCE You Gentlewoman— 380

DOLL What says your Grace?

FALSTAFF His Grace says that which his Flesh rebels against.

*Peto knocks at the Door.*

387    **Westminster**   *site of the royal palace, now a part of central London.*

388    **Posts**   *messengers. We should notice that Peto, speaking in verse, introduces a new note of gravity and urgency, a reminder that a more serious world awaits beyond the leisurely rooms of the Tavern.*

393    **too blame**   *too blameworthy.*

394    **profane**   *use in a wasteful, unholy fashion.*

395    **South**   *south wind.*

396    **Borne with black Vapor**   *laden with black storm clouds.*

397    **our bare unarmed Heads**   *The Prince's imagery conveys a sudden sense of emergency. To be at ease in times of "Tempest" is to be "unarmed" (unprovided). The Prince's wording echoes Lord Bardolph's remarks in I.iii.60–62.*

399–    **the sweetest Morsel of the Night**   *the lovemaking that*
400    *Falstaff and Doll have been anticipating.*

403    **presently**   *right away.*

405    **Pay . . . Sirrah.**   *Falstaff probably addresses this line to his Page, who would be carrying his Master's purse.*

HOSTESS   Who knocks so loud at Door? Look to th'
   Door there, Francis.                                         385

                    *Enter Peto.*

PRINCE   Peto, how now, what News?
PETO   The King your Father is at Westminster,
   And there are twenty weak and weari'd Posts
   Come from the North. And as I came along
   I met and overtook a dozen Captains,                         390
   Bareheaded, sweating, knocking at the Taverns,
   And asking ev'ry one for Sir John Falstaff.
PRINCE   By Heaven, Poins, I feel me much too blame
   So idly to profane the precious Time
   When Tempest of Commotion, like the South                    395
   Borne with black Vapor, doth begin to melt
   And drop upon our bare unarmed Heads.
   Give me my Sword and Cloak. —Falstaff, good
     night.
            *Exeunt Prince and Poins with Peto and Bardolph.*
FALSTAFF   Now comes in the sweetest Morsel of the
   Night, and we must hence and leave it unpick'd.              400
                                      *Knocking within.*
   More knocking at the Door?

                *Re-enter Bardolph.*

   —How now, what's the Matter?
BARDOLPH   You must away to Court, Sir, presently;
   A dozen Captains stay at Door for you.
FALSTAFF   —Pay the Musicians, Sirrah. —Farewell,              405

119

---

406-9 You see . . . on. *Falstaff's remarks echo what he has said earlier (I.ii.235–39) about his transcendent merits. They anticipate (and provide an ironic counterpoint to) the King's reflections on sleep in the scene that follows.*

410 post *immediately.*

417 Peascod Time *peapod time (early summer).*

424 blubber'd *sobbing.*

Hostess. —Farewell, Doll. You see, my good
Wenches, how Men of Merit are sought after.
The Undeserver may sleep when the Man of
Action is call'd on. Farewell, good Wenches.
If I be not sent away post, I will see you                    410
again ere I go.

DOLL   I cannot speak: if my Heart be not ready to
burst— Well, sweet Jack, have a care of thy
self.

FALSTAFF   Farewell, farewell.                               415

*Exeunt Falstaff, Bardolph, and Page.*

HOSTESS   Well, fare thee well; I have known thee
these twenty-nine years, come Peascod Time,
but an honester and truer-hearted man—Well,
fare thee well.

*Re-enter Bardolph.*

BARDOLPH   Mistress Tearsheet!                               420
HOSTESS   What's the matter?
BARDOLPH   Bid Mistress Tearsheet come to my Master.
HOSTESS   —O run, Doll, run! Run, good Doll! Come!
—She comes blubber'd. —Yea! Will you come,
Doll?                                         *Exeunt.*   425

III.i    *This scene takes place at the royal Palace in Westminster.*

6    soft Nurse    *The King is probably thinking of the kind of gentle nurse who cared for him and rocked him to sleep as an infant.*

8    steep    *soak, saturate.*

9    smoky Cribs    *smoke-filled hovels, the dwellings of the poor. But the word* Cribs *also recalls the manger in which the Christ-child was placed; by doing so, it reminds us of the contrast between the innocence of the sleeping baby Jesus and the tormenting guilt of the sleepless King.*

10    uneasy Pallets    *hard, uncomfortable beds.*

11    hush'd    *This is a beautifully appropriate word for this context. Its sound imitates both (a) the humming of the "Night-flies," and (b) the shushing of a Nurse urging her baby to be calm and snooze. In the process it reinforces the other sibilants (s-sounds) in a passage whose every phrase seems to whisper "fall asleep, please fall asleep."*

# Scene 1

*Enter the King in his Nightgown, followed by a Page.*

KING   Go call the Earls of Surrey and of Warwick;
But ere they come, bid them o'er-read these
    Letters
And well consider of them. Make good speed.

                           *Exit Page.*

  —How many thousand of my poorest Subjects
Are at this Hour asleep? O Sleep, O gentle
    Sleep!                             5
Nature's soft Nurse, how have I frighted thee,
That thou no more wilt weigh my Eyelids down
And steep my Senses in Forgetfulness?
Why rather, Sleep, li'st thou in smoky Cribs,
Upon uneasy Pallets stretching thee,         10
And hush'd with buzzing Night-flies to thy
    Slumber,

13     costly State    *magnificent pomp.*

15     dull God    *The King calls the God of Sleep (Morpheus) "dull"*
          *because (a) his effect is to dull the senses, and (b) his preference*
          *for "smoky Cribs" over "perfum'd Chambers" would seem to*
          *be the kind of choice only a dull (foolish) God would make.*
         Vile    *the lowest of Earth's creatures.*

17     Watch-case    *the case enclosing a ticking clock. In this meta-*
          *phor the King becomes both (a) the moving parts of the watch,*
          *and (b) the night-watchman standing sentry over the opera-*
          *tion. The King's image also recalls an earlier King's descrip-*
          *tion of himself as Bullingbrook's "Jack o' th' Clock" in* Rich-
          ard II, *V.v. 48–59.*
         'Larum-bell    *alarm bell.*

18     giddy    *dizzying, from its height and motion.*

20     rude imperious Surge    *rough, all-powerful tide.*

22     Ruffian Pillows    *rough, white-capped waves.*

24     deafing    *deafening.*
         in the slipp'ry Clouds    *The King is talking about waves so*
          *high that they seem to hang suspended from the clouds.*

25     Hurly    *tumult.*

27     rude    *rough, filled with commotion.*

29     Appliances    *implements (the comforts listed in lines 12–14).*

30     Low    *low-born, common people.*

37     the Body of our Kingdom    *the Body Politic.*

Than in the perfum'd Chambers of the Great
Under the Canopies of costly State,
And lull'd with sound of sweetest Melody?
O thou dull God, why li'st thou with the Vile          15
In loathsome Beds and leav'st the Kingly Couch
A Watch-case or a common 'Larum-bell?
Wilt thou upon the high and giddy Mast
Seal up the Ship-boy's Eyes and rock his Brains
In Cradle of the rude imperious Surge                  20
And in the Visitation of the Winds,
Who take the Ruffian Pillows by the Top,
Curling their monstrous Heads and hanging them
With deafing Clamor in the slipp'ry Clouds
That, with the Hurly, Death itself awakes?             25
Canst thou, O partial Sleep, give thy Repose
To the wet Sea-boy in an Hour so rude,
And in the calmest and most stillest Night,
With all Appliances and Means to boot,
Deny it to a King? —Then happy Low, lie down:          30
Uneasy lies the Head that wears a Crown.

*Enter Warwick, Surrey, and Sir John Blunt.*

WARWICK    Many good morrows to your Majesty.
KING    Is it good morrow, Lords?
WARWICK                        'Tis one a' clock, and past.
KING    Why then good morrow to you all, my Lords.
    Have you read o'er the Letter that I sent you?      35
WARWICK    We have, my Liege.
KING    Then you perceive the Body of our Kingdom,

38    foul   *ugly, loathsome, as if splotched with sores.*
      rank   *festering, unchecked.*

40    yet distemper'd   *subject only to a temporary imbalance of the humours, not fatally diseased.*

43    My . . . cool'd.   *Warwick's implication is that Northumberland and his allies are like an excess of the choleric humour (the effect of too much yellow bile, a hot, dry substance); once they are "cool'd," the system will return to its normal "temper" (harmonious balance).*

45    the Revolution of the Times   *the changes in the face of the earth brought about by vast geological movements.*

46    the Continent   *the land; literally, that which contains [the sea].*

47    melt   *dissolve.*

50    Neptune   *the Roman name for Poseidon, the God of the Sea.*

52–55  O . . . die.   *These lines occur only in the second issue of the First Quarto. They are not found in the Folio text, which thus has a metrically regular line ("With divers . . . gone") rather than the short line (56) in the Quarto. It is difficult to determine whether lines 52–55 were a late addition or a passage marked for deletion, and thus omitted from all but one of the early printings.*

54    what Crosses to ensue   *what hardships are to come.*

59    since   *ago.*

64    by   *there.*

65    Nevil   *Warwick.*

How foul it is, what rank Diseases grow,
And with what Danger near the Heart of it.

WARWICK    It is but as a Body yet distemper'd,                    40
Which to his former Strength may be restor'd
With good Advice and little Medicine.
My Lord Northumberland will soon be cool'd.

KING    O God, that one might read the Book of Fate
And see the Revolution of the Times                               45
Make Mountains level, and the Continent,
Weary of solid Firmness, melt itself
Into the Sea; and other Times to see
The beachy Girdle of the Ocean
Too wide for Neptune's Hips! How Chance's Mocks      50
And Changes fill the Cup of Alteration
With divers Liquors! O if this were seen,
The happiest Youth, viewing his Progress
  through
What Peril's past, what Crosses to ensue,
Would shut the Book and sit him down and die.           55
            'Tis not ten years gone
Since Richard and Northumberland, great
  Friends,
Did Feast together, and in two year after
Were they at Wars. It is but eight years since
This Percy was the Man nearest my Soul,                    60
Who like a Brother toil'd in my Affairs
And laid his Love and Life under my Foot,
Yea for my sake, ev'n to the Eyes of Richard,
Gave him Defiance. But which of you was by
—You, Cousin Nevil, as I may remember—              65
When Richard with his Eye brimful of Tears,

67      check'd and rated   *rebuked and scolded. The King may be thinking of the Abdication Scene (IV.i) in* Richard II, *where Northumberland kept badgering Richard to read a statement in which he would publicly acknowledge the crimes that made it necessary for him to yield the crown. But he is more likely to be thinking of Northumberland's role in V.i, when he enters to tell Richard and his Queen that they will be dispatched to different destinations.*

69–76    "Northumberland . . . Corruption."   *The King paraphrases the words Richard spoke in* Richard II, *V.i.55–59.*

70      Bullingbrook   *In this one instance in the First Quarto, the future King's name is spelled* Bolingbrooke; *at this point in the First Folio the name is spelled the usual way,* Bullingbrooke.

71      then . . . intent   *In* Richard II *Shakespeare makes it difficult, if not impossible, for the audience to determine just when Bullingbrook decided to take the Crown rather than content himself with the restoration of his dukedom.*

78      Amity   *friendship.*

80      Figuring   *imitating the pattern of.*

82      Main Chance   *highest probability.*

85      Hatch and Brood   *birth and progeny.*

93      cries out on us   *cries out to us for action.*

Then check'd and rated by Northumberland,
Did speak these words now prov'd a Prophecy:
"Northumberland, thou Ladder by the which
My Cousin Bullingbrook ascends my Throne" 70
(Though then, God knows, I had no such intent,
But that Necessity so bow'd the State
That I and Greatness were compell'd to kiss),
"The Time shall come," thus did he follow it,
"The Time will come, that foul Sin, gath'ring
 Head, 75
Shall break into Corruption." So went on,
Foretelling this same Time's Condition
And the Division of our Amity.
WARWICK    There is a History in all Men's Lives
Figuring the Natures of the Times deceas'd: 80
The which observ'd, a Man may prophesy
With a near Aim of the Main Chance of Things
As yet not come to Life, who in their Seeds
And weak Beginning lie intreasured.
Such things become the Hatch and Brood of Time, 85
And by the Necessary Form of this
King Richard might create a perfect Guess
That great Northumberland, then false to him,
Would of that Seed grow to a greater Falseness
Which should not find a Ground to root upon 90
Unless on you.
KING              Are these things then Necessities?
Then let us meet them like Necessities.
And that same word ev'n now cries out on us:
They say the Bishop and Northumberland
Are fifty thousand strong.

96    **Rumor** *Unlike his counterparts on the Rebel side of the conflict, Warwick is too level-headed to be taken in by false rumors.*

102    **A certain Instance** *definite proof.*

104    **these unseason'd Hours** *our meeting "out of season" (at an abnormal hour) rather than sleeping at this time of night.*

106    **these inward Wars** *The King refers to the civil wars that he and his Council have just discussed. But his phrase reminds us that the other "inward Wars"—the conflict within his "little Kingdom" (*Julius Caesar, *II.i.67), his uneasy conscience— cannot be put "out of hand" so easily.*

III.ii    *This scene takes place in Gloucestershire, in front of the house of Justice Shallow.*

3    **early Stirrer** *early riser. This phrase links this scene to the early stirring in the preceding scene.*
    **Rood** *Cross.*
    **dooth** *doth. This spelling occurs often enough to suggest that Shakespeare is attempting to capture a local accent (or perhaps reflecting his own). So also with* **Coosin** *in line 6 and elsewhere.*

6    **Coosin your Bedfellow** *your wife. In Shakespeare's time the word "cousin" was used much more broadly than in our own. Any kind of relative, whether by blood or by marriage, could be referred to as a cousin.*

WARWICK                    It cannot be, my Lord.                95
    Rumor doth double, like the Voice and Echo,
    The Numbers of the fear'd. Please it your Grace
    To go to Bed. Upon my Soul, my Lord,
    The Pow'rs that you already have sent forth
    Shall bring this Prize in very easily.                      100
    To comfort you the more, I have receiv'd
    A certain Instance that Glendow'r is dead.
    Your Majesty hath been this fortnight ill,
    And these unseason'd Hours perforce must add
    Unto your Sickness.
KING                       I will take your Counsel.            105
    And were these inward Wars once out of hand,
    We would, dear Lords, unto the Holy Land.    *Exeunt.*

# Scene 2

*Enter Justice Shallow and Justice Silence, meeting;*
*with Mouldy, Shadow, Wart, Feeble, Bullcalf,*
*and Servants behind.*

SHALLOW   Come on, come on, come on, Sir; give me
    your Hand, Sir; give me your Hand, Sir. An
    early Stirrer, by the Rood! And how dooth my
    good Cousin Silence?
SILENCE   Good morrow, good Cousin Shallow.                      5
SHALLOW   And how dooth my Coosin your Bedfellow?

131

9    Woosel   *ousel, blackbird. Silence is probably speaking with modest self-deprecation here. At a time when ladies were ideally "fair" (blonde), to describe one's daughter as "black" was to say that she was not as pretty as one might wish.*

14   Inns a' Court   *The four Inns of Court were the legal colleges in London that provided access to the best careers in law.*

15   Clement's Inn   *one of the Inns of Chancery, for pre-law students unprepared for or unable to obtain admission to the Inns of Court.*

16   mad Shallow   *Shallow is very proud of his youth as a madcap, and it becomes clear from the ensuing dialogue that he has often told his nephew of the wild times he had before settling down.*

20   roundly   *unrestrainedly.*

22   Cotsole   *Cotswold, a hilly region in Gloucestershire.*

23   Swinge-bucklers   *swashbucklers.* Swinge *(pronounced to rhyme with* hinge*) refers to swinging blows.*

25   Bona-robes   *bona-robas, "good stuff" (high-quality prostitutes).*

26   at Commandement   *at our beck and call.*

32   Scoggin   *Shakespeare may have been thinking of John Skoggon, a Court jester during the period to which Shallow refers.*

33   Crack   *young lad.*

35   Gray's Inn   *one of the Inns of Court.*

And your fairest Daughter and mine, my
Goddaughter Ellen?

SILENCE   Alas, a black Woosel, Cousin Shallow.

SHALLOW   By yea and no, Sir, I dare say my Coosin        10
William is become a good Scholar. He is at
Oxford still, is he not?

SILENCE   Indeed Sir, to my Cost.

SHALLOW   'A must then to the Inns a' Court shortly.
I was once of Clement's Inn, where I think          15
they will talk of mad Shallow yet.

SILENCE   You were call'd Lusty Shallow then, Cousin.

SHALLOW   By the Mass, I was call'd any thing, and I
would have done any thing indeed too, and
roundly too. There was I, and little John Doit       20
of Staffordshire, and Black George Barnes, and
Francis Pickbone, and Will Squeale, a Cotsole
man; you had not four such Swinge-bucklers in
all the Inns a' Court again; and I may say to
you, we knew where the Bona-robes were, and         25
had the best of them all at Commandement.
Then was Jack Falstaff, now Sir John, a Boy,
and Page to Thomas Mowbray, Duke of Norfolk.

SILENCE   Coosin, this Sir John that comes hither
anon about Soldiers?                                30

SHALLOW   The same Sir John, the very same. I see
him break Scoggin's Head at the Court-gate,
when 'a was a Crack, not thus high; and the
very same day did I fight with one Samson
Stockfish, a Fruiterer, behind Gray's Inn.          35
Iesu, Iesu, the mad days that I have spent!
And to see how many of my old Acquaintance

41    the Psalmist   *Shallow may be thinking of Psalm 89:7, "What man is he that liveth, and shall not see death?"*

42–43    How . . . Fair?   *How much was a good pair of bullocks (oxen) at the Stamford market? Shallow's change of subject allows him a brief respite from what is really on his mind this morning: the passing of youth and the inevitability of death. In line 55 he interrupts his reflections on the past for another question on the current price for "a score of Ewes."*

49    John a' Gaunt   *Duke of Lancaster and father of King Henry IV.*

51–52    'A would . . . twelvescore   *He was able to hit the target at a distance of 240 yards.* Clout *(cloth) refers to the square canvas on which the target (a small white circle with a peg, or "pin," in the center) was drawn.*

52–53    and carri'd . . . half   *and shot an arrow straight for 280–90 yards. A "Forehand Shaft" was an arrow designed for straightforward aiming rather than for shooting on a curved trajectory over a long distance.*

54–55    it would . . . see   *Shallow's memories of a more glorious past are no doubt exaggerated. But it obviously does his "heart good" now to remember that there were once "old Doobles" on the earth. Shallow's remarks provide a touchingly homely illustration of the literary convention known as the "ubi sunt meditation" (a series of elegiac "where are they now?" questions, all leading to the melancholy conclusion that "all shall die").*

63    Esquire   *a gentleman just below a knight in rank.*

are dead!

SILENCE   We shall all follow, Coosin.

SHALLOW   Certain, 'tis certain; very sure, very          40
sure; Death, as the Psalmist saith, is certain
to all; all shall die. How a good Yoke of
Bullocks at Samforth Fair?

SILENCE   By my troth, I was not there.

SHALLOW   Death is certain. Is old Dooble of your         45
Town living yet?

SILENCE   Dead, Sir.

SHALLOW   Iesu, Iesu, dead! 'A drew a good Bow, and
dead! 'A shot a fine Shoot: John a' Gaunt
lov'd him well, and betted much Money on his        50
Head. Dead! 'A would have clapp'd i' th' Clout
at twelvescore, and carri'd you a Forehand
Shaft a' fourteen and fourteen and a half,
that it would have done a man's heart good to
see. How a score of Ewes now?                        55

SILENCE   Thereafter as they be, a score of good
Ewes may be worth ten Pounds.

SHALLOW   And is old Dooble dead?

SILENCE   Here come two of Sir John Falstaff's Men
as I think.                                          60

*Enter Bardolph and One with him.*

—Good morrow, honest Gentlemen.

BARDOLPH   I beseech you, which is Justice Shallow?

SHALLOW   I am Robert Shallow, Sir, a poor Esquire
of this County, and one of the King's Justices
of the Peace. What is your pleasure with me?         65

135

67    tall   *brave.*

69    He greets me well   *He sends a worthy ambassador to greet me in his stead.*

70    Backsword-man   *fencer. A backsword was a fencing stick with a basket-hilt to protect the fencer's hand.*

73    accommodate   *accommodated. Bardolph's implication is that a soldier has his needs met in a much more sophisticated way than do ordinary men who settle for conventional marriage. As the Justice's reply makes clear,* accommodate *was a pretentious word that was evidently in vogue during Shakespeare's time.*

78    accommodo   *a Latin word meaning to adjust or apply something to a situation.*

79    Phrase   *Shakespeare often has his characters use* phrase *to refer to a single word.*

84    of exceeding good Command   *commanding exceeding respect.*

87    whereby . . . accommodated   *where he may be expected to be "accommodated." Bardolph's innuendo makes it clear that "accommodate" and "occupy" were closely associated terms (see the note to II.iv.161).*

91    By my troth   *by my truth, in all sincerity.*
       you like well   *you appear to be well; you thrive.*

BARDOLPH   My Captain, Sir, commends him to you: my
    Captain Sir John Falstaff, a tall Gentleman,
    by Heaven, and a most gallant Leader.

SHALLOW   He greets me well, Sir; I knew him a good
    Backsword-man. How doth the good Knight? May I     70
    ask how my Lady his Wife doth?

BARDOLPH   Sir, pardon, a Soldier is better
    accommodate than with a Wife.

SHALLOW   It is well said, in faith, Sir, and it is
    well said indeed too; "better accommodated";     75
    it is good, yea indeed is it. Good Phrases are
    surely, and ever were, very commendable.
    "Accommodated": it comes of *accommodo;* very
    good, a good Phrase.

BARDOLPH   Pardon me, Sir, I have heard the Word;     80
    Phrase you call it? By this good Day, I know
    not the Phrase, but I will maintain the Word
    with my Sword to be a Soldier-like Word, and a
    Word of exceeding good Command, by Heaven.
    "Accommodated": that is when a man is, as they     85
    say, accommodated; or when a man is being
    whereby 'a may be thought to be accommodated,
    which is an excellent thing.

*Enter Sir John Falstaff.*

SHALLOW   It is very just. Look, here comes good Sir
    John. —Give me your good Hand; give me your     90
    Worship's good Hand. By my troth, you like well
    and bear your Years very well. Welcome, good
    Sir John.

95     Soccard   *This may be Falstaff's pronunciation of "Surecard," the name that appears in the First Folio printing. "Surecard" seems to have meant something like "safe bet" or "sure thing."*

96–97    in Commission with me   *serving with me as Justice of the Peace.*

106     Roll   *roster of potential inductees.*

113     of good Friends   *of good family and worthy acquaintance.*

116     'Tis . . . us'd.   *Falstaff is having a little joke at the expense of Mouldy's name (which can mean stale, decaying, and rusty, as well as covered with fungus mold).*

121     Prick him   *Falstaff tells Shallow to place a prick-mark next to Mouldy's name on the roll.*

122–25    I was . . . Drudgery.   *Mouldy's "old Dame" is his wife (his "old lady" in modern parlance), not his mother.* Husbandry *and* Drudgery *are probably terms for all of a husband's "chores," not just the unpleasant ones associated with maintaining a farm and household. Mouldy may be concerned that the ones that will be "undone" by him will be "done" by another man (thus cuckolding Mouldy). If so, in this context* prick'd *probably has the sense that Shakespeare gives it in Sonnet 20, where he describes the young man he is addressing as "prick'd out for Woman's Pleasure." But* prick'd *can also mean turning sour; so Mouldy's first clause is probably meant to pick up on Falstaff's joke, with the implication that "I was mouldy enough already if you had only left well enough alone."*

FALSTAFF    I am glad to see you well, good Maister
    Robert Shallow. —Master Soccard, as I think.                95
SHALLOW    No Sir John, it is my Coosin Silence, in
    Commission with me.
FALSTAFF    Good Maister Silence, it well befits you
    should be of the Peace.
SILENCE    Your good Worship is welcome.                         100
FALSTAFF    Fie, this is Hot Weather, Gentlemen! Have
    you provided me here half a dozen sufficient
    Men?
SHALLOW    Marry have we, Sir; will you sit?
FALSTAFF    Let me see them, I beseech you.                      105
SHALLOW    Where's the Roll? Where's the Roll? Where's
    the Roll? Let me see, let me see: so, so, so,
    so, so, so, so. Yea, marry Sir. —Rafe Mouldy.
    —Let them appear as I call; let them do so,
    let them do so. Let me see, where is Mouldy?          110
MOULDY    Here and it please you.
SHALLOW    What think you, Sir John? A good-limb'd
    Fellow, young, strong, and of good Friends.
FALSTAFF    Is thy name Mouldy?
MOULDY    Yea, and 't please you.                                115
FALSTAFF    'Tis the more time thou wert us'd.
SHALLOW    Ha, ha, ha, most excellent i' faith!
    Things that are Mouldy lack Use. Very singular
    good i' faith; well said, Sir John, very well
    said.                                                          120
FALSTAFF    Prick him.
MOULDY    I was prick'd well enough before, and you
    could have let me alone; my old Dame will be
    undone now for one to do her Husbandry and

126    **go out**   *go to war. But "go out" probably continues the sexual wordplay as well. It may imply the same thing as "go off" (ejaculate), as in II.iv.146–47; but it seems more likely to refer either to withdrawal or to an inability to perform sexually.*

127    Go to   *hush, don't argue with me.*

128    **spent**   *used, consumed. Falstaff is probably combining two metaphorical senses here: (a) "done," in a post-ejaculatory state (as in the first clause of Sonnet 129, "Th' Expense of Spirit in a Waste of Shame / Is Lust in Action"), and (b) dead in a more permanent sense.*

131    other   *others.*

134    **cold**   *Falstaff is playing on the idea that Shadow will provide cool shade. But* cold *can also mean (a) unwilling to fight, lacking in valor, and (b) dead.*

140    Shadow   *likeness, with puns on Shadow's name and on the kind of shadow cast by the Sun. Such shadows consume a father's "substance" (wealth).*

145    Shadows   *"ghosts," names of recruits who are listed (and thus pad the officer's expense allotment) but who do not appear because they have paid off the recruiting officer.*

154    It were superfluous   *It would be redundant to do so.*

154–56    for 's Apparel . . . Pins   *for his ragged clothes are pricked (fastened) together by pins, like the pegs that hold together a wooden frame.*

her Drudgery. You need not to have prick'd me; 125
there are other men fitter to go out than I.

FALSTAFF   Go to; peace, Mouldy. You shall go,
Mouldy. It is time you were spent.

MOULDY   Spent?

SHALLOW   Peace, Fellow, peace. Stand aside. Know 130
you where you are? —For th' other, Sir John,
let me see. —Simon Shadow.

FALSTAFF   Yea marry, let me have him to sit under:
he's like to be a cold Soldier.

SHALLOW   Where's Shadow? 135

SHADOW   Here Sir.

FALSTAFF   Shadow, whose Son art thou?

SHADOW   My Mother's Son, Sir.

FALSTAFF   Thy Mother's Son: like enough, and thy
Father's Shadow. So the Son of the Female is 140
the Shadow of the Male—it is often so
indeed—but much of the Father's Substance.

SHALLOW   Do you like him, Sir John?

FALSTAFF   Shadow will serve for Summer. Prick him,
for we have a number of Shadows fill up the 145
Muster-book.

SHALLOW   Thomas Wart.

FALSTAFF   Where's he?

WART   Here Sir.

FALSTAFF   Is thy name Wart? 150

WART   Yea Sir.

FALSTAFF   Thou art a very ragged Wart.

SHALLOW   Shall I prick him, Sir John?

FALSTAFF   It were superfluous, for 's Apparel is
built upon his Back, and the whole Frame 155

164 **prick'd you** *both (a) fitted you with a suit of clothes, and (b) stuck you with a tailor's needle or pin. The word* **Pins** *is frequently used with phallic implication, and here the phrase "stands upon Pins" would have carried bawdy innuendo in the Elizabethan theatre.*

165 **Battail** *battalions, battle-lines.*

166 **in a Woman's Petticoat** *In addition to its literal meaning, this phrase probably refers as well to sexual "pricking." Like* **tail**, **Tailor** *was a term for the male member. So was* **will** *(line 167). Falstaff's "Well said, good Woman's Tailor" in line 169 makes it clear that he and Feeble are talking about more than one kind of tailoring.*

171 **wrathful Dove** *Falstaff's oxymoron is a reminder that woman's tailors were generally regarded as effeminate creatures.*
    **magnanimous** *great-souled, a term normally applied only to those strong enough to be gentle or condescending.*

177 **put him** *turn him into.*

178 **the Leader of so many thousands** *Falstaff probably refers to the lice and other vermin that infest Wart and look to him as their "Leader."*

142

stands upon Pins. Prick him no more.

SHALLOW   Ha, ha, ha, you can do it, Sir; you can do
    it, I commend you well. —Francis Feeble.

FEEBLE   Here Sir.

SHALLOW   What Trade art thou, Feeble?          160

FEEBLE   A Woman's Tailor, Sir.

SHALLOW   Shall I prick him, Sir?

FALSTAFF   You may, but if he had been a Man's
    Tailor he'd 'a prick'd you. —Wilt thou make
    as many Holes in an Enemy's Battail as thou     165
    hast done in a Woman's Petticoat?

FEEBLE   I will do my good will, Sir; you can have
    no more.

FALSTAFF   Well said, good Woman's Tailor, well said,
    courageous Feeble. Thou wilt be as valiant as    170
    the wrathful Dove, or most magnanimous Mouse.
    —Prick the Woman's Tailor. Well, Master
    Shallow; deep Master Shallow.

FEEBLE   I would Wart might have gone, Sir.

FALSTAFF   I would thou wert a Man's Tailor, that    175
    thou mightst mend him and make him fit to go.
    I cannot put him to a private Soldier that is
    the Leader of so many thousands. Let that
    suffice, most forcible Feeble.

FEEBLE   It shall suffice, Sir.          180

FALSTAFF   I am bound to thee, Reverend Feeble.
    —Who is next?

SHALLOW   Peter Bullcalf o' th' Green.

FALSTAFF   Yea marry, let's see Bullcalf.

BULLCALF   Here Sir.          185

FALSTAFF   'Fore God, a likely Fellow! Come prick

143

187    till he roar again   *Bulls were proverbial for their bellowing.*

194–   Ringing . . . Coronation Day   *ringing the church bells in*
95         *honor of the anniversary of the King's coronation.*

196    Gown   *nightgown.*

197–   take such order   *make arrangements.*
98

198–   thy Friends . . . thee   *Falstaff means that Bullcalf's*
99         *friends will ring bells at his funeral.*

204    tarry   *stay for.*
       Dinner   *It is now midday.*

206    since   *when.*

207    Windmill   *probably a brothel. Saint George's Field was an*
           *area south of the Thames where such establishments*
           *abounded.*

213    away with me   *put up with me.*

217    Bona-roba   *high-class prostitute.*

Bullcalf till he roar again.

BULLCALF    O Lord, good my Lord Captain!

FALSTAFF    What, dost thou roar before thou art
    prick'd?                                                            190

BULLCALF    O Lord, Sir, I am a Diseas'd Man.

FALSTAFF    What Disease hast thou?

BULLCALF    A whoreson Cold, Sir, a Cough, Sir, which
    I caught with Ringing in the King's Affairs
    upon his Coronation Day, Sir.                          195

FALSTAFF    Come, thou shalt go to the Wars in a Gown.
    We will have away thy Cold, and I will take
    such order that thy Friends shall ring for
    thee. —Is here all?

SHALLOW    Here is two more call'd than your Number;      200
    you must have but four here, Sir. And so I
    pray you go in with me to Dinner.

FALSTAFF    Come, I will go drink with you, but I
    cannot tarry Dinner. I am glad to see you, by
    my troth, Master Shallow.                               205

SHALLOW    O Sir John, do you remember since we lay
    all Night in the Windmill in Saint George's
    Field?

FALSTAFF    No more of that, Master Shallow.

SHALLOW    Ha, 'twas a merry Night! And is Jane            210
    Nightwork alive?

FALSTAFF    She lives, Master Shallow.

SHALLOW    She never could away with me.

FALSTAFF    Never never; she would always say she
    could not abide Master Shallow.                       215

SHALLOW    By the Mass, I could anger her to th'
    Heart; she was then a Bona-roba. Doth she hold

145

221    Robin    *the name of the Nightworks' son.*

226    that that    *that which.*

228    We have heard the Chimes at Midnight    *What Falstaff means is that we have been up late many a time, carousing and wenching together. But the phrase "Chimes at Midnight" is a haunting reminder of the church bells that interrupt such holiday revelry and eventually call us all away for good. In 1966 Orson Welles used this evocative phrase as the title for his touching black-and-white film on the fortunes of Falstaff.*

232    Hem-boys!    *This phrase literally means "Clear your throat, Boys!" It was a tavern salute, with the implication "Down the hatch!"*

233    Iesus    *Jesus.*

235    Corporate    *Bullcalf means "Corporal."*
       stand    *be counted as.*

236    Harry Ten-shillings    *ten-shilling coins first minted in the time of King Henry VII, several decades after the period depicted in this play. Characteristically, Shakespeare is not concerned about a minor anachronism.*

237    French Crowns    *coins worth four shillings apiece.*

238    as live    *as lief, as soon.*

her own well?

FALSTAFF   Old old, Master Shallow.

SHALLOW   Nay she must be old; she cannot choose          220
  but be old; certain she's old, and had Robin
  Nightwork by old Nightwork before I came to
  Clement's Inn.

SILENCE   That's fifty-five year ago.

SHALLOW   Ha, Cousin Silence, that thou hadst seen        225
  that that this Knight and I have seen! —Ha,
  Sir John, said I well?

FALSTAFF   We have heard the Chimes at Midnight,
  Master Shallow.

SHALLOW   That we have, that we have, that we have;        230
  in faith, Sir John, we have. Our Watchword was
  "Hem-boys!" Come let's to Dinner, come let's
  to Dinner. Iesus, the Days that we have seen!
  Come, come.

*Exeunt Shallow, Silence, and Falstaff.*

BULLCALF   Good Maister Corporate Bardolph, stand        235
  my Friend; and here's four Harry Ten-shillings in
  French Crowns for you. In very truth, Sir, I
  had as live be hang'd, Sir, as go; and yet for
  mine own part, Sir, I do not care, but rather
  because I am unwilling, and for mine own part        240
  have a desire to stay with my Friends. Else,
  Sir, I did not care for mine own part so much.

BARDOLPH   Go to, stand aside.

MOULDY   And good Master Corporal Captain, for my
  old Dame's sake stand my Friend; she has no          245
  body to do any thing about her when I am gone,
  and she is old and cannot help her self. You

248    forty   *forty shillings.*

255    quit   *relieved, answered.*

262    Go to   *Here the phrase seems to mean "go to it, get on with it"
       (good job).*

268    past Service   *too far gone to be used (another play on
       Mouldy's name).*

269    grow   *Falstaff puns on Bullcalf's name, suggesting that he
       grow up and become an adult bull before he enters the King's
       service.*

272    likeliest   *most capable of serving as good soldiers.*

275    Thews   *muscular strength.*

shall have forty, Sir.

BARDOLPH  Go to, stand aside.

FEEBLE  By my troth I care not, a Man can die but      250
    once, we owe God a Death; I'll ne'er bear a
    Base Mind. And 't be my Destiny, so; and 't be
    not, so; no Man's too good to serve 's Prince,
    and let it go which way it will, he that dies
    this year is quit for the next.      255

BARDOLPH  Well said, th' art a good Fellow.

FEEBLE  Faith, I'll bear no Base Mind.

*Enter Falstaff and the Justices.*

FALSTAFF  Come Sir, which Men shall I have?

SHALLOW  Four of which you please.

BARDOLPH  Sir, a word with you: [*aside*] I have      260
    three Pound to free Mouldy and Bullcalf.

FALSTAFF  Go to, well.

SHALLOW  Come, Sir John, which four will you have?

FALSTAFF  Do you choose for me.

SHALLOW  Marry then, Mouldy, Bullcalf, Feeble, and      265
    Shadow.

FALSTAFF  Mouldy and Bullcalf. —For you, Mouldy,
    stay at home till you are past Service. —And
    for your part, Bullcalf, grow till you come
    unto it; I will none of you.      270

SHALLOW  Sir John, Sir John, do not your self wrong:
    they are your likeliest Men, and I would have
    you serv'd with the best.

FALSTAFF  Will you tell me, Master Shallow, how to
    choose a Man? Care I for the Limb, the Thews,      275

149

276    big Assemblance    *large frame.*

277    Give me the Spirit    *Falstaff alludes to 1 Samuel 16:7, where
       "the Lord said unto Samuel, Look not on his countenance, or
       on the height of his stature; because I have refused him: for the
       Lord seeth not as man seeth; for man looketh on the outward
       appearance, but the Lord looketh on the heart."*

279–   'a shall . . . Hammer    *he shall load and fire for you with
80     the efficiency of a craftsman pounding pewter.*

280–   come off . . . Bucket    *fire and reload ammunition more
82     swiftly than a brewer who hoists ("gibbets") the yoke that
       enables him to carry two buckets of liquid on his shoulders.*

286    Retrait    *retreat, withdrawal.*

289    Caliver    *musket.*

290    traverse    *step forward.*
       thas    *Bardolph's pronunciation of "thus."*

293–   chopp'd, bald Shot    *rough-hewn, bald, "shot" (discarded)
94     marksman.*

295    Tester    *both (a) a sixpence, and (b) a "headpiece" for your
       baldness.*

299    Arthur's Show    *a demonstration in which archers would as-
       sume the roles of Arthurian knights (Sir Dragonet being a
       Fool).*

302    come you in    *move in for the attack with a thrust.*

306    wool    *will.*

the Stature, Bulk, and big Assemblance of a
Man? Give me the Spirit, Master Shallow. Here's
Wart: you see what a ragged Appearance it is;
'a shall charge you and discharge you with
the motion of a Pewterer's Hammer, come off     280
and on swifter than he that gibbets on the
Brewer's Bucket. And this same half-fac'd
fellow, Shadow, give me this Man: he presents
no Mark to the Enemy; the Foeman may with as
great Aim level at the edge of a Penknife. And     285
for a Retrait, how swiftly will this Feeble
the Woman's Tailor run off? O give me the
Spare Men, and spare me the Great Ones; put me
a Caliver into Wart's Hand, Bardolph.

BARDOLPH   Hold, Wart; traverse: thas, thas, thas.     290

FALSTAFF   Come manage me your Caliver. So, very
well, go to, very good, exceeding good. —O
give me always a little lean, old, chopp'd,
bald Shot. —Well said, i' faith, Wart, th' art
a good Scab. Hold, there's a Tester for thee.     295

SHALLOW   He is not his Craft's Master; he doth not
do it right. I remember at Mile-end Green,
when I lay at Clement's Inn: I was then Sir
Dragonet in Arthur's Show. There was a little
Quiver-fellow, and 'a would manage you his     300
Piece thus, and 'a would about and about, and
come you in, and come you in. "Rah, tah, tah,"
would 'a say; "Bounce," would 'a say; and away
again would 'a go; and again would 'a come. I
shall ne'er see such a Fellow.     305

FALSTAFF   These Fellows wool do well, Master

151

309    I must    *I must travel.*

315    peradventure    *perhaps.*

318    Go to . . . word    *don't worry, I mean what I say.*

322    fetch off    *Falstaff probably puns on three meanings of this phrase: (a) deliver (of their excess wealth), (b) get the better of, and (c) drink off; drain, as of a draft of brew. Falstaff plays on the third implication in his next sentence, where he compares Shallow to a drinking vessel whose "Bottom" is easily plumbed.*

325    starv'd    *both (a) thin, and (b) empty of substance.*

326    prate    *talk idly.*

328    Turnbull Street    *a street notorious for its vice and crime.*

329    duer    *more duly (conscientiously and punctually).*

329–    the Turk's Tribute    *The Sultan of Turkey was famous for the*
30      *strict fees he demanded of those who used his trade routes or were otherwise subject to him.*

333    fork'd Redish    *a radish carved into the fork-legged shape of a man.*

334    fantastically    *with fanciful abandon.*

335    forlorn    *lost (like an object too tiny to be found).*

Shallow. God keep you, Master Silence. I will
not use many words with you. Fare you well,
Gentlemen both, I thank you; I must a dozen
Mile tonight. —Bardolph, give the Soldiers          310
Coats.

SHALLOW   Sir John, the Lord bless you, God prosper
your Affairs, God send us Peace; at your
Return visit our House, let our old
Acquaintance be renew'd; peradventure I will          315
with ye to the Court.

FALSTAFF   'Fore God, would you would.

SHALLOW   Go to, I have spoke at a word; God keep
you.

FALSTAFF   Fare you well, gentle Gentlemen.          320
                    *Exeunt Shallow and Silence.*

SHALLOW   On, Bardolph; lead the Men away.
                    *Exeunt Bardolph and the Men.*

As I return I will fetch off these Justices. I
do see the Bottom of Justice Shallow. Lord,
Lord, how subject we Old Men are to this Vice
of Lying! This same starv'd Justice hath done          325
nothing but prate to me of the Wildness of his
Youth, and the Feats he hath done about
Turnbull Street, and every third word a Lie,
duer paid to the Hearer than the Turk's
Tribute. I do remember him at Clement's Inn          330
like a Man made after Supper of a Cheese-
paring: when 'a was naked, he was for all the
World like a fork'd Redish with a Head
fantastically carv'd upon it with a Knife. 'A
was so forlorn that his Dimensions to any          335

336    invincible   *invulnerable to injury because impossible to perceive.*

337    Genius   *personifying spirit.*

338    Mandrake   *a plant whose root was thought to resemble the shape of a man (complete with "privie parts," according to one source) and whose medicinal powers were thought to enhance sexual desire and performance.*

338–    'A came . . . Fashion   *he was hopelessly out of fashion.*
39

340    over-scutch'd Huswives   *What Shallow thinks of as "Bona-robas" (adopting the escutcheons of respectable housewives) are really cheap whores who have been whipped ("scutch'd") many times over.*

341    Car-men   *carters, wagon-drivers.*

342    Fancies, Goodnights   *types of serenades.*

343    Vice's Dagger   *the comical lath weapon used by the Vice, a character in morality plays.*

351    Hoboy   *oboe.*

355    Philosopher's two Stones   *Falstaff puns on (a) the philosopher's stone, supposedly used by alchemists to turn base metals into gold, and (b) the "stones" (testicles) of a philosopher. His implication is that Shallow's gold will preserve Falstaff's youth and support his lechery.*

356    Old Pike   *both (a) Falstaff, as the large fish that will devour the smaller one (the "Dace"), and (b) Falstaff's "Pike" (as in II.iv.53).*

Thick Sight were invincible. 'A was the very
Genius of Famine, yet lecherous as a Monkey,
and the Whores call'd him Mandrake. 'A came
over in the Rearward of the Fashion, and sung
those Tunes to the over-scutch'd Huswives that          340
he heard the Car-men whistle, and sware they
were his Fancies or his Goodnights. And now is
this Vice's Dagger become a Squire, and talks
as familiarly of John a' Gaunt as if he had
been sworn Brother to him; and I'll be sworn          345
'a ne'er saw him but once in the Tilt-yard,
and then he burst his Head for Crowding among
the Marshal's Men. I saw it, and told John a'
Gaunt he beat his own Name. For you might have
thrust him and all his Apparel into an Eelskin;          350
the Case of a Treble Hoboy was a Mansion for
him, a Court; and now he has Land and Beefs!
Well, I'll be acquainted with him if I return,
and 't shall go hard but I'll make him a
Philosopher's two Stones to me. If the Young          355
Dace be a Bait for the Old Pike, I see no
reason in the Law of Nature but I may snap at
him till Time shape, and there an end.          *Exeunt.*

IV.i    *This scene takes place in Gaultree Forest north of York.*

1    What . . . call'd?    *The Archbishop's line is indented in this edition to indicate that, as is often the case, we begin "eavesdropping" on the scene in mid-conversation—indeed, in midline.*

3    Discov'rers    *scouts.*

9    Tenure    *tenor, import.*

10    Here doth he wish his Person    *He wishes he could be here. This phrasing echoes Northumberland's words in II.iii.65.*

11    hold sortance with his Quality    *be fitting for a man of his position and resources.*

# Act Four

## Scene 1

*Enter the Archbishop, Mowbray, Hastings, and*
*Others within the Forest of Gaultree.*

ARCHBISHOP                           What is this Forest call'd?
HASTINGS   'Tis Gaultree Forest, and 't shall please
    your Grace.
BISHOP   Here stand, my Lords, and send Discov'rers
    forth
To know the numbers of our Enemies.
HASTINGS   We have sent forth already.
ARCHBISHOP                           'Tis well done.        5
    My Friends and Brethren in these great Affairs,
    I must acquaint you that I have receiv'd
    New-dated Letters from Northumberland,
    Their cold Intent, Tenure, and Substance thus:
    Here doth he wish his Person, with such Pow'rs        10
    As might hold sortance with his Quality,

12    levy    *raise, draw together.*

13    ripe    *ripen, augment.*

17    touch Ground    *both (a) reach the bottom, and (b) fall to the ground with all the force of gravity.*

20    In goodly Form    *in fine condition.*

21    by the Ground they hide    *by the amount of ground their forces cover.*

23    The just Proportion that we gave them out    *precisely the number that we estimated.*

24    sway on    *move forward with a sense of command.*

25    well-appointed    *well-attired and well-equipped.*
      fronts    *confronts, comes face to face with.*

29    in peace    *without fear for your safety.*

The which he could not levy; whereupon
He is retir'd, to ripe his growing Fortunes,
To Scotland, and concludes in hearty Prayers
That your Attempts may over-live the Hazard                    15
And fearful Meeting of their Opposite.

MOWBRAY    Thus do the Hopes we have in him touch
    Ground
And dash themselves in pieces.

*Enter a Messenger.*

HASTINGS                                Now what News?
MESSENGER    West of this Forest, scarcely off a Mile,
In goodly Form, comes on the Enemy;                            20
And by the Ground they hide, I judge their
    Number
Upon or near the rate of thirty thousand.

MOWBRAY    The just Proportion that we gave them out:
Let us sway on, and face them in the Field.

*Enter Westmerland.*

ARCHBISHOP    What well-appointed Leader fronts us
    here?                                               25
MOWBRAY    I think it is my Lord of Westmerland.
WESTMERLAND    Health and fair Greeting from our
    General,
The Prince Lord John and Duke of Lancaster.
ARCHBISHOP    Say on, my Lord of Westmerland, in
    peace:
What doth concern your coming?

33      Came like itself    *appeared in its true colors.*
        base and abject Routs    *rioting mobs (rather than orderly ranks).*

34      guarded with Rage    *attempting to defend itself with irrational fury.*

35      countenanc'd by Boys and Beggary    *approved and maintained by immature boys and irresponsible beggars.*

36      damn'd Commotion    *condemned rebellion ("damn'd" because of the Church's admonition to "be subject unto the higher powers . . . that be ordained of God," as expounded in Romans 13:1–8).*

42      See    *ecclesiastical jurisdiction (literally, "oversight").*

43      Whose Beard . . . touch'd    *whose gray beard would appear to be a sign of peace.*

44      good Letters    *literary training.*

45      Investments    *vestments, clerical robes.*
        figure    *symbolize.*

47      translate    *a complex word that here combines three senses: (a) remove physically, (b) move from one "language" to another, and (c) transform.*

52      Point of War    *Westermerland's primary meaning has to do with "Point" as a short burst of notes sounded as a signal of battle. But he is probably also thinking of the Archbishop's "Tongue Divine" (line 51) as an organ that has been "translated" into a sharp weapon.*

55      Surfeiting    *overindulgent, overfeeding.*

WESTMERLAND                    Then, my Lord,                    30
    Unto your Grace do I in chief address
    The substance of my Speech. If that Rebellion
    Came like itself, in base and abject Routs,
    Led on by bloody Youth, guarded with Rage,
    And countenanc'd by Boys and Beggary,          35
    I say, if damn'd Commotion so appear
    In his true, native, and most proper Shape,
    You, Reverend Father, and these Noble Lords
    Had not been here to dress the ugly Form
    Of base and bloody Insurrection                40
    With your fair Honors. You, Lord Archbishop,
    Whose See is by a Civil Peace maintain'd,
    Whose Beard the Silver Hand of Peace hath
        touch'd,
    Whose Learning and good Letters Peace hath
        tutor'd,
    Whose white Investments figure Innocence,      45
    The Dove, and very blessed Spirit of Peace,
    Wherefore do you so ill translate your Self
    Out of the Speech of Peace, that bears such
        Grace,
    Into the harsh and boistrous Tongue of War,
    Turning your Books to Graves, your Ink to
        Blood,                                     50
    Your Pens to Launces, and your Tongue Divine
    To a loud Trumpet and a Point of War?
ARCHBISHOP   Wherefore do I this? So the Question
    stands.
    Briefly to this End: we are all Diseas'd,
    And with our Surfeiting and Wanton Hours       55

57    bleed   *The Archbishop refers to the medical practice of opening a patient's veins to release blood and thus purge the body of disease.*

60    I take . . . Physician   *I do not assume the role of a doctor.*

63    show a while like   *assume for a period the costume of.*

64    To diet rank Minds   *to administer a dietary regimen to swollen minds.*

65    purge   *remove.*

71    And are . . . there   *and are forced thereby from our quietest position.*

76    And might . . . Audience   *and were unable, despite our requests, to obtain a hearing.*

77    unfold   *lay out, present.*
       our Griefs   *our grievances, the wrongs that have been done us.*

80    The Dangers . . . newly gone   *The Archbishop refers to the insurrection that removed Richard II from the throne and installed Bullingbrook as Henry IV.*

82    yet appearing   *still-evident.*

83    ev'ry Minute's Instance   *provided by every minute that passes.*

84    ill-beseeming   *unbecoming, unfitting.*

Have brought our selves into a burning Fever
And we must bleed for it; of which Disease
Our late King Richard, being infected, died.
But, my most Noble Lord of Westmerland,
I take not on me here as a Physician,                           60
Nor do I as an Enemy to Peace
Troop in the Throngs of Military Men,
But rather show a while like fearful War
To diet rank Minds sick of Happiness
And purge th' Obstructions which begin to stop         65
Our very Veins of Life. Hear me more plainly.
I have in equal Balance justly weigh'd
What Wrongs our Arms may do, what Wrongs we
    suffer,
And find our Griefs heavier than our Offenses.
We see which way the Stream of Time doth run,        70
And are enforc'd from our most Quiet there
By the rough Torrent of Occasion,
And have the Summary of all our Griefs,
When Time shall serve, in Articles,
Which long ere this we offer'd to the King                 75
And might by no Suit gain our Audience;
When we are wrong'd, and would unfold our
    Griefs,
We are denied Access unto his Person,
Ev'n by those Men that most have done us Wrong.
The Dangers of the Days but newly gone,                 80
Whose Memory is written on the Earth
With yet appearing Blood, and the Examples
Of ev'ry Minute's Instance, present now,
Hath put us in these ill-beseeming Arms:

86   a Peace indeed   *a true peace, rather than the mere appearance of one.*

88   Appeal   *request for a hearing of your grievances.*

89   galled   *chafed, irritated.*

90   suborn'd to grate on you   *instigated to annoy you.*

91–92   this lawless . . . Rebellion   *Westmerland says that the document justifying the rebellion is an illegal forgery (because there is no legitimate basis for the action it pledges its parties to undertake).*

92   Seal Divine   *divine sanction. Westmerland may also be alluding to the role that prelates had in licensing books for publication.*

93   general   *the general population.*

94   I make my Quarrel in particular   *I cite as the justification for my own personal dispute with the King.*

97   in part   *as one of many injured parties.*

98   That feel . . . Before   *who still bear bruises from the days when we were all oppressed by Richard's injustices.*

99   suffer   *permit.*

102   Construe . . . Necessities   *interpret the times in accordance with the necessities they impose upon us.*

109   Signories   *rights of inheritance (seniority) in estates and titles.*

Not to break Peace, or any Branch of it,                    85
But to establish here a Peace indeed,
Concurring both in Name and Quality.

WESTMERLAND   When ever yet was your Appeal
    denied?
Wherein have you been galled by the King?
What Peer hath been suborn'd to grate on you,              90
That you should seal this lawless bloody Book
Of forg'd Rebellion with a Seal Divine?

ARCHBISHOP   My Brother general, the Commonwealth,
I make my Quarrel in particular.

WESTMERLAND   There is no need of any such Redress:        95
Or if there were, it not belongs to you.

MOWBRAY   Why not to him in part, and to us all,
That feel the Bruises of the Days Before,
And suffer the Condition of these Times
To lay a heavy and unequal Hand                           100
Upon our Honors?

WESTMERLAND             O my good Lord Mowbray,
Construe the Times to their Necessities,
And you shall say indeed it is the Time,
And not the King, that doth you Injuries.
Yet for your part, it not appears to me,                  105
Eith'r from the King or in the present Time,
That you should have an inch of any Ground
To build a Grief on. Were you not restor'd
To all the Duke of Norfolk's Signories,
Your noble and right well-rememb'red Father's?            110

MOWBRAY   What thing, in Honor, had my Father lost
That need to be reviv'd and breath'd in me?
The King that lov'd him, as the State stood then,

116    roused in their Seats    *in their saddles and eager to fight. The scene the Archbishop describes is dramatized in I.iii of* Richard II.

117    daring of the Spur    *challenging their riders to spur them into battle.*

118    Staves in charge    *lances braced for the charge.*
       Beavers    *metal visors.*

124    His, he    *Both pronouns refer to King Richard.*
       the Staff    *the King's warder (baton).*

126    Indictment    *formal accusation.*
       dint    *force (but probably with a pun on* dent).

127    miscarri'd    *been carried away.*

131    Fortune    *Its metrical position suggests that* Fortune *is here to be accented on the second syllable, as in the Latin word* Fortuna.

133    He ne'er had borne it    *He would never have carried his triumph (because he would have been apprehended and killed by those who hated him).*
       Coventry    *site of the royal lists where Mowbray and Bullingbrook were set to settle their dispute in a trial by combat.*

134–   For all . . . him    *Westmerland is saying that the whole country considered Mowbray responsible for carrying out the King's orders to kill his uncle Thomas of Woodstock, Duke of Gloucester, who was in Mowbray's custody at Calais in Brittany.*
35

166

Was forc'd, perforce compell'd, to banish him.
And then, that Henry Bullingbrook and he          115
Being mounted and both roused in their Seats,
Their neighing Coursers daring of the Spur,
Their armed Staves in charge, their Beavers
    down,
Their Eyes of Fire, sparkling through sights
    of Steel,
And the loud Trumpet blowing them together,      120
Then, then, when there was nothing could have
    stay'd
My Father from the Breast of Bullingbrook,
O when the King did throw his Warder down,
His own Life hung upon the Staff he threw,
Then threw he down himself, and all their
    Lives                                        125
That by Indictment and by dint of Sword
Have since miscarri'd under Bullingbrook.

WESTMERLAND   You speak, Lord Mowbray, now you
    know not what.
The Earl of Herford was reputed then
In England the most valiant Gentleman.           130
Who knows on whom Fortune would then have
    smil'd?
But if your Father had been Victor there,
He ne'er had borne it out of Coventry:
For all the Country, in a gen'ral Voice,
Cried Hate upon him; and all their Pray'rs and
    Love                                         135
Were set on Herford, whom they doted on

143    enjoy them    *receive what you've requested.*

143–   ev'ry thing . . . Enemies    *with every just complaint re-*
44     *moved from consideration that might so much as imply that*
       *you remain enemies.*

146    Policy    *political cunning.*

147    over-ween    *presume too much on the basis of what you sup-*
       *pose to be the case.*

149    within a Ken    *within sight of us here.*

152    Battail    *battalion, army.*
       Names    *men of noble rank.*

153    perfect    *skilled.*

155    Then Reason will    *therefore reason would suggest that.*

157    admit no Parley    *permit no discussion of negotiations.*

159    A rotten . . . Handling.    *A rotten container (such as a*
       *box) will not permit one to handle it. What Westmerland refers*
       *to is the "Case" (justification, cause) for the rebellion. He may*
       *also be using* rotten Case *in a bawdy sense, to refer to a*
       *diseased whore.*

160    a full Commission    *complete authority; here pronounced*
       com-mís-si-òn.

161    In very ample Virtue    *in true and sufficient power. Lines*
       *160–63 are deliberately redundant: Hastings wants to be*
       *absolutely certain that the Rebels are negotiating, in effect,*
       *with the King himself.*

And bless'd, and grac'd, and did more than the
   King.
But this is mere Digression from my Purpose.
Here come I from our Princely General
To know your Griefs; to tell you, from his Grace,     140
That he will give you Audience; and wherein
It shall appear that your Demands are just,
You shall enjoy them, ev'ry thing set off
That might so much as think you Enemies.

MOWBRAY    But he hath forc'd us to compel this Offer,   145
And it proceeds from Policy, not Love.

WESTMERLAND    Mowbray, you over-ween to take it so:
This Offer comes from Mercy, not from Fear.
For lo, within a Ken our Army lies,
Upon mine Honor, all too confident     150
To give admittance to a thought of Fear.
Our Battail is more full of Names than yours,
Our Men more perfect in the use of Arms,
Our Armor all as strong, our Cause the best;
Then Reason will our Hearts should be as good.   155
Say you not then our Offer is compell'd.

MOWBRAY    Well, by my will, we shall admit no Parley.

WESTMERLAND    That argues but the Shame of your
   Offense:
A rotten Case abides no Handling.

HASTINGS    Hath the Prince John a full Commission,   160
In very ample Virtue of his Father,
To hear and absolutely to determine
Of what Conditions we shall stand upon?

WESTMERLAND    This is intended in the General's
   Name:

169

165   I muse . . . Question.   *I'm surprised you ask such a silly question.*

166   Schedule   *list, roster.*

168   sev'ral   *individual.*
      redress'd   *addressed and remedied.*

169   hence   *elsewhere.*

170   ensinew'd   *committed with our power.*

171–73   Acquitted . . . confin'd   *pardoned in a substantive and formal document that executes the granting of what we have demanded, with all of this limited to us and to what we purpose.*

174–75   We come . . . Peace   *[like a river,] we will flow once more within our banks of reverence and obedience, and knit our armies [like a badge or insignia] to "the Arm of Peace."*

177   Battails   *armed battalions.*

178   frame   *execute, bring about.*

179   the place of Diff'rence   *the battlefield.*

181   There . . . me   *In Shakespeare, misgivings like this are usually well-founded.*

185   consist upon   *both (a) consist of, and (b) insist upon.*

188   false-derived   *falsely conceived or interpreted.*

189   idle, nice, and wanton   *capricious, petty, and irresponsible.*

I muse you make so slight a Question. 165
ARCHBISHOP   Then take, my Lord of Westmerland,
    this Schedule,
    For this contains our gen'ral Grievances:
    Each sev'ral Article herein redress'd,
    All members of our Cause, both here and hence,
    That are ensinew'd to this Action 170
    Acquitted by a true substantial Form
    And present Execution of our Wills,
    To us and to our Purposes confin'd,
    We come within our aweful Banks again
    And knit our Powers to the Arm of Peace. 175
WESTMERLAND   This will I show the General. Please
    you, Lords,
    In sight of both our Battails we may meet
    At either end in Peace, which God so frame,
    Or to the place of Diff'rence call the Swords
    Which must decide it.
ARCHBISHOP                 My Lord, we will do so. 180
                        *Exit Westmerland.*
MOWBRAY   There is a thing within my Bosom tells me
    That no Conditions of our Peace can stand.
HASTINGS   Fear you not that, if can we make our
    Peace
    Upon such large terms and so absolute
    As our Conditions shall consist upon, 185
    Our Peace shall stand as firm as rocky
    Mountains.
MOWBRAY   Ay, but our Valuation shall be such
    That ev'ry slight and false-derived Cause,
    Yea, ev'ry idle, nice, and wanton Reason,

171

190     taste of   *be interpreted as flavored by.*

191     That, were . . . Love   *so that even if our fidelity to the King made us patriotic martyrs.*

192     winnow'd   *sifted, sorted out (to separate the grain from the chaff).*

193     Corn   *grain.*

194     Partition   *division, line of demarcation.*

196     dainty   *minute, petty.*
        picking   *nit-picking, trifling.*

197     Doubt   *both (a) questions about him by his adversaries, and (b) his fear of the motives and power of those who raise questions.*

198     the Heirs of Life   *those who remain alive (including, but not limited to, the heirs of those executed for treason).*

199     Tables   *records.*

201     history   *narrate.*

203     precisely   *cleanly and completely.*

205     enrooted with   *mingled with. This imagery recalls III.iv of Richard II.*

209     offer   *threaten, initiate. So also in line 217.*

211     hangs   *suspends.*

217     hold   *hold to his resolve, execute his intentions.*

Shall to the King taste of this Action,                    190
That, were our Royal Faiths Martyrs in Love,
We shall be winnow'd with so rough a Wind
That ev'n our Corn shall seem as light as
    Chaff,
And Good from Bad find no Partition.
ARCHBISHOP   No, no, my Lord, note this: the
    King is weary                                          195
Of dainty and such picking Grievances:
For he hath found, to end one Doubt by Death
Revives two greater in the Heirs of Life.
And therefore will he wipe his Tables clean
And keep no Tell-tale to his Memory                        200
That may repeat and history his Loss
To new Remembrance. For full well he knows
He cannot so precisely weed this Land
As his Misdoubts present Occasion.
His Foes are so enrooted with his Friends                  205
That plucking to unfix an Enemy
He doth unfasten so and shake a Friend:
So that this Land, like an offensive Wife
That hath enrag'd him on to offer Strokes,
As he is striking, holds his Infant up                     210
And hangs resolv'd Correction in the Arm
That was uprear'd to Execution.
HASTINGS   Besides, the King hath wasted all his
    Rods
On late Offenders, that he now doth lack
The very Instruments of Chastisement:                      215
So that his Pow'r, like to a Fangless Lion,
May offer, but not hold.

173

219    Atonement    *"at-onement," reconciliation.*

224    just distance    *midway.*

226    Before    *no, you go first.*

IV.ii    *This scene follows immediately at the site specified in line 224 of the previous scene.*

1    You are well encount'red    *I am glad to see you.*

ARCHBISHOP                    'Tis very true:
    And therefore be assur'd, my good Lord Marshal,
    If we do now make our Atonement well,
    Our Peace will, like a Broken Limb united,                    220
    Grow stronger for the Breaking.
MOWBRAY                              Be it so:
    Here is return'd my Lord of Westmerland.

*Enter Westmerland.*

WESTMERLAND   The Prince is here at hand: pleaseth
    your Lordship
    To meet his Grace just distance 'tween our
    Armies?
MOWBRAY   Your Grace of York, in Heav'n's Name
    then set forward.                                                    225
ARCHBISHOP   Before, and greet his Grace, my Lord:
    we come.

# Scene 2

*Enter Prince John and his Army.*

PRINCE JOHN   You are well encount'red here, my
    Cousin Mowbray.
    —Good day to you, gentle Lord Archbishop.
    —And so to you, Lord Hastings, and to you all.

175

8      Iron-man    *Prince John implies that the Archbishop's unaccustomed, ill-beseeming military armor shows him to be a man whose "iron" heart is deficient in grace, obedience, and Christian love.*

10      the Word to Sword    *Prince John is probably thinking of such passages as Ephesians 6:17, where the "word of God" is called "the sword of the Spirit," and Hebrews 4:12, where it is described as "quick and powerful, and sharper than any two-edged sword, piercing even to the dividing asunder of soul and spirit, and of the joints and marrow, and . . . a discerner of the thoughts and intents of the heart." If so, his point is that the Archbishop is wielding the wrong kind of sword and thus abusing the "Count'nance" (line 13), the true image and nature, of his office.*

13      Count'nance    *here, both (a) visage or name, and (b) trust.*

14      set abroach    *break open and set flowing.*

15      In shadow of    *both (a) under the protection of, and (b) while seeming to represent.*

18      Speaker in His Parliament    *the one who interprets the will of the Monarch (here, God) to the Commons (the officers of the Church).*

19      imagine    *imaginary, substitute.*

22      Dull Workings    *unenlightened mental operations.*

30      upswarm'd them    *made them swarm like angry bees or hornets.*

—My Lord of York, it better show'd with you
When that your Flock, assembled by the Bell,     5
Encircled you to hear with reverence
Your Exposition on the Holy Text
Than now to see you here an Iron-man talking,
Cheering a rout of Rebels with your Drum,
Turning the Word to Sword, and Life to Death.     10
That Man that sits within a Monarch's Heart
And ripens in the Sunshine of his Favor,
Would he abuse the Count'nance of the King,
Alack what Mischiefs might he set abroach
In shadow of such Greatness? With you, Lord
    Bishop,     15
It is ev'n so; who hath not heard it spoken
How deep you were within the Books of God,
To us the Speaker in His Parliament,
To us th' imagine Voice of God Himself,
The very Op'ner and Intelligencer,     20
Between the Grace, the Sanctities of Heav'n,
And our Dull Workings? O who shall believe
But you misuse the Rev'rence of your Place,
Employ the Countenance and Grace of Heav'n,
As a false Fav'rite doth his Prince's Name,     25
In Deeds Dishon'rable? You have ta'en up
Under the counterfeited Zeal of God,
The Subjects of his Substitute, my Father,
And both against the Peace of Heav'n and him
Have here upswarm'd them.

ARCHBISHOP         Good my Lord of Lancaster,     30
    I am not here against your Father's Peace;
    But, as I told my Lord of Westmerland,

33    in Common Sense   *in keeping with the dictates of common sense (the prudence of men who feel threatened by the King's demeanor).*

34    this Monstrous Form   *The Archbishop probably means both (a) his own appearance, and (b) a rebel army that looks like a portentous monster (as explained in lines 38–39).*

36    parcels   *individual complaints.*

38    this Hydra Son of War   *this many-headed multitude, which is the offspring of War. The Archbishop alludes to a multi-headed serpent that would grow two heads for every one that Hercules severed with his sword.*

39    Whose . . . asleep   *With this line the Archbishop combines the image of Hydra with a feature of Argus, the hundred-eyed creature assigned by the jealous Hera to keep watch and prevent her husband Zeus from making love to the maiden Io. Zeus circumvented Hera's plans by having the God Hermes disguise himself as a shepherd, pipe and talk to Argus, and eventually charm all the monster's eyes to sleep so that Hermes could kill him. The Archbishop's allusion to a creature whose "Eyes" may be "charm'd asleep" will prove ironically apt.*

45    Supplies   *reinforcements.*
       second   *support, back up.*

47    Success of Mischief   *a succession of rebellions. Hastings recalls the Hydra image of line 39; he also echoes Exodus 20:5 and Richard II, IV.i.135–48.*

The Time misord'red doth in Common Sense
Crowd us and crush us to this Monstrous Form
To hold our Safety up. I sent your Grace                35
The parcels and partic'lars of our Grief,
The which hath been with Scorn shov'd from the
    Court,
Whereon this Hydra Son of War is born,
Whose dang'rous Eyes may well be charm'd
    asleep
With grant of our most just and right Desires,         40
And true Obedience, of this Madness cur'd,
Stoop tamely to the Foot of Majesty.
MOWBRAY   If not, we ready are to try our Fortunes
To the last Man.
HASTINGS            And though we here fall down,
We have Supplies to second our Attempt;                45
If they miscarry, theirs shall second them;
And so Success of Mischief shall be born,
And Heir from Heir shall hold his Quarrel up
Whiles England shall have Generation.
PRINCE JOHN   You are too shallow, Hastings, much
    too shallow,                                        50
To sound the Bottom of the After-times.
WESTMERLAND   Pleaseth your Grace to answer them
    directly
How far forth you do like their Articles.
PRINCE JOHN   I like them all, and do allow them
    well,
And swear here, by the Honor of my Blood,              55
My Father's Purposes have been mistook,
And some about him have too lavishly

65   Amity   *friendship.*

71   Hie   *haste.*

74   breed   *conceive.*

80   something   *somewhat, for some reason.*

81   Against Ill Chances   *in advance of bad fortune.*

Wrested his Meaning and Authority.
My Lord, these Griefs shall be with speed
    redress'd,
Upon my Soul they shall. If this may please
    you,                                                    60
Discharge your Pow'rs unto their sev'ral
    Counties,
As we will ours, and here between the Armies
Let's drink together friendly and embrace,
That all their Eyes may bear those Tokens home
Of our restored Love and Amity.                            65
ARCHBISHOP   I take your Princely Word for these
    Redresses;
I give it you, and will maintain my Word,
And thereupon I drink unto your Grace.
PRINCE JOHN   —Go Captain, and deliver to the Army
This News of Peace; let them have Pay and part.            70
I know it will well please them. Hie thee,
    Captain.                                    *Exit Captain.*
ARCHBISHOP   To you, my Noble Lord of Westmerland.
WESTMERLAND   I pledge your Grace, and if you knew
    what Pains
I have bestow'd to breed this present Peace
You would drink freely. But my Love to ye                  75
Shall show itself more openly hereafter.
ARCHBISHOP   I do not doubt you.
WESTMERLAND                       I am glad of it.
    —Health to my Lord and gentle Cousin Mowbray.
MOWBRAY   You wish me Health in very happy Season,
For I am on the sudden something Ill.                       80
ARCHBISHOP   Against Ill Chances men are ever Merry,

181

82     Heaviness   *melancholy, foreboding.*

85     passing Light   *surpassingly jovial. But* Light *is a word that can also mean (a) frivolous, and (b) foolish.*

93     Trains   *armies.*

95     We should have cop'd withal   *we would have contended with.*

98     wherefore . . . still?   *why is our army still on duty?*

But Heaviness foreruns the Good Event.

WESTMERLAND   Therefore be Merry, Coz, since
    sudden Sorrow
    Serves to say thus: some Good Thing comes
    tomorrow.

ARCHBISHOP   Believe me, I am passing Light in
    Spirit.                                                    85

MOWBRAY   So much the worse if your own Rule be
    true.                                               *Shout.*

PRINCE JOHN   The word of Peace is rend'red. Hark
    how they shout!

MOWBRAY   This had been cheerful after Victory.

ARCHBISHOP   A Peace is of the nature of a Conquest,
    For then both Parties nobly are subdu'd,                   90
    And neither party Loser.

PRINCE JOHN                    —Go, my Lord,
    And let our Army be discharged too.

                                        *Exit Westmerland.*

    —And, good my Lord, so please you let our Trains
    March by us, that we may peruse the Men
    We should have cop'd withal.

ARCHBISHOP                    Go, good Lord Hastings,         95
    And ere they be dismiss'd let them march by.

                                        *Exit Hastings.*


                *Enter Westmerland.*


PRINCE JOHN   I trust, Lords, we shall lie tonight
    together:
    —Now, Cousin, wherefore stands our Army still?

112    I pawn'd thee none. *Here* pawn'd *means "pledged,"* *"promised." Prince John's words are delivered with a stark* *directness that is chillingly reinforced by his momentary shift* *from* you *to* thee. *"Thee," "thou," and "thy" are the pro-* *nouns upper-class Elizabethans used when addressing rela-* *tives and close friends (social familiars) or servants and com-* *moners (social inferiors). During most of this scene everyone* *uses the more "reserved," "respectful," and "distancing" pro-* *nouns and accompanying verb forms: "you," "your," and* *"yours." Prince John's shift to* thee, *then, is a significant* *linguistic indication (like calling an equal "Sirrah") that he* *has now gained the upper hand with the Archbishop and his* *allies. Having made his point, he immediately shifts back to a* *less contemptuous mode of address, just as Westmerland has* *done in the previous speech after shocking Hastings with "I do* *arrest thee, Traitor, of high Treason."*

113    I promis'd you Redress   *Prince John is correct. A look back* *at what he and Westmerland say from line 54 on will show* *that their assurances are deliberately couched in ambiguity.* *The Archbishop has been charmed to sleep immediately, hear-* *ing only what he wants to hear and demanding no guarantees* *of good faith from his adversaries. Hastings' intuitions have* *made him more dubious; but because he has been too timid to* *act on the misgivings he has expressed, he too now finds himself* *a "naked Subject" (I.iii.61) on his way to execution.*

118    shallowly   *without a substantive foundation. Prince John's* *words echo Lord Bardolph's speech in I.iii.41–62.*

119    Fondly   *foolishly.*

WESTMERLAND  The Leaders, having charge from
    you to stand,
  Will not go off until they hear you speak.          100
PRINCE JOHN  They know their Duties.

*Enter Hastings.*

HASTINGS  My Lord, our Army is dispers'd already.
  Like youthful Steers unyok'd, they take their
    Courses,
  East, West, North, South; or like a School
    broke up,
  Each hurries toward his Home and Sporting-
    place.                                            105
WESTMERLAND  Good Tidings, my Lord Hastings: for
    the which
  I do arrest thee, Traitor, of high Treason.
  —And you, Lord Archbishop, and you, Lord
    Mowbray:
  Of cap'tal Treason I attach you both.
MOWBRAY  Is this Proceeding just and hon'rable?      110
WESTMERLAND  Is your Assembly so?
ARCHBISHOP  Will you thus break your Faith?
PRINCE JOHN                      I pawn'd thee none.
  I promis'd you Redress of these same Grievances
  Whereof you did complain, which by mine Honor
  I will perform with a most Christian Care.          115
  But for you Rebels, look to taste the Due
  Meet for Rebellion and such Acts as yours.
  Most shallowly did you these Arms commence,
  Fondly brought here and foolishly sent hence.

185

120     Stray   *the soldiers who have left the battlefield.*

IV.iii    *This scene takes place in the Forest of Gaultree shortly after the preceding scene.*

S.D.    **Alarum**   *a trumpet call to tell troops to advance.*
      **Excursions**   *sorties, movements about the battlefield.*

1       **Condition**   *rank.*

10     **Colevile of the Dale**   *Here and in his preceding lines, Falstaff puns on Colevile's name, noting that it will be appropriate for him to be placed in a vile, coal-black dungeon that will only be a darker and more enclosed "Dale" (valley) than the one from which Colevile hails. Lines 67 and 68, which appear to be in verse, suggest that* **Colevile** *is to be pronounced as a three-syllable word (Coal-a-vile).*

14     thy **Lovers**   *those who love you. Sensing that Colevile is on the verge of yielding to him, Falstaff shifts from* your *to* thy.

15–16    **rouse up Fear and Trembling**   *Falstaff is being facetious, of course: "rouse up" is normally an exhortation to summon up courage.*

—Strike up our Drums, pursue the scatt'red
  Stray.                                           120
God and not we hath safely fought today.
Some guard these Traitors to the Block of
  Death,
Treason's true Bed, and yielder-up of Breath.

*Exeunt.*

# Scene 3

*Alarum. Excursions. Enter Falstaff, meeting Colevile.*

FALSTAFF   What's your Name, Sir? Of what Condition
  are you, and of what Place?
COLEVILE   I am a Knight, Sir, and my name is
  Colevile of the Dale.
FALSTAFF   Well then, Colevile is your Name, a Knight    5
  is your Degree, and your Place the Dale.
  Colevile shall be still your Name, a Traitor
  your Degree, and the Dungeon your Place, a
  place deep enough so shall you be still
  Colevile of the Dale.                          10
COLEVILE   Are not you Sir John Falstaff?
FALSTAFF   As good a Man as he, Sir, who e'er I am.
  Do ye yield, Sir, or shall I sweat for you? If
  I do sweat, they are the drops of thy Lovers,
  and they weep for thy Death: therefore rouse    15

18–19  in that Thought  *based on that premise. Colevile is evidently one of the Rebels who have been misled by "Rumor": he believes Falstaff to be the valiant soldier who slew the mighty Hotspur at Shrewsbury.*

20  School of Tongues  *Falstaff's description of himself recalls the play's first stage direction: "Enter Rumor painted full of Tongues." Falstaff probably means by lines 20–22 that the notorious size of his belly proclaims his identity wherever he goes.*

23  Indifferency  *lacking in differentiation, distinction. What Falstaff means is "a belly of any normal dimensions."*

24  active  *The immediate context would suggest that one of Falstaff's meanings here is "active militarily." But* active *can also refer to what Shylock calls "the work of Generation" in I.iii of* The Merchant of Venice, *and that kind of activity is probably what Falstaff has primarily in mind.*

25  my Womb undoes me  *my belly keeps me from "doing." Compare the similar wordplay on "undone" in III.ii.124.*

27  The Heat is past  *Prince John means "the need for hot pursuit is over now." But in the context of Falstaff's words about being undone by his "Womb," Prince John's remarks are also a humorous reminder of the Falstaffian condition that Poins has remarked upon in II.iv.283–84: "Is it not strange that Desire should so many years outlive Performance?"*

38–39  with . . . Possibility  *as expeditiously (rapidly) as possible.*

up Fear and Trembling, and do Observance to my
Mercy.

COLEVILE    I think you are Sir John Falstaff, and in
that Thought yield me.

FALSTAFF    I have a whole School of Tongues in this     20
Belly of mine, and not a Tongue of them all
speaks any other word but my Name. And I had
but a Belly of any Indifferency, I were simply
the most active Fellow in Europe; my Womb, my
Womb, my Womb undoes me. Here comes our     25
General.

*Enter Prince John, Westmerland, Blunt,*
*and the rest.*

PRINCE JOHN    The Heat is past: follow no further
now.
Call in the Powers, good Cousin Westmerland.
                              *Exit Westmerland.*
—Now Falstaff, where have you been all this
while?
When every thing is ended, then you come.     30
These tardy Tricks of yours will, on my Life,
One time or other break some Gallows' back.

FALSTAFF    I would be sorry, my Lord, but it should
be thus: I never knew yet but Rebuke and Check
was the Reward of Valor. Do you think me a     35
Swallow, an Arrow, or a Bullet? Have I in my
poor and old Motion the Expedition of Thought?
I have speeded hither with the very extremest
inch of Possibility; I have found'red ninescore

40    Posts  *post-horses. Post-horses were normally furnished at ten-mile intervals along major routes, so Falstaff is claiming to have traveled more than 1800 miles.*

41    immaculate  *spotless.*

45    the hook-nos'd Fellow of Rome there  *Julius Caesar. Falstaff goes on to quote Caesar's most famous line:* "Veni, vidi, vici." *Caesar's words were sometimes cited in reference to amorous conquests, and that sense is reinforced here by the description of Caesar's nose ("hook" being a word with phallic implications).*

52    particular Ballad  *a ballad about myself.*

55    show  *appear, come across.*

56    gilt Twopences  *gilded twopences (silver coins colored gold to be passed off as half-crowns, which were the same size and were worth a great deal more).*

58    Cinders of the Element  *a reductive description of the stars in the sky.*

61    mount  *Falstaff means "ascend" to the skies and be fixed in one of the spheres of the "Element." But Prince John probably plays on another sense (mount a horse) in line 62. Meanwhile the audience would probably supply a third sense ("mount" a woman, as implied in II.i.82–83).*

64    thick  *both (a) lacking in brightness or clarity, and (b) heavy.*

and odd Posts, and here, Travel-tainted as I          40
am, have in my pure and immaculate Valor taken
Sir John Colevile of the Dale, a most furious
Knight and valorous Enemy. But what of that?
He saw me and yielded, that I may justly say
with the hook-nos'd Fellow of Rome there,          45
Cousin, "I came, saw, and overcame."

PRINCE JOHN   It was more of his Courtesy than your
Deserving.

FALSTAFF   I know not; here he is, and here I yield
him; and I beseech your Grace let it be book'd          50
with the rest of this day's Deeds, or by the
Lord I will have it in a particular Ballad
else, with mine own Picture on the top on 't
(Colevile kissing my Foot), to the which course
if I be enforc'd, if you do not all show like          55
gilt Twopences to me, and I in the clear Sky
of Fame o'ershine you as much as the full
Moon doth the Cinders of the Element (which
show like Pin's-heads to her), believe not the
Word of the Noble. Therefore let me have Right,          60
and let Desert mount.

PRINCE JOHN   Thine's too heavy to mount.

FALSTAFF   Let it shine then.

PRINCE JOHN   Thine's too thick to shine.

FALSTAFF   Let it do some thing, my good Lord, that          65
may do me good, and call it what you will.

PRINCE JOHN   Is thy name Colevile?

COLEVILE                              It is, my Lord.

PRINCE JOHN   A famous Rebel art thou, Colevile.

FALSTAFF   —And a famous True Subject took him.

191

70–72 I am . . . have.  *It is a mark of Colevile's "Courtesy" (line 47) that he responds to Prince John's questions in verse rather than in prose. Falstaff's impudence in this scene is highlighted by his refusal or inability to rise above the prose which is his habitual element.*

72 dearer  *at a higher price.*

75 gratis  *free of charge. But this word is also a reminder of the "grace" (courtesy) of Colevile's behavior throughout the scene.*

77 Retrait . . . stay'd.  *Retreat has been sounded by the trumpets, and execution of the order to pursue has been suspended.*

79 present  *instant. Prince John's disposition of Colevile stands in stark contrast with the magnanimity of Prince Hal's treatment of the noble Douglas at the end of the Battle of Shrewsbury (*1 Henry IV, *V.v).*

81 dispatch we  *let us proceed immediately.*

82 sore  *grievously.*

85 sober  *deliberate.*

87 Gloucestershire  *Falstaff plans to pay another visit to Justice Shallow (as he has indicated in III.ii.353–58).*

88 stand my good Lord  *represent me as a faithful sponsor.*

91 condition  *disposition.*

93–94 'twere . . . Dukedom  *what I deserve is a position higher than yours.*

COLEVILE    —I am, my Lord, but as my Betters are          70
    That led me hither. Had they been rul'd by me,
    You should have won them dearer than you have.
FALSTAFF   I know not how they sold themselves, but
    thou like a Kind Fellow gav'st thy self away
    gratis, and I thank thee for thee.                          75

*Enter Westmerland.*

PRINCE JOHN   Now, have you left Pursuit?
WESTMERLAND    Retrait is made, and Execution stay'd.
PRINCE JOHN   Send Colevile with his Confederates
    To York, to present Execution.
    —Blunt, lead him hence, and see you guard him
    sure.              *Exeunt Blunt and Guards with Colevile.*    80
    —And now dispatch we toward the Court, my
    Lords.
    I hear the King my Father is sore sick:
    Our News shall go before us to his Majesty,
    Which, Cousin, you shall bear to comfort him,
    And we with sober speed will follow you.                     85
FALSTAFF   My Lord, I beseech you give me leave to
    go through Gloucestershire, and when you come
    to Court, stand my good Lord in your good
    Report.
PRINCE JOHN   Fare you well, Falstaff. I, in my            90
    condition, shall better speak of you than you
    deserve.                      *Exeunt all but Falstaff.*
FALSTAFF   I would you had the Wit: 'twere better
    than your Dukedom. —Good Faith, this same
    young, sober-blooded Boy doth not love me, nor              95

193

98    demure    *correctly behaved.*
      come to any Proof    *prove to be anything good, stand up to the trial.*

99    Thin Drink    *drink with little or no alcohol.*

100   making    *eating.*

101   Green-sickness    *an anemia normally associated with lovesick maidens.*

102   get Wenches    *beget girls. That is, they are too effeminate to be capable of conceiving male heirs.*

104   Inflammation    *"heating" of the blood through the consumption of alcohol.*

105   Sherris-sack    *white sherry, a wine whose name derives from its origin: Jerez in Spain.*

107   cruddy    *curdled, thick.*

108   apprehensive    *quick to grasp or perceive ideas.*

109   forgetive    *creative. This adjective derives from* forge *and is probably to be pronounced with a soft g. In* The Merry Wives of Windsor, *IV.ii.235–36, Mistress Page says "Come to the Forge with it, then; shape it." Similarly, in* Henry V *the Chorus introduces the play with a reference to "the quick Forge and Working-house of Thought" (Prologue, line 5).*

110   Shapes    *both (a) ideas, and (b) the words to express them.*

116   Pusillanimity    *"smallness of soul," faintheartedness (the opposite of magnanimity, greatness of soul).*

a Man cannot make him laugh. But that's no
Marvel: he drinks no Wine. There's never none
of these demure Boys come to any Proof: for
Thin Drink doth so over-cool their Blood, and
making many Fish-meals, that they fall into a                    100
kind of male Green-sickness; and then when
they marry, they get Wenches. They are
generally Fools and Cowards, which some of us
should be too but for Inflammation. A good
Sherris-sack hath a twofold Operation in it:                     105
it ascends me into the Brain, dries me there
all the foolish and dull and cruddy Vapors
which environ it, makes it apprehensive, quick,
forgetive, full of nimble, fiery, and
delectable Shapes, which, deliver'd o'er to                      110
the Voice, the Tongue, which is the Birth,
becomes excellent Wit. The Second Property of
your excellent Sherris is the Warming of the
Blood, which before, cold and settl'd, left
the Liver white and pale, which is the Badge                     115
of Pusillanimity and Cowardice. But the Sherris
warms it, and makes it course from the Inwards
to the Parts' Extremes; it illumineth the Face,
which as a Beacon gives Warning to all the
rest of this Little Kingdom, Man, to arm, and                    120
then the Vital Commoners and Inland Petty
Spirits muster me all to their Captain, the
Heart, who, great and puff'd up with this
Retinue, doth any deed of Courage. And this
Valor comes of Sherris, so that skill in the                     125
Weapon is nothing without Sack (for that sets

127–  a mere . . . Divel  *Falstaff's association of gold with the*
28    *Devil recalls several Biblical passages, among them Matthew*
      *6:19–20 ("Lay not up for yourselves treasures upon earth,*
      *where moth and rust doth corrupt, and where thieves break*
      *through and steal: But lay up for yourselves treasures in*
      *heaven") and 1 Timothy 6:10 ("the love of money is the root*
      *of all evil"). It probably relates as well to the medieval super-*
      *stition that buried treasure was guarded by evil spirits or by*
      *dragons.*

128   commences it  *sets it free, enables it to become effectual. Fal-*
      *staff is probably thinking of the granting of a university de-*
      *gree, which allows a scholar who has built a "Hoard" of*
      *"Learning" to go into the world and put his knowledge to use.*
      *Behind Falstaff's images are the parables of stewardship in the*
      *Gospels: the Parable of the Talents (Matthew 25:14–30) and*
      *the Parable of the Servants (Luke 12:42–48), both of which*
      *illustrate the moral that "unto whomsoever much is given, of*
      *him shall be much required: and to whom men have committed*
      *much, of him they will ask the more" (Luke 12:48).*

133   husbanded  *cultivated, tended.*

134   good and good store  *high-quality and large quantities.*

137   Humane  *The Elizabethan spelling combines (a) human, and*
      *(b) humane.*

138   Potations  *drinks.*

144   temp'ring  *softening from being warmed (like the sealing wax*
      *alluded to in lines 145–46).*

196

it a-work), and Learning a mere Hoard of Gold
kept by a Divel till Sack commences it and
sets it in Act and Use. Hereof comes it that
Prince Harry is Valiant, for the Cold Blood he          130
did naturally inherit of his Father he hath,
like lean, sterile, and bare Land, manur'd,
husbanded, and till'd, with excellent endeavor
of Drinking good and good store of fertile
Sherris, that he is become very Hot and              135
Valiant. If I had a thousand Sons, the first
Humane Principle I would teach them should
be to forswear Thin Potations and to addict
themselves to Sack.

*Enter Bardolph.*

—How now, Bardolph?                       140
BARDOLPH   The Army is discharged all, and gone.
FALSTAFF   Let them go: I'll through Gloucestershire,
and there will I visit Master Robert Shallow,
Esquire. I have him already temp'ring between
my Finger and my Thumb, and shortly will I       145
seal with him. Come, away.              *Exeunt.*

197

IV.iv   *This scene takes place in the Jerusalem Chamber in Westminster Abbey.*

2   **Debate**   *The King refers to the civil war with the rebels.*

3   **Higher Fields**   *Once again the King is thinking about a Crusade to the Holy Land.*

4   sanctified   *made holy by the cause in which they are used.*

5   address'd   *prepared to sail.*

6   invested   *deputized, vested with authority to act in the King's stead while he is absent.*

7   level to our Wish   *in accordance with our desires.*

8   we want   *I lack. The King is employing the royal plural.*

13   the Prince your Brother   *Prince Hal.*

# Scene 4

*Enter the King carried in a Chair, Warwick,*
*Thomas Duke of Clarence, Humphrey of Gloucester,*
*and Others.*

KING   Now, Lords, if God doth give successful End
To this Debate that bleedeth at our Doors,
We will our Youth lead on to Higher Fields
And draw no Swords but what are sanctified.
Our Navy is address'd, our Pow'r collected,                   5
Our Substitutes in Absence well invested,
And ev'ry thing lies level to our Wish;
Only we want a little pers'nal Strength,
And pause us till these Rebels now afoot
Come underneath the Yoke of Government.                       10
WARWICK   Both which we doubt not but your Majesty
Shall soon enjoy.
KING                    Humphrey, my Son of Gloucester,
Where is the Prince your Brother?
GLOUCESTER                        I think he's gone
To hunt, my Lord, at Windsor.
KING                          And how accompanied?
GLOUCESTER   I do not know, my Lord.
KING                              Is not his Brother          15
Thomas of Clarence with him?

199

17  in presence here *present, in attendance at Court.*

24  Offices thou may'st effect *duties you may discharge.*

27  omit *neglect, fail to pay attendance to.*

30  observ'd *treated solicitously and respectfully.*

32  meting Charity *dispensing love and grace.*

33  incens'd *angered.*
   Flint *as hard and unyielding as flint (a proverbial symbol for the cold, unfeeling heart).*

34  Humourous *subject to being seized capriciously by a mood of inflexible coldness.*

35  Flaws congealed in the Spring of Day *flakes of ice formed in the early hours of a cold morning.*

36  Temper *temperament, disposition.*
   observ'd *both (a) noted, and (b) interpreted as a guide to one's own actions.*

37  rev'rently *with respect and grace.*

39  being Moody *when he is moody (angry).*

41  Confound themselves with Working *exhaust themselves in struggles that do no one else any harm.*

GLOUCESTER                    No, my good Lord,
    He is in presence here.
CLARENCE                      What would my Lord
    And Father?
KING    Nothing but well to thee, Thomas of Clarence.
    How chance thou art not with the Prince thy
        Brother?                                              20
    He loves thee, and thou dost neglect him,
        Thomas.
    Thou hast a better place in his Affection
    Than all thy Brothers: cherish it, my Boy,
    And Noble Offices thou may'st effect
    Of Mediation after I am dead                              25
    Between his Greatness and thy other Brethren.
    Therefore omit him not, blunt not his Love,
    Nor lose the good Advantage of his Grace
    By seeming Cold or Careless of his Will.
    For he is gracious if he be observ'd;                     30
    He hath a Tear for Pity, and a Hand
    Open as Day for meting Charity;
    Yet notwithstanding, being incens'd, he's
        Flint,
    As Humourous as Winter, and as Sudden
    As Flaws congealed in the Spring of Day.                  35
    His Temper therefore must be well observ'd.
    Chide him for Faults, and do it rev'rently,
    When you perceive his Blood inclin'd to Mirth;
    But, being Moody, give him Time and Scope
    Till that his Passions, like a Whale on Ground,           40
    Confound themselves with Working. Learn this,
        Thomas,

44    **united**   *unleaking, secure, self-contained. The King compares his sons to a barrel: Clarence is the hoop binding the staves (the other brothers) together; and the liquid corresponds to the Lancastrian bloodline they represent.*

45    **Venom of Suggestion**   *poisonous innuendo and incitement to discord.*

46    **Force perforce**   *of necessity, inevitably.*

47    **it**   *suggestion.*

48    **Aconitum**   *wolf's bane, a potent poison.*
      **rash**   *quick-acting, violent.*

54    **Fattest**   *most fertile, richest.*

58    **shape**   *conceive mental pictures.*

59    **unguided Days**   *days without landmarks or counselors to mark the way.*

63    **Rage**   *uncontrolled passions; here equivalent to "headstrong Riot" (line 62).*

64    **When Means . . . together**   *when he has the wherewithal to live as lavishly (unrestrainedly) as he wishes.*

65    **Affections**   *inclinations, desires, drives.*

66    **fronting**   *confronting, challenging.*
      **oppos'd Decay**   *opposing forces that will undo him and all he has, and leave his estate in ruins.*

67    **look beyond him quite**   *completely overlook his true nature.*

And thou shalt prove a Shelter to thy Friends,
A Hoop of Gold to bind thy Brothers in,
That the united Vessel of their Blood,
Mingled with Venom of Suggestion                    45
(As Force perforce the Age will pour it in),
Shall never leak, though it do work as strong
As Aconitum or rash Gunpowder.

CLARENCE   I shall observe him with all Care and
    Love.

KING   Why art thou not at Windsor with him, Thomas?   50

CLARENCE   He is not there today: he dines in London.

KING   And how accompanied? Canst thou tell that?

CLARENCE   With Poins and other his continual
    Followers.

KING   Most subject is the Fattest Soil to Weeds,
And he, the Noble Image of my Youth,                 55
Is overspread with them. Therefore my Grief
Stretches itself beyond the Hour of Death;
The Blood weeps from my Heart when I do shape,
In Forms Imaginary, th' unguided Days
And Rotten Times that you shall look upon            60
When I am sleeping with my Ancestors.
For when his headstrong Riot hath no Curb,
When Rage and Hot Blood are his Counselors,
When Means and Lavish Manners meet together,
O with what Wings shall his Affections fly           65
Towards fronting Peril and oppos'd Decay?

WARWICK   My gracious Lord, you look beyond him
    quite.
The Prince but studies his Companions

203

69    strange Tongue  *foreign language.*
       gain the Language  *master the vocabulary and idioms.*

73    Gross Terms  *indecent, coarse words.*

77    mete  *measure, calculate and evaluate.*
       Other  *others like "his Foll'wers."*

78    Turning past Evils to Advantages  *Warwick's lines recall two of the Prince's speeches in* 1 Henry IV: *(a) the soliloquy in I.ii.216–38, where Hal promises to "throw off" his "Loose Behavior" and redeem the time that appears to have been totally wasted, and (b) his comment in II.iv.4–22 that he "can drink with any Tinker in his own Language" and will thus be able to "command all the good Lads in Eastcheap" when he is King.*

79–80    'Tis seldom . . . Carrion.  *The King is skeptical about Warwick's sanguine assessment of the future: he notes that once a bee has established a honeycomb in a piece of rotting carrion, she tends to remain there.*

87    Olive  *The olive branch was a traditional symbol of peace.*

Like a strange Tongue wherein, to gain the
    Language,
'Tis needful that the most Immodest Word          70
Be look'd upon and learnt, which, once
    attain'd,
Your Highness knows, comes to no further Use
But to be known and hated: so, like Gross
    Terms,
The Prince will in the perfectness of Time
Cast off his Foll'wers, and their Memory          75
Shall as a Pattern or a Measure live,
By which his Grace must mete the Lives of
    Other,
Turning past Evils to Advantages.

KING   'Tis seldom when the Bee doth leave her Comb
In the dead Carrion.

*Enter Westmerland.*

                    Who's here, Westmerland?     80
WESTMERLAND   Health to my Sov'reign, and new
    Happiness
Added to that that I am to deliver.
Prince John your Son doth kiss your Grace's
    Hand.
Mowbray, the Bishop Scroop, Hastings, and all
Are brought to the Correction of your Law;        85
There is not now a Rebel's Sword unsheath'd,
But Peace puts forth her Olive ev'ry where.
The Manner how this Action hath been borne
Here at more Leisure may your Highness read,

90    With . . . particular   *with all the particulars spelled out in order.*

92    the Haunch of Winter   *the end (literally, the buttocks) of Winter. After a number of late-summer and autumnal images, this image signals a change of atmosphere; interestingly, it occurs in the context of an image of the dawn. A similar image complex has been used in lines 34–35.*

99    Shrieve   *Sheriff.*

101   at large   *with full detail. Shakespeare compresses into a single historical moment a pair of triumphs that were actually separated by three years: (a) the events at Gaultree Forest (1405), and (b) the Battle of Bramham Moor (1408), where the King's forces defeated Northumberland. Historically, the King himself supervised the executions of the Gaultree rebels and then led the campaign north against Northumberland. It was three years later (in 1411) that he died.*

104   wet . . . Terms   *Here* wet *may mean "dipped in ink" (to pen the "Fair Words"); if so, the phrase "Foulest Terms" refers to the color of that ink. In view of the food images that follow,* wet *may involve a play on* whet *(sharpen), of which* wet *was a variant spelling. Most modern editions follow the First Folio and substitute "write" for "wet"; some also adopt the Folio's "Letters" in place of the Quarto's "Terms."*

108   Aboundance   *abundance.*

113   look up   *both (a) buck up, and (b) look to Heaven for aid and comfort. Toward the end of* King Lear *a similar exhortation seems to be a way of saying "don't surrender to despair."*

With ev'ry course in his particular.                    90
KING    O Westmerland, thou art a Summer Bird,
Which ever in the Haunch of Winter sings
The lifting up of Day.

*Enter Harcourt.*

Look, here's more News.
HARCOURT    From Enemies Heav'ns keep your Majesty;
And when they stand against you, may they fall    95
As those that I am come to tell you of:
The Earl Northumberland and the Lord Bardolph,
With a great Pow'r of English and of Scots,
Are by the Shrieve of Yorkshire overthrown.
The Manner and true Order of the Fight           100
This Packet, please it you, contains at large.
KING    And wherefore should these Good News make me
    Sick?
Will Fortune never come with both Hands full,
But wet her Fair Words still in Foulest Terms?
She either gives a Stomach and no Food           105
(Such are the Poor in Health) or else a Feast
And takes away the Stomach (such are the Rich,
That have Aboundance and enjoy it not).
I should rejoice now at this Happy News;
And now my Sight fails and my Brain is giddy.     110
O me, come near me: now I am much ill!
GLOUCESTER    Comfort, your Majesty.
CLARENCE                        O my Royal Father!
WESTMERLAND    My Sov'reign Lord, cheer up your self;
    look up.

207

114    Fits   *spells, seizures.*

116    from   *away from.*
        straight   *quickly.*

117    Pangs   *pains. But Shakespeare's word choice associates the King's pains with the "Labor" of childbirth (line 118) as well as with impending death.*

119    wrought the Mure   *rendered the wall.*

121    fear   *frighten.*

122    Unfather'd Heirs   *children born without the mother having been impregnated by a man.*
        loathly Births   *loathsome (deformed) offspring.*

123    as   *as if.*

125    flow'd   *risen to successively higher tides, without ebb tides to separate them. According to Holinshed's* Chronicles, *in October 1411, just before the death of King Henry IV, there were "three floods in the Thames, the one following upon the other, and no ebbing between: which thing no man then living could remember the like to be seen."*

126    doting Chronicles   *foolish (gullible, superstitious) storytellers.*

126–    And . . . died   *None of the chronicles mentions such a portent in connection with the death of Edward III; this detail, then, is probably Shakespeare's invention.*
28

128    sick'd   *grew sick.*

130    Apoplex'   *apoplexy, a paralysis, probably brought on by a stroke.*

WARWICK    Be patient, Princes: you do know these
    Fits
    Are with his Highness very ordinary.                        115
    Stand from him, give him Air; he'll straight
    be well.
CLARENCE    No, no, he cannot long hold out these
    Pangs:
    Th' incessant Care and Labor of his Mind
    Hath wrought the Mure that should confine it
    in
    So thin that Life looks through and will break
    out.                                                         120
GLOUCESTER    The People fear me, for they do observe
    Unfather'd Heirs and loathly Births of Nature;
    The Seasons change their Manners, as the Year
    Had found some Months asleep and leapt them
    over.
CLARENCE    The River hath thrice flow'd, no Ebb
    between,                                                     125
    And the Old Folk, Time's doting Chronicles,
    Say it did so a little time before
    That our Great-grandsire Edward sick'd and
    died.
WARWICK    Speak lower, Princes, for the King
    recovers.
GLOUCESTER    This Apoplex' will certain be his End.    130
KING    I pray your take me up, and bear me hence
    Into some other Chamber. Softly, pray.
            *The King is carried to a Bed on the Stage.*

IV.v    *In performance there would be no break between Scenes iv and v. But moving the King from his chair to a bed would have the effect of shifting the location from the Jerusalem Room to a more private chamber.*

2       dull    *sleep-inducing.*
        favorable    *doing favors.*

6       changes    *Here as frequently elsewhere, this word means "for the worse."*

7       saw    *has seen.*

9       abroad    *outside.*

13      Physic    *medical assistance.*

14      low    *softly.*

# Scene 5

KING   Let there be no Noise made, my gentle Friends,
    Unless some dull and favorable Hand
    Will whisper Music to my weary Spirit.
WARWICK   Call for the Music in the other Room.
KING   Set me the Crown upon my Pillow here.          5
CLARENCE   His Eye is hollow, and he changes much.
WARWICK   Less Noise, less Noise.

*Enter Harry.*

PRINCE                  Who saw the Duke of Clarence?
CLARENCE   I am here, Brother, full of Heaviness.
PRINCE   How now? Rain within doors, and none abroad?
    How doth the King?
HUMPHREY                  Exceeding ill.          10
PRINCE   Heard he the Good News yet? Tell it him.
HUMPHREY   He alter'd much upon the hearing it.
PRINCE   If he be sick with Joy, he'll recover
    without Physic.
WARWICK   Not so much Noise, my Lords. —Sweet
    Prince, speak low:
    The King your Father is dispos'd to sleep.          15
CLARENCE   Let us withdraw into the other Room.

211

22    Ports of Slumber    *eyes.*

23    watchful    *wakeful.*

25    Biggen    *the coarse nightcap worn by the poor.*

26    the Watch of Night    *both (a) the period when Night is stand-ing sentinel over the world, and (b) the period when night watchmen are on duty.*

27    pinch    *confine, squeeze tight.*

29    scald'st with Safety    *burns the wearer while securing him from other injuries.*
      Gates of Breath    *mouth. This image is similar to that of line 22. Both reinforce the tidal imagery of IV.iv.125–28, and together they suggest that the King is at the threshold separat-ing life from death.*

30    dowlny    *downy. This spelling may well preserve Shakespeare's own pronunciation of the word. It also suggests a link with "dowl," the word for a filament of a feather or a very thin, soft feather.*

34    Rigol    *circle. The Prince is probably playing on "regal."*

35    Dew    *here a metaphor for both (a) tears, and (b) due (that which is owed another). The Prince picks up the second mean-ing in line 39.*

37    Filial Tenderness    *a son's love for his father.*

40    immediate    *the nearest (eldest) offspring.*

WARWICK    Will 't please your Grace to go along with
    us?
PRINCE    No, I will sit and watch here by the King.

*Exeunt all but the Prince.*

Why doth the Crown lie there upon his Pillow,
Being so troublesome a Bedfellow?                          20
—O polish'd Perturbation! Golden Care,
That keep'st the Ports of Slumber open wide
To many a watchful Night! —Sleep with it now,
Yet not so sound, and half so deeply sweet,
As he whose Brow, with homely Biggen bound,                25
Snores out the Watch of Night. —O Majesty,
When thou dost pinch thy Bearer, thou dost sit
Like a rich Armor worn in Heat of Day,
That scald'st with Safety. —By his Gates of
    Breath
There lies a dowlny Feather which stirs not;              30
Did he suspire, that light and weightless Dowln
Perforce must move. —My gracious Lord, my
    Father,
This Sleep is sound indeed; this is a Sleep
That from this golden Rigol hath divorc'd
So many English Kings. Thy Dew from me                    35
Is Tears and heavy Sorrows of the Blood,
Which Nature, Love, and Filial Tenderness
Shall, O dear Father, pay thee plenteously;
My Due from thee is this imperial Crown,
Which, as immediate from thy Place and Blood,             40
Derives itself to me.

*He takes the Crown and places it on his Head.*

---

42      put    *even if you put.*

44      lineal    *lineally descended, inherited according to the laws of primogeniture.*

45      to mine    *to my heir.*

51–52   The Prince . . . here.    *Here* Wales *is probably to be pronounced as a two-syllable word, making line 51 an alexandrine (an iambic line with six metrical feet, one more than the normal five). The next line, on the other hand, is three metrical feet short of the pentameter norm. The effect, dramatically, is to give line 51 unusual urgency as the King's emotions overflow the bounds that would normally contain them, and then to follow with a moment's pause as the King's eyes sweep the room in search of his son and Warwick looks around long enough to discover that "The Door is open."*

                    Lo where it sits,
     Which God shall guard; and, put the World's
          whole Strength
     Into one giant Arm, it shall not force
     This lineal Honor from me. This from thee
     Will I to mine leave as 'tis left to me.          *Exit.*     45
KING    Warwick, Gloucester, Clarence!


          *Enter Warwick, Gloucester, Clarence.*


CLARENCE                    Doth the King call?
WARWICK    What would your Majesty? How fares your
     Grace?
KING    Why did you leave me here alone, my Lords?
CLARENCE    We left the Prince my Brother here, my
     Liege,
     Who undertook to sit and watch by you.          50
KING    The Prince of Wales, where is he? Let me
     see him:
                         He is not here.
WARWICK    The Door is open, he is gone this way.
GLOUCESTER    He came not through the Chamber
     where we stay'd.
KING    Where is the Crown? Who took it from my
     Pillow?                                          55
WARWICK    When we withdrew, my Liege, we left it
     here.
KING    The Prince hath ta'en it hence: go seek him
     out.
     Is he so hasty that he doth suppose
     My Sleep my Death? Find him, my Lord of Warwick,

60     Part   *role, deed. The King seems to be thinking of the Prince and his disease as co-conspirators in an assassination plot.*

64     careful   *both (a) cautious, prudent, and (b) full of cares.*

67     **Engrossed**   *amassed.*
cank'red   *corrupted, tarnished.*

68     **strange-achieved**   *hard-earned. The King probably refers to gold that has to be acquired rather than gold that is inherited and only has to be preserved. According to this reading,* strange *means "alien" (not one's own) until "achieved." But the association with "cank'red" suggests that the King may also be referring to unusual (and perhaps crooked) means of acquisition, which of course would be pertinent to the "Gold" (the Crown) that now concerns him.*

69     invest . . . Arts   *to prepare their sons with proper educations.*

71     **Tolling**   *gathering (as in the collection of tolls).*

74     murd'red   *The King implies that the worker bees are the ones that get killed after the gathering of the harvest; in fact, the bees that get murdered are the drones, the non-working male bees.*

74–75  This bitter Taste . . . Father.   *This bitter knowledge is what the dying father has for all his efforts to amass an estate.*

77     Hands   *Most editors follow the Folio and substitute* hath *here. But the Quarto reading, suggesting that Sickness is laying violent hands on his victim, is more compatible with the King's imagery of murder. Here* determin'd *means "terminated."*

216

Chide him hither.

*Exit Warwick.*

     —This Part of his conjoins    60
With my Disease, and helps to end me. —See,
 Sons,
What things you are! How quickly Nature falls
Into Revolt when Gold becomes her object!
For this the foolish over-careful Fathers
Have broke their Sleep with Thoughts, their
 Brains with Care,        65
Their Bones with Industry. For this they have
Engrossed and pil'd up the cank'red Heaps
Of strange-achieved Gold. For this they have
Been thoughtful to invest their Sons with Arts
And Martial Exercises when, like the Bee  70
Tolling from ev'ry Flow'r the virtuous Sweets,
Our Thighs pack'd with Wax, our Mouths with
 Honey,
We bring it to the Hive, and, like the Bees,
Are murd'red for our Pains. This bitter Taste
Yields his Engrossments to the ending Father. 75

*Enter Warwick.*

   —Now where is he that will not stay so long
 Till his Friend Sickness' Hands determin'd me.
WARWICK My Lord, I found the Prince in the next
 Room,
 Washing with kindly Tears his gentle Cheeks
 With such a deep Demeanor in great Sorrow 80
 That Tyranny, which never quaff'd but Blood,

87    thought   *expected.*

89    by   *with.*

90    Chair   *throne.*

94    Stay   *wait.*

98    Were   *would have been.*
      without Offense   *without your having to commit an offense to
      obtain it.*

99    seal'd up my Expectation   *confirmed me in my worst fears.*

100   Thy Life did manifest   *your way of life made it clear.*

103   whetted   *sharpened.*
      stony Heart   *The King is probably thinking of a heart of flint.*

105   forbear   *indulge, put up with.*

Would by beholding him have wash'd his Knife
With gentle Eyedrops. He is coming hither.

KING But wherefore did he take away the Crown?

*Enter Harry.*

Lo where he comes. —Come hither to me Harry.          85
—Depart the Chamber; leave us here alone.
                    *Exeunt all but the King and the Prince.*

PRINCE I never thought to hear you speak again.

KING Thy Wish was Father, Harry, to that Thought.
I stay too long by thee, I weary thee.
Dost thou so hunger for mine empty Chair          90
That thou wilt needs invest thee with my
    Honors
Before thy Hour be ripe? O foolish Youth,
Thou seek'st the Greatness that will overwhelm
    thee.
Stay but a little, for my Cloud of Dignity
Is held from falling with so weak a Wind          95
That it will quickly drop. My Day is dim.
Thou hast stol'n that which after some few
    Hours
Were thine without Offense; and at my Death
Thou hast seal'd up my Expectation.
Thy Life did manifest thou lov'dst me not,          100
And thou wilt have me die assur'd of it.
Thou hadst a thousand Daggers in thy Thoughts,
Whom thou hast whetted on thy stony Heart
To stab at Half an Hour of my Life.
What, canst thou not forbear me Half an Hour?          105

109     Hearse    *coffin.*

110     Balm    *anointing oil consecrated for use in coronation ceremonies.*

111     compound    *mingle.*

114     Form    *order and degree.*

115     Fift    *Fifth.*
        Vanity    *empty folly.*

116     State    *dignity and ceremony.*

118     Apes of Idleness    *both (a) ape-like fools and wastrels, and (b) imitators aping such models of indecorum.*

119     Neighbor Confines    *nearby countries.*

120     Ruffin    *ruffian.*

124     double-gild . . . Gilt    *make him a counterfeit five layers deep. The King is also punning on* guilt, *of course.*

126     curbed License    *restrained licentiousness.*

129     Civil Blows    *self-inflicted wounds. The King uses "Civil" to refer to blows that Englishmen inflict on other Englishmen.*

130     Riots    *both (a) ungoverned, licentious behavior, and (b) civil disorder.*

131     when Riot is thy Care    *when the very embodiment of Riot (the Prince) is your custodian and protector from Riot. The King can see nothing ahead but anarchy and a return to the law of the jungle.*

Then get thee gone, and dig my Grave thy self,
And bid the merry Bells ring to thine Ear
That thou art crowned, not that I am dead.
Let all the Tears that should bedew my Hearse
Be drops of Balm to sanctify thy Head;    110
Only compound me with forgotten Dust.
Give that which gave thee Life unto the Worms;
Pluck down my Officers, break my Decrees,
For now a Time is come to mock at Form.
— "Harry the Fift is crown'd: Up, Vanity!   115
Down, Royal State! All you Sage Couns'lors
 hence!
And to the English Court assemble now
From ev'ry Region, Apes of Idleness!
Now Neighbor Confines, purge you of your Scum!
Have you a Ruffin that will swear, drink,
 dance,            120
Revel the Night, rob, murder, and commit
The oldest Sins the newest kind of Ways?
Be happy, he will trouble you no more:
England shall double-gild his treble Gilt;
England shall give him Office, Honor, Might.  125
For the fift Harry from curbed License plucks
The Muzzle of Restraint, and the Wild Dog
Shall flesh his Tooth on ev'ry Innocent."
—O my poor Kingdom! Sick with Civil Blows!
When that my Care could not withhold thy
 Riots,            130
What wilt thou do when Riot is thy Care?
O thou wilt be a Wilderness again,
Peopled with Wolves, thy old Inhabitants.

140    affect    *desire, love.*

142    this Obedience    *this kneeling posture. Just when the Prince kneels is not specified in the original texts. He may kneel as early as line 134.*

153    as having Sense    *as if it could hear and feel what I spoke.*

154    on thee depending    *literally, "hanging from you" (resulting from the responsibilities you impose). But the Prince also seems to be depicting "Care" as a dependent (a child), like the baby pelican that devours its own parent. Lear refers to his "Pelican Daughters" in III.iv of* King Lear; *John of Gaunt alludes to the same concept in II.i.126 of* Richard II. *The Prince's emphasis on Care recalls* Richard II, *IV.i.192–97.*

157    Charract    *carat, a measure of purity. For this line the Folio text seems the better and is adopted by all modern editions. Its spelling of "carat," reproduced here (the Quarto has* karrat), *preserves the word's connections with "character" (integrity or quality). Then as now, the purity of gold was measured in fractions of twenty-four (so that, for example, a twenty-carat piece of gold contained twenty parts gold to four parts alloy), a number that corresponded to the number of letters (characters) in early versions of the English alphabet (before* i/j *and* u/v *had become firmly differentiated).*

158    Med'cine potable    *The Prince refers to* aurum potabile *("drinkable gold"), a cordial containing a small amount of gold, which was said by some to be capable of healing "every disease that is thought uncurable."*

PRINCE    O pardon me, my Liege: but for my Tears,
   The moist Impediments unto my Speech,    135
   I had forestall'd this dear and deep Rebuke
   Ere you with Grief had spoke and I had heard
   The course of it so far. There is your Crown,
   And He that wears the Crown immortally
   Long guard it yours. If I affect it more    140
   Than as your Honor and as your Renown,
   Let me no more from this Obedience rise,
   Which my most inward true and duteous Spirit
   Teacheth this prostrate and exterior Bending.
   God witness with me, when I here came in   145
   And found no course of Breath within your
    Majesty,
   How cold it strook my Heart! If I do feign,
   O let me in my present Wildness die,
   And never live to show th' incred'lous World
   The Noble Change that I have purposed.    150
   Coming to look on you, thinking you dead,
   And dead almost, my Liege, to think you were,
   I spake unto this Crown as having Sense
   And thus upbraided it: "The Care on thee
    depending
   Hath fed upon the Body of my Father;    155
   Therefore thou Best of Gold art Worst of Gold.
   Other, less fine in Charract, is more precious,
   Preserving Life in Med'cine potable;
   But thou, most fine, most honor'd, most
    renown'd,
   Hast eat thy Bearer up." Thus, my most Royal
    Liege,    160

162    try with it    *contend with it, make a trial of it.*

163    murd'red my Father    *The Prince, too, speaks of murder. For him, however, the "assassin" is the Crown, not Sickness or the Crown Prince.*

164    a true Inheritor    *an heir who truly loves his father and would feel it his duty to avenge his death. Claudius alludes to this definition of a true "Father's Son" in IV.vii of* Hamlet.

166    strain    *This word probably combines several senses: (a) effort to reach or grasp for the object of proud ambition, (b) streak or trace, and (c) emotional pitch.*

169    Entertainment    *consideration, hospitality.*

171    Vassail    *vassal (servant or peasant).*

173    O my Son!    *This ejaculation occurs only in the Folio text. Its indented placement here is meant to suggest a dramatic pause while the King registers the full import of what the Prince has said.*

176    so wisely    *with such wisdom.*

178    latest    *last, final.*

181    I met    *The King's verb is significant: he does not deny that he took steps in the direction of the Crown, but he also does not say that he knew that the Crown would be around the next bend of the "indirect crook'd Ways" his course involved.*

182    sate    *sat.*

185    Soil    *stain. But the King's image suggests that he believes his guilt will be buried with him like the soil that "goes / With me into the Earth."*

224

Accursing it, I put it on my Head
To try with it as with an Enemy
That had before my Face murd'red my Father:
The Quarrel of a true Inheritor.
But if it did infect my Blood with Joy,                    165
Or swell my Thoughts to any strain of Pride,
If any Rebel or vain Spirit of mine
Did with the least Affection of a Welcome
Give Entertainment to the Might of it,
Let God for ever keep it from my Head,                    170
And make me as the poorest Vassail is
That doth with Awe and Terror kneel to it.
KING                          O my Son!
God put it in thy Mind to take it hence,
That thou mightst win the more thy Father's
    Love                                                   175
Pleading so wisely in excuse of it.
Come hither, Harry, sit thou by my Bed,
And hear, I think, the very latest Counsel
That ever I shall breathe. God knows, my Son,
By what By-paths and indirect crook'd Ways               180
I met this Crown; and I my self know well
How troublesome it sate upon my Head.
To thee it shall descend with better Quiet,
Better Opinion, better Confirmation:
For all the Soil of the Achievement goes                 185
With me into the Earth. It seem'd in me
But as an Honor snatch'd with boist'rous Hand,
And I had many living to upbraid
My Gain of it by their Assistances,
Which daily grew to Quarrel and to Bloodshed,            190

191    bold Fears   *Here the King seems to personify "Fears," so that it becomes an abstract quality in addition to its embodiment in the bold Rebels who have tried to strike fear into the King's heart and take his Crown away.*

192    with Peril I have answered   *I have responded to the peril of my challengers.*

194    Acting that Argument   *dramatizing that theme (plot).*

195    purchas'd   *acquired by my own efforts (compare "strange-achieved," line 68).*

196    in a more fairer sort   *in a manner that makes you less suspect.*

197    successively   *by due succession (inheritance).*

198    sure   *secure, with a clearer claim to the title.*

199    Griefs are green   *grievances are still fresh.*

200    thy . . . thy   *Many editors emend the first* thy *to* my.

202    fell   *fierce (as with wasps and wolves).*

208    State   *throne.*

209    Giddy   *unstable, unreliable.*

210    hence borne out   *carried out elsewhere.*

211    waste   *use up, waste away.*

213    utterly   *both (a) totally, and (b) because of my uttering (speaking aloud).*

226

Wounding supposed Peace. All these bold Fears
Thou seest with Peril I have answered:
For all my Reign hath been but as a Scene
Acting that Argument. And now my Death
Changes the Mood: for what in me was purchas'd     195
Falls upon thee in a more fairer sort,
So thou the Garland wear'st successively.
Yet though thou stand'st more sure than I
    could do,
Thou art not firm enough, since Griefs are
    green,
And all thy Friends, which thou must make thy
    Friends,                                        200
Have but their Stings and Teeth newly ta'en
    out,
By whose fell working I was first advanc'd,
And by whose Pow'r I well might lodge a Fear
To be again displac'd, which, to avoid,
I cut them off and had a Purpose now             205
To lead out many to the Holy Land,
Lest Rest, and Lying Still, might make them
    look
Too near unto my State. Therefore, my Harry,
Be it thy course to busy Giddy Minds
With Foreign Quarrels, that Action hence borne
    out                                            210
May waste the Memory of the Former Days.
More would I, but my Lungs are wasted so
That Strength of Speech is utterly denied me.
How I came by the Crown, O God forgive,
And grant it may with thee in true Peace live.   215

227

218    plain and right   *The verbs in the Prince's preceding line would seem to have more to do with the assertion of might than with the exercise of right. But if the Prince is going to maintain the "Possession," it is important for him to believe that a course that was "indirect" and "crook'd" for his father will be "plain and right" (straight, correct, and rightful) for the King's heir.*

219    Pain   *effort. But "pain" in the other sense will be part of that effort.*

225    bare wither'd Trunk   *The King compares himself to a leafless, dying tree.*

229    swound   *swoon.*

231    Laud   *praise.*

234    vainly   *both (a) foolishly, and (b) in vain.*

236    In that Jerusalem   *The fact that the King ends up in a different Jerusalem from the one he thought he was aiming for gives a final, ironic twist to the "indirect crook'd" path his life has coursed.*

PRINCE                    My gracious Liege,
    You won it, wore it, kept it, gave it me;
    Then plain and right must my Possession be,
    Which I with more than with a common Pain
    'Gainst all the World will rightfully maintain.                    220

                *Enter Prince John of Lancaster.*

KING   Look, look, here comes my John of Lancaster.
PRINCE JOHN   Health, Peace, and Happ'ness to my
        Royal Father.
KING   Thou bring'st me Happiness and Peace, Son
        John,
    But Health, alack, with youthful Wings is flown
    From this bare wither'd Trunk. Upon thy Sight                    225
    My Worldly Business makes a Period.
    Where is my Lord of Warwick?
PRINCE                    My Lord of Warwick!

                *Enter Warwick.*

KING   Doth any Name particular belong
    Unto the Lodging where I first did swound?
WARWICK   'Tis call'd Jerusalem, my Noble Lord.                    230
KING   Laud be to God, ev'n there my Life must end.
    It hath been proph'sied to me many years
    I should not die but in Jerusalem,
    Which vainly I suppos'd the Holy Land.
    But bear me to that Chamber, there I'll lie:                    235
    In that Jerusalem shall Harry die.                *Exeunt.*

229

V.i    *This scene takes place at Shallow's house in Gloucestershire.*

1    **By Cock and Pie**   *This oath was probably a corruption of "by God and Pie." "Pie" was the name of a Roman Catholic liturgical manual. Shallow addresses this line to Falstaff, insisting that he and his men agree to accept Shallow's hospitality for the night.*

2    **What . . . say!**   *Shallow calls for his servingman.*

11    **William Cook**   *Shallow's cook.*

# Act Five

## Scene 1

*Enter Shallow, Falstaff, Bardolph, and Page.*

SHALLOW   By Cock and Pie, Sir, you shall not away
tonight. —What, Davy, I say!
FALSTAFF   You must excuse me, Master Robert Shallow.
SHALLOW   I will not excuse you, you shall not be
excus'd. Excuses shall not be admitted, there                    5
is no Excuse shall serve, you shall not be
excus'd. —Why Davy!

*Enter Davy.*

DAVY   Here Sir.
SHALLOW   Davy, Davy, Davy, Davy; let me see, Davy;
let me see, Davy; let me see. Yea marry,                          10
William Cook, bid him come hither. —Sir John,
you shall not be excus'd.

231

13–14     those Precepts cannot be serv'd    *Davy is probably refer-ring to some legal documents and telling his Master he is unable to serve (deliver) them.*

14–15     Hade Land    *unploughed strips.*

16     Red Wheat    *a variety of wheat normally sown in the late summer.*

18     the Smith's Note    *the Blacksmith's bill.*

20     cast    *added up, calculated.*

22     a new Link to the Bucket    *a new rope or chain for a pail or yoke.*

24–25     the Sack he lost at Hinckley Fair    *probably a sack of farm produce to have been sold at the Hinckley Fair market near Coventry.*

28     Kickshaws    *side dishes (from the French* quelques choses, *somethings).*

30     Man of War    *soldier. Davy refers to Falstaff.*

31     use    *treat. But it is clear from what Shallow goes on to confide to Davy that he plans to "use" Falstaff in other ways as well.*

35     backbitten    *Davy refers to the lice that infest Falstaff's men.*

36     marvailes    *marvelous.*

37     Well conceited    *Shallow commends Davy for his witty word-play.*

39     countenance    *show favor to.*

40     Woncote    *probably Woodmancote, a town in Gloucestershire.*

DAVY  Marry Sir thus; those Precepts cannot be
    serv'd; and again, Sir, shall we sow the Hade
    Land with Wheat?                                    15
SHALLOW  With Red Wheat, Davy. But for William
    Cook, are there no young Pigeons?
DAVY  Yes Sir, here is now the Smith's Note for
    Shoeing and Plough-irons.
SHALLOW  Let it be cast and paid. —Sir John, you     20
    shall not be excus'd.
DAVY  Now Sir, a new Link to the Bucket must needs
    be had; and Sir, do you mean to stop any of
    William's Wages, about the Sack he lost at
    Hinckley Fair?                                      25
SHALLOW  'A shall answer it. Some Pigeons, Davy, a
    couple of short-legg'd Hens, a Joint of Mutton,
    and any pretty little tiny Kickshaws, tell
    William Cook.
DAVY  Doth the Man of War stay all Night, Sir?        30
SHALLOW  Yea Davy, I will use him well. A Friend
    i' th' Court is better than a Penny in Purse.
    Use his Men well, Davy, for they are arrant
    Knaves, and will backbite.
DAVY  No worse than they are backbitten, Sir, for     35
    they have marvailes foul Linen.
SHALLOW  Well conceited, Davy; about thy Business,
    Davy.
DAVY  I beseech you, Sir, to countenance William
    Visor of Woncote against Clement Perkes a' th'     40
    Hill.
SHALLOW  There is many Complaints, Davy, against

233

51    bear out   *take the side of, obtain support for.*

53    Credit   *standing, influence.*

54    honest   *faithful, true.*

56    have no wrong   *not be found guilty and punished.*

63    tall   *brave. Shallow is addressing the Page, who is anything but "tall" in the usual modern sense.*

68    Quantities   *vertical slices.*

69    Staves   *staffs, posts.*

70    wonderful   *to be wondered or marveled at.*

71    semblable Coherence of   *close similarities between.*

72    observing   *both (a) watching, and (b) attending to.*

that Visor; that Visor is an arrant Knave, on
my knowledge.

DAVY   I grant your Worship that he is a Knave, Sir.          45
But yet God forbid, Sir, but a Knave should
have some Countenance at his Friend's Request.
An Honest Man, Sir, is able to speak for
himself, when a Knave is not. I have serv'd
your Worship truly, Sir, this eight years; and          50
I cannot once or twice in a quarter bear out a
Knave against an Honest Man, I have little
Credit with your Worship. The Knave is mine
honest Friend, Sir, therefore I beseech you
let him be countenanc'd.          55

SHALLOW   Go to, I say, he shall have no wrong; look
about, Davy.          *Exit Davy.*
—Where are you, Sir John? Come, come, come,
off with your Boots. —Give me your Hand,
Master Bardolph.          60

BARDOLPH   I am glad to see your Worship.

SHALLOW   I thank thee with my Heart, kind Master
Bardolph. —And welcome, my tall Fellow.
—Come Sir John.

FALSTAFF   I'll follow you, good Maister Robert          65
Shallow.          *Exit Shallow.*
—Bardolph, look to our Horses.          *Exit Bardolph.*
If I were saw'd into Quantities, I should make
four dozen of such bearded Hermit's Staves as
Maister Shallow. It is a wonderful thing to          70
see the semblable Coherence of his Men's
Spirits and his. They, by observing him, do
bear themselves like foolish Justices; he, by

74    conversing    *interacting.*

76–77    with . . . Society    *through the time they spend in one anoth-
         er's company.*

77    in consent    *in agreement, consensus.*

79–80    I would . . . Maister    *I would flatter the vanity of his men
         by marveling at how much influence they have over their
         master.*

81    curry with    *flatter, smooth (as when currying a horse).*

86    take heed of their Company    *be careful about the company
      they keep. The "moral" in lines 83–86, recalling similar
      statements by Falstaff elsewhere (for example, 1 Henry IV,
      I.ii.103–5, II.ii.17–20, II.iv.437–51, and III.iii.11–12),
      and echoing a number of the King's statements to the Prince, is
      one of the thematic keys to 2 Henry IV.*

88–89    the . . . Fashions    *for as long as it takes for fashions in
         dress and manners to change six times.*

89    four Terms    *one year. The legal calendar was organized into
      four quarters.*

90    Actions    *legal actions, lawsuits.*

91    Intervallums    *intervals between terms.*

92    Sad Brow    *sober countenance.*

95    ill laid up    *tossed to one side (not folded or hung to prevent
      wrinkles).*

conversing with them, is turn'd into a Justice-
like Servingman. Their Spirits are so married                    75
in conjunction with the participation of
Society that they flock together in consent,
like so many Wild Geese. If I had a Suit to
Master Shallow, I would humour his Men with
the Imputation of being near their Maister; if                    80
to his Men, I could curry with Maister Shallow,
that no Man could better command his Servants.
It is certain that either Wise Bearing or
Ignorant Carriage is caught, as Men take
Diseases one of another: therefore let Men                        85
take heed of their Company. I will devise
Matter enough out of this Shallow to keep
Prince Harry in continual Laughter the wearing
out of six Fashions, which is four Terms or
two Actions; and 'a shall laugh without                           90
Intervallums. O it is much that a Lie with a
Slight Oath and a Jest with a Sad Brow will
do with a Fellow that never had the Ache in
his Shoulders! O you shall see him laugh till
his Face be like a Wet Cloak ill laid up.                         95

SHALLOW   Sir John?
FALSTAFF   I come, Maister Shallow; I come, Master
    Shallow.                                                *Exit.*

V.ii    *This scene takes place either in or near the Palace in Westminster.*

2       **Exceeding** well   *exceeding what we normally mean by "well." It was conventional to speak of those who had gone to their eternal reward as "well." The King has finally put off the Cares he took from the head of Richard II.*

7       truly   *faithfully, responsibly.*

11      welcome   *meet and greet.*
        Condition   *disposition.*

13      drawn it in my Fantasy   *imagined it to be.*

14      heavy Issue   *grieving sons.*

# Scene 2

*Enter Warwick, meeting the Lord Chief Justice.*

WARWICK  How now, my Lord Chief Justice, whither
    away?

JUSTICE  How doth the King?

WARWICK                  Exceeding well: his Cares
    Are now all ended.

JUSTICE  I hope not dead.

WARWICK             He's walk'd the Way of Nature,
    And to our Purposes he lives no more.         5

JUSTICE  I would his Majesty had call'd me with him:
    The Service that I truly did his Life
    Hath left me open to all Injuries.

WARWICK  Indeed I think the young King loves you
    not.

JUSTICE  I know he doth not, and do arm my self     10
    To welcome the Condition of the Time,
    Which cannot look more hideously upon me
    Than I have drawn it in my Fantasy.

*Enter Prince John, Thomas of Clarence, Humphrey
of Gloucester, Westmerland, and Others.*

WARWICK  Here come the heavy Issue of dead Harry:

239

15    living Harry    *Prince Hal, soon to be crowned King Henry V.*
      Temper    *self-control, disciplined bearing, disposition.*

16    he the worst    *the very worst.*

17    hold their Places    *retain their positions and honors.*

18    strike sail to    *lower their sails to (as a ship does when subjected
      to high winds that would otherwise capsize it), submit to.*

22    forgot    *forgotten how.*

23    Argument    *theme, topic of conversation.*

26    heavier    *both (a) sadder, and (b) more grievously afflicted.*

29    Of seeming Sorrow    *from the mere pretense of sorrow.*
      sure    *surely.*

30    what Grace to find    *what favor to expect.*

31    in coldest Expectation    *in the position least likely to benefit
      from a warm reception.*

33    speak . . . fair    *say kind things about Sir John Falstaff.*

34    your Stream of Quality    *the stream of your integrity.*

35    in Honor    *in keeping with the dictates of my honor (sense of
      personal rectitude).*

36    impartial    *unbiased, immune to favoritism or special pleading.*

38    A ragged . . . Remission    *a beggarly forgiveness that
      would surely be denied before I requested it.*

O that the living Harry had the Temper 15
Of he the worst of these three Gentlemen!
How many Nobles then should hold their Places
That must strike sail to Spirits of Vile Sort!

JUSTICE   O God, I fear all will be over-turn'd.

PRINCE JOHN   Good morrow, Cousin Warwick, good
morrow. 20

GLOUCESTER, CLARENCE   Good morrow, Cousin.

PRINCE JOHN   We meet like men that had forgot to
speak.

WARWICK   We do remember, but our Argument
Is all too heavy to admit much Talk.

PRINCE JOHN   Well, Peace be with him that hath made
us heavy. 25

JUSTICE   Peace be with us, lest we be heavier.

GLOUCESTER   O good my Lord, you have lost a Friend
indeed,
And I dare swear you borrow not that Face
Of seeming Sorrow: it is sure your own.

PRINCE JOHN   Though no man be assur'd what Grace
to find, 30
You stand in coldest Expectation.
I am the sorrier, would 'twere otherwise.

CLARENCE   Well, you must now speak Sir John Falstaff
fair,
Which swims against your Stream of Quality.

JUSTICE   Sweet Princes, what I did I did in Honor, 35
Led by th' impartial Conduct of my Soul.
And never shall you see that I will beg
A ragged and forestall'd Remission.
If Truth and Upright Innocency fail me,

40    I'll . . . dead    *I'll be sent as an ambassador to the place where the late King now holds court (a euphemistic way of saying "I'll be executed by the new King").*

45    easy    *comfortably.*

48    Amurath    *The Prince alludes to Murad III, a Turkish Sultan who, upon becoming King in 1574, strangled his five younger brothers to forestall any threats to his throne. His son Mahomat, succeeding Murad III in 1596, promptly executed his younger brothers as well.*

57    Father    *It was not uncommon for the monarch to be likened to a father, indeed to the Heavenly Father, in whose place he served as a deputy on earth.*

60    that    *who.*

63    strangely    *as if you thought us strangers to one another. Having set his brothers' minds at rest, the Prince now addresses the others in the gathering.*

I'll to the King my Maister that is dead,                    40
And tell him who hath sent me after him.

*Enter the Prince and Blunt.*

WARWICK   Here comes the Prince.
JUSTICE   Good morrow, and God save your Majesty.
PRINCE   This new and gorgeous Garment, Majesty,
 Sits not so easy on me as you think.                    45
 —Brothers, you mix'd your Sadness with some
  Fear.
 This is the English, not the Turkish, Court:
 Not Amurath an Amurath succeeds,
 But Harry Harry. Yet be sad, good Brothers,
 For by my faith it very well becomes you:                50
 Sorrow so Royally in you appears
 That I will deeply put the Fashion on
 And wear it in my Heart. Why then be Sad,
 But entertain no more of it, good Brothers,
 Than a joint Burden laid upon us all.                    55
 For me, by Heav'n, I bid you be assur'd,
 I'll be your Father and your Brother too:
 Let me but bear your Love, I'll bear your
  Cares.
 Yet weep that Harry's dead, and so will I;
 But Harry lives, that shall convert those
  Tears                                                 60
 By number into Hours of Happiness.
BROTHERS   We hope no oth'rwise from your Majesty.
PRINCE   You all look strangely on me. —And you
 most:

243

65 **if I be measur'd rightly** *if a just measure is taken of my character.*

70 **easy** *easy to take and forget. The Prince alludes to an occasion when he struck the Lord Chief Justice and was sent to jail for his insolence to the chief magistrate of England.*

71 **Lethe** *the River of Forgetfulness in the Hades of classical mythology.*

72 **use the Person of your Father** *act in behalf of your father, as if you had violated his person (dignity) by your disrespect for mine.*

75 **busy for** *working industriously for, employed in the service of.*

78 **presented** *represented, stood in the place of.*

79 **strook** *struck.*

80 **as . . . Father** *This phrase refers to the Prince, not to the Justice.*

84 **set . . . naught** *treat your Decrees as if they were nothing.*

85 **your aweful Bench** *your awesome seat of power.*

88 **spurn** *kick.*

89 **in a Second Body** *in the person of a second embodiment of your Royal Majesty. Here the Lord Chief Justice probably refers to himself rather than to the King's son and heir apparent.*

91 **propose** *imagine for hypothetical purposes.*

You are, I think, assur'd I love you not.

JUSTICE   I am assur'd, if I be measur'd rightly,                    65
    Your Majesty hath no just Cause to hate me.

PRINCE   No? How might a Prince of my great Hopes
    forget
    So great Indignities you laid upon me?
    What, Rate, Rebuke, and roughly send to Prison
    Th' immediate Heir of England? Was this easy?                    70
    May this be wash'd in Lethe and forgotten?

JUSTICE   I then did use the Person of your Father:
    The Image of his Pow'r lay then in me,
    And in th' administration of his Law,
    Whiles I was busy for the Commonwealth,                          75
    Your Highness pleased to forget my Place,
    The Majesty and Pow'r of Law and Justice,
    The Image of the King whom I presented,
    And strook me in the very Seat of Judgment,
    Whereon, as an Offender to your Father,                          80
    I gave bold Way to my Authority
    And did commit you. If the Deed were ill,
    Be you contented, wearing now the Garland,
    To have a Son set your Decrees at naught,
    To pluck down Justice from your aweful Bench,                    85
    To trip the course of Law and blunt the Sword
    That guards the Peace and Safety of your
        Person,
    Nay more, to spurn at your most Royal Image
    And mock your workings in a Second Body?
    Question your Royal Thoughts, make the Case
        yours;                                                       90
    Be now the Father and propose a Son,

245

93  dreadful *treated with respect, feared.*

96  soft *gently.*

97  cold Consid'rance *dispassionate consideration.*

98  in your State *both (a) in your royal capacity, and (b) from your throne as you speak to your council.*

101  weigh *The Prince alludes to the balance scales that were a traditional symbol of Justice. His point is that the Justice has spoken wisely, justly, and impartially, as a man in his high office should.*

108  proper *own.*

111  commit *sentence, "hand over" to the jailer. In the next line, the Prince uses* commit *to mean "hand over a responsibility."*

113  unstained *unblemished, pure.*
  Sword *Just as the Balance symbolized the Justice's duty to arrive at a proper determination of the truth in a legal case, the Sword symbolized the Justice's duty to sentence those found guilty.*
  have us'd *have been accustomed.*

117  Father *Now that his natural father is dead, the Prince adopts the Lord Chief Justice as his surrogate father.*

118  sound *both (a) speak, and (b) be based (bottomed) on wise counsel. One meaning of* sound *is to plumb the depths of a body of water.*

Hear your own Dignity so much profan'd,
See your most dreadful Laws so loosely
    slighted,
Behold your Self so by a Son disdained,
And then imagine me taking your part                95
And in your Pow'r soft silencing your Son;
After this cold Consid'rance sentence me,
And as you are a King, speak in your State
What I have done that misbecame my Place,
My Person, or my Liege's Sov'reignty.               100
PRINCE   You are right, Justice, and you weigh this
    well:
Therefore still bear the Balance and the Sword,
And I do wish your Honors may increase
Till you do live to see a Son of mine
Offend you and obey you as I did.                   105
So shall I live to speak my Father's Words:
"Happy am I that have a Man so bold
That dares do Justice on my proper Son;
And not less happy, having such a Son,
That would deliver up his Greatness so              110
Into the Hands of Justice." You did commit me,
For the which I do commit into your Hand
Th' unstained Sword that you have us'd to bear,
With this Remembrance, that you use the same
With the like bold, just, and impartial Spirit      115
As you have done 'gainst me. There is my Hand.
You shall be as a Father to my Youth:
My Voice shall sound as you do prompt mine Ear,
And I will stoop and humble mine Intents
To your well-practic'd wise Directions.             120

122    wild   *untamed, ungoverned. The Prince means that what has been buried with the late King is all the wildness of his son's youth; what remains above the ground is the majestic sobriety that properly befits a King's legitimate successor.*

123    Affections   *passions, unruly desires.*

124    sadly   *soberly, gravely.*

126    race out   *uproot, erase.*

127    writ me down   *recorded me in its account book.*

129    proudly   *arrogantly, impudently.*

131    State of Floods   *majesty of the ocean.*

135    go   *walk, proceed.*

139    Father   *the Lord Chief Justice.*

140    accite   *summon, call together.*

141    rememb'red   *noted, reminded you.*
        all our State   *all the men of rank in the nation.*

142    consigning to   *consenting to, supporting.*

144    happy   *well-ordered, blessed.*

—And Princes all, believe me, I beseech you,
My Father is gone wild into his Grave:
For in his Tomb lie my Affections,
And with his Spirits sadly I survive,
To mock the Expectation of the World,                    125
To frustrate Prophecies, and to race out
Rotten Opinion, who hath writ me down
After my Seeming. The Tide of Blood in me
Hath proudly flow'd in Vanity till now;
Now doth it turn and ebb back to the Sea,                130
Where it shall mingle with the State of Floods
And flow henceforth in Formal Majesty.
Now call we our High Court of Parliament,
And let us choose such Limbs of Noble Counsel
That the Great Body of our State may go                   135
In equal Rank with the best-govern'd Nation,
That War or Peace, or both at once, may be
As things acquainted and familiar to us,
In which you, Father, shall have foremost Hand.
Our Coronation done, we will accite,                      140
As I before rememb'red, all our State,
And, God consigning to my good Intents,
No Prince nor Peer shall have just Cause to say
God shorten Harry's happy Life one Day.      *Exeunt.*

V.iii   *This scene takes place in the Orchard of Shallow's house in Gloucestershire.*

2   Pippin   *high-quality apple. Pippins were often picked before they ripened and then eaten several months later.*

3   Caraways   *Caraway seeds or biscuits containing them were frequently eaten with apples.*

4   Coosin   *cousin.*

7   Barrain   *barren, poor.*

9   spread   *Davy is spreading a cloth for the use of the picnickers.*
    well said   *well done.*

11   Husband   *steward, overseer of the estate.*

12   Varlet   *valet, servant.*

19   Flesh   *meat.*
     dear   *Here this word probably means "expensive," perhaps because these females are not for sale (because they are virtuous, or "dear" in a sense implying their chastity).*

# Scene 3

*Enter Sir John Falstaff, Shallow, Silence, Davy,*
*Bardolph, and Page.*

SHALLOW    Nay you shall see my Orchard, where in an
    Arbor we will eat a last-year's Pippin of mine
    own graffing, with a Dish of Caraways and so
    forth. —Come Coosin Silence, and then to Bed.

FALSTAFF    'Fore God, you have here good Dwelling,    5
    and rich.

SHALLOW    Barrain, barrain, barrain, Beggars all,
    Beggars all, Sir John. —Marry, good Air:
    spread, Davy; spread, Davy; well said, Davy.

FALSTAFF    This Davy serves you for good Uses; he is    10
    your Servingman and your Husband.

SHALLOW    A good Varlet, a good Varlet, a very good
    Varlet, Sir John. By the Mass, I have drunk
    too much Sack at Supper. A good Varlet. Now
    sit down, now sit down. —Come, Cousin.    15

SILENCE    Ah Sirrah, quoth 'a, we shall    *Sings.*
    "Do nothing but eat and make good Cheer,
    And praise God for the merry Year,
    When Flesh is cheap and Females dear,
    And lusty Lads roam here and there    20
        So merrily,

23     anon   *right away.*

27     Proface!   *Welcome to it! A formulaic phrase similar to "Bon appetit!"*
       want in Meat   *lack in food.*

28     bear   *be content.*

33     Shrows   *This spelling captures the normal pronunciation of shrew (a disagreeable, scolding woman).*

34     when . . . all   *when everyone sports a beard.*

35     Shrovetide   *the carnival season just before the beginning of Lent.*

37     Metal   *mettle, virtue. Falstaff is impressed by Silence's merry-making.*

38     twice and once   *Silence uses a proverbial expression normally associated with large numbers. He probably believes that he has made merry with reckless abandon.*

40     Leather-coats   *russet apples (known for their rough, mottled skins).*

45     Leman   *sweetheart.*

And ever among so merrily."

FALSTAFF   There's a Merry Heart, good Master
Silence! I'll give you a Health for that anon.

SHALLOW   Give Master Bardolph some Wine, Davy.

DAVY   Sweet Sir, sit; I'll be with you anon, most          25
sweet Sir, sit. —Master Page, good Master
Page, sit. Proface! What you want in Meat,
we'll have in Drink; but you must bear, the
Heart's all.                                                    *Exit.*

SHALLOW   Be merry, Master Bardolph. —And my          30
little Soldier there, be merry.

SILENCE   "Be merry, be merry. My Wife has all,
For Women are Shrows, both short and tall;
'Tis merry in Hall when Beards wags all,
And welcome Merry Shrovetide; be merry,
be merry."                                                       35

FALSTAFF   I did not think Master Silence had been
a Man of this Metal.

SILENCE   Who, I? I have been Merry twice and once
ere now.

*Enter Davy.*

DAVY   There's a Dish of Leather-coats for you.          40

SHALLOW   Davy?

DAVY   Your Worship, I'll be with you straight.
—A Cup of Wine, Sir?

SILENCE   "A Cup of Wine that's brisk and fine,
And drink unto the Leman mine,                              45
And a merry Heart lives long-a."

FALSTAFF   Well said, Master Silence.

253

48–49   now . . . Night   *Silence's phrase recalls Falstaff's in II.iv. 399–400. But see Patrick Stewart's foreword (page vii) for a discussion of the differences between the two expressions.*

51   let it come   *let it come around (pass it around).*

52   I'll . . . Bottom.   *I'll keep drinking with you (exchanging toasts), even if it's a mile to the bottom of the cup.*

57   Cabileros   *gallants; a variant of the Spanish word for knightly gentlemen.*

60   crack a Quart   *drink a quart of beverage.*

62   Pottle-pot   *two-quart tankard.*

63   By God's Liggens   *an oath unique to Shallow. It has been explained as a variant of "lidkins" (a diminutive for "lids," eyelids); another possibility is "leggings."*

64   stick by thee   *keep up with you (in your drinking bouts).*

64–65   'a will not out   *he won't quit on you.*

71   Do me right   *a drinking expression meaning "pledge me properly."*

72   dub me Knight   *It was customary to "knight" someone who had shown a special ability to hold his own in pledging healths.*

73   Samingo   *a character in "Monsier Mingo," the drinking song from which Silence is quoting. The name is probably a contraction of Santo Domingo.*

254

SILENCE   And we shall be merry, now comes in the
        Sweet a' th' Night.
FALSTAFF   Health and Long Life to you, Master
        Silence.                                          50
SILENCE   "Fill the Cup, and let it come;
                I'll pledge you a Mile to th' Bottom."
SHALLOW   Honest Bardolph, welcome; if thou want'st
        any thing, and wilt not call, beshrew thy Heart.
        —Welcome, my little tiny Thief, and welcome       55
        indeed too. I'll drink to Master Bardolph, and
        to all the Cabileros about London.
DAVY   I hope to see London once ere I die.
BARDOLPH   And I might see you there, Davy!
SHALLOW   By the Mass, you'll crack a Quart together,     60
        ha, will you not, Master Bardolph?
BARDOLPH   Yes Sir, in a Pottle-pot.
SHALLOW   By God's Liggens, I thank thee; the Knave
        will stick by thee; I can assure thee that 'a
        will not out; ah 'tis true bred!                  65
BARDOLPH   And I'll stick by him, Sir.
SHALLOW   Why there spoke a King: lack nothing, be
        merry.                           *One knocks at the Door.*
        —Look who's at Door there, ho! Who knocks?
                                                *Exit Davy.*
FALSTAFF   Why now you have done me right.                70
SILENCE   "Do me right,
                And dub me Knight,
                        Samingo."
        Is't not so?
FALSTAFF   'Tis so.                                       75


255

77        somewhat    *something.*

87–88   Goodman . . . Barson    *Silence may be quoting from an-*
          *other lost song; otherwise he is probably referring to a fat*
          *yeoman (goodman) from a nearby village. In either case, he*
          *casts Falstaff in a satirical light and prompts Pistol to defend*
          *him.*

90        Puff . . . Teeth    *I'll shove that "Puff" in your teeth.*
          recreant    *faithless, reprobate.*

92        helter-skelter    *at a recklessly rapid pace.*

95–96   like a Man of this World    *like an ordinary fellow. Falstaff*
          *probably means both (a) in plain language rather than the*
          *rant you usually employ, and (b) in a calm demeanor.*

97        Foutre    *a derivative from Latin with the same implications as*
          *a well-known four-letter imprecation of Anglo-Saxon origins.*
          *It reappears in Princess Katherine's English lesson in*
          *III.iv.55 of Henry V.*

98        Africa    *a continent fabled for its exotic treasures.*

99        Assyrian Knight    *Falstaff is probably making fun of Pistol's*
          *extravagance with a bit of his own Orientalism.*

100      King Covetua    *Falstaff refers to the ballad about "King Co-*
          *phetua and the Beggar Maid." Shakespeare alludes to it in*
          *several plays. Here the spelling is probably a reminder of the*
          *covetousness that has brought Falstaff back to Shallow's house*
          *for a second visit.*

SILENCE   Is't so? Why then say an Old Man can do
   somewhat.

*Re-enter Davy.*

DAVY   And 't please your Worship, there's one Pistol
   come from the Court with News.
FALSTAFF   From the Court? Let him come in.                    80

*Enter Pistol.*

   —How now Pistol?
PISTOL   Sir John, God save you.
FALSTAFF   What Wind blew you hither, Pistol?
PISTOL   Not the Ill Wind which blows no Man to Good:
   Sweet Knight, thou art now one of the Greatest          85
   Men in this Realm.
SILENCE   By'r Lady I think 'a be but Goodman Puff
   of Barson.
PISTOL   Puff?
   Puff i' thy Teeth, most recreant Coward Base!           90
   Sir John, I am thy Pistol and thy Friend,
   And helter-skelter have I rode to thee,
   And Tidings do I bring, and Lucky Joys,
   And Golden Times, and Happy News of price.
FALSTAFF   I pray thee now deliver them like a Man          95
   of this World.
PISTOL   A Foutre for the World and Worldlings Base;
   I speak of Africa and Golden Joys.
FALSTAFF   O base Assyrian Knight, what is thy News?
   Let King Covetua know the Truth thereof.               100

257

101    **And . . . John**  *Silence quotes from a ballad about Robin Hood and two of his companions. Robin Hood stole from the rich and gave to the poor; Falstaff's thievery is less noble.*

102    **Shall . . . Helicons?**  *Pistol asks whether the kinds of foul dogs who hang around dunghills are going to be permitted to compete with the Muses who dwell on Mount Helicon.*

103    **baffled**  *disgraced, treated with scorn.*

111    **Besonian**  *a variant of the Spanish word for "ignoramus."*

116    **do this and Fig me**  *Pistol probably inserts his thumb through his fist to illustrate the obscene gesture to which he refers.*

118    **just**  *true.*

122    **double-charge . . . Dignities**  *overload you with honors. Falstaff puns on Pistol's name.*

123    **Knight**  *knighthood.*

126    **Carry . . . Bed.**  *Evidently Shallow's young cousin has been put to silence by his heavy carousing.*

SILENCE   "And Robin Hood, Scarlet, and John."

PISTOL   Shall Dunghill Curs confront the Helicons?
     And shall Good News be baffled? Then Pistol,
     Lay thy Head in Furies' Lap.

SHALLOW   Honest Gentleman, I know not your Breeding.   105

PISTOL   Why then lament therefore.

SHALLOW   Give me Pardon, Sir. If, Sir, you come with
     News from the Court, I take it there's but two
     ways, either to utter them or conceal them. I
     am, Sir, under the King in some Authority.   110

PISTOL   Under which King, Besonian? Speak or die!

SHALLOW   Under King Harry.

PISTOL                      Harry the Fourth, or Fift?

SHALLOW   Harry the Fourth.

PISTOL                      A Foutre for thine Office!
     —Sir John, thy tender Lambkin now is King.
     Harry the Fift's the Man. I speak the Truth.   115
     When Pistol lies, do this and Fig me like
     The bragging Spaniard.

FALSTAFF                      What, is the old King dead?

PISTOL   As Nail in Door; the things I speak are just.

FALSTAFF   Away, Bardolph, saddle my Horse. —Master
     Robert Shallow, choose what Office thou wilt   120
     in the Land, 'tis thine. —Pistol, I will
     double-charge thee with Dignities.

BARDOLPH   O Joyful Day! I would not take a Knight
     for my Fortune.

PISTOL   What? I do bring Good News.   125

FALSTAFF   Carry Master Silence to Bed. —Master
     Shallow, my Lord Shallow, be what thou wilt,

128    **I am Fortune's Steward**   *Falstaff imagines himself to be in a position to preside over all the new King's possessions, spending lavishly and bestowing gifts and titles on anyone he fancies.*

131    **withal**   *while doing so.*

134    **sick for me**   *dying to see me.*

134–   **the Laws . . . Commandement**   *This clause recalls the*
35    *King's nightmarish vision of Vanity triumphant in IV.v.115–28.*

138    **Let Vultures . . . also.**   *Pistol alludes to the myth of Prometheus, the God who incurred Zeus's wrath and was chained to a rock where vultures gnawed perpetually at his intestines.*

139    **Where . . . led?**   *Pistol alludes to a ballad (also quoted by Petruchio in IV.i of* The Taming of the Shrew) *whose singer longs for the good old days. For Pistol, Bardolph, and Falstaff, it now appears that happy days are here at last. There is no need to think of either yesterday or tomorrow; the watchword of the moment is "Seize today!"*

V.iv   *This scene takes place on a street in London.*

S.D.   **Beadle**   *Beadles were officers who took petty offenders into custody.*

1–2    **I would . . . hang'd!**   *The Hostess assumes that if the officer were to kill her, he would be hanged for police brutality.*

5    **Whipping-cheer**   *"Cheer" normally refers to a bountiful meal; here it indicates a full serving with the whip, a punishment for whores.*

I am Fortune's Steward. Get on thy Boots,
we'll ride all Night. —O sweet Pistol! —Away,
Bardolph!                                    *Exit Bardolph.*    130
—Come, Pistol, utter more to me, and withal
devise something to do thy self good. —Boot,
boot, Master Shallow! I know the young King is
sick for me. Let us take any man's Horses: the
Laws of England are at my Commandement.                  135
Blessed are they that have been my Friends, and
woe to my Lord Chief Justice!

PISTOL   Let Vultures vile seize on his Lungs also.
"Where is the Life that late I led?" say they.
Why here it is. Welcome these Pleasant Days!             140
                                           *Exeunt.*

# Scene 4

*Enter Beadle and three or four Officers with
Mistress Quickly and Doll Tearsheet.*

HOSTESS   No, thou arrant Knave! I would to God
that I might die, that I might have thee hang'd!
Thou hast drawn my Shoulders out of joint.

BEADLE   —The Constables have deliver'd her over
to me, and she shall have Whipping-cheer, I              5
warrant her. There hath been a Man or two
kill'd about her.

8     Nuthook   *a term for constable or beadle, based on the analogy between their weapons and the hooked sticks used to shake nuts down.*

9     Tripe-visag'd   *sallow-faced. Tripe is a dish prepared from the stomach or intestines of sheep or oxen.*

12    Paper-fac'd   *both (a) as white, and (b) as thin as paper.*

16–17  If . . . now.   *What the Beadle means is that if Doll "mis-carries" (drops one of her cushions), that "Fruit of her Womb" can be added to the eleven the Hostess has under her own dress.*

20    Thin Man in a Censor   *Doll may be referring to a low-relief embossed figure on the lid of a perfuming pan. But it is also possible that* Censor *is a variant of "scissor," a reading that would relate to the paper image in line 12.*

21    swing'd   *beaten.* Swinged *rhymes with* hinged.

22    Blue-bottle   *Beadles wore blue coats.*

24    forswear half-Kirtles   *swear off skirts.*

25    arrant   *arrogant, with puns on "Knight-errant" and "Night-errant."*

27    of Sufferance comes Ease   *a proverbial saying encouraging one to endure suffering with patience.*

31    Atomy   *The Hostess probably means "anatomy" (that is, skeleton); but "atomy" (a tiny particle) would fit the occasion equally well.*

DOLL   Nuthook, Nuthook, you lie! Come on, I'll tell
        thee what, thou damn'd Tripe-visag'd Rascal!
        And the Child I go with do miscarry, thou wert        10
        better thou hadst strook thy Mother, thou
        Paper-fac'd Villain!
HOSTESS   O the Lord, that Sir John were come! I
        would make this a Bloody Day to some body. But
        I pray God the Fruit of her Womb miscarry.        15
BEADLE   If it do, you shall have a dozen of Cushions
        again; you have but eleven now. Come, I charge
        you both go with me, for the Man is dead that
        you and Pistol beat amongst you.
DOLL   I'll tell you what, you Thin Man in a Censor!        20
        I'll have you as soundly swing'd for this, you
        Blue-bottle Rogue, you filthy famish'd
        Correctioner; if you be not swing'd, I'll
        forswear half-Kirtles!
BEADLE   Come, come, you she-Knight-arrant, come!        25
HOSTESS   O God, that Right should thus overcome
        Might! Well, of Sufferance comes Ease.
DOLL   Come, you Rogue; come bring me to a Justice!
HOSTESS   Ay, come, you starv'd Bloodhound!
DOLL   Goodman Death, Goodman Bones!        30
HOSTESS   Thou Atomy, thou!
DOLL   Come, you Thin-thing! Come, you Rascal!
BEADLE   Very well.        *Exeunt.*

263

V.v    *This final scene takes place in Westminster, probably near the entrance to Westminster Abbey.*

1    Rushes   *Rushes (grass-like plants from the edge of rivers and streams) were strewn on floors or streets to mark ceremonial occasions.*

6    do you grace   *treat you with favor.*
leer   *look familiarly and proudly.*

8    Countenance   *both (a) facial expression, and (b) acceptance and approval.*

11    Liveries   *uniforms signifying one's service to a lord or monarch.*

12    bestow'd   *spent.*

12–13    the thousand Pound . . . you   *Falstaff has accomplished his mission in Gloucestershire.*

14    Poor Show   *humble appearance.*
infer   *indicate.*

# Scene 5

*Enter Strewers of Rushes.*

FIRST STREWER   More Rushes, more Rushes!
SECOND STREWER   The Trumpets have sounded twice.
THIRD STREWER   'Twill be two a' clock ere they come
    from the Coronation. Dispatch, dispatch!    *Exeunt.*

*Trumpets sound, and the King and his Train pass over
the Stage; after them enter Falstaff, Shallow,
Pistol, Bardolph, and the Page.*

FALSTAFF   Stand here by me, Maister Shallow. I will    5
    make the King do you grace. I will leer upon
    him as 'a comes by, and do but mark the
    Countenance that he will give me.
PISTOL   God bless thy Lungs, good Knight.
FALSTAFF   Come here, Pistol, stand behind me. —O    10
    if I had had time to have made new Liveries, I
    would have bestow'd the thousand Pound I
    borrow'd of you. But 'tis no matter, this
    Poor Show doth better; this doth infer the
    Zeal I had to see him.    15
SHALLOW   It doth so.
FALSTAFF   It shows my earnestness of Affection.

23      to shift me    *to change my clothes.*

25      Travail    *both (a) travel, and (b) arduous effort.*

28      Oblivion    *forgetfulness.*

30      semper idem    *Latin for "always the same."*
        obsque hoc nihil est    *Latin for "apart from this is nothing." Here* obsque *is probably Pistol's erroneous rendering of* absque.

33      Liver    *here treated as the seat of anger. Like many of Pistol's speeches, this one has passages that scan as verse.*

34      Helen    *Helen of Troy, who was stolen from her husband Menelaus by Paris, became a symbol for high-class mistresses or prostitutes (such as the "bona-robas" of Shallow's youth).*

35      Durance    *imprisonment.*

37      mechanical    *a term associated with manual laborers.*

38      Ebon Den    *Hell (*ebon *means black).*
        fell Alecto's Snake    *Alecto was one of the Furies (traditionally depicted as women with bloody eyes and serpents for hair); they haunted evildoers until vengeance had been rendered.*

41      There roar'd the Sea    *By juxtaposing Falstaff's promise (to "deliver her") with the "Shouts within," Shakespeare achieves the comic effect of having Pistol's statement appear to refer to both "roars."*

S.D.      Enter the King and his Train.    *The new King and his entourage are emerging from Westminster Abbey following the Coronation.*

| | |
|---|---|
| SHALLOW | It doth so. |
| FALSTAFF | My Devotion. |
| SHALLOW | It doth, it doth, it doth. | 20 |

FALSTAFF As it were, to ride Day and Night, and
not to deliberate, not to remember, not to
have patience to shift me.

SHALLOW It is best, certain.

FALSTAFF But to stand tainted with Travail, and 25
sweating with Desire to see him, thinking of
nothing else, putting all Affairs else in
Oblivion, as if there were nothing else to be
done but to see him.

PISTOL 'Tis *semper idem,* for *obsque hoc nihil est;* 30
'tis all in every part.

SHALLOW 'Tis so indeed.

PISTOL My Knight, I will inflame thy Noble Liver
and make thee rage. Thy Doll, and Helen of thy
Noble Thoughts, is in base Durance and 35
contagious Prison, haul'd thither by most
mechanical and dirty Hand. Rouse up Revenge
from Ebon Den, with fell Alecto's Snake, for
Doll is in. Pistol speaks nought but Truth.

FALSTAFF I will deliver her. 40

*Shouts within. Trumpets sound.*

PISTOL There roar'd the Sea, and Trumpet Clangor
sounds.

*Enter the King and his Train.*

FALSTAFF God save thy Grace, King Hal, my Royal
Hal!

267

43      **Imp**    *scion, offspring. Like "Hal" (line 42) and "Boy" (line 44), it is now an inappropriate form of address.*

45      **Vain**    *This is a word with a complex of meanings here, among them (a) foolish, (b) empty (lacking in substance or gravity), (c) overweening (arrogant), and (d) doomed to defeat (in vain).*

47      **My King . . . Heart!**    *Once again Falstaff refuses to acknowledge or speak directly to the Lord Chief Justice (as in I.ii and II.i). Falstaff continues to believe himself immune from all authority.*

48      **Old Man**    *Drawing on the concepts and much of the language of Ephesians 5:17–32, the new King addresses Falstaff not merely as a man who is physically old, but more fundamentally as the embodiment of a fallen spiritual condition that must now be shed, buried, and replaced with the kind of "new man" the King aspires to be.*

60      **So will . . . Company**    *With this utterance the new King establishes a fresh context for all the previous references to "Company" in the two parts of* Henry IV.

65      **As . . . Misleaders**    *This line suggests that the King had already made arrangements for all of his old companions before Falstaff interrupted the Coronation procession. From here on in the speech the King appears to be referring not only to Falstaff but to the rest of Falstaff's "Company."*

67      **For . . . you**    *I will provide a small allowance to maintain all of you in a modest way of life.*

PISTOL   The Heav'ns thee guard and keep, most Royal
        Imp of Fame!

FALSTAFF   God save thee, my sweet Boy!

KING   My Lord Chief Justice, speak to that Vain Man.      45

JUSTICE   —Have you your Wits? Know you what 'tis
        you speak?

FALSTAFF   —My King, my Jove, I speak to thee, my
        Heart!

KING   I know thee not, Old Man: fall to thy Prayers.
        How ill White Hairs become a Fool and Jester!
        —I long have dreamt of such a kind of Man,       50
        So Surfeit-swell'd, so Old, and so Profane;
        But, being awak'd, I do despise my Dream.
        —Make less thy Body hence, and more thy Grace;
        Leave Gourmandizing; know the Grave doth gape
        For thee thrice wider than for other Men.         55
        Reply not to me with a Fool-borne Jest.
        Presume not that I am the Thing I was,
        For God doth know, so shall the World perceive,
        That I have turn'd away my former Self;
        So will I those that kept me Company.             60
        When thou dost hear I am as I have been,
        Approach me, and thou shalt be as thou wast,
        The Tutor and the Feeder of my Riots.
        Till then I banish thee on pain of Death,
        As I have done the rest of my Misleaders,         65
        Not to come near our Person by ten Mile.
        For Competence of Life I will allow you,
        That lack of Means enforce you not to Evils;
        And as we hear you do reform your selves,

269

72    tenure   *tenor, intent.*

77    have home with me   *have to take home with me.*

79    grieve at this   *worry about this.*

81    your Advancements   *the exalted responsibilities I have promised to secure for you (in exchange for the "thousand Pound" you have paid for my services).*

82    Great   *exalted in titles and wealth. But in his reply Shallow reinterprets* Great *to mean "fat."*

88    a Color   *a pretense (to preserve the King's image as an upholder of order and decorum).*

89    A Color . . . die in   *Shallow's reply involves two kinds of wordplay: (a) he implies that the King has shown Falstaff his true colors, his true identity as a King who will rule in accordance with law and justice; and (b) he implies that if Falstaff doesn't adjust his behavior accordingly, he will soon find himself outfitted with a Hangman's collar.*

91    Fear no Colors.   *Falstaff puns on "colors" as the banner (insignia) of a battalion. He picks up on Shallow's reference to danger and says, in effect, "fear no enemy attacks."*

92    Lieftenant   *lieutenant. The Quarto spelling captures the pronunciation that remains current in Britain.*

94    the Fleet   *the London prison just north of Fleet Street.*

We will, according to your Strengths and
   Qualities,                                 70
Give you Advancement. —Be it your Charge, my
   Lord,
To see perform'd the tenure of my Word.
—Set on.              *Exeunt the King and his Train.*

FALSTAFF   Master Shallow, I owe you a thousand
   Pound.                                 75

SHALLOW   Yea marry, Sir John, which I beseech you
to let me have home with me.

FALSTAFF   That can hardly be, Master Shallow. Do
not you grieve at this: I shall be sent for in
private to him. Look you, he must seem thus to     80
the World. Fear not your Advancements; I will
be the Man yet that shall make you Great.

SHALLOW   I cannot perceive how, unless you give me
your Doublet, and stuff me out with Straw. I
beseech you, good Sir John, let me have five     85
hundred of my thousand.

FALSTAFF   Sir, I will be as good as my Word; this
that you heard was but a Color.

SHALLOW   A Color that I fear you will die in, Sir
John.                                   90

FALSTAFF   Fear no Colors. Go with me to Dinner.
—Come, Lieftenant Pistol, come Bardolph.
—I shall be sent for soon at Night.

*Enter the Lord Chief Justice and Prince John,*
*accompanied by Officers.*

JUSTICE   Go carry Sir John Falstaff to the Fleet;

97    I cannot now speak    *The Lord Chief Justice probably relishes the opportunity to repay Falstaff for the occasions when his old thorn in the flesh has refused to listen to him.*

99    Si . . . contenta.    *Here Pistol uses a more correct version of the expression he employed in II.iv: "If Fortune torments me, Hope contents me."*

101    wonted    *former, accustomed.*

103    Conversations    *ways of life.*

110    I heard a Bird so sing    *Fittingly, a play that began with "Rumor painted full of Tongues" ends with another rumor. This one, however, will prove to be "Music" from a reliable source.*

112    Come, will you hence?    *This line is addressed to the Lord Chief Justice, but it could almost be interpreted in addition as an invitation to the audience to return for the next installment in this historical sequence.*

Take all his Company along with him.                              95
FALSTAFF   My Lord, my Lord—
JUSTICE   I cannot now speak; I will hear you soon.
      —Take them away.
PISTOL   *Si fortuna me tormenta, spero contenta.*
            *Exeunt Falstaff and his Companions under Guard.*
PRINCE JOHN   I like this Fair Proceeding of the
      King's;                                                     100
      He hath intent his wonted Followers
      Shall all be very well provided for;
      But all are banish'd till their Conversations
      Appear more wise and modest to the World.
JUSTICE   And so they are.                                       105
PRINCE JOHN   The King hath call'd his Parliament,
      my Lord.
JUSTICE   He hath.
PRINCE JOHN   I will lay Odds that ere this Year
      expire
      We bear our Civil Swords and Native Fire
      As far as France. I heard a Bird so sing,                  110
      Whose Music, to my thinking, pleas'd the King.
      Come, will you hence?                           *Exeunt.*

273

EPILOGUE    *Fittingly, a play that began with a prologue from an unreliable source, Rumor, concludes with an epilogue from the most reliable source possible, the author or an actor serving as his surrogate.*

1       Cur'sy    *curtsy, a bow.*

6       what I . . . Making    *This clause is probably meant to be paradoxical. Even though the speaker of the Epilogue is presumably uttering words written by the playwright, he comes before the audience now as one who is to be regarded as a spokesman for the play and who stands outside the world (the play) where actors speak only as "characters" created by an external "maker" (the playwright). In other words, the actor who speaks these words is playing the character of an actor who has stepped out of character (and out of the play itself) to speak words of his "own Making." In reality, if what the actor says is true, he must either be the playwright himself or someone else who steps forward to speak on his own behalf. Otherwise what he has to say is not of his own making.*

8       Marring    *undoing (or at least injuring), unmaking. If the maker creates a "figure" (artistic representation) of reality, he risks being "disfigured" if the audience rejects his work.*

11      a displeasing Play    *What this was is not certain. One possibility is that the speaker refers to the displeasure occasioned by the name Shakespeare originally gave to Falstaff: Sir John Oldcastle.*

14      break    *go broke financially.*

# *Epilogue*

First my Fear; then my Cur'sy; last my
Speech.

My Fear is your Displeasure; my Cur'sy, my
Duty; and my Speech, to beg your Pardons. If
you look for a good Speech now, you undo me,      5
for what I have to say is of mine own Making.
And what indeed I should say will, I doubt,
prove mine own Marring. But to the Purpose,
and so to the Venture. Be it known to you, as
it is very well, I was lately here in the end      10
of a displeasing Play, to pray your Patience
for it and to promise you a better. I meant
indeed to pay you with this, which if like
an ill Venture it come unluckily home, I break,
and you, my Gentle Creditors, lose. Here I      15
promis'd you I would be, and here I commit my

17      **Bate me some**   *abate me somewhat; let me off the hook.*

20      **but . . . Queen**   *This can be interpreted as a jest that he is not really begging the audience for mercy but instead kneeling in prayer for the health of the Queen.*

22      **use my Legs**   *either (a) to dance, or (b) to run away in fear.*

23      **light**   *Here* light *means (a) easy, (b) inadequate, (c) frivolous, and (d) irresponsible.*

31      **Fat Meat**   *a reference to Falstaff.*

31–32    **our humble Author**   *Although the speaker of the Epilogue functions as one who apologizes for the play (makes the case for it and defends it where necessary), this line makes it clear that he is to be regarded as a "character" (even though the actor playing him may have been William Shakespeare) and not as the author (the maker) in his own person. Most editors assume that the Epilogue was originally confined to the first paragraph, with the remainder a subsequent addition. There is nothing to compel such an interpretation.*

36–37    **For Oldcastle . . . Man.**   *This sounds like an oblique apology to those in the audience who were offended by the scandal of attributing to a noble "Martyr" the base motives and frivolous behavior now associated with Sir John Falstaff.*

38      **when my Legs are too**   *Presumably the speaker is dancing as he speaks these last words. Once he has finished his dance, he will bid the audience farewell.*

Body to your Mercies. Bate me some, and I will pay you some, and, as most Debtors do, promise you infinitely. And so I kneel down before you; but indeed to pray for the Queen.　　　　　　　　　20

If my Tongue cannot entreat you to acquit me, will you command me to use my Legs? And yet that were but light Payment, to dance out of your Debt. But a good Conscience will make any possible Satisfaction, and so would I. All　　25 the Gentlewomen here have forgiven me; if the Gentlemen will not, then the Gentlemen do not agree with the Gentlewomen, which was never seen in such an Assembly.

One word more, I beseech you. If you be not　　30 too much cloy'd with Fat Meat, our humble Author will continue the Story, with Sir John in it, and make you merry with fair Katharine of France, where (for any thing I know) Falstaff shall die of a Sweat, unless already 'a be　　35 kill'd with your hard Opinions. For Oldcastle died Martyr, and this is not the Man. My Tongue is weary; when my Legs are too, I will bid you Good Night.

FINIS

277

# HENRY V

# NAMES OF THE ACTORS

KING HENRY THE FIFTH

HUMPHREY, DUKE OF GLOUCESTER
JOHN, DUKE OF BEDFORD          Brothers to the King
DUKE OF CLARENCE

DUKE OF EXETER, Uncle to the King
DUKE OF YORK, Cousin to the King
EARL OF SALISBURY
EARL OF WESTMERLAND
EARL OF WARWICK
ARCHBISHOP OF CANTERBURY
BISHOP OF ELY
EARL OF CAMBRIDGE
LORD SCROOP
SIR THOMAS GREY

SIR THOMAS ERPINGHAM
GOWER
FLUELLEN                        Officers in the English Army
MACMORRICE
JAMY

BATES
COURT                           Soldiers in the English Army
WILLIAMS

PISTOL
NYM
BARDOLPH
BOY
HERALD

HOSTESS (formerly MISTRESS QUICKLY)

CHARLES THE SIXTH, KING OF FRANCE
ISABEL, QUEEN OF FRANCE
KATHERINE, their Daughter

LEWIS, THE DOLPHIN (DAUPHIN)
DUKE OF BOURGOGNE
DUKE OF ORLEANCE
DUKE OF BERRY
DUKE OF BOURBON
DUKE OF BEAUMONT
DUKE OF BRITAINE
CONSTABLE OF FRANCE

RAMBURES        French Lords
GRANDPRE

GOVERNOR OF HARFLEW (HARFLEUR)
MONTJOY, the French Herald
AMBASSADORS to the King of England

ALICE, a Lady attending on Princess Katherine

CHORUS

LORDS, LADIES, OFFICERS, SOLDIERS, CITIZENS,
    MESSENGERS, and ATTENDANTS

PROLOGUE   *In the First Folio text the initial stage direction is "Enter Prologue." The Prologue is not identified as such, and there is no speaker designation for "Chorus." It is clear, however, that the actor who speaks these opening lines is the same "Chorus" who speaks similar lines later in the play. He functions as an official "apologist" for the acting company and sometimes as a surrogate for the playwright himself.*

1   Muse of Fire   *Fire was the most "heavenly" of the elements. Associated with the ethereal realms and with spirit, it was an apt symbol for poetic "Invention" (creativity).*

3–4   A Kingdom . . . Scene   *What the Chorus wishes for is a theatrical spectacle as "swelling" (large) as the magnificent personalities and grand events it reenacts.*

6   the Port of Mars   *the bearing of the God of War.*

8   Crouch for Employment   *wait for orders.*

9   flat unraised Spirits   *ordinary, uninspired human beings; mere actors. This phrase also suggests the kinds of aspiring "Spirits" that "bring forth" (line 10) other kinds of "great" objects. As such, it suggests that this will be a play about various kinds of action and conception.*

11   this Cockpit   *like "this unworthy Scaffold" (line 10), a self-deprecating reference to the inadequate resources of the theatre. Its "Wooden O" was quite similar to the architecture of other amphitheatres used for cockfighting and bear-baiting.*

13   Casques   *helmets.*

14   Agincourt   *the village in northern France where Henry V won his great victory on October 25, 1415.*

# Prologue

*Enter Chorus.*

CHORUS   O for a Muse of Fire, that would ascend
    The brightest Heaven of Invention:
    A Kingdom for a Stage, Princes to act,
    And Monarchs to behold the swelling Scene.
    Then should the Warlike Harry, like himself,       5
    Assume the Port of Mars, and at his Heels
    (Leash'd in, like Hounds) should Famine, Sword,
       and Fire
    Crouch for Employment. But pardon, Gentles all,
    The flat unraised Spirits that hath dar'd
    On this unworthy Scaffold to bring forth       10
    So great an Object. Can this Cockpit hold
    The vasty Fields of France? Or may we cram
    Within this Wooden O the very Casques
    That did affright the Air at Agincourt?

283

15    a crooked Figure    *both (a) a human figure, and (b) a numerical symbol, such as the "Ciphers" (zeros) referred to in line
17. The Chorus reminds us that, following a number, a short
string of these "nothings" can "Attest" (represent) "a Million."*

17    Accompt    *account, playing on (a) a story, (b) a numerical
sum or calculation, (c) "Cipher," and (d) "Wooden O."*

18    your Imaginary Forces    *your powers of imagination.*

21    abutting Fronts    *The Chorus refers to the cliffs of Dover
(England) and Calais (France), but he personifies them as the
foreheads of two proud warriors. They are called "abutting"
(a) because they are separated only by the narrow English
Channel, and (b) because they will soon be "butting" heads
like two beasts establishing their territorial rights.*

22    per'lous    *perilous; probably pronounced "parlous" here.*

23    Piece out    *augment, extrapolate from.*

25    Puissance    *power, forces; here pronounced "pú-ee-sance."*

28    deck    *dress, outfit.*

31    for the which supply    *to provide which. The Chorus will
function as the "Hourglass" through which the sands (the
action presented on the stage) representing several years of
"History" will be poured. The play treats events that span the
period from 1414 to 1420.*

34    hear    *Discriminating playgoers "heard" rather than "saw" a
play.*

O pardon, since a crooked Figure may                15
Attest in little place a Million,
And let us, Ciphers to this great Accompt,
On your Imaginary Forces work.
Suppose within the Girdle of these Walls
Are now confin'd two mighty Monarchies,                20
Whose high upreared and abutting Fronts
The per'lous narrow Ocean parts asunder.
Piece out our Imperfections with your Thoughts:
Into a thousand Parts divide one Man,
And make imaginary Puissance.                25
Think, when we talk of Horses, that you see
    them
Printing their proud Hoofs i' th' receiving Earth.
For 'tis your Thoughts that now must deck our
    Kings,
Carry them here and there, jumping o'er Times,
Turning th' accomplishment of many Years                30
Into an Hourglass: for the which supply,
Admit me Chorus to this History;
Who, Prologue-like, your humble Patience pray,
Gently to hear, kindly to judge, our Play.        *Exit.*

I.i  *The opening scene takes place in an antechamber of one of the royal palaces. According to Raphael Holinshed's* Chronicles of England, Scotland, and Ireland *(Shakespeare's principal source for the play), the events depicted in this scene took place in two sites: Kenilworth and Leicester. Most editors place the scene in London. Since the play specifies no location, it seems clear that Shakespeare was content to leave the matter to his audience's "Imaginary Forces."*

1  self  *same.*

2  Which . . . Reign  *The Archbishop of Canterbury refers to a bill that was introduced in Parliament in 1410, the eleventh year of the reign of King Henry IV. It would have provided for the Crown's seizure of lands held by the Church for the purposes specified in lines 7–19. Here Shakespeare follows Holinshed's account with great fidelity.*

3  Was like  *was likely (to be adopted).*

4  scrambling  *disorderly, turbulent.*

9  Temp'ral Lands  *estates bequeathed to the Church for uses not confined to religious purposes.*

286

# Scene 1

*Enter the two Bishops of Canterbury and Ely.*

CANTERBURY   My Lord, I'll tell you, that self Bill is urg'd
    Which in th' eleventh year of th' last King's Reign
    Was like, and had indeed against us pass'd,
    But that the scrambling and unquiet Time
    Did push it out of farther Question.          5
ELY   But how, my Lord, shall we resist it now?
CANTERBURY   It must be thought on: if it pass against us,
    We lose the better half of our Possession.
    For all the Temp'ral Lands which Men Devout
    By Testament have given to the Church          10
    Would they strip from us, being valu'd thus:
    As much as would maintain, to the King's Honor,

15    Lazars    *lepers and other diseased persons.*

16    past corp'ral Toil    *too old and infirm for any kind of physical labor.*

21    what Prevention?    *what can be done to prevent it?*

26    mortified    *put to death.*

28    Consideration    *responsibility and good judgment.*

29    th' offending Adam    *the manifestations of the "old Adam" (human nature as corrupted by original sin).*

30    Paradise    *Canterbury refers to the "Paradise within," the renewed spirit of those who have been infused by the "new Adam" (Christ). Sources for the doctrine include 1 Corinthians 15:45 and Ephesians 4:22–24.*

32    Scholar    *student of things spiritual.*

34    heady Currance    *powerful (headlong) current.*
      scouring    *cleansing.*

35    Hydra    *a multi-headed serpent killed by Hercules.*

36    Seat    *throne, source of power.*

37    Change    *both (a) transformation, and (b) exchange (of an "old man" for a "new man").*

38    Divinity    *theology, religion.*

Full fifteen Earls and fifteen hundred Knights;
Six thousand and two hundred good Esquires;
And to relief of Lazars and weak age                        15
Of indigent faint Souls past corp'ral Toil,
A hundred Alms-houses right well supplied;
And to the Coffers of the King beside,
A hundred thousand Pounds by th' Year. Thus
    runs the Bill.

ELY   This would drink deep.

CANTERBURY            'Twould drink the Cup and all.      20

ELY   But what Prevention?

CANTERBURY   The King is full of Grace and fair
    Regard.

ELY   And a true Lover of the holy Church.

CANTERBURY   The Courses of his Youth promis'd it
    not.
The Breath no sooner left his Father's Body              25
But that his Wildness, mortified in him,
Seem'd to die too: yea, at that very moment
Consideration like an Angel came
And whipp'd th' offending Adam out of him,
Leaving his Body as a Paradise                           30
T' envelop and contain Celestial Spirits.
Never was such a sudden Scholar made;
Never came Reformation in a Flood
With such a heady Currance scouring Faults;
Nor never Hydra-headed Willfulness                       35
So soon did lose his Seat, and all at once,
As in this King.

ELY              We are blessed in the Change.

CANTERBURY   Hear him but reason in Divinity,

39     admiring   *both (a) impressed, and (b) wondering in astonishment.*

41     Commonwealth   *political, pertaining to the state.*

43     List   *listen to.*

45     Cause of Policy   *case of political affairs or statecraft.*

46     Gordian Knot   *an intricate knot devised by King Gordius of Phrygia and cut through by the youthful Alexander the Great.*

48     charter'd Libertine   *licensed freeman, one at liberty to go at will.*

50     Sentences   *sententiae, wise sayings.*

51–52  So that . . . Theoric   *so that the part of life that has to do with art (skill) and practice must be subservient to this theoretical understanding. Here* Mistress *is usually interpreted to mean "patroness" or "authoress"; but the context would seem to suggest that "Theoric" is in a position of mastery rather than subservience.*

54     Vain   *worthless, idle, irresponsible.*

58     Sequestration   *separation, secreting.*

59     open Haunts   *common gathering places.*

63     obscur'd   *hid; literally, shadowed.*

66     crescive in his faculty   *growing in its natural mode.*

And, all-admiring, with an inward wish
You would desire the King were made a Prelate.          40
Hear him debate of Commonwealth Affairs:
You would say it hath been all in all his Study.
List his discourse of War, and you shall hear
A fearful Battle rend'red you in Music.
Turn him to any Cause of Policy,                        45
The Gordian Knot of it he will unloose,
Familiar as his Garter: that when he speaks,
The Air, a charter'd Libertine, is still,
And the mute Wonder lurketh in Men's Ears
To steal his sweet and honey'd Sentences,               50
So that the Art and Practic part of Life
Must be the Mistress to this Theoric;
Which is a wonder how his Grace should glean
  it,
Since his Addiction was to Courses Vain,
His Companies unletter'd, rude, and shallow,            55
His Hours fill'd up with Riots, Banquets,
  Sports;
And never noted in him any Study,
Any Retirement, any Sequestration
From open Haunts and Popularity.

ELY   The Strawberry grows underneath the Nettle,       60
And wholesome Berries thrive and ripen best
Neighbor'd by Fruit of Baser Quality:
And so the Prince obscur'd his Contemplation
Under the Veil of Wildness; which (no doubt)
Grew like the Summer Grass, fastest by Night,          65
Unseen, yet crescive in his faculty.

68     admit   *acknowledge.*
    Means   *Canterbury here refers to the natural causes for what might otherwise be thought to be a miraculous transformation.*

69     perfected   *brought to pass; here accented on the first syllable.*

72     Indifferent   *undecided, impartial.*

74     th' exhibiters against us   *those who present arguments against us.*

76     Upon . . . Convocation   *as a result of our ecclesiastical deliberations.*

78     at large   *in detail.*

79     As touching   *pertaining to.*

81     withal   *with.*

85     would fain have done   *would have liked to do.*

86     sev'rals   *particulars, details.*
    unhidden Passages   *manifest (clear and open) lines of descent.*

89     Edward   *Edward III. His maternal grandfather was King Philip IV of France.*

91     Embassador   *ambassador (a common spelling of the word).*
    upon that Instant   *immediately.*

95     Embassy   *mission, message.*

CANTERBURY    It must be so: for Miracles are ceas'd,
          And therefore we must needs admit the Means
          How things are perfected.
ELY                              But my good Lord,
          How now for Mitigation of this Bill                          70
          Urg'd by the Commons? Doth his Majesty
          Incline to it or no?
CANTERBURY            He seems Indifferent,
          Or rather swaying more upon our part
          Than cherishing th' exhibiters against us.
          For I have made an Offer to his Majesty,                     75
          Upon our Spiritual Convocation
          And in regard of Causes now in hand
          Which I have open'd to his Grace at large,
          As touching France, to give a greater Sum
          Than ever at one time the Clergy yet                         80
          Did to his Predecessors part withal.
ELY    How did this Offer seem receiv'd, my Lord?
CANTERBURY    With good acceptance of his Majesty:
          Save that there was not time enough to hear,
          As I perceiv'd his Grace would fain have done,               85
          The sev'rals and unhidden Passages
          Of his true Titles to some certain Dukedoms
          And generally to the Crown and Seat of France,
          Deriv'd from Edward, his great-Grandfather.
ELY    What was th' Impediment that broke this off?                    90
CANTERBURY    The French Embassador upon that Instant
          Crav'd Audience; and the Hour, I think, is come
          To give him Hearing. Is it four a' Clock?
ELY    It is.
CANTERBURY    Then go we in, to know his Embassy,                      95

293

I.ii    *This scene, which follows immediately upon I.i, takes place in the Presence Chamber of the royal Palace.*

4    **we would be resolv'd**   *I would like to be clear in my mind. The King uses the royal plural.*

6    **task**  *burden, tax.*

8    **Sure**  *surely.*

Which I could with a ready Guess declare
Before the Frenchman speak a word of it.
ELY    I'll wait upon you, and I long to hear it.

*Exeunt.*


# Scene 2

*Enter the King, Humphrey, Duke of Gloucester,
Bedford, Clarence, Warwick, Westmerland, and Exeter.*

KING    Where is my gracious Lord of Canterbury?
EXETER    Not here in presence.
KING                                    Send for him, good Uncle.
WESTMERLAND    Shall we call in th' Ambassador, my
        Liege?
KING    Not yet, my Cousin: we would be resolv'd,
    Before we hear him, of some things of weight          5
    That task our thoughts concerning us and
        France.

*Enter the two Bishops.*

CANTERBURY    God and his Angels guard your sacred
        Throne
    And make you long become it!
KING                                    Sure we thank you.
    My learned Lord, we pray you to proceed

295

10   religiously   *in accordance with the teachings of religion.*

11   Law Salic   *As explained in lines 35–95, the French had a law whose purpose was to award the Crown only to male heirs and their descendents. At issue here is the fact that it had been used by France to deny King Edward III the throne when he had claimed it through his mother, Isabella. The name Salic derives from the river Sala (one of the mouths of the Rhine), and it here refers to a tribe of Franks who lived in the region.*

14   Reading   *interpretation.*

15   nicely . . . Soul   *put your rational faculties under an inappropriate strain and become guilty of excessive subtlety.*

16   With . . . miscreate   *by setting forth spuriously fabricated titles.*

19   drop   *spill.*
      in approbation   *in proving the truth.*

21   impawn   *pledge, commit.*

28   Waste in brief Mortality   *expenditure of lives made brief by war.*

29   Conjuration   *adjuration, injunction, order.*

35   Bar   *objection, impediment.*

And justly and religiously unfold 10
Why the Law Salic that they have in France
Or should or should not bar us in our Claim.
And God forbid, my dear and faithful Lord,
That you should fashion, wrest, or bow your
   Reading,
Or nicely charge your understanding Soul 15
With op'ning Titles miscreate, whose Right
Suits not in Native Colors with the Truth:
For God doth know how many now in Health
Shall drop their Blood in approbation
Of what your Rev'rence shall incite us to. 20
Therefore take heed how you impawn our Person,
How you awake our sleeping Sword of War.
We charge you in the Name of God take heed:
For never two such Kingdoms did contend
Without much fall of Blood, whose guiltless
   Drops 25
Are ev'ry one a Woe, a sore Complaint,
'Gainst him whose Wrongs give edge unto the
   Swords
That makes such Waste in brief Mortality.
Under this Conjuration speak, my Lord:
For we will hear, note, and believe in Heart 30
That what you speak is in your Conscience wash'd
As pure as Sin with Baptism.
CANTERBURY   Then hear me, gracious Sov'reign, and
   you Peers
That owe your Selves, your Lives, and Services
To this Imperial Throne. There is no Bar 35

37 **Pharamond** *an ancient king of the Salian Franks.*

40 **gloze** *gloss, interpret.*

42 **Female Bar** *prohibition against female succession. We should bear in mind that when* Henry V *was first performed, England's own monarch was a woman.*

45 **Floods** *rivers (literally, "flows").*
  **Elve** *spelled "Elbe" in Holinshed's* Chronicles *and so rendered in most modern editions. Shakespeare's spelling may have derived from Edward Hall, an earlier historian.*

49 **Dishonest** *unchaste.*

51 **Inheritrix** *heiress.*

58 **defunction** *death.*

59 **Idly** *incorrectly, foolishly, vainly.*

To make against your Highness' Claim to France
But this which they produce from Pharamond,
*In terram Salicam Mulieres ne succedant,*
"No Woman shall succeed in Salic Land,"
Which Salic Land the French unjustly gloze                40
To be the Realm of France, and Pharamond
The Founder of this Law and Female Bar.
Yet their own Authors faithfully affirm
That the Land Salic is in Germany
Between the Floods of Sala and of Elve,                   45
Where Charles the Great, having subdu'd the
    Saxons,
There left behind and settled certain French;
Who, holding in disdain the German Women
For some Dishonest Manners of their Life,
Establish'd then this Law: to wit, No Female              50
Should be Inheritrix in Salic Land,
Which Salic, as I said, 'twixt Elve and Sala,
Is at this day in Germany call'd Meisen.
Then doth it well appear, the Salic Law
Was not devised for the Realm of France,                  55
Nor did the French possess the Salic Land
Until four hundred one and twenty years
After defunction of King Pharamond,
Idly suppos'd the Founder of this Law,
Who died within the year of our Redemption               60
Four hundred twenty-six; and Charles the Great
Subdu'd the Saxons, and did seat the French
Beyond the River Sala, in the year
Eight hundred five. Besides, their Writers say,
King Pepin, which deposed Childeric,                      65

299

66    Heir General    *an heir whose right of succession was not lim-
      ited to the male line.*

72    To find . . . Truth    *to discover a basis for his title with some
      appearance of truth.*

73    Naught    *worthless.*

74    Convey'd    *misrepresented.* Convey *often meant "steal."*

75    Charlemain    *Charlemagne, or Charles the Great. Shake-
      speare follows an error in both Hall's and Holinshed's histo-
      ries; the King referred to here was actually Charles the Bald.*

77    Lewis the Tenth    *actually Louis IX. Here and elsewhere,*
      Lewis *is to be pronounced as a single-syllable word (some-
      thing like "Loose").*

82    Lineal of    *a direct descendent of.*

88    Lewis his    *Lewis's.*
      Satisfaction    *resolution of the question about his title.*

Did as Heir General, being descended
Of Blithild, which was Daughter to King
   Clothair,
Make Claim and Title to the Crown of France.
Hugh Capet also, who usurp'd the Crown
Of Charles the Duke of Lorraine, sole Heir male       70
Of the true Line and Stock of Charles the
   Great,
To find his Title with some Shows of Truth,
Though in pure Truth it was Corrupt and Naught,
Convey'd himself as th' Heir to th' Lady Lingare,
Daughter to Charlemain, who was the Son        75
To Lewis the Emperor, and Lewis the Son
Of Charles the Great; also King Lewis the
   Tenth,
Who was sole Heir to the Usurper Capet,
Could not keep quiet in his Conscience,
Wearing the Crown of France, till satisfied        80
That fair Queen Isabel, his Grandmother,
Was Lineal of the Lady Ermengare,
Daughter to Charles, the foresaid Duke of
   Lorraine,
By the which Marriage the Line of Charles the
   Great
Was reunited to the Crown of France.        85
So that as clear as is the Summer's Sun,
King Pepin's Title, and Hugh Capet's Claim,
King Lewis his Satisfaction, all appear
To hold in Right and Title of the Female.
So do the Kings of France unto this day.        90

91     Howbeit   *nevertheless.*

93     hide them in a Net   *try in vain to hide themselves from you by entangling themselves in a net of transparent contradictions.*

94     amply to imbar   *Canterbury's use of* imbar *is deliberately ambiguous here: his point is that the only way the French can sufficiently ("amply") protect their "Titles" is by resort to a way of "imbarring" (barring out) Henry V that has the effect of imbarring themselves at the same time.*

     crooked   *both (a) derived by indirect, circuitous routes, and (b) derived by wickedly devious means. By recalling the "indirect crook'd Ways" by which Henry IV obtained his crown (2 Henry IV, IV.v.180), this adjective reminds us that the French are not alone in clinging to "crooked Titles."*

98     Numbers   *Canterbury refers to Numbers 27:8, which Holinshed rendered as follows: "When a man dyeth and hath no son, ye shall turn his inheritance unto his daughter."*

101    Stand for   *stand up for, maintain.*

103    great-Grandsire's   *Edward III's.*

106    play'd a Tragedy   *wrought a tragic defeat on the French (at the Battle of Crécy in 1346).*

110    Forage in   *search in, like preying animals.*

114    cold for Action   *cold waiting for a call to action.*

Howbeit they would hold up this Salic Law
To bar your Highness claiming from the Female,
And rather choose to hide them in a Net
Than amply to imbar their crooked Titles,
Usurp'd from you and your Progenitors.                    95

KING   May I with Right and Conscience make this
    Claim?

CANTERBURY   The Sin upon my Head, dread Sovereign:
For in the Book of Numbers is it writ,
When the Man dies, let the Inheritance
Descend unto the Daughter. Gracious Lord,                 100
Stand for your own, unwind your bloody Flag,
Look back into your mighty Ancestors.
Go, my dread Lord, to your great-Grandsire's
    Tomb,
From whom you claim; invoke his Warlike Spirit,
And your great-Uncle's, Edward the Black
    Prince,                                                105
Who on the French ground play'd a Tragedy,
Making defeat on the full Pow'r of France,
Whiles his most mighty Father on a Hill
Stood smiling to behold his Lion's Whelp
Forage in Blood of French Nobility.                       110
O Noble English, that could entertain
With half their Forces the full Pride of
    France,
And let another half stand laughing by,
All out of Work and cold for Action!

ELY   Awake Remembrance of these Valiant Dead,            115
And with your puissant Arm renew their Feats:
You are their Heir, you sit upon their Throne;

119      thrice-puissant   *Here as elsewhere in* Henry V, thrice *is used, apparently, to echo both the Spanish word* trés *(three) and the French word* très, *usually rendered "very." (See IV.iv.63 for an instance of direct translation.) But there is also the implication that the King carries in his veins the strength of his "renowned" forebears: Edward III, Edward the Black Prince, and Henry IV.*

120      Youth   *Henry was twenty-seven at this time.*

126      So hath your Highness   *so your Highness has.*

128–
29      Whose . . . France   *who are so eager to be in France on this great mission that their hearts are already "pavilion'd" (encamped in their tents) there.*

132      Spiritualty   *clergy.*

137      lay . . . Proportions   *make provisions.*

138      make road   *invade, make inroads.*

139      With all Advantages   *with every advantage offered him.*

140      Marches   *borders.*

The Blood and Courage that renowned them
Runs in your Veins; and my thrice-puissant Liege
Is in the very May-morn of his Youth,                    120
Ripe for Exploits and mighty Enterprises.

EXETER   Your Brother Kings and Monarchs of the
       Earth
Do all expect that you should rouse your Self
As did the former Lions of your Blood.

WESTMERLAND   They know your Grace hath Cause,
       and Means, and Might;                             125
So hath your Highness. Never King of England
Had Nobles richer and more loyal Subjects,
Whose Hearts have left their Bodies here in
       England
And lie pavilion'd in the Fields of France.

CANTERBURY   O let their Bodies follow, my dear         130
       Liege,
With Blood, and Sword, and Fire, to win your
       Right;
In aid whereof we of the Spiritualty
Will raise your Highness such a mighty Sum
As never did the Clergy at one time
Bring in to any of your Ancestors.                       135

KING   We must not only arm t' invade the French,
But lay down our Proportions to defend
Against the Scot, who will make road upon us
With all Advantages.

CANTERBURY   They of those Marches, gracious
       Sovereign,                                        140
Shall be a Wall sufficient to defend
Our Inland from the pilf'ring Borderers.

305

143 Coursing Snatchers *quick-riding raiders. The King's metaphor derives from the sport of "coursing," where greyhounds chased their prey (usually rabbits) until they "snatched" them with their teeth.* Snatchers *is probably used with sexual innuendo here, to compare the Scots to barbarian rapists. As a noun, "snatch" often referred to another kind of "Breach (line 149) subject to "hot Assays" (line 151).*

144 Main Intendment *both (a) general hostility, and (b) main forces.*

145 still *always.*
   giddy *unreliable, unstable.*

149 Breach *opening.*

151 Galling *chafing, injuring.*
   gleaned *cleaned out, stripped bare of defenders.*
   Assays *attempts, forays.*

152 Girding *encircling.*

154 ill Neighborhood *behavior ill becoming a neighbor.*

155 fear'd *frightened.*

157 Chevalry *chivalry, knights in armor.*

161 King of Scots *King David II, who was captured by the English in 1346 when Edward III was fighting in France. This "Stray" creature was actually imprisoned in London, not France.*

164 Owse *ooze.*

165 Wrack *wrecked ships.*

KING   We do not mean the Coursing Snatchers only,
But fear the Main Intendment of the Scot,
Who hath been still a giddy Neighbor to us:     145
For you shall read that my great-Grandfather
Never went with his Forces into France
But that the Scot on his unfurnish'd Kingdom
Came pouring like the Tide into a Breach,
With ample and brim fullness of his Force     150
Galling the gleaned Land with hot Assays,
Girding with grievous Siege Castles and Towns:
That England, being empty of Defense,
Hath shook and trembled at th' ill Neighborhood.

CANTERBURY   She hath been then more fear'd than
     harm'd, my Liege,     155
For hear her but exampled by her Self:
When all her Chevalry hath been in France,
And she a mourning Widow of her Nobles,
She hath her Self not only well defended
But taken and impounded as a Stray     160
The King of Scots, whom she did send to France
To fill King Edward's Fame with pris'ner Kings
And make their Chronicle as rich with Praise
As is the Owse and Bottom of the Sea
With sunken Wrack and sum-less Treasuries.     165

ELY   But there's a Saying very old and true:
     If that you will France win,
     Then with Scotland first begin.
For once the Eagle (England) being in prey,
To her unguarded Nest the Weasel (Scot)     170
Comes sneaking, and so sucks her Princely Eggs,

307

173     tame   *either (a) subdue, capture, or (b) pierce (from "at-*
          *tame").*
         havoc   *tear to pieces, ravage.*

175     a crush'd Necessity   *either (a) a threat that we can squash,*
         *or (b) a strained reading of our necessities.*

177     pretty   *quaint, so small as to seem toy-like.*

179     advised   *prudent, wise.*

180     Government   *the maintenance of order and harmony*
         *(whether in the state, in the individual soul, or in a musical*
         *composition).*

180–    though . . . parts   *though divided into three estates or*
81       *ranks.*

181     doth keep in one Consent   *consists in the preservation of a*
         *single thought, intention, or theme.*

182     Congreeing   *agreeing, harmonizing.*
         Close   *both (a) cadence, and (b) conclusion.*

186     Aim or Butt   *target.*

188     Rule   *kingdom, ordered realm.*

189     a peopled Kingdom   *a kingdom of human beings.*

191     correct   *maintain the rule of law.*

192     venter Trade   *venture to conduct trade.*

194     Make boot upon   *pillage, obtain booty from.*

Playing the Mouse in absence of the Cat,
To tame and havoc more than she can eat.

EXETER   It follows then the Cat must stay at home;
Yet that is but a crush'd Necessity,                              175
Since we have Locks to safeguard Necessaries
And pretty Traps to catch the petty Thieves.
While that the armed Hand doth fight Abroad,
Th' advised Head defends itself at Home:
For Government, though High and Low and Lower          180
Put into parts, doth keep in one Consent,
Congreeing in a full and nat'ral Close,
Like Music.

CANTERBURY   Therefore doth Heav'n divide
The State of Man in divers Functions,
Setting Endeavor in continual Motion,                          185
To which is fixed, as an Aim or Butt,
Obedience: for so work the Honey-bees,
Creatures that by a Rule in Nature teach
The Act of Order to a peopled Kingdom.
They have a King, and Officers of sorts:                        190
Where some like Magistrates correct at home,
Others like Merchants venter Trade abroad;
Others like Soldiers, armed in their Stings,
Make boot upon the Summer's velvet Buds,
Which Pillage they with merry March bring home          195
To the Tent-royal of their Emperor,
Who, busied in his Majesties, surveys
The singing Masons building Roofs of Gold,
The civil Cit'zens kneading up the Honey,
The poor Mechanic Porters crowding in                         200
Their heavy Burthens at his narrow Gate,

309

202    sad-eyed    *sober-faced.*

203    Executors    *executioners.*

206    contrariously    *individually but to a common purpose.*

207    loosed sev'ral Ways    *shot from different angles.*

210    the Dial's Center    *the center of the sundial.*

211    a foot    *on foot, launched.*

216    withal    *therewith.*
       Gallia    *France.*

220    Hardiness and Policy    *strength and political wisdom.*

224    bend it to our Awe    *make it bow in reverence to us.*

225    Or there    *either there.*

226    Empery    *sovereignty, imperial power.*

228    Urn    *grave.*

229    Tombless    *without a burial monument.*
       Remembrance    *memorial, epitaph.*

231    freely    *uninhibitedly, proudly.*

The sad-eyed Justice with his surly Hum
Deliv'ring o'er to Executors pale
The lazy yawning Drone. I this infer,
That Many Things, having full reference                    205
To One Consent, may work contrariously;
As many Arrows loosed sev'ral Ways
Come to one Mark, as many Ways meet in one Town,
As many fresh Streams meet in one salt Sea,
As many Lines close in the Dial's Center,                  210
So may a thousand Actions once a foot
End in one Purpose, and be all well borne
Without Defeat. Therefore to France, my Liege:
Divide your happy England into four,
Whereof take you one quarter into France,                  215
And you withal shall make all Gallia shake.
If we with thrice such Powers left at Home
Cannot defend our own Doors from the Dog,
Let us be worri'd, and our Nation lose
The Name of Hardiness and Policy.                          220
KING    —Call in the Messengers sent from the
     Dolphin.                    *Exeunt some Attendants.*
  —Now are we well resolv'd, and by God's Help
And yours, the noble Sinews of our Power,
France being ours, we'll bend it to our Awe
Or break it all to pieces. Or there we'll sit,             225
Ruling in large and ample Empery
O'er France and all her almost Kingly Dukedoms,
Or lay these Bones in an unworthy Urn,
Tombless, with no Remembrance over them.
Either our History shall with full Mouth                   230
Speak freely of our Acts, or else our Grave,

232    Like Turkish mute . . . Mouth   *The King alludes to the Turkish practice of cutting out the tongues of slaves in the royal palace to ensure the security of state secrets.*

233    Not . . . Epitaph   *Here* waxen *probably means "with full Mouth" (line 230), fully articulated. Another possibility (the usual explanation) is that the King means "not even adorned with an epitaph of wax, let alone one engraved in stone."*

235    Dolphin   *Shakespeare's rendering of the French "Dauphin."*

238    what we have in charge   *what we have been commissioned to convey.*

239    show you far off   *communicate our message indirectly and tactfully.*

240    Embassy   *purpose in coming.*

242    Grace   *imperial bearing, magnanimity.*
        Passion   *personal feelings.*

243    Wretches   *convicts.*

245    in few   *in a few words, briefly.*

250    savor too much   *have too much of the flavor.*

251    bids you be advis'd   *suggests that you take note.*

252    Galliard   *a merry, sprightly dance.*

253    revel   *sport your way.*

Like Turkish mute, shall have a Tongueless
    Mouth,
Not worshipp'd with a waxen Epitaph.

*Enter the Ambassadors of France, attended.*

—Now are we well prepar'd to know the Pleasure
Of our fair Cousin Dolphin. For we hear      235
Your Greeting is from him, not from the King.
AMBASSADOR   May 't please your Majesty to give us
    leave
Freely to render what we have in charge,
Or shall we sparingly show you far off
The Dolphin's Meaning and our Embassy?      240
KING  We are no Tyrant, but a Christian King,
Unto whose Grace our Passion is as subject
As is our Wretches fett'red in our Prisons:
Therefore with frank and with uncurbed
    Plainness
Tell us the Dolphin's Mind.
AMBASSADOR            Thus then in few:    245
Your Highness, lately sending into France,
Did claim some certain Dukedoms, in the Right
Of your great Predecess'r, King Edw'rd the
    Third.
In answer of which Claim the Prince our Master
Says that you savor too much of your Youth      250
And bids you be advis'd: there's nought in
    France
That can be with a nimble Galliard won;
You cannot revel into Dukedoms there.

313

254      meeter for your Spirit    *more suitable for your disposition.*

255      Tun    *barrel.*
        in lieu of this    *in return for this, with this as a substitute.*

263      Crown    *both (a) the French throne, and (b) a coin represent-*
        *ing the sum customarily wagered on the outcome of a match.*
        into the Hazard    *both (a) into jeopardy, and (b) into one of*
        *the openings in the wall surrounding the tennis court (thereby*
        *scoring a point, according to the rules of Renaissance tennis).*

264      Wrangler    *opponent, disputant.*

266      Chaces    *both (a) hunting pursuits (chases), and (b) points*
        *scored when one's opponent fails to return tennis balls.*

267      comes o'er    *taunts, ridicules.*

270      hence    *away from the "Seat" (throne), such as in the Boar's*
        *Head Tavern.*

273      keep my State    *both (a) stay on my throne, and (b) maintain*
        *the bearing befitting a monarch.*

274      show . . . Greatness    *The King compares his "Greatness"*
        *to a sail swollen to the full with wind. The sexual suggestive-*
        *ness of this "rousing" image is fulfilled in the final scene of the*
        *play.*

276      For that    *for.*

277      like a Man for Working-days    *like a common day-laborer.*

282      his Balls    *tennis balls. If the King intends a pun on testicles as*
        *well (compare II.iv.131–32), his image anticipates another*
        *modern idiom ("balls" as a symbol of manhood or resolve).*

He therefore sends you, meeter for your Spirit,
This Tun of Treasure, and in lieu of this                    255
Desires you let the Dukedoms that you claim
Hear no more of you. This the Dolphin speaks.

KING  —What Treasure, Uncle?

EXETER                Tennis-balls, my Liege.

KING  We are glad the Dolphin is so pleasant with us.
His Present and your Pains we thank you for:               260
When we have match'd our Rackets to these Balls,
We will in France, by God's Grace, play a Set
Shall strike his Father's Crown into the Hazard.
Tell him he hath made a Match with such a
   Wrangler
That all the Courts of France will be disturb'd            265
With Chaces. And we understand him well,
How he comes o'er us with our Wilder Days,
Not measuring what use we made of them.
We never valu'd this poor Seat of England,
And therefore, living hence, did give our self             270
To barb'rous License, as 'tis ever common
That Men are merriest when they are from home.
But tell the Dolphin I will keep my State,
Be like a King, and show my Sail of Greatness
When I do rouse me in my Throne of France.                 275
For that I have laid by my Majesty
And plodded like a Man for Working-days,
But I will rise there with so full a Glory
That I will dazzle all the Eyes of France,
Yea strike the Dolphin blind to look on us.                280
And tell the pleasant Prince this Mock of his
Hath turn'd his Balls to Gunstones, and his Soul

315

283     sore charged    *gravely responsible.*

287     ungotten    *unconceived.*

292     as I may    *as I am able to do.*

297     Convey . . . Conduct.    *The King addresses this line to those who will escort the Ambassadors back to their ship.*

298     merry    *Here, as is usually the case, the word refers to a biting jest.*

299     blush at it    *be ashamed of it, and embarrassed by it.*

300     omit no happy Hour    *waste no time, neglect no opportunity.*

301     Expedition    *Here the King refers to the upcoming journey, but his word also conveys the idea of urgency (as in "expedite," hasten).*

303     run before    *precede. In lines 302–3 the King probably refers to the prayers that will be offered to request a successful undertaking.*
        our Business    *the work we have to do, but* business *often refers specifically to a man's "business," and in view of the earlier wordplay on "Balls," an assertion of sexual machismo is very much to the point here.*

304     Proportions    *forces and supplies.*

307     God before    *with God in our vanguard, leading us on.*

309     task his Thought    *engage his mind and will.*

Shall stand sore charged for the wasteful Vengeance
That shall fly with them: for many a thousand
      Widows
Shall this his Mock mock out of their dear
      Husbands,                                                      285
Mock Mothers from their Sons, mock Castles down;
And some are yet ungotten and unborn
That shall have cause to curse the Dolphin's Scorn.
But this lies all within the Will of God,
To whom I do appeal, and in whose Name            290
Tell you the Dolphin I am coming on
To venge me as I may, and to put forth
My rightful Hand in a well-hallow'd Cause.
So get you hence in peace: and tell the Dolphin
His Jest will savor but of shallow Wit               295
When thousands weep more than did laugh at it.
—Convey them with safe Conduct. —Fare you
      well.                                    *Exeunt Ambassadors.*
EXETER   This was a merry Message.
KING   We hope to make the Sender blush at it.
      Therefore, my Lords, omit no happy Hour       300
      That may give furth'rance to our Expedition:
      For we have now no Thought in us but France,
      Save those to God, that run before our Business.
      Therefore let our Proportions for these Wars
      Be soon collected, and all things be thought upon   305
      That may with reasonable Swiftness add
      More Feathers to our Wings. For God before,
      We'll chide this Dolphin at his Father's Door.
      Therefore let ev'ry Man now task his Thought
      That this fair Action may on Foot be brought. *Exeunt.*   310

3¹7

II. Chorus   *Here as elsewhere, the Chorus stands outside the action of the play, "containing" and commenting on it.*

2   silken Dalliance   *luxurious idleness, here personified as a silken garment that has been stored away in the "Wardrobe."*

3   Honor's Thought   *thoughts ruled by Honor (military valor).*

4   solely   *alone, without competition from other thoughts.*

6   Mirror   *model, ideal image.*

7   Mercuries   *an allusion to the winged messenger of the Gods.*

9   hides   *carries in a sheath.*
    Hilts   *hilt, usually treated as a plural in Shakespeare's time and referring to the arms of the crosspiece protecting the hand.*

10   Crowns Imperial   *crowns worn by kings who rule more than one kingdom, as Henry V aspires to do.*
     Coronets   *the small crowns worn by noblemen.*

12   advis'd   *informed.*

13   dreadful   *frightening.*

14   pale Policy   *bloodless (cowardly) political cunning rather than forthright, honorable valor.*

318

# Act Two

*Flourish. Enter Chorus.*

CHORUS   Now all the Youth of England are on fire,
And silken Dalliance in the Wardrobe lies;
Now thrive the Armorers, and Honor's Thought
Reigns solely in the Breast of ev'ry Man.
They sell the Pasture now to buy the Horse,                    5
Foll'wing the Mirror of all Christian Kings
With winged Heels as English Mercuries.
For now sits Expectation in the Air
And hides a Sword, from Hilts unto the Point,
With Crowns Imperial, Crowns, and Coronets,                   10
Promis'd to Harry and his Followers.
The French, advis'd by good Intelligence
Of this most dreadful Preparation,
Shake in their Fear, and with pale Policy
Seek to divert the English Purposes.                          15

3¹9

16    Model to    *image of. In lines 16–17 the Chorus refers to England's small size, as contrasted with her large role in world affairs.*

19    kind    *here, a near synonym for "natural," referring to the "kind" of children a great nation like England fittingly produces.*

20    Fault    *fissure, breach, point of weakness.*

21    hollow    *empty of fidelity and valor.*
       Bosoms    *both (a) hearts, and (b) upper garments.*

26    Gilt    *gold-plated coins (the "Crowns" referred to in line 22).*

27    Confirm'd    *agreed to, plotted.*
       fearful    *frightened, cowardly.*

28    this Grace of Kings    *this emblem of the grace (kingly virtues) that should characterize a monarch.*

31–32 digest . . . Distance    *summarize the ways in which our play abuses the classical doctrine that a dramatic work should all take place within a single setting. This was one of the "three unities"; the other two pertained to time (the notion that a play should cover no more than a 24-hour period) and action (the notion that a play should have only a single, unified plot).*

38    charming    *taming, subduing.*

39    gentle Pass    *easy passage. The English Channel was proverbial for its rough waters and treacherous currents.*

—O England, Model to thy inward Greatness,
Like little Body with a mighty Heart,
What mightst thou do that Honor would thee do
Were all thy Children kind and natural!
But see, thy Fault France hath in thee found
   out,                               20
A Nest of hollow Bosoms, which he fills
With treach'rous Crowns; and three corrupted
   Men,
One, Richard, Earl of Cambridge, and the second,
Henry, Lord Scroop of Masham, and the third,
Sir Thomas Grey, Knight, of Northumberland,    25
Have for the Gilt of France (O Guilt indeed!)
Confirm'd Conspiracy with fearful France,
And by their Hands this Grace of Kings must
   die,
If Hell and Treason hold their Promises,
Ere he take ship for France, and in Southampton.   30
—Linger your Patience on, and we'll digest
Th' abuse of Distance, force a Play.
The Sum is paid, the Traitors are agreed,
The King is set from London, and the Scene
Is now transported, Gentles, to Southampton.   35
There is the Playhouse now, there must you sit,
And thence to France shall we convey you safe
And bring you back, charming the narrow Seas
To give you gentle Pass: for if we may,
We'll not offend one Stomach with our Play.   40
But till the King come forth, and not till then,
Unto Southampton do we shift our Scene.    *Exit.*

II.i     *Even though the Chorus has just told us that the scene is now Southampton (a port city to the south and west of London), this episode appears to occur on a street in London.*

2     Lieutenant    *In* 2 Henry IV *Bardolph is called a corporal; here he appears to have both titles (compare III.ii.3).*

3     Ancient    *ensign, the officer who bore the standard (the military colors).*

8     wink    *shut my eyes (presumably to disregard the prohibitions against private dueling).*
       hold out    *thrust. Nym seems to be saying that although he will not initiate a quarrel, he will not decline one if it is offered him.*

9     what though?    *what of that?*

9–10     It will toast Cheese    *Swords were frequently described as "smoking" and as causing their victims to smoke. Nym's image is a variation on that metaphor for hot thrusting. He may also be alluding to the heating and cooling process involved in tempering steel for durable swords.*

10     endure Cold    *tolerate inaction.*

13–14     sworn Brothers to France    *loyal friends as we depart for France. The "brotherhood" that has characterized these "Friends" in the past is the fraternity of thieves, and there is a suggestion that that fellowship will now be restored.*

18     Rendezvous    *resort or refuge.*

21     Troth-plight    *betrothed, promised to marry.*

322

# Scene 1

*Enter Corporal Nym and Lieutenant Bardolph.*

BARDOLPH   Well met, Corporal Nym.

NYM   Good morrow, Lieutenant Bardolph.

BARDOLPH   What, are Ancient Pistol and you Friends
yet?

NYM   For my part, I care not. I say little; but when          5
Time shall serve, there shall be Smiles. But
that shall be as it may. I dare not fight, but
I will wink and hold out mine Iron; it is a
simple one, but what though? It will toast
Cheese, and it will endure Cold, as another          10
man's Sword will, and there's an end.

BARDOLPH   I will bestow a Breakfast to make you
Friends, and we'll be all three sworn Brothers
to France. Let 't be so, good Corporal Nym.

NYM   Faith, I will live so long as I may, that's          15
the certain of it; and when I cannot live any
longer, I will do as I may. That is my Rest,
that is the Rendezvous of it.

BARDOLPH   It is certain, Corporal, that he is
married to Nell Quickly, and certainly she did          20
you wrong, for you were Troth-plight to her.

NYM   I cannot tell. Things must be as they may: Men

23–25   **and . . . Edges**   *Nym implies that he is harboring thoughts of revenge.*

25–26   **though . . . plod**   *Nym compares Patience (here meaning "forbearance") to a worn-out jade; his implication is that, even though she is reputed to be slow to be moved (presumably to wrath), she will eventually come to "Conclusions" (an act of vengeance). Most editors here adopt the reading of the First Quarto and substitute "Mare" for the Folio text's "Name."*

31   **Tike**   *cur, mongrel.*
     **Host**   *Pistol assumes that by "Host" Bardolph means "bawd." In the following speech the Hostess also rejects the implication that she is the proprietress of a brothel.*

36–37   **by the prick . . . Needles**   *The Hostess' image comically undercuts the point she wishes to make. "Needles" can refer either (a) to the male instruments that "prick" these "Gentlewomen" or (b) to the female "eyes" that get pricked. In either case, what the Hostess intends as an image of respectable domestic employment becomes an unintended reminder of another means of livelihood.*

39   **welliday, Lady**   *a mild oath, referring to the Virgin Mary.*
     **hewn**   *cut down. Most editors emend to either "drawn" or "here."*

42–43   **offer nothing**   *do not offer (threaten) to fight.*

45   **Iseland dog**   *probably a reference to an Iceland terrier.*

47–48   **put up**   *put away.*

may sleep, and they may have their Throats
about them at that time; and some say Knives
have Edges. It must be as it may; though
Patience be a tired Name, yet she will plod;
there must be Conclusions. Well, I cannot tell.

*Enter Pistol and Quickly.*

BARDOLPH   Here comes Ancient Pistol and his Wife.
  Good Corporal, be patient here. —How now,
  mine Host Pistol?
PISTOL   Base Tike, call'st thou me Host? Now by
    this Hand,
  I swear I scorn the term; nor shall my Nell
  Keep Lodgers.
HOSTESS   No, by my troth, not long. For we cannot
  lodge and board a dozen or fourteen
  Gentlewomen that live honestly by the prick
  of their Needles but it will be thought we
  keep a Bawdy-house straight.
                              *Nym and Pistol draw.*
  O welliday, Lady, if he be not hewn now, we
  shall see willful Adultery and Murther
  committed!
BARDOLPH   Good Lieutenant, good Corporal, offer
  nothing here!
NYM   Pish!
PISTOL   Pish for thee, Iseland Dog! Thou prick-ear'd
  Cur of Iseland!
HOSTESS   Good Corporal Nym, show thy Valor and put
  up your Sword.

25

30

35

40

45

325

49      shog off   *come along, step aside (to fight with me).*
        solus   *alone.*

51      mervailous   *marvelous.*

53      Maw   *stomach.*
        perdy   *a corruption of the French "par Dieu" (by God).*

55      retort   *reply, counter; literally, return.*

56      take   *take you, harm you.*
        and   *Pistol probably means "if" here.*
        Pistol's Cock is up   *Pistol is cocked, ready for firing. The
            image also has sexual implications, but here Pistol refers pri-
            marily to the arousal of his valor.*

58      Barbason   *the name of a devil. Pistol's preceding speech has
            been a parody of the rite employed by priests to exorcise demons,
            conjuring them out of the bodies they possess (inhabit).*

59      indifferently well   *tolerably. In contrast to Pistol's bombastic
            hyperbole, Nym's language is ludicrously mild.*

64      the Humour of it   *the disposition I'm in.*

65      Wight   *man (a "poetically" archaic term).*

71      mickle   *great.*

72      Fist   *hand.*

73      tall   *valiant.*

76      Couple a gorge!   *corrupt French for "cut the throat!"*

78      Spittle   *probably " 'spital" (hospital).*

NYM    Will you shog off? I would have you solus.

PISTOL    Solus, egregious Dog? O Viper vile!    50
  The Solus in thy most mervailous Face;
  The Solus in thy Teeth, and an' thy Throat,
  And in thy hateful Lungs, yea in thy Maw perdy;
  And, which is worse, within thy nasty Mouth!
  I do retort the Solus in thy Bowels,    55
  For I can take, and Pistol's Cock is up,
  And flashing Fire will follow.

NYM    I am not Barbason, you cannot conjure me. I
  have an humour to knock you indifferently well.
  If you grow foul with me, Pistol, I will scour    60
  you with my Rapier, as I may, in fair Terms.
  If you would walk off, I would prick your Guts
  a little in good Terms, as I may, and that's
  the Humour of it.

PISTOL    O Braggard vile, and damned furious Wight,    65
  The Grave doth gape, and doting Death is near:
  Therefore exhale.

BARDOLPH    Hear me, hear me what I say: he that
  strikes the first Stroke, I'll run him up to
  the Hilts, as I am a Soldier.    *He draws.*    70

PISTOL    An Oath of mickle Might, and Fury shall
  abate.
  —Give me thy Fist, thy Fore-foot to me give:
  Thy Spirits are most tall.

NYM    I will cut thy Throat one time or other in
  fair Terms; that is the Humour of it.    75

PISTOL    *Couple a gorge!* That is the Word. I thee
  Defy again. O Hound of Crete, think'st thou
  My Spouse to get? No, to the Spittle go,

79     Powd'ring-tub   *a sweating tub used to treat venereal disease.*

80     Lazar Kite of Cressid's kind   *diseased prostitute.*

81     espouse   *marry.*

82     Quondam   *former (with the implication that she has now taken on her new husband's name).*

84     Pauca   *in a few words.*

88     do the Office   *serve the function.*

91     yield the Crow a Pudding   *a proverbial expression for dying on the gallows and thus becoming food for predatory birds. The Hostess refers to Falstaff's cheeky Page, who has just made a gratuitous gibe at Bardolph, suggesting that his fire-like complexion would make his face a good warming-pan for a bed.*

92–93     The King . . . Heart.   *The Hostess suggests that Falstaff is dying of a broken heart because of his rejection by the new King.*

93     presently   *right away.*

96     keep Knives   *keep our knives in readiness.*

97     Let Floods . . . on!   *Pistol's rant carries the implication that his wrath is no more controllable than overflowing rivers and ravenous fiends.*

102     As Manhood shall compound   *[that will be] as valor shall determine.*

And from the Powd'ring-tub of Infamy
Fetch forth the Lazar Kite of Cressid's kind,                80
Doll Tearsheet, she by name, and her espouse.
I have and I will hold the Quondam Quickly
For the only She.
And *Pauca,* there's enough to go to.

*Enter the Boy.*

BOY   Mine Host Pistol, you must come to my Maister,     85
and your Hostess: he is very sick, and would
to Bed. —Good Bardolph, put thy Face between
his Sheets and do the Office of a Warming-pan.
Faith, he's very ill.

BARDOLPH   Away you Rogue!                                90

HOSTESS   By my troth, he'll yield the Crow a Pudding
one of these days. The King has kill'd his
Heart. —Good Husband, come home presently.
                                   *Exit, with Boy.*

BARDOLPH   Come, shall I make you two Friends? We
must to France together. Why the Divel should     95
we keep Knives to cut one another's Throats?

PISTOL   Let Floods o'er-swell, and Fiends for Food
howl on!

NYM   You'll pay me the eight Shillings I won of you
at Betting?

PISTOL   Base is the Slave that pays.                     100

NYM   That now I will have: that's the Humour of it.

PISTOL   As Manhood shall compound: push home!
              *They draw, and Bardolph draws to part them.*

BARDOLPH   By this Sword, he that makes the first

329

106    and    *if.*

111    A Noble    *a third of a pound, equivalent to six shillings, eight pence.*
       present Pay    *immediate payment.*

113    shall combine    *shall come with it.*

115    Sutler    *seller of food and other provisions.*

123    quotidian Tertian    *The Hostess combines two types of fever: the quotidian ague came every day, the tertian every other day.*

125    hath . . . Knight    *Nym's language for "has treated the Knight badly."*

126    the Even of it    *the plain truth.*

128    fracted    *fractured.*
       corroborate    *This word normally means "strengthened" or "supported"; Pistol probably means the opposite of that: corrupted and broken to pieces.*

130    he passes . . . Careers    *What Nym probably means is that the King sometimes gets carried away and goes too far. To pass a career in horsemanship was to gallop for a short distance at full speed.*

Thrust, I'll kill him; by this Sword I will!

PISTOL   Sword is an Oath, and Oaths must have their
    Course.                                                        105

BARDOLPH   Corporal Nym, and thou wilt be Friends,
    be Friends; and thou wilt not, why then be
    Enemies with me too: prethee put up.

NYM   I shall have my eight Shillings I won from
    you at Betting?                                                110

PISTOL   A Noble shalt thou have, and present Pay,
    And Liquor likewise will I give to thee,
    And Friendship shall combine, and Brotherhood.
    I'll live by Nym, and Nym shall live by me:
    Is not this just? For I shall Sutler be                        115
    Unto the Camp, and Profits will accrue.
    Give me thy Hand.

NYM   I shall have my Noble?

PISTOL   In Cash, most justly paid.

NYM   Well then, that's the Humour of 't.                          120

*Enter Hostess.*

HOSTESS   As ever you come of Women, come in quickly
    to Sir John! Ah poor Heart, he is so shak'd of
    a burning quotidian Tertian, that it is most
    lamentable to behold. Sweet Men, come to him!

NYM   The King hath run bad Humours on the Knight,                 125
    that's the Even of it.

PISTOL   Nym, thou hast spoke the Right:
    His Heart is fracted and corroborate.

NYM   The King is a good King, but it must be as it
    may: he passes some Humours and Careers.                       130

33¹

131     condole    *comfort, sympathize with.*

131–    for . . . live    *What Pistol seems to mean is that eventually*
32         *we will all be in need of the same comforting Falstaff now*
           *requires. He may also be implying that sooner or later the King*
           *will treat his other former companions with just as little com-*
           *passion as they believe he has shown to Falstaff.*

II.ii     *We now proceed to Southampton, where the King and his forces*
          *are preparing to set sail for France.*

1       bold    *daring, confident of his security.*

4       sate    *sat.*

6       hath note    *has been notified.*

8       Bedfellow    *dearest friend. Exeter refers to Lord Scroop, of*
           *whom Holinshed says that in his "fidelity the King reposed*
           *such trust that when any private or public council was in*
           *hand, this Lord had much in the determination of it."*

9       dull'd and cloy'd    *satiated (satisfied and surfeited).*

12      aboord    *aboard. The ships are ready to set sail.*

332

PISTOL   Let us condole the Knight, for, Lambkins,
   we will live.                                         *Exeunt.*


# Scene 2

*Enter Exeter, Bedford, and Westmerland.*

BEDFORD   'Fore God, his Grace is bold to trust
   these Traitors.
EXETER   They shall be apprehended by and by.
WESTMERLAND   How smooth and even they do bear
   themselves,
   As if Allegiance in their Bosoms sate,
   Crowned with Faith and constant Loyalty.                    5
BEDFORD   The King hath note of all that they intend,
   By Interception which they dream not of.
EXETER   Nay, but the Man that was his Bedfellow,
   Whom he hath dull'd and cloy'd with gracious
   Favors:
   That he should for a Foreign Purse so sell                 10
   His Sov'reign's Life to Death and Treachery!

*Sound Trumpets. Enter the King, Scroop, Cambridge,
   and Grey, with Attendants.*

KING   Now sits the Wind fair, and we will aboord.


333

13    Lord of Masham    *Henry, third Baron Scroop of Masham.*

14    Knight    *Sir Thomas Grey of Northumberland.*

15    Pow'rs    *armed forces.*

16    Force    *armies, defensive forces.*

17    Doing . . . Act    *performing the mission.*

22    fair Consent    *perfect agreement.*

27    Heart-grief    *discontent.*

30    steep'd their Galls    *soaked their bitterness.*

31    create    *created, newly born.*
      Zeal    *fervent loyalty.*

33–35  And . . . Worthiness    *The King is saying that before he
       fails to reward those who deserve it, he will cease to function as
       king. His expression may allude to Psalm 137:5, "If I forget
       thee, O Jerusalem, let my right hand forget her cunning."*
       Quittance *means payment, recompense.*

36    steeled Sinews    *strength of steel-like durability.*

—My Lord of Cambridge, and my kind Lord of
  Masham,
And you, my gentle Knight, give me your Thoughts:
Think you not that the Pow'rs we bear with us            15
Will cut their passage through the Force of
  France,
Doing the Execution and the Act
For which we have in head assembled them?

SCROOP  No doubt, my Liege, if each Man do his best.

KING  I doubt not that, since we are well persuaded      20
  We carry not a Heart with us from hence
  That grows not in a fair Consent with ours,
  Nor leave not one behind that doth not wish
  Success and Conquest to attend on us.

CAMBRIDGE  Never was Monarch better fear'd and
  lov'd                                                  25
  Than is your Majesty; there's not, I think, a
    Subject
  That sits in Heart-grief and Uneasiness
  Under the sweet Shade of your Government.

GREY  True: those that were your Father's Enemies
  Have steep'd their Galls in Honey and do serve
    you                                                  30
  With Hearts create of Duty and of Zeal.

KING  We therefore have great Cause of Thankfulness
  And shall forget the Office of our Hand
  Sooner than Quittance of Desert and Merit
  According to the Weight and Worthiness.                35

SCROOP  So Service shall with steeled Sinews toil,
  And Labor shall refresh itself with Hope

38   incessant   *unceasing.*

40   Enlarge   *release.*

41   rail'd   *spoke out, complained.*

43   on his more Advice   *now that he has come to his senses and reconsidered what he said.*

44   Security   *Scroop means "false security," a self-confidence that results from a foolish lack of caution.*

46   by his Suff'rance   *by his crime being suffered (tolerated) without punishment.*

47   yet   *nevertheless, still.*

49–50   Sir . . . Correction.   *Grey is saying that the King would still be showing mercy if he punished the man and then released him.*

52   heavy Orisons   *weighty pleas.*

53   proceeding on Distemper   *resulting from an imbalance of the humours or from a failure to govern his passions by reason.*

54   wink'd at   *disregarded (literally, looked at with closed eyes).*
     stretch our Eye   *open our eye wide to see.*

57   dear   *priceless because heartfelt.*

60   the late Commissioners   *the newly commissioned officers (to act in the King's stead while he is away in France).*

To do your Grace incessant Services.

KING    We judge no less. —Uncle of Exeter,
    Enlarge the Man committed yesterday                          40
    That rail'd against our Person: we consider
    It was excess of Wine that set him on,
    And on his more Advice we pardon him.

SCROOP    That's Mercy, but too much Security:
    Let him be punish'd, Sov'reign, lest Example                 45
    Breed by his Suff'rance more of such a kind.

KING    O let us yet be merciful.

CAMBRIDGE    So may your Highness, and yet punish
    too.

GREY    Sir, you show great Mercy if you give him Life
    After the taste of much Correction.                          50

KING    Alas, your too much Love and Care of me
    Are heavy Orisons 'gainst this poor Wretch:
    If little Faults, proceeding on Distemper,
    Shall not be wink'd at, how sh'll we stretch
      our Eye
    When Cap'tal Crimes, chew'd, swallow'd, and
      digested,                                                 55
    Appear before us? We'll yet enlarge that Man,
    Though Cambridge, Scroop, and Grey, in their
      dear Care
    And tender Preservation of our Person,
    Would have him pun'sh'd. And now to our French
      Causes:
    Who are the late Commissioners?

CAMBRIDGE                          I one, my Lord:               60
    Your Highness bade me ask for it today.

SCROOP    So did you me, my Liege.

337

68     aboord    *aboard.*

70     Complexion    *skin color. But in this instance the word also retains its original psychological sense, referring to the composition (ideally in balance) of the four humours in the human body. The three conspirators have suddenly exhibited a deficiency in the humour known as Blood (a hot, moist substance derived from the element Air).*

73     Apparance    *"Apparentness," visibility.*

76     quick    *both (a) alive, and (b) rapid.*

78     for Shame    *because of your sense of shame.*

80     Maisters    *masters. This spelling, which occurs frequently in Shakespeare, is a reminder that the modern word derives from the Latin* magister.
        worrying    *baiting, harassing, tearing at.*

82     English Monsters    *monstrosities, freaks; deformed versions of true Englishmen.*

83     apt    *eager, ready.*
        accord    *agree, consent.*

84     appertinents    *appurtenances, things pertaining to.*

86     lightly    *easily, without considering the grave consequences.*

GREY                          And I, my royal Sovereign.

KING   Then Richard, Earl of Cambridge, there is
    yours.
    —There yours, Lord Scroop of Masham. —And
    Sir Knight,
    Grey of Northumberland, this same is yours.        65
    Read them, and know I know your Worthiness.
    —My Lord of Westmerland, and Uncle Exeter,
    We will aboord tonight. —Why how now,
    Gentlemen?
    What see you in those Papers, that you lose
    So much Complexion? —Look ye how they change:   70
    Their Cheeks are Paper! —Why, what read you
    there
    That have so cowarded and chas'd your Blood
    Out of Apparance?

CAMBRIDGE              I do confess my Fault,
    And do submit me to your Highness' Mercy.

GREY, SCROOP   To which we all appeal.               75

KING   The Mercy that was quick in us but late
    By your own Counsel is suppress'd and kill'd.
    You must not dare, for Shame, to talk of Mercy,
    For your own Reasons turn into your Bosoms,
    As Dogs upon their Maisters, worrying you.        80
    —See you, my Princes, and my Noble Peers,
    These English Monsters. My Lord of Cambridge
    here,
    You know how apt our Love was, to accord
    To furnish him with all appertinents
    Belonging to his Honor; and this Man              85
    Hath for a few light Crowns lightly conspir'd

339

87    Practices    *intrigues, plots.*

88    Hampton    *Southampton.*

92    inhumane    *the normal Elizabethan spelling for* inhuman, *and one that usually contains the sense of the other modern word as well.*

95    coin'd me into Gold    *As Lord Treasurer, Scroop was responsible for the coining of money bearing the King's image. The King suggests that he has now tried to convert the King himself into currency by selling him and his royal Crown for "a few light Crowns" of French money.*

99    annoy    *injure (a much stronger word in Shakespeare's time).*

100    gross    *starkly obvious.*

103    Yoke-divels    *devils yoked together like oxen.*

104    Working . . . Cause    *working so openly in a cause in which they are natural allies.*

105    That Admiration . . . them    *that astonishment did whoop (cry out) at the disclosure of what they had done.*

109    prepost'rously    *literally, putting first what should be last; against nature, in defiance of all conceptions of normality. The King's phrasing suggests that the "Fiend" that "wrought upon" Scroop did so "grossly" (line 104).*

110    the Voice . . . Excellence    *the acknowledged preeminence in Hell.*

111    suggest by Treasons    *tempt to acts of treachery.*

And sworn unto the Practices of France
To kill us here in Hampton. To the which,
This Knight, no less for Bounty bound to us
Than Cambridge is, hath likewise sworn. —But O,     90
What shall I say to thee, Lord Scroop, thou
    cruel,
Ingrateful, savage, and inhumane Creature?
Thou, that didst bear the Key of all my
    Counsels,
That knew'st the very Bottom of my Soul,
That almost might'st have coin'd me into Gold,     95
Would'st thou have practic'd on me for thy
    Use?
May it be possible that Foreign Hire
Could out of thee extract one spark of Evil
That might annoy my Finger? 'Tis so strange
That, though the truth of it stands off as
    gross     100
As Black and White, my Eye will scarcely see
    it.
Treason and Murther ever kept together,
As two Yoke-divels sworn to either's purpose,
Working so grossly in a nat'ral Cause
That Admiration did not hoop at them.     105
But thou, 'gainst all Proportion, didst bring
    in
Wonder to wait on Treason and on Murther.
And whatsoever cunning Fiend it was
That wrought upon thee so prepost'rously
Hath got the Voice in Hell for Excellence;     110
And other Divels that suggest by Treasons

34¹

112–  botch . . . Piety  *clumsily patch together a pretext for dam-*
14  *nable temptations from an assortment of seemingly pious mo-*
*tives.*

115  temper'd  *molded, worked on.*
bade thee stand up  *urged you to raise your head in rebellion.*

116  Instance  *reason, argument.*

117  dub thee . . . Traitor  *knight you as a member of the Order*
*of Traitors.*

118  Daemon  *demon, inner spirit.*

119  Lion-gait  *an allusion to 1 Peter 5:8, "your adversary the*
*devil, as a roaring lion, walketh about, seeking whom he may*
*devour."*

120  vasty Tartar  *vast Hell. Tartarus was the pit of torment in*
*Hades.*

121  Legions  *an allusion to Mark 5:9, where the "unclean spirit"*
*conjured out of the demon-possessed man tells Jesus "My name*
*is Legion."*

123  Jealousy  *suspicion.*

124  Affiance  *faith, trust.*
Show Men Dutiful?  *Do men appear to be dutiful?*

131  modest Complement  *a well-mannered, decorous demeanor.*

134  bolted  *sifted, and thus pure and refined.*

136  full-fraught  *fully laden, bountifully endowed.*
indued  *clothed.*

Do botch and bungle up Damnation
With Patches, Colors, and with Forms being
  fetch'd
From glist'ring Semblances of Piety;
But he that temper'd thee, bade thee stand up,      115
Gave thee no Instance why thou shouldst do
  Treason,
Unless to dub thee with the Name of Traitor.
If that same Daemon that hath gull'd thee thus
Should with his Lion-gait walk the whole World,
He might return to vasty Tartar back      120
And tell the Legions "I can never win
A Soul so easy as that Englishman's."
O, how hast thou with Jealousy infected
The Sweetness of Affiance? Show Men Dutiful?
Why so didst thou. Seem they Grave and Learned?    125
Why so didst thou. Come they of Noble Family?
Why so didst thou. Seem they Religious?
Why so didst thou. Or are they spare in Diet,
Free from gross Passion, or of Mirth or Anger?
Constant in Spirit, not swerving with the
  Blood?      130
Garnish'd and deck'd in modest Complement?
Not working with the Eye without the Ear,
And but in purged Judgment trusting neither?
Such and so finely bolted didst thou seem:
And thus thy Fall hath left a kind of Blot      135
To make thee, full-fraught Man and best,
  indued
With some Suspicion. I will weep for thee,
For this Revolt of thine, methinks, is like

139     open    *manifest, beyond any doubt.*

141     acquit . . . Practices    *forgive them for their treachery.*

148     discover'd    *uncovered, revealed.*

150     Which    *Scroop refers to "my Fault" (crime).*

153     admit . . . Motive    *accept it as a means of effecting my aims. Cambridge's true motive was to remove Henry V from the throne and replace him with the Earl's brother-in-law, Edmund Mortimer, the fifth Earl of March, who had a better claim to the title. This issue had emerged earlier (see* 1 Henry IV, *I.iii.138–57), and it would prove to be the seed for the conflict between the houses of York and Lancaster that would result in the Wars of the Roses. If Cambridge had succeeded in his plot, he might have eventually become King himself: Mortimer was childless, and the crown would have descended to Cambridge through his marriage to Mortimer's sister, Anne Mortimer.*

156     in Suff'rance    *in my suffering.*

163     our Royal Person    *Here the King refers to himself not merely as a man but as an embodiment of the institution of kingship: the monarch as the mystical epitome of the Body Politic.*

166     Earnest of    *down payment for.*

Another Fall of Man. —Their Faults are open:
Arrest them to the Answer of the Law, 140
And God acquit them of their Practices.

EXETER  —I arrest thee of High Treason, by the
Name of Richard, Earl of Cambridge.
  —I arrest thee of High Treason, by the Name
of Henry, Lord Scroop of Masham. 145
  —I arrest thee of High Treason, by the Name
of Thomas Grey, Knight, of Northumberland.

SCROOP  Our Purposes God justly hath discover'd,
And I repent my Fault more than my Death,
Which I beseech your Highness to forgive, 150
Although my Body pay the Price of it.

CAMBRIDGE  For me the Gold of France did not
  seduce,
Although I did admit it as a Motive,
The sooner to effect what I intended.
But God be thanked for Prevention, 155
Which I in Suff'rance heart'ly will rejoice,
Beseeching God, and you, to pardon me.

GREY  Never did faithful Subject more rejoice
At the Discov'ry of most dang'rous Treason
Than I do at this Hour joy o'er my self, 160
Prevented from a damned Enterprise.
My Fault, but not my Body, pardon, Sov'reign.

KING  God quit you in his Mercy. Hear your Sentence.
You have conspir'd against our Royal Person,
Join'd with an Enemy proclaim'd, and from his
  Coffers 165
Receiv'd the Golden Earnest of our Death,

171    Touching   *concerning, with respect to.*

172    tender   *hold in regard.*

180    like   *alike, equally.*

185    But   *but that.*
       Rub   *impediment. The King alludes to the game of bowls, where a "rub" was anything in the path of the bowled ball that might send it off course.*

187    Puissance   *power; here pronounced "pú-ee-sance."*

188    straight in Expedition   *immediately into swift motion.*

189    Signs   *banners, insignia, carried by ensigns.*
       advance   *hold aloft.*

Wherein you would have sold your King to
   Slaughter,
His Princes and his Peers to Servitude,
His Subjects to Oppression and Contempt,
And his whole Kingdom into Desolation.                    170
Touching our Person, seek we no Revenge,
But we our Kingdom's Safety must so tender,
Whose Ruin you have sought, that to her Laws
We do deliver you. Get you therefore hence,
Poor miserable Wretches, to your Death,                   175
The taste whereof God of His Mercy give
You Patience to endure, and true Repentance
Of all your dear Offenses. —Bear them hence.
        *Exeunt Cambridge, Scroop, and Grey under Guard.*
—Now Lords, for France: the Enterprise whereof
Shall be to you as us, like glorious.                     180
We doubt not of a fair and lucky War,
Since God so graciously hath brought to light
This dang'rous Treason lurking in our way
To hinder our Beginnings. We doubt not now
But ev'ry Rub is smoothed on our way.                     185
Then forth, dear Countrymen: let us deliver
Our Puissance into the Hand of God,
Putting it straight in Expedition.
Cheerly to Sea; the Signs of War advance!
No King of England if not King of France!                 190
        *Flourish and Exeunt.*

347

II.iii   *This scene takes place on a street in London.*

2        Staines   *a small town on the Thames between London and Southampton.*

3        ern   *grieve.*

9–10     Arthur's Bosom   *The Hostess is thinking of Abraham's bosom (Luke 16:22), a symbol of Heaven. The soul of the legendary King Arthur was said to reside in Avalon, another paradisal realm.*

11–12    and . . . Child   *as innocently as a just-christened child.*

12–13    just between . . . Tide   *The time of Falstaff's death recalls 2 Henry IV, III.ii.228–29, where Falstaff says "We have heard the Chimes at Midnight, Master Shallow."*

17–18    as sharp . . . Fields   *This famous passage is here rendered as it appears in the First Folio. Since the middle of the eighteenth century most editors have adopted Lewis Theobald's emendation and substituted " 'a babbl'd" for "a Table." But "Table" and "Pen" can be related in various ways. The Hostess could be referring to a pen on a decorated writing tablet, for example; or she could be referring to a pen (enclosure) on a picture (tabula) of green fields. Or, more simply, she could be thinking of a writing pen on a table covered with green baize (a coarse cloth often used to protect flat surfaces). If so, both objects could be equally distinct to her, the pen with its fine point, the table with its keen edges and sharp corners.*

# Scene 3

*Enter Pistol, Nym, Bardolph, Boy, and Hostess.*

HOSTESS  'Prythee, honey-sweet Husband, let me bring
    thee to Staines.
PISTOL  No: for my manly Heart doth ern. —Bardolph,
    Be blithe. —Nym, rouse thy vaunting Veins.
      —Boy, bristle
    Thy Courage up. For Falstaff he is dead,         5
    And we must ern therefore.
BARDOLPH  Would I were with him, wheresome'er he is,
    either in Heaven or in Hell.
HOSTESS  Nay sure he's not in Hell. He's in Arthur's
    Bosom if ever man went to Arthur's Bosom: 'a    10
    made a finer end, and went away and it had been
    any Christom Child; 'a parted ev'n just between
    Twelve and One, ev'n at the Turning of the Tide.
    For after I saw him fumble with the Sheets, and
    play with Flowers, and smile upon his Finger's    15
    end, I knew there was but one way: for his Nose
    was as sharp as a Pen, and a Table of Green
    Fields. "How now, Sir John," quoth I, "what
    Man, be a' good Cheer." So 'a cried out, "God,
    God, God!" three or four times. Now I, to    20
    comfort him, bid him 'a should not think of

349

27     up-peer'd    *This spelling is usually interpreted as a rendering of "up'ard." But the spelling also suggests "peered up."*

28     cold as any Stone    *a delicate reminder that by this point the Hostess' fingers have probably arrived at Falstaff's own cold "stones."*

29     of    *on (meaning "against").*

34     incarnate    *both (a) in the flesh, and (b) red (for prostitutes).*

39     handle    *The Hostess means "talk about." But of course the literal meaning is also apropos.*

40     rheumatic    *The Hostess probably means "grievously ill." She may be thinking of "lunatic" (delirious), but "rheumatic" (which was often pronounced "romatic") is more in keeping with the image of "the Whore of Babylon" (Revelation 17:3–6), widely interpreted by Protestants as a prophecy of the Roman Catholic Church.*

45     Fuel    *the recompense Bardolph received as one of Falstaff's retainers.*

48     shog    *jog, move along.*

51     Chattels    *property.*
        Moveables    *furniture.*

52     Let Senses rule.    *Let common sense (prudence) prevail.*
        Pitch and Pay    *put down your money (an expression meaning "no credit").*

God; I hop'd there was no need to trouble
himself with any such Thoughts yet. So 'a bade
me lay more Clothes on his Feet. I put my Hand
into the Bed, and felt them, and they were as          25
cold as any Stone; then I felt to his Knees,
and so up-peer'd, and upward, and all was as
cold as any Stone.

NYM   They say he cried out of Sack.

HOSTESS   Ay, that 'a did.          30

BARDOLPH   And of Women.

HOSTESS   Nay, that 'a did not.

BOY   Yes that 'a did, and said they were Dev'ls
incarnate.

HOSTESS   'A could never abide Carnation, 'twas a          35
Color he never lik'd.

BOY   'A said once, the Dev'l would have him about
Women.

HOSTESS   'A did in some sort, indeed, handle Women;
but then he was rheumatic, and talk'd of the          40
Whore of Babylon.

BOY   Do you not remember 'a saw a Flea stick upon
Bardolph's Nose, and 'a said it was a black
Soul burning in Hell.

BARDOLPH   Well, the Fuel is gone that maintain'd          45
that Fire: that's all the Riches I got in his
Service.

NYM   Shall we shog? The King will be gone from
Southampton.

PISTOL   Come, let's away. My Love, give me thy Lips.          50
Look to my Chattels and my Moveables.
Let Senses rule. The World is "Pitch and Pay":

35<sup>1</sup>

53     Wafer-cakes   *cakes that are wafer-thin (and thus subject to breaking and crumbling).*

54     Hold-fast . . . Dog   *Pistol alludes to a proverb counseling modesty and prudence: "Brag is a good dog, but Hold-fast is better."*

55     Caveto   *a Latinate term meaning "beware."*

56     clear thy Crystals   *Pistol probably means "dry your eyes."*

57     Horse-leeches   *parasites. Pistol may be alluding to Proverbs 30:15, "The horseleach hath two daughters, crying, Give, give."*

62     I cannot kiss   *Evidently Nym is still too hurt by the Hostess' marriage to Bardolph to be able to bring himself to kiss her.*

64     Let Huswifery . . . command.   *Conduct yourself as a prudent, sober housewife; stay home and don't gad about.*

II.iv     *This scene takes place in France at the King's Palace.*

1     FRANCE   *the King of France.*

4     Berry   *Berri.*
       Britaine   *Brittany.*

5     Orleance   *Orleans.*
       make forth   *proceed.*

Trust none. For Oaths are Straws, Men's Faiths
  are Wafer-cakes,
And Hold-fast is the only Dog, my Duck;
Therefore Caveto be thy Counselor.            55
Go, clear thy Crystals. —Yokefellows in Arms,
Let us to France like Horse-leeches, my Boys,
To suck, to suck, the very Blood to suck!

BOY   And that's but unwholesome Food, they say.

PISTOL   Touch her soft Mouth, and march.       60

BARDOLPH   Farewell, Hostess.        *He kisses her.*

NYM   I cannot kiss, that is the Humour of it; but
  adieu.

PISTOL   Let Huswifery appear: keep close, I thee
  command.

HOSTESS   Farewell; adieu.        *Exeunt.*  65

# Scene 4

*Flourish. Enter the French King, the Dolphin, the Dukes
of Berry and Britaine, the Constable, and Others.*

FRANCE   Thus comes the English with full Pow'r
  upon us,
And more than carefully it us concerns
To answer Royally in our Defenses.
Therefore the Dukes of Berry and of Britaine,
Of Brabant and of Orleance, shall make forth,    5

7     line and new repair   *fortify and reinforce.*

11     provident   *prepared, resourceful.*

12     late Examples   *The King probably refers to the French losses at the battles of Crécy (Cressy, line 54) in 1346 and Poitiers in 1356.*

13     the fatal and neglected English   *the English whom we neglected to take seriously, and with fatal consequences.*

14     redoubted   *feared, held in great respect.*

15     meet   *appropriate.*

18     Musters   *summoning of troops for military exercises.*

25     Whitsun   *Whitsunday (Pentecost, fifty days after Easter).*
       Morris-dance   *folk-dance in which performers blackened their faces (like Moors) and wore bells to celebrate the coming of spring.*

26     idly King'd   *ruled by a frivolous King.*

27     so fantastically borne   *borne by a man so given to indulgence of his fantasies (fancies and light whims).*

28     giddy   *silly, unstable.*
       humourous   *ruled by his passions and fancies rather than by his reason.*

32     State   *majesty, monarchial bearing.*
       Embassy   *message.*

And you, Prince Dolphin, with all swift dispatch,
To line and new repair our Towns of War
With Men of Courage and with Means Defendant:
For England his Approaches makes as fierce
As Waters to the sucking of a Gulf. 10
It fits us then to be as provident
As Fear may teach us, out of late Examples
Left by the fatal and neglected English
Upon our Fields.

DOLPHIN    My most redoubted Father,
It is most meet we arm us 'gainst the Foe: 15
For Peace itself should not so dull a Kingdom
(Though War nor no known Quarrel were in
  question)
But that Defenses, Musters, Preparations
Should be maintain'd, assembled, and collected
As were a War in expectation. 20
Therefore, I say, 'tis meet we all go forth
To view the sick and feeble parts of France;
And let us do it with no show of Fear,
No, with no more than if we heard that England
Were busied with a Whitsun Morris-dance. 25
For my good Liege, she is so idly King'd,
Her Scepter so fantastically borne,
By a vain, giddy, shallow, humourous Youth,
That Fear attends her not.

CONSTABLE    O peace, Prince Dolphin,
You are too much mistaken in this King: 30
Question, your Grace, the late Embassadors,
With what great State he heard their Embassy,

34 **modest in Exception** *unlike a braggart in his manner of disagreeing.*

35 **terrible . . . Resolution** *intimidating in the firmness of his resolve.*

36 **forespent** *past. The Constable may also mean "forspent" (exhausted).*

37–38 **the outside . . . Folly** *the external manner of Lucius Junius Brutus, the Roman Consul who pretended to be an idiot in order to deflect the suspicions of his tyrannical uncle, King Tarquinius Superbus. In 509 B.C., Brutus led a popular uprising against the Tarquins and banished them (and kingship) from Rome.*

38 **Discretion** *intelligence, prudence.*

39 **Ordure** *manure.*

46–48 **Which . . . Cloth** *Here "Which" refers to "Proportions of Defense." The Dolphin is saying that to skimp on defensive preparations is as foolish as to ruin a coat by economizing on the cloth to be used.*

48 **Think . . . strong** *I believe that King Henry is indeed strong.*

50 **flesh'd** *a hunting term, referring to the taste of blood or flesh by which hounds or hawks were incited to bloodthirsty pursuit of the prey.*

52 **in our familiar Paths** *on our own soil.*

57 **Mountain Sire** *King Edward III, born in the Welsh mountains.*

356

How well supplied with Noble Counselors,
How modest in Exception, and withal
How terrible in constant Resolution,                                35
And you shall find his Vanities forespent
Were but the outside of the Roman Brutus,
Covering Discretion with a Coat of Folly,
As Gard'ners do with Ordure hide those Roots
That shall first spring and be most delicate.                       40

DOLPHIN    Well, 'tis not so, my Lord High Constable.
But though we think it so, it is no matter.
In cases of Defense 'tis best to weigh
The Enemy more mighty than he seems,
So the Proportions of Defense are fill'd,                           45
Which, of a weak and niggardly Projection,
Doth like a Miser spoil his Coat with scanting
A little Cloth.

FRANCE              Think we King Harry strong;
And Princes, look you strongly arm to meet him.
The Kindred of him hath been flesh'd upon us,                       50
And he is bred out of that bloody Strain
That haunted us in our familiar Paths.
Witness our too much memorable Shame
When Cressy Battle fatally was struck,
And all our Princes captiv'd, by the Hand                           55
Of that black Name, Edward, Black Prince of
    Wales,
Whiles that his Mountain Sire, on Mountain
    standing
Up in the Air, crown'd with the Golden Sun,
Saw his Heroical Seed, and smil'd to see him,
Mangle the Work of Nature and deface                                60

61 Patterns *faces (in the image of their fathers).*

64 native *inherited.*
Fate of him *destiny that attends him.*

67 present *immediate.*

69 Turn Head *turn and face him instead of running away.*

70 Most spend their Mouths *bark most vigorously.*

72 Take up the English short *surprise the English by standing up to them and facing them down.*

75 Self-neglecting *failing to assert one's own self-interest.*

78 divest your Self *remove the garments of kingship.*
lay apart *set aside.*

79–80 The borrow'd Glories . . . Nations *Exeter invokes every kind of law—divine, natural, and human—in support of King Henry's claim that the French King is wearing "borrow'd Glories" (dignities that properly belong to a more rightful heir to his throne).*

80 'longs *belongs.*

358

The Patterns that by God and by French Fathers
Had twenty years been made. This is a Stem
Of that Victorious Stock, and let us fear
The native Mightiness and Fate of him.

*Enter a Messenger.*

MESSENGER  Embassadors from Harry, King of England,    65
　Do crave admittance to your Majesty.
FRANCE  We'll give them present audience: go and
　　bring them.          *Exit Messenger, with Attendants.*
　—You see the Chase is hotly follow'd, Friends.
DOLPHIN  Turn Head and stop Pursuit: for coward
　Dogs
　Most spend their Mouths when what they seem to
　　threaten                                            70
　Runs far before them. Good my Sovereign,
　Take up the English short, and let them know
　Of what a Monarchy you are the Head:
　Self-love, my Liege, is not so vile a Sin
　As Self-neglecting.

*Enter Exeter and his Train, attended.*

FRANCE                  —From our Brother of England?    75
EXETER  From him, and thus he greets your Majesty:
　He wills you, in the Name of God Almighty,
　That you divest your Self and lay apart
　The borrow'd Glories that by Gift of Heaven,
　By Law of Nature and of Nations, 'longs           80
　To him and to his Heirs; namely, the Crown

83    the Ordinance of Times   *ancient ordinances (such as the Salic Law).*

85    sinister   *literally, left-handed; figuratively, "not right" (and hence "wrong"); here pronounced "sin-ís-ter."*
    awkward   *irregular; literally, "turned backward."*

86    Pick'd . . . Days   *culled selectively from worm-eaten pages of dead history.*

87    Oblivion   *that which is long forgotten.*

88    memorable Line   *pedigree worthy of remembrance, and thus respect.*

89    demonstrative   *proven, attested to be true.*

90    overlook   *look over, examine.*

91    evenly deriv'd   *lawfully descended.*

94    indirectly held   *held by means of an indirect line, as distinguished from King Henry's direct descent.*

97    Constraint   *compulsion, force.*

101    requiring   *Here this word hovers between two possible meanings: (a) requesting, and (b) demanding.*

102    in the Bowels of the Lord   *in keeping with God's mercy. The bowels were considered to be a seat of compassion, as illustrated by Philippians 1:8, "in the bowels of Jesus Christ."*

107    privy   *private, lonely.*

And all wide-stretched Honors that pertain
By Custom and the Ordinance of Times
Unto the Crown of France. That you may know
'Tis no sinister nor no awkward Claim,                                    85
Pick'd from the Worm-holes of long-vanish'd
    Days,
Nor from the Dust of old Oblivion rak'd,
He sends you this most memorable Line,

*He presents a Document.*

In ev'ry Branch truly demonstrative,
Willing you overlook this Pedigree,                                       90
And when you find him evenly deriv'd
From his most fam'd of famous Ancestors,
Edward the Third, he bids you then resign
Your Crown and Kingdom, indirectly held
From him, the Native and True Challenger.                                 95

FRANCE   Or else what follows?

EXETER   Bloody Constraint: for if you hide the
    Crown
Ev'n in your Hearts, there will he rake for it.
Therefore in fierce Tempest is he coming,
In Thunder and in Earthquake, like a Jove,                               100
That, if requiring fail, he will compel;
And bids you, in the Bowels of the Lord,
Deliver up the Crown, and to take Mercy
On the poor Souls for whom this hungry War
Opens his vasty Jaws; and on your Head                                   105
Turning the Widow's Tears, the Orphan's Cries,
The Dead-men's Blood, the privy Maiden's
    Groans,
For Husbands, Fathers, and betrothed Lovers

361

115    Back to    *carried back to.*

119    prize you at    *apprise you to be, hold you to be worth.*

121    at large    *in full*

124    Womby Vaultages    *womb-like vaults (caverns and other large enclosures).*

126    second Accent    *echo.*

127    render fair Return    *reply with a peaceful message.*

132    Paris Lover    *Picking up on the sexual sense of "Paris-balls," Exeter puns on* Louvre, *the name of the royal palace in Paris. He continues the sexual wordplay in the next line with the phrase "Mistress Court."*

133    Court    *Exeter plays on two senses: (a) tennis court, and (b) royal court. There is probably also a hint of wordplay on* court *as a verb meaning "make love" (woo).*

135    in Wonder    *to our amazement.*

136    Greener Days    *youth. Cleopatra uses a similar image when she refers to her "Salad Days" in I.v.69 of* Antony and Cleopatra.

That shall be swallow'd in this Controversy.
This is his Claim, his Threat'ning, and my
    Message;                                110
Unless the Dolphin be in presence here,
To whom expressly I bring Greeting too.

FRANCE   For us, we will consider of this further:
Tomorrow shall you hear our full Intent
Back to our Broth'r of England.

DOLPHIN                  For the Dolphin,   115
I stand here for him: what to him from England?

EXETER   Scorn and Defiance, Slight Regard, Contempt,
And any thing that may not mis-become
The mighty Sender, doth he prize you at.
Thus says my King: and if your Father's
    Highness                                  120
Do not, in grant of all Demands at large,
Sweeten the bitter Mock you sent his Majesty,
He'll call you to so hot an Answer of it
That Caves and Womby Vaultages of France
Shall chide your Trespass and return your Mock   125
In second Accent of his Ordinance.

DOLPHIN   Say: if my Father render fair Return,
It is against my Will, for I desire
Nothing but Odds with England. To that end,
As matching to his Youth and Vanity,          130
I did present him with the Paris-balls.

EXETER   He'll make your Paris Lover shake for it,
Were it the Mistress Court of mighty Europe;
And be assur'd you'll find a Difference,
As we his Subjects have in Wonder found,      135
Between the Promise of his Greener Days

137    weighs   *In addition to its literal sense in terms of Exeter's metaphor, this verb means "takes full account of, treats with the utmost gravity."*

138    read   *interpret, calculate.*

141    Dispatch us   *send us back with your answer.*

145    small Breath   *a short breathing space.*

And these he masters now. Now he weighs Time
Ev'n to the utmost Grain: that you shall read
In your own Losses if he stay in France.

FRANCE    Tomorrow shall you know our Mind at full.    140

*Flourish.*

EXETER    Dispatch us with all speed, lest that our
  King
Come here himself to question our Delay:
For he is footed in this Land already.

FRANCE    You shall be soon dispatch'd, with fair
  Conditions.
A Night is but small Breath, and little Pause,    145
To answer Matters of this Consequence.    *Exeunt.*

III. Chorus  *In this appearance the Chorus transports us with the King and his forces to France.*

1  imagin'd Wing  *both (a) an imaginary wing, and (b) the wings of our imaginations.*

2  Celerity  *speed.*

4  Dover  *This is probably a mistake for "Hampton," an emendation all modern editions substitute for the Folio reading.*

6  Streamers  *sails.*
   young Phoebus fayning  *feigning (imitating) the youthful Sun God. Other possible readings (if the Folio spelling is also meant to convey "faining") are (a) making the morning sun rejoice, and (b) wooing the morning sun. Assuming that the manuscript was difficult to decipher, modern editors normally emend the word to "fanning."*

8  hempen Tackle  *rope rigging.*

9  shrill Whistle  *the signal of the ship's master.*

10  To Sounds confus'd  *to the accompaniment of a medley of sounds.*
    threaden  *woven of thread.*

11  creeping  *stealthy, moving with a low profile.*

12  Bottoms  *large ships.*

# Act Three

*Flourish. Enter Chorus.*

CHORUS   Thus with imagin'd Wing our swift Scene
　　　　flies,
　　　In Motion of no less Celerity
　　　Than that of Thought. Suppose that you have
　　　　seen
　　　The well-appointed King at Dover Pier
　　　Embark his Royalty; and his brave Fleet,                    5
　　　With silken Streamers, the young Phoebus
　　　　fayning.
　　　Play with your Fancies and in them behold,
　　　Upon the hempen Tackle, Ship-boys climbing;
　　　Hear the shrill Whistle, which doth Order give
　　　To Sounds confus'd. Behold the threaden Sails,           10
　　　Borne with th' invisible and creeping Wind,
　　　Draw the huge Bottoms through the furrow'd Sea

14     Rivage    *bank, shore.*

15     City    *a metaphor for the English fleet, which numbered a thousand, according to Holinshed's* Chronicles.

17     Harflew    *Harfleur, a town on the French coast at the mouth of the Seine.*

18     Grapple . . . Navy    *affix your minds to the sterns of this navy.*

19     as dead Midnight still    *as deserted and quiet as if it were midnight.*

21     Pith and Puissance    *mature strength.*

24     cull'd and choice-drawn    *carefully selected for quality.*

26     Ord'nance    *artillery.*

27     fatal Mouths    *The Chorus depicts the cannons as beasts of prey, prepared to devour the besieged town.*
       girded    *surrounded.*

30     to Dowry    *as a marriage settlement.*

32     likes    *pleases.*

33     Linstock    *a staff (stock) with a match (lunt) at one end to be used to fire the cannon. The match was a small bundle of combustible material.*

S.D.     Chambers    *stage cannons.*

35     eche out    *eke out, fill out.*

Breasting the lofty Surge. O, do but think
You stand upon the Rivage, and behold
A City on th' inconstant Billows dancing:                    15
For so appears this Fleet Majestical,
Holding due course to Harflew. Follow, follow;
Grapple your Minds to sternage of this Navy,
And leave your England as dead Midnight still,
Guarded with Grandsires, Babies, and old Women,             20
Eith'r past or not arriv'd to Pith and Puissance.
For who is he whose Chin is but enrich'd
With one appearing Hair that will not follow
These cull'd and choice-drawn Cavaliers to
    France?
Work, work your Thoughts, and therein see a
    Siege;                                                   25
Behold the Ord'nance on their Carriages,
With fatal Mouths gaping on girded Harflew.
Suppose th' Embass'dor from the French comes
    back,
Tells Harry that the King doth offer him
Kath'rine his Daughter, and with her to Dowry               30
Some petty and unprofitable Dukedoms.
The Offer likes not; and the nimble Gunner
With Linstock now the div'lish Cannon touches,
                    *Alarum, and Chambers go off.*
And down goes all before them. Still be kind,
And eche out our Performance with your Mind.                35
                                            *Exit.*

369

III.i   *This scene takes place outside the walls of Harfleur.*

S.D.   Alarum   *trumpet call to battle.*

1   unto the Breach   *into the opening, battlefront (but with a sexual analogy reinforced by the imagery in line 7).*

4   modest Stillness   *humble quietness.*

7   commune up the Blood   *summon up your passion. Here* commune *(pronounced "cóm-mune") probably combines such meanings as "communicate with" and "draw together." Modern editions normally emend to either "summon" or "conjure"; both of those senses can be derived from the word that appears in the First Folio.*

8   hard-favor'd   *stern-featured, ugly (as contrasted with "fair," lovely, beautiful).*

9   terrible Aspect   *terrifying expression.*

10   Portage of the Head   *eye-sockets, here likened to the openings or emplacements for the cannons.*

11   o'erwhelm   *overhang.*

12   galled   *jagged; worn away by the waves.*

13   jutty his confounded Base   *jut out over its eroded base.*

14   Swill'd   *swallowed up.*
wasteful   *wasting, wearing away.*

16   bend up   *tense up.*

# Scene 1

*Enter the King, Exeter, Bedford, and Gloucester.*
*Alarum. Enter Soldiers with Scaling-ladders*
*at Harflew.*

KING   Once more unto the Breach, dear Friends, once
    more;
    Or close the Wall up with our English Dead.
    In Peace there's nothing so becomes a Man
    As modest Stillness and Humility;
    But when the Blast of War blows in our Ears,     5
    Then imitate the Action of the Tiger:
    Stiffen the Sinews, commune up the Blood,
    Disguise fair Nature with hard-favor'd Rage.
    Then lend the Eye a terrible Aspect:
    Let it pry through the Portage of the Head     10
    Like the Brass Cannon; let the Brow o'erwhelm
      it
    As fearfully as doth a galled Rock
    O'erhang and jutty his confounded Base,
    Swill'd with the wild and wasteful Ocean.
    Now set the Teeth, and stretch the Nostril
      wide,     15
    Hold hard the Breath, and bend up ev'ry Spirit

18    fet  *fetched, derived.*
of War-proof  *of armor tested and proven by warfare.*

19    Alexanders  *The King alludes to Alexander the Great (356–323 B.C.), who was such an aggressive warrior that he is said to have wept when he realized that there were no further realms for him to conquer.*

21    Argument  *both (a) resistance, and (b) reason to continue fighting.*

22    attest  *prove.*

24    Be Copy . . . Blood  *serve as models now to men of less than noble extraction.*

25    Yeomen  *small landowners, below the rank of gentlemen.*

27    mettle of your Pasture  *quality of your breeding. But the King puns on both* mettle *("metal") and* Pasture *(the grassy meadows on which cattle are pastured).*

29    mean and base  *of low estate in the social order.*

31    Slips  *leashes.*

32    Straying  *refusing to stand still. Modern editions normally emend to "straining," a sense contained in the word to be found in the Folio.*

S.D.    Chambers  *stage cannon.*

372

To his full Height. —On, on, you Noblest
  English,
Whose Blood is fet from Fathers of War-proof:
Fathers that, like so many Alexanders,
Have in these parts from Morn till Even fought,     20
And sheath'd their Swords for lack of Argument.
Dishonor not your Mothers: now attest
That those whom you call'd Fathers did beget
  you.
Be Copy now to Men of grosser Blood,
And teach them how to war. —And you, good
  Yeomen,     25
Whose Limbs were made in England, show us here
The mettle of your Pasture; let us swear
That you are worth your Breeding, which I
  doubt not:
For there is none of you so mean and base
That hath not Noble Luster in your Eyes.     30
I see you stand like Greyhounds in the Slips,
Straying upon the Start. The Game's afoot:
Follow your Spirit, and upon this Charge
Cry "God for Harry, England, and Saint George!"
        *Alarum, and Chambers go off. Exeunt.*

III.ii    *The scene remains at Harfleur.*

3    Knocks    *blows, military encounters.*

4    Case    *set.*

5    The Humour of it    *Nym uses this phrase habitually, often with no particular significance; in this instance he seems to mean "it."*

6    Plain-song    *a simple melody, without elaboration or variations. The indented verses that follow may well be lyrics from such contemporary songs. If so, they are probably meant to be sung. Another possibility is that they are ad hoc rhymes here set to familiar tunes.*

10    Vassals    *servants.*

15    Fame    *the glory to be won in military valor.*

19    hie    *hasten.*

20    duly    *punctually, surely.*
      truly    *faithfully. The Boy's point is that if Pistol had his wish, he would be "untrue" to his duty as a soldier.*

374

# Scene 2

*Enter Nym, Bardolph, Pistol, and Boy.*

BARDOLPH   On, on, on, on, on, to the Breach, to the
    Breach!

NYM   'Pray thee, Corporal, stay: the Knocks are too
    hot; and for mine own part, I have not a Case
    of Lives. The Humour of it is too hot, that is       5
    the very Plain-song of it.

PISTOL   The Plain-song is most just,
       For Humours do abound.
       Knocks go and come;
       God's Vassals drop and die;       10
         And Sword and Shield,
         In Bloody Field,
       Doth win immortal Fame.

BOY   Would I were in an Ale-house in London! I would
    give all my Fame for a Pot of Ale, and Safety.       15

PISTOL   And I:
       If Wishes would prevail with me,
       My Purpose should not fail with me,
        But thither would I hie.

BOY   As duly, but not as truly,       20
       As Bird doth sing on Bough.

22 Avaunt *begone*
  Cullions *ne'er-do-wells; literally, testicles.*

23 Men of Mould *men of earth, ordinary mortals.*

24 Abate *diminish, cease. In line 26* bate *is an abbreviated form of* abate.

26 Bawcock *fine fellow (from the French* beau coq, *handsome cock).*

27 Chuck *a term of endearment.*

28–29 These . . . Humours. *Nym seems to be saying that he likes Pistol's words and disapproves of Fluellen's.*

31 Swashers *swashbucklers, bragging swaggerers.*
  Boy to *both (a) page or servant to, and (b) younger than.*

33 Man to *both (a) servant to, and (b) examples of manly behavior in comparison with my boyish nature.*
  Antics *buffoons, grotesques (spelled* Antiques *in the Folio, as is frequently the case in Shakespeare).*

34 amount to *add up to.*

35 White-liver'd *cowardly. The Boy's point is that all of Bardolph's "blood" (courage) is in his face.*

36 faces it out *feigns courage, acts brazen.*

39 keeps whole Weapons *keeps weapons whole (unbroken), by not using them.*

48 twelve Leagues *thirty-six miles.*

376

*Enter Fluellen.*

FLUELLEN   Up to the Breach, you Dogs! Avaunt, you
    Cullions!

PISTOL   Be merciful, great Duke, to Men of Mould.
    Abate thy Rage, abate thy manly Rage;
      Abate thy Rage, great Duke.               25
      Good Bawcock, bate thy Rage:
      Use Lenity, sweet Chuck.

NYM   These be Good Humours; your Honor wins Bad
    Humours.                   *Exit, with Bardolph and Pistol.*
                            *Fluellen steps aside.*

BOY   As young as I am, I have observ'd these three    30
    Swashers. I am Boy to them all three, but all
    they three, though they would serve me, could
    not be Man to me: for indeed three such Antics
    do not amount to a Man. For Bardolph, he is
    White-liver'd and Red-fac'd; by the means      35
    whereof 'a faces it out but fights not. For
    Pistol, he hath a killing Tongue and a quiet
    Sword; by the means whereof 'a breaks Words
    and keeps whole Weapons. For Nym, he hath
    heard that Men of Few Words are the Best Men,    40
    and therefore he scorns to say his Prayers,
    lest 'a should be thought a Coward; but his
    few Bad Words are match'd with as few Good
    Deeds; for 'a never broke any Man's Head but
    his own, and that was against a Post when he    45
    was drunk. They will steal any thing and call
    it Purchase. Bardolph stole a Lute-case, bore
    it twelve Leagues, and sold it for three

50     Filching    *stealing.*
          Callice    *Calais, a French town on the coast of the English Channel.*

51     piece of Service    *a euphemism comparing a theft to an act of valor.*

52     carry Coals    *be cowards. Like "Pocketing up of Wrongs" (line 57), this expression refers to one's tolerating insults and injuries and holding in one's anger rather than defending one's honor.*

52–53    They . . . Pockets    *The Boy says that Nym and Bardolph have tried to train him as a pickpocket.*

60     cast it up    *vomit it.*

61     presently    *immediately.*

62     the Mines    *excavations to undermine an enemy's fortress or encampment.*

66–67    Disciplines of the War    *Fluellen is obsessed with the military science of the ancient Romans.*

67     Concavities    *depth.*

68     Athversary    *adversary.*

71     Cheshu    *Jesu.*
          plow    *blow.*

72     Directions    *leadership.*

76     MacMorrice    *MacMorris.*

Halfpence. Nym and Bardolph are sworn Brothers
in Filching, and in Callice they stole a Fire-                         50
shovel. I knew by that piece of Service the
Men would carry Coals. They would have me as
familiar with Men's Pockets as their Gloves or
their Handkerchers; which makes much against
my Manhood if I should take from another's                            55
Pocket to put into mine, for it is plain
Pocketing up of Wrongs. I must leave them, and
seek some better Service: their Villainy goes
against my weak Stomach, and therefore I must
cast it up.                                                *Exit.*    60

*Enter Gower. Fluellen comes forward.*

GOWER   Captain Fluellen, you must come presently to
the Mines: the Duke of Gloucester would speak
with you.
FLUELLEN   To the Mines? Tell you the Duke, it is not
so good to come to the Mines: for look you, the                       65
Mines is not according to the Disciplines of
the War. The Concavities of it is not
sufficient: for look you, th' Athversary (you
may discuss unto the Duke, look you) is digg't
himself four Yard under the Countermines. By                          70
Cheshu, I think 'a will plow up all if there
is not better Directions.
GOWER   The Duke of Gloucester, to whom the Order
of the Siege is given, is altogether directed by
an Irishman, a very valiant Gentleman i' faith.                       75
FLUELLEN   It is Captain MacMorrice, is it not?

379

79    verify as much in his Beard   *make good on my words by telling him so to his face.*

80    Directions   *Fluellen probably means "discretion," knowledge, and judgment.*

85    falorous   *valorous, valiant.*

87    Expedition   *efficiency, readiness.*
aunchiant   *ancient. Fluellen's comments are a comic reflection of one of the major debates of Renaissance culture: whether the Moderns can ever measure up to the Ancients in any significant aspect of human achievement.*

89    maintain his Argument   *both (a) argue for the position he is maintaining (as a military theoretician), and (b) defend his position on the battlefield. Fluellen's phrasing would also have carried an unintended reminder of another way for a soldier to maintain his "Argument" (a word used elsewhere to refer to a woman's "Case").*

91    Pristine   *both (a) ancient, and (b) pure, ideal.*

93    Good-den   *good evening (an expression used after noon).*

96    Pioners   *miners, diggers.*
given o'er   *given up.*

97    By Chrish Law   *either (a) by Christ's law, or (b) by Christ, la.*
'tish   *'tis.*

GOWER   I think it be.

FLUELLEN   By Cheshu he is an Ass as in the World;
I will verify as much in his Beard. He has no
more Directions in the true Disciplines of the                    80
Wars, look you, of the Roman Disciplines, than
is a Puppy-dog.

*Enter MacMorrice and Captain Jamy.*

GOWER   Here 'a comes, and the Scots Captain, Captain
Jamy, with him.

FLUELLEN   Captain Jamy is a marvelous falorous             85
Gentleman, that is certain, and of great
Expedition and Knowledge in th' aunchiant Wars,
upon my particular knowledge of his Directions.
By Cheshu he will maintain his Argument as
well as any Military Man in the World, in the            90
Disciplines of the Pristine Wars of the Romans.

JAMY   I say gud-day, Captain Fluellen.

FLUELLEN   Good-den to your Worship, good Captain
James.

GOWER   How now, Captain MacMorrice, have you quit      95
the Mines? Have the Pioners given o'er?

MACMORRICE   By Chrish Law, 'tish ill done! The Work
ish give over, the Trompet sound the Retreat. By
my Hand I swear, and my Father's Soul, the Work
ish ill done; it ish give over. I would have blowed      100
up the Town, so Chrish save me la, in an Hour.
O 'tish ill done, 'tish ill done; by my Hand 'tish
ill done!

FLUELLEN   Captain MacMorrice, I beseech you now,

381

105    voutsafe   *vouchsafe, grant.*

106    Disputations   *discussions. Shakespeare often uses this word without the adversarial connotations normal in modern usage. So also with "Argument" (line 108).*

114    sall quit you with gud leve   *shall give you (repay you with) welcome (good leave, permission).*

115    mary   *marry, indeed; an expression that originated as an oath referring to the Virgin Mary.*

117    the Day is hot   *MacMorrice probably means "the fighting is fierce."*

119    beseech'd   *besieged.*

121    be   *by.*

122    sa'   *save.*

126    Mess   *Mass.*

127    de   *do.*

128    lig i' th' Grund   *lie in the ground (be dead and buried).*

130    Breff   *brief.*

131    I wad full fain heard   *I would very much like to have heard.*

132    tway   *two.*

134    under your Correction   *begging your pardon.*

will you voutsafe me, look you, a few                                105
Disputations with you, as partly touching or
concerning the Disciplines of the War, the
Roman Wars, in the way of Argument, look you,
and friendly Communication; partly to satisfy
my Opinion, and partly for the Satisfaction,           110
look you, of my Mind, as touching the Direction
of the Military Discipline, that is the Point.

JAMY   It sall be vary gud, gud feith, gud Capten's
Bath, and I sall quit you with gud leve, as I
may pick Occasion; that sall I mary.                                 115

MACMORRICE   It is no time to discourse, so Chrish
save me: the Day is hot, and the Weather, and
the Wars, and the King, and the Dukes. It is no
time to discourse. The Town is beseech'd; and
the Trumpet call us to the Breach, and we              120
talk, and, be Chrish, do nothing; 'tis Shame
for us all. So God sa' me 'tis Shame to stand
still, it is Shame by my Hand. And there is
Throats to be cut, and Works to be done, and
there ish nothing done, so Christ sa' me la.                         125

JAMY   By the Mess, ere theise Eyes of mine take
themselves to slomber, ay'll de gud Service,
or I'll lig i' th' Grund for it; ay, or go to
Death; and I'll pay 't as valorously as I may.
That sall I suerly do, that is the Breff and            130
the Long. Mary, I wad full fain heard some
Question 'tween you tway.

FLUELLEN   Captain MacMorrice, I think, look you,
under your Correction, there is not many of
your Nation—                                                         135

383

142    use    *treat.*

143    Affability    *friendliness.*

151    you will mistake each other    *you are mis-taking (misunder-standing) each other's meanings.*

153    sounds a Parley    *signals a desire to cease fighting and pause for negotiations.*

157    and there is an end    *and that's all I have to say on the subject for now.*

MACMORRICE  Of my Nation? What ish my Nation?
      Ish a Villain, and a Basterd, and a Knave,
      and a Rascal! What ish my Nation? Who talks
      of my Nation?
FLUELLEN  Look you, if you take the Matter otherwise        140
      than is meant, Captain MacMorrice, peradventure
      I shall think you do not use me with that
      Affability as in Discretion you ought to use me,
      look you, being as good a Man as your self,
      both in the Disciplines of War, and in the            145
      Derivation of my Birth, and in other
      Particularities.
MACMORRICE  I do not know you so good a Man as
      my self: so Chrish save me, I will cut off your
      Head.                                                   150
GOWER  Gentlemen both, you will mistake each other.
JAMY  Ah, that's a foul Fault.               *A Parley.*
GOWER  The Town sounds a Parley.
FLUELLEN  Captain MacMorrice, when there is more
      better Opportunity to be required, look you, I         155
      will be so bold as to tell you, I know the
      Disciplines of War: and there is an end.    *Exeunt.*

III.iii     *The setting remains outside the walls of Harfleur.*

2     latest Parle    *last conversation. In accordance with military law of the time, the King is announcing that the point has now been reached when the city must either surrender or risk being destroyed, whether or not its inhabitants subsequently lay down their arms.*

4     proud of    *enamored of, given over to.*

5     to    *to do.*

6     A Name . . . best    *the name I most wish to be known by.*

8     half-achieved    *The King implies that the city is already half-won.*

11     flesh'd    *eager for prey, having had a taste of flesh and blood to incite him to fury.*

12     range    *move without restraint.*

13     With Conscience wide as Hell    *with no moral or spiritual restraints.*

14     flow'ring    *growing, flourishing.*

17     smirch'd    *blackened, as with smoke.*
       fell Feats    *fierce deeds.*

18     Enlink'd to    *connected with.*

# Scene 3

*Enter the King and all his Train before the Gates.*

KING    How yet resolves the Gov'rnor of the Town?
This is the latest Parle we will admit.
Therefore to our best Mercy give your selves,
Or like to Men proud of Destruction,
Defy us to our worst. For as I am a Soldier,                    5
A Name that in my Thoughts becomes me best,
If I begin the Batt'ry once again
I will not leave the half-achieved Harflew
Till in her Ashes she lies buried.
The Gates of Mercy shall be all shut up,                        10
And the flesh'd Soldier, rough and hard of
    Heart,
In liberty of Bloody Hand shall range
With Conscience wide as Hell, mowing like
    Grass
Your fresh fair Virgins, and your flow'ring
    Infants.
What is it then to me if impious War,                           15
Array'd in Flames like to the Prince of Fiends,
Do with his smirch'd Complexion all fell Feats
Enlink'd to Waste and Desolation?

387

21      hot and forcing Violation   *savage rape.*

23      Career   *gallop, headlong descent.*

24      bootless   *useless, to no avail.*
        vain   *in vain.*

25      in their Spoil   *as they despoil (loot, destroy).*

26      Precepts   *teachings, instructions.*
        Leviathan   *whale. The King alludes to Job 41:1–4.*

29      in my Command   *under my control.*

31      O'erblows   *blows over or away.*
        filthy and contagious Clouds   *Fog and mist were thought to harbor contagion and disease.*

32      headly   *headlong, unrestrained (given head).*

34      blind and bloody   *blinded with fury, frenzied.*

35      Desire   *Modern editions normally emend to "defile." That notion is implicit in the word to be found in the Folio text.*
        shriking   *shrieking.*

38      spitted upon Pikes   *spiked on sharp-bladed spears.*

40–41      as . . . Slaughter-men   *an allusion to the Slaughter of the Innocents, as described in Matthew 2:16–18.*

42      avoid   *forestall, prevent.*

What is't to me, when you your selves are
   Cause,
If your pure Maidens fall into the Hand         20
Of hot and forcing Violation?
What Rein can hold licentious Wickedness
When down the Hill he holds his fierce Career?
We may as bootless spend our vain Command
Upon th' enraged Soldiers in their Spoil        25
As send Precepts to the Leviathan
To come ashore. Therefore, you Men of Harflew,
Take pity of your Town and of your People,
Whiles yet my Soldiers are in my Command,
Whiles yet the cool and temp'rate Wind of Grace    30
O'erblows the filthy and contagious Clouds
Of headly Murther, Spoil, and Villainy.
If not, why in a moment look to see
The blind and bloody Soldier with foul Hand
Desire the Locks of your shrill-shriking
   Daughters;                     35
Your Fathers taken by the silver Beards,
And their most rev'rend Heads dash'd to the
   Walls;
Your naked Infants spitted upon Pikes,
Whiles the mad Mothers, with their Howls
   confus'd,
Do break the Clouds, as did the Wives of Jewry   40
At Herod's bloody-hunting Slaughter-men.
What say you? Will you yield, and this avoid?
Or, guilty in Defense, be thus destroy'd?

*Enter Governor.*

389

44    Expectation    *hope.*

45    whom . . . entreated    *whom we begged for help.*

46    Returns us    *replies to us.*

47    raise    *lift, remove.*

50    are defensible    *are capable of self-defense.*

54    for us    *in our behalf.*

55    growing    *increasing.*

56    retire    *withdraw, retreat.*

58    address'd    *prepared.*

III.iv    *This scene takes place in the French Palace at Rouen. Princess Katherine is receiving her first English lesson. Modern editions normally modernize the French to be found in the First Folio. Here, with a few minor exceptions, it is reproduced as it stands.*

1–6    Alice . . . Anglois?    *"Alice, thou hast been in England, and thou speakest the language well." "A little, Madam." "I pray thee, teach me; it is necessary that I learn to speak. What do you call the hand in English?"*

GOVERNOR   Our Expectation hath this day an end:
    The Dolphin, whom of Succors we entreated,                    45
    Returns us that his Pow'rs are not yet ready
    To raise so great a Siege. Therefore, great
      King,
    We yield our Town and Lives to thy soft Mercy.
    Enter our Gates, dispose of us and ours,
    For we no longer are defensible.                              50
KING   Open your Gates. —Come, Uncle Exeter,
    Go you and enter Harflew. There remain
    And fortify it strongly 'gainst the French.
    Use Mercy to them all for us, dear Uncle.
    The Winter coming on, and Sickness growing                    55
    Upon our Soldiers, we will retire to Callice.
    Tonight in Harflew will we be your Guest;
    Tomorrow for the March are we address'd.
                        *Flourish, and enter the Town.*


# Scene 4

*Enter Katherine and Alice, an old Gentlewoman.*

KATHERINE   *Alice, tu as este en Angleterre, and tu
    bien parles le Langage.*
ALICE   *Un peu, Madame.*
KATHERINE   *Je te prie, m'enseignez; il faut que
    j'apprend a parler. Comment appele vous la*                   5

391

7–36  La main . . . menton?  *"The hand? It is called de Hand."*
*"De Hand. And the fingers?" "The Fingers? My faith, I have
forgotten the fingers, but I will remember. The fingers? I think
they are called de Fingres; yes, de Fingres." "The hand, d'
Hand; the fingers, de Fingres. I think that I am a good
scholar; I have learned two words in English quickly. How do
you say the nails?" "The nails. They are called de Nailes."
"De Nailes. Listen, tell me if I speak well: de hand, de Fingres, and de Nailes." "It is well said, Madam, it is very good
English." "Tell me the English for the arm." "De Arma,
Madam." "And the elbow?" "D' Elbow." "D' Elbow. I am
going to repeat all the words that you have taught me thus
far." "That is too difficult, Madam, as I think." "Excuse me,
Alice; listen: d' Hand, de Fingre, de Nailes, d' Arma, de
Bilbow." "D' Elbow, Madam." "O Lord God, I am forget-
ting d' Elbow! What do you call the neck?" "De Nick,
Madam." "De Nick. And the chin?"*

*main en Anglois?*

ALICE    *La main? Elle est appelee de Hand.*

KATHERINE    *De Hand. Et les doigts?*

ALICE    *Les doigts? Ma foi, j'oublie les doigts,*
*mais je me souviendray. Les doigts? Je pense*        10
*qu'ils sont appeles de Fingres; ouy, de*
*Fingres.*

KATHERINE    *La main, d' Hand; les doigts, de Fingres.*
*Je pense que je suis le bon escolier; j'ai*
*gagne deux mots d'Anglois vitement. Comment*        15
*appele vous les ongles?*

ALICE    *Les ongles? Les appelons de Nailes.*

KATHERINE    *De Nailes. Escoutez, dites moy si je*
*parle bien: de Hand, de Fingres, et de Nailes.*

ALICE    *C'est bien dict, Madame, il est fort bon*        20
*Anglois.*

KATHERINE    *Dites moy l'Anglois pour le bras.*

ALICE    *De Arma, Madame.*

KATHERINE    *Et le coude?*

ALICE    *D' Elbow.*        25

KATHERINE    *D' Elbow. Je m'en fais la repetition de*
*tous les mots que vous m'aves apprins des a*
*present.*

ALICE    *Il est trop dificile, Madame, comme je pense.*

KATHERINE    *Excuse moy, Alice; escoute: d' Hand, de*        30
*Fingre, de Nailes, d' Arma, de Bilbow.*

ALICE    *D'Elbow, Madame.*

KATHERINE    *O Seigneur Dieu, je m'en oublie d' Elbow!*
*Comment appele vous le col?*

ALICE    *De Nick, Madame.*        35

KATHERINE    *De Nick. Et le menton?*

393

37–66 **De Chin . . . diner.** *"De Chin." "De Sin. The neck, de Nick; the chin, the Sin." "Yes. Saving your Honor, in truth, you pronounce the words as correctly as the natives of England." "I doubt not that I can learn, by the grace of God, and in a little time." "You haven't already forgotten that which I have taught you?" "No, I will recite to you quickly: d' Hand, de Fingre, de Mailes." "De Nailes, Madam." "De Nailes, de Arma, de Ilbow." "Save your Honor, d' Elbow." "So I said: d' Elbow, de Nick, and de Sin. What do you call the foot and the coat?" "The Foot, Madam, and the Count." "The Foot and the Count! O dear Lord! These are words that are nasty, corrupt, gross, and immodest, and not for honorable Ladies to use. I would not speak these words before the Gentlemen of France for all the world. Foh! The Foot and the Count! Nevertheless, I will recite another time my whole lesson: d' Hand, de Fingre, de Nailes, d' Arma, d' Elbow, de Nick, de Sin, de Foot, the Count." "Excellent, Madam!" "That is enough for one time: let us go to dinner."*

60 **Le Foot et le Count** *indecent French words equivalent to the four-letter English words they resemble. A number of other words here are also likely to have had sexual implications for an Elizabethan audience:* **Nailes** *and* **Bilbo** *(a type of sword) are probably phallic,* **Nick** *is probably vaginal, and* **Sin** *is what proper maidens are not supposed to be aware of.*

ALICE    *De Chin.*

KATHERINE    *De Sin. Le col, de Nick; le menton, de*
    *Sin.*

ALICE    *Ouy. Sauf vostre honneur, en verite, vous*    40
    *prononcies les mots aussi droict que les Natifs*
    *d' Angleterre.*

KATHERINE    *Je ne doute point d' apprendre, par la*
    *grace de Dieu, et en peu de temps.*

ALICE    *N'ave vous desia oublie ce que je vous ai*    45
    *enseigne?*

KATHERINE    *Non, je reciterai a vous promptement:*
    *d' Hand, de Fingre, de Mailes—*

ALICE    *De Nailes, Madame.*

KATHERINE    *De Nailes, de Arma, de Ilbow.*    50

ALICE    *Sauf vostre honneur, d' Elbow.*

KATHERINE    *Ainsi dis je; d' Elbow, de Nick, et de*
    *Sin. Comment appele vous le pied et la robe?*

ALICE    *Le Foot, Madame, et le Count.*

KATHERINE    *Le Foot et le Count! O Seigneur Dieu!*    55
    *Ils son le mots de son mauvais, corruptible,*
    *gros, et impudique, et non pour les Dames des*
    *Honneur d'user. Je ne voudray prononcer ces*
    *mots devant les Seigneurs de France pour tout*
    *le Monde. Foh! Le Foot et le Count! Neany moys,*    60
    *je reciterai un autre foys ma lecon ensemble:*
    *d' Hand, de Fingre, de Nailes, d' Arma,*
    *d' Elbow, de Nick, de Sin, de Foot, le Count.*

ALICE    *Excellent, Madame!*

KATHERINE    *C'est asses pour un foyes: allons nous*    65
    *a diner.*                                    *Exeunt.*


395

III.v    *This scene takes place in the presence chamber of the French Palace at Rouen.*

1    he hath pass'd the River Somme    *The King of France notes that the English forces have retreated toward Calais, on the English Channel.*

2    withal    *with.*

3    quit all    *all leave.*

5    Dieu vivant    *living God.*
     Sprays of us    *offshoots of the French. The Dolphin alludes to the fact that many of the English are descendants of the Norman William the Conqueror and his soldiers, who invaded England in 1066.*

6    Luxury    *both (a) lechery, and (b) excess wealth.*

7    Scions    *shoots, grafted into other trees ("Stock").*

8    Spirt    *sprout, spurt.*

11    Mort du ma vie    *Depending on whether* du *is thought to represent* de *or* Dieu, *this phrase means either (a) "Death of my life!" or (b) "God's death, my life!" (an oath referring to the Crucifixion).*

13    slobb'ry    *unkempt, muddy.*

14    Nook-shotten Isle of Albion    *nook-ridden isle of England.*

17    Despight    *spite, contempt.*

18    sodden    *both (a) dull, or dulling, and (b) boiled.*

396

# Scene 5

*Enter the King of France, the Dolphin, the Duke
of Britaine, the Constable of France, and Others.*

FRANCE  'Tis certain he hath pass'd the River Somme.

CONSTABLE   And if he be not fought withal, my Lord,
  Let us not live in France; let us quit all,
  And give our Vineyards to a barb'rous People.

DOLPHIN  *O Dieu vivant!* Shall a few Sprays of us,                5
  The emptying of our Fathers' Luxury,
  Our Scions, put in wild and savage Stock,
  Spirt up so suddenly into the Clouds
  And over-look their Grafters?

BRITAINE   Normans, but bastard Normans, Norman
  Bastards!                                                         10
  *Mort du ma vie,* if they march along
  Unfought withal, but I will sell my Dukedom
  To buy a slobb'ry and a dirty Farm
  In that Nook-shotten Isle of Albion.

CONSTABLE   *Dieu de Batailles,* where have they this
  Mettle?                                                          15
  Is not their Climate foggy, raw, and dull,
  On whom, as in Despight, the Sun looks pale,
  Killing their Fruit with Frowns? Can sodden
  Water,

397

19     Drench    *a medicinal ale ("Barley Broth") given to horses to refresh them.*
        sur-rein'd Jades    *over-ridden, weary nags.*

20     Decoct    *boil to refine or purify.*

21     Quick    *living, lively.*

23     roping    *long and rope-like.*

29     bred out    *exhausted by excessive in-breeding.*

31     new-store    *replenish.*

33     Lavoltas    *dances in which swift turns were followed by high leaps.*
        Corantos    *galloping dances.*

35     lofty    *pretentious, arrogant.*

40     High Constable    *the chief military officer of France.*

42     Burgony    *Bourgogne; usually rendered "Burgundy" in English today. All three forms occur in the Folio text; they probably reflect the pronunciations Shakespeare preferred in particular contexts, and are retained in this edition as they appear in the original printing.*

A Drench for sur-rein'd Jades, their Barley
   Broth,
Decoct their Cold Blood to such Valiant Heat?     20
And shall our Quick Blood, spirited with Wine,
Seem frosty? O, for Honor of our Land,
Let us not hang like roping Icicles
Upon our Houses' Thatch whiles a more frosty
   People
Sweat Drops of gallant Youth in our rich Fields.   25
Poor we call them in their Native Lords.
DOLPHIN   By Faith and Honor,
   Our Madames mock at us, and plainly say
   Our Mettle is bred out, and they will give
   Their Bodies to the Lust of English Youth,    30
   To new-store France with Bastard Warriors.
BRITAINE   They bid us to the English Dancing-
   schools,
   And teach Lavoltas high, and swift Corantos,
   Saying our Grace is only in our Heels,
   And that we are most lofty Runaways.     35
FRANCE   Where is Montjoy the Herald? Speed him
   hence,
   Let him greet England with our sharp Defiance.
   Up, Princes, and with Spir't of Honor edg'd
   More sharper than your Swords, hie to the
   Field!
   Charles Delabreth, High Constable of France,   40
   You Dukes of Orleance, Bourbon, and of Berry,
   Alanson, Brabant, Bar, and Burgony,
   Jacques Chatillion, Rambures, Vandemont,

47    For . . . Shames.    *In keeping with your noble positions,
      now rid your honors of the shames the English have made you
      suffer.*

49    Pennons    *pennants (pointed or swallow-tailed flags).*

50    Host    *army.*

51    Vassal Seat    *subservient position.*

54    Roan    *Rouen.*

55    This becomes the Great.    *This is in keeping with true maj-
      esty.*

60    for Achievement    *both (a) to achieve his escape, and (b) as
      the sum of his achievements for this ill-advised mission.*
      his Ransom    *the price he is willing to pay in exchange for our
      allowing him to return to England.*

Beaumont, Grandpre, Roussi, and Faulconbridge,
Loys, Lestrale, Bouciqualt, and Charoloyes,          45
High Dukes, great Princes, Barons, Lords, and
   Kings:
For your great Seats now quit you of great
   Shames.
Bar Harry England, that sweeps through our Land
With Pennons painted in the Blood of Harflew;
Rush on his Host as doth the melted Snow           50
Upon the Valleys, whose low Vassal Seat
The Alps doth spit and void his Rheum upon.
Go down upon him, you have Pow'r enough,
And in a Captive Chariot into Roan
Bring him our Prisoner.

CONSTABLE               This becomes the Great.     55
Sorry am I his Numbers are so few,
His Soldiers sick, and famish'd in their March:
For I am sure, when he shall see our Army,
He'll drop his Heart into the Sink of Fear
And for Achievement offer us his Ransom.           60

FRANCE   Therefore Lord Constable, haste on Montjoy,
And let him say to England that we send
To know what willing Ransom he will give.
—Prince Dolphin, you shall stay with us in
   Roan.

DOLPHIN   Not so, I do beseech your Majesty.         65

FRANCE   Be patient, for you shall remain with us.
—Now forth, Lord Constable, and Princes all,
And quickly bring us word of England's Fall.

*Exeunt.*

III.vi  *This scene takes place at the English camp in Picardy. The King has sent a detachment ahead of his army to capture a bridge over the River Ternoise at Blangy, on the way to Calais. The French were attempting to destroy the bridge and thereby cut off the English escape route.*

S.D.  Welch  *This word is spelled with both a "c" and an "s" in the Folio text. In this edition the Folio's inconsistency (which may reflect Shakespeare's own) is retained; so also with the spellings* Divel *and* Devil.

4  Services committed  *valor demonstrated.*

6  magnanimous  *literally, great of spirit; valiant.*

7  Agamemnon  *the general of the victorious Greek forces during the Trojan War.*

9  Live  *life.*

13  aunchient  *ensign.*

15  Anthony  *probably pronounced "Antony," as the name is consistently spelled in the Folio edition of* Julius Caesar. *"Anthony" is the spelling used throughout the Folio printing of* Antony and Cleopatra.

16  Estimation  *fame, reputation.*

# Scene 6

*Enter Captains, English and Welch (Gower and Fluellen).*

GOWER   How now, Captain Fluellen, come you from
the Bridge?

FLUELLEN   I assure you, there is very excellent
Services committed at the Bridge.

GOWER   Is the Duke of Exeter safe?                              5

FLUELLEN   The Duke of Exeter is as magnanimous as
Agamemnon, and a Man that I love and honor
with my Soul, and my Heart, and my Duty, and
my Live, and my Living, and my uttermost
Power. He is not, God be praised and blessed,      10
any Hurt in the World, but keeps the Bridge
most valiantly, with excellent Discipline.
There is an aunchient Lieutenant there at the
Pridge, I think in my very Conscience he is as
valiant a Man as Mark Anthony, and he is a Man    15
of no Estimation in the World, but I did see
him do as gallant Service.

GOWER   What do you call him?

FLUELLEN   He is call'd Aunchient Pistol.

GOWER   I know him not.                                          20

403

24      and  *if.*

27      buxom  *Pistol probably means "robust."*

28      giddy  *unstable, dizzy.*
        furious  *frenzied. Pistol combines at least three traditional im-*
        *ages of Fortune: (a) a woman turning a large wheel, (b) a*
        *woman riding the wheel, and (c) a woman standing on a*
        *rolling stone. The first two images focus on Fortune's cyclical*
        *changes; the third one focuses on Fortune's instability. Fluel-*
        *len picks up on these images in his next speech.*

32      Muffler  *blindfold.*

33      his Eyes  *In Shakespeare's time "his" alternates with "it" to*
        *convey what we now render as "its." Many editors emend*
        *"his" to "her" here; that is unnecessary.*

43      Pax  *a small metal tablet or plate stamped with the Crucifix and*
        *used during the celebration of the Mass. The Priest kissed the*
        *Pax (Latin for "peace") and passed it to each member of the*
        *congregation. Bardolph has stolen one of these objects from a*
        *local church.*

44      'A  *he.*

44–45  Let . . . Dog  *let dogs instead of men be hanged.*

*Enter Pistol.*

FLUELLEN   Here is the Man.

PISTOL   Captain, I thee beseech to do me Favors:
The Duke of Exeter doth love thee well.

FLUELLEN   I praise God and I have merited some
Love at his Hands.                                                    25

PISTOL   Bardolph, a Soldier firm and sound of Heart,
And of buxom Valor, hath by cruel Fate,
And giddy Fortune's furious fickle Wheel,
That Goddess blind, that stands upon the
   rolling,
Restless Stone—                                                      30

FLUELLEN   By your patience, Aunchient Pistol,
Fortune is painted blind, with a Muffler afore
his Eyes, to signify to you that Fortune is
blind; and she is painted also with a Wheel,
to signify to you, which is the Moral of it,          35
that she is turning, and inconstant, and
mutability, and variation; and her Foot, look
you, is fixed upon a Spherical Stone, which
rolls, and rolls, and rolls. In good truth,
the Poet makes a most excellent Description   40
of it: Fortune is an excellent Moral.

PISTOL   Fortune is Bardolph's Foe, and frowns on
   him:
For he hath stol'n a Pax, and hanged must
'A be, a damned Death. Let Gallows gape
For Dog; let Man go free, and let not Hemp     45
His Windpipe suffocate. But Exeter

405

50    Penny-cord   *cheap rope.*

51    requite   *reward.*

60    Figo   *Like "Fig of Spain" (line 61), an insulting gesture made either by thrusting the thumb between the fingers or by putting the thumb in the mouth and flicking it against the backs of the upper front teeth.*

63    Bawd   *pander or pimp.*
       Cutpurse   *thief.*

67–68    when Time is serve   *when an appropriate time presents itself [I'll respond to him].*

69    'tis   *he is.*
       Gull   *Normally this word refers to a dupe, a foolish victim; here it appears to denote Pistol as one who gulls (dupes) others.*

70    grace himself   *make himself seem respectable or valiant.*

71    under the form of   *in the guise of.*

Hath giv'n the Doom of Death, for Pax of
　　little Price.
Therefore go speak (the Duke will hear thy
　　Voice),
And let not Bardolph's vital Thread be cut
With edge of Penny-cord and vile Reproach.　　50
Speak, Captain, for his Life, and I will thee
　　requite.

FLUELLEN　Aunchient Pistol, I do partly understand
　　your Meaning.

PISTOL　Why then rejoice therefore.

FLUELLEN　Certainly, Aunchient, it is not a thing　　55
　　to rejoice at: for if, look you, he were my
　　Brother, I would desire the Duke to use his
　　good pleasure and put him to Execution. For
　　Discipline ought to be used.

PISTOL　Die and be damn'd, and Figo for thy
　　Friendship!　　60

FLUELLEN　It is well.

PISTOL　　　　　The Fig of Spain.　　　　　*Exit.*

FLUELLEN　　　　　　　　　Very good.

GOWER　Why, this is an arrant counterfeit Rascal!
　　I remember him now: a Bawd, a Cutpurse.

FLUELLEN　I'll assure you, 'a utt'red as prave words
　　at the Pridge as you shall see in a Summer's　　65
　　Day. But it is very well: what he has spoke to
　　me, that is well, I warrant you, when Time is
　　serve.

GOWER　Why 'tis a Gull, a Fool, a Rogue, that now
　　and then goes to the Wars to grace himself at　　70
　　his return into London under the form of a

407

72     perfit   *perfect, in the sense of having committed something to memory.*

75     Sconce   *fortification, often of earthwork.*
       Breach   *break in a line of forces.*

77     stood on   *held out for, insisted upon in negotiations.*

78     con   *learn by heart, memorize.*

79     trick up   *outfit, embellish.*
       new-tun'd   *newly composed.*

80     of the General's Cut   *of the style favored by the General.*

81     horrid Suit of the Camp   *This phrase probably refers to a uniform that is so bloodied and battle-scarred that it strikes awe into anyone who thinks about how it attained its frightful condition.*

81–82 foaming Bottles   *bottles of ale.*

84     Slanders of the Age   *disgraces to our times.*

85     mistook   *misled, deceived.*

88–89 a Hole in his Coat   *Fluellen probably means this literally, with reference to a cut that Pistol will put in his garment to enable himself to masquerade as a soldier who has been struck by a sword. But he may also mean it figuratively, with reference to a blemish in his figurative coat of arms (his honor).*

97     gone off   *retreated.*

Soldier. And such Fellows are perfit in the
Great Commanders' Names, and they will learn
you by rote where Services were done: at such
and such a Sconce, at such a Breach, at such                    75
a Convoy; who came off bravely, who was shot,
who disgrac'd, what terms the Enemy stood on;
and this they con perfitly in the Phrase of
War, which they trick up with new-tun'd Oaths.
And what a Beard of the General's Cut and a                     80
horrid Suit of the Camp will do among foaming
Bottles and Ale-wash'd Wits is wonderful to be
thought on. But you must learn to know such
Slanders of the Age, or else you may be
marvelously mistook.                                            85

FLUELLEN   I tell you what, Captain Gower: I do
perceive he is not the Man that he would gladly
make show to the World he is. If I find a Hole
in his Coat, I will tell him my Mind.

*A Drum sounds.*

Heark you, the King is coming, and I must speak                 90
with him from the Pridge.

*Drum and Colors. Enter the King and his
poor Soldiers.*

—God pless your Majesty!
KING   How now, Fluellen, cam'st thou from the
Bridge?
FLUELLEN   Ay, so please your Majesty. The Duke               95
of Exeter has very gallantly maintain'd the
Pridge. The French is gone off, look you, and

409

105    Perdition    *losses.*

108    like to be executed    *likely to be executed by now.*

110    Bubukles and Whelks    *carbuncles and pimples.*

116    Charge    *orders.*

117    compell'd    *extorted, forced.*

120    Lenity    *restraint, gentleness. The Folio prints "Leuitie" (Levity), but that reading is difficult to square with the context in which the word occurs. All modern editions emend to "Lenity."*

121    play for    *compete or gamble for.*

S.D.    Tucket    *a trumpet call to announce an entrance.*
       Montjoy    *the name of France's chief herald.*

123    Habit    *uniform, here a sleeveless coat bearing a coat of arms.*

124    of    *from.*

there is gallant and most prave Passages.
Marry, th' Athversary was have possession of
the Pridge, but he is enforced to retire, and          100
the Duke of Exeter is Master of the Pridge.
I can tell your Majesty, the Duke is a prave
Man.

KING   What Men have you lost, Fluellen?

FLUELLEN   The Perdition of th' Athversary hath been     105
very great, reasonable great. Marry for my
part, I think the Duke hath lost never a Man
but one that is like to be executed for robbing
a Church: one Bardolph, if your Majesty know
the Man. His Face is all Bubukles and Whelks,      110
and Knobs, and Flames a' Fire, and his Lips
blows at his Nose, and it is like a Coal of
Fire, sometimes plue and sometimes red; but
his Nose is executed, and his Fire's out.

KING   We would have all such Offenders so cut off:     115
and we give express Charge that in our Marches
through the Country there be nothing compell'd
from the Villages, nothing taken but paid for,
none of the French upbraided or abused in
disdainful Language; for when Lenity and       120
Cruelty play for a Kingdom, the gentler
Gamester is the soonest Winner.

*Tucket. Enter Montjoy.*

MONTJOY   You know me by my Habit.

KING   Well then, I know thee: what shall I know of
thee?

411

126   Unfold   *disclose.*

129   Advantage   *awaiting the proper opportunity.*

132   bruise   *squeeze, crush, as with a festering boil or pimple.*

135   admire our Sufferance   *wonder at our patience and re-
       straint.*

137   proportion   *equal.*

139   in Weight to re-answer   *to make equivalent on the scale.*

141   Exchequer   *treasury.*
       Effusion   *out-flowing, loss.*

142   the Muster of his Kingdom   *the assembling of a throng the
       size of his kingdom's entire population.*

145   Satisfaction   *repayment.*

149   Quality   *rank and merit.*

151   Thou . . . fairly.   *You carry out your duty in a fitting man-
       ner.*

152   seek him   *seek to fight him.*

154   Impeachment   *resistance.*
       Sooth   *truth.*

MONTJOY   My Master's Mind.

KING   Unfold it.

MONTJOY   Thus says my King. "Say thou to Harry
   of England, though we seem'd dead, we did
   but sleep. Advantage is a better Soldier than
   Rashness. Tell him we could have rebuk'd him   130
   at Harflew, but that we thought not good to
   bruise an Injury till it were full ripe. Now
   we speak upon our Cue, and our Voice is
   Imperial. England shall repent his Folly, see
   his Weakness, and admire our Sufferance. Bid   135
   him therefore consider of his Ransom, which
   must proportion the Losses we have borne, the
   Subjects we have lost, the Disgrace we have
   digested, which in Weight to re-answer, his
   Pettiness would bow under. For our Losses, his   140
   Exchequer is too Poor; for th' Effusion of our
   Blood, the Muster of his Kingdom too faint a
   Number; and for our Disgrace, his own Person
   kneeling at our Feet but a weak and worthless
   Satisfaction. To this add Defiance; and tell   145
   him, for Conclusion, he hath betrayed his
   Followers, whose Condemnation is pronounc'd."
   So far my King and Master; so much my Office.

KING   What is thy Name? I know thy Quality.

MONTJOY   Montjoy.   150

KING   Thou doo'st thy Office fairly. Turn thee back
   And tell the King I do not seek him now
   But could be willing to march on to Callice
   Without Impeachment: for to say the Sooth,
   Though 'tis no Wisdom to confess so much   155

159    Almost . . . French   *Even in his seeming modesty, the King puts in a jab at the prowess of his adversary.*

166    Trunk   *body.*

168    God before   *with God leading us on.*

172    pass   *pass through to Calais, and thence back to England.*

Unto an Enemy of Craft and Vantage,
My People are with Sickness much enfeebled,
My Numbers lessen'd, and those Few I have
Almost no better than so many French;
Who, when they were in Health, I tell thee,
   Herald, 160
I thought upon one pair of English Legs
Did march three Frenchmen. —Yet forgive me,
   God,
That I do brag thus. —This your Air of France
Hath blown that Vice in me: I must repent.
Go therefore, tell thy Master here I am; 165
My Ransom is this frail and worthless Trunk;
My Army but a weak and sickly Guard;
Yet, God before, tell him we will come on,
Though France himself, and such another
   Neighbor,
Stand in our way. There's for thy Labor,
   Montjoy. 170
Go bid thy Master well advise himself.
If we may pass, we will; if we be hind'red,
We shall your tawny Ground with your red Blood
Discolor. And so, Montjoy, fare you well.
The Sum of all our Answer is but this: 175
We would not seek a Battle as we are;
Nor, as we are, we say we will not shun it.
So tell your Master.
MONTJOY   I shall deliver so. Thanks to your
   Highness. *Exit.*
GLOUCESTER   I hope they will not come upon us now. 180
KING   We are in God's Hand, Brother, not in theirs.

III.vii   *This scene takes place at the French camp, near Agincourt.*

12     change   *exchange.*

13     Postures   *The Dolphin means "pasterns." A horse's pastern is the part of the leg between the fetlook and the hoof. Shakespeare's spelling may reflect a wry pun: like his horse, the Dolphin "treads but on . . . posture." Indeed, Shakespeare presents the French nobility in general as little more than a collection of blustering impostors.*
    Ch'ha!   ça ha, *a French equivalent of "ha, ha."*

14     as if his Entrails were Hairs   *like a tennis ball. Tennis balls were stuffed with hair.*

14–15  le Cheval volant   *the flying horse.*

15     Pegasus   *a winged horse from Greek mythology. He served a hero named Bellerephon and helped him kill the Chimaera, a fire-breathing dragon with features of both a lion and a goat. Through a stamp of his hoof on Mount Helicon, Pegasus also opened up Hippocrene, the spring of the Muses. He thus became a symbol of both heroic exploits and poetic inspiration. For the Dolphin, Pegasus is more apt as a symbol of poetic embellishment than as an embodiment of transcendent valor.*

15–16  ches les narines de feu   *with nostrils of fire.*

18     the basest Horn of his Hoof   *both (a) the lowest part of his hoof, and (b) the lowest note sounded by his hoof as he prances.*

416

March to the Bridge, it now draws toward Night;
Beyond the River we'll encamp our selves,
And on tomorrow bid them march away.     *Exeunt.*

# Scene 7

*Enter the Constable of France, the Lord Rambures,*
*Orleance, and the Dolphin, with Others.*

CONSTABLE   Tut, I have the best Armor in the World.
  Would it were Day!
ORLEANCE   You have an excellent Armor; but let my
  Horse have his due.
CONSTABLE   It is the best Horse of Europe.                   5
ORLEANCE   Will it never be Morning?
DOLPHIN   My Lord of Orleance, and my Lord High
  Constable, you talk of Horse and Armor?
ORLEANCE   You are as well provided of both as any
  Prince in the World.                                        10
DOLPHIN   What a long Night is this! I will not
  change my Horse with any that treads but on
  four Postures. Ch'ha! He bounds from the
  Earth as if his Entrails were Hairs: *le*
  *Cheval volant,* the Pegasus, *ches les narines*           15
  *de feu.* When I bestride him, I soar, I am a
  Hawk! He trots the Air; the Earth sings when
  he touches it; the basest Horn of his Hoof is

19      the Pipe of Hermes    *Hermes (identical with the Roman Mercury) was the messenger of the Gods and the inventor of the pipe. In Book I of the* Metamorphoses *Ovid tells how Hermes played his pipe to charm to sleep all the eyes of the monster Argus, thereby allowing Hermes to slay him.*

22      Perseus    *According to Book IV of Ovid's* Metamorphoses, *Perseus was riding Pegasus when he rescued Andromeda from a dragon.*

       Air and Fire    *Air and fire were the elements associated with mind and spirit; they were thought to be free of the base limitations of the two lower elements (Earth and Water).*

24      but only in    *except in.*

29      Palfreys    *saddle horses. Palfreys were the horses normally ridden by ladies.*

35      vary deserved Praise    *praise with elegant rhetorical variations.*

36      Theme    *poetic subject.*

       fluent    *literally, flowing, and thus inspiring.*

37      Argument    *theme. But since "Argument" is also a term that can be associated with a man's "Mistress" (line 45), the Dolphin's phrasing opens him to ridicule.*

39      reason on    *contemplate and discourse about.*

41–42    to . . . Functions    *to set aside their individual responsibilities.*

49      bears    *carries. Orleance puns on the sexual sense of "Mistress."*

more Musical than the Pipe of Hermes!

ORLEANCE   He's of the Color of the Nutmeg.                    20

DOLPHIN   And of the Heat of the Ginger. It is a
Beast for Perseus. He is pure Air and Fire;
and the dull Elements of Earth and Water never
appear in him but only in patient Stillness
while his Rider mounts him. He is indeed a            25
Horse, and all other Jades you may call Beasts.

CONSTABLE   Indeed, my Lord, it is a most absolute
and excellent Horse.

DOLPHIN   It is the Prince of Palfreys. His Neigh is
like the Bidding of a Monarch, and his                 30
Countenance enforces Homage.

ORLEANCE   No more, Cousin.

DOLPHIN   Nay, the Man hath no Wit that cannot,
from the rising of the Lark to the lodging of the
Lamb, vary deserved Praise on my Palfrey. It is       35
a Theme as fluent as the Sea: turn the Sands
into eloquent Tongues, and my Horse is Argument
for them all. 'Tis a Subject for a Sovereign
to reason on, and for a Sovereign's Sovereign
to ride on; and for the World, familiar to us          40
and unknown, to lay apart their particular
Functions and wonder at him. I once writ a
Sonnet in his Praise, and began thus: "Wonder
of Nature."

ORLEANCE   I have heard a Sonnet begin so to one's      45
Mistress.

DOLPHIN   Then did they imitate that which I compos'd
to my Courser, for my Horse is my Mistress.

ORLEANCE   Your Mistress bears well.

50 prescript *prescribed, ideal.*

51 particular *individual, exclusively reserved for a single "master."*

53 shrewdly . . . Back *gave you a rough ride—a "shrewd" (shrewish, unruly) thing for a horse to do, but not necessarily a undesirable thing for a lusty mistress to do.*

55 Mine . . . bridled. *The Constable is saying that "mine was not a horse" (and therefore what my Mistress gave me was a "good" kind of back-shaking). He may also be saying "mine was not forced to bear me."*

56 belike *probably, in all likelihood.*

57 a Kern of Ireland *The kerns were swift-riding raiders proverbial for the lightness of the armor they bore into conflict.*

57 French Hose *wide, baggy breeches.*

58 strait Strossers *tight-fitting trousers.*

61 fall into foul Bogs *both (a) fall into stinking marshes and mudholes, and (b) fall into latrines (or their anatomical equivalent).*

63 as live *as lief, as soon.*
   Jade *both (a) a worn-out nag, and (b) a common whore.*

68–69 Le chien . . . bourbier. *A paraphrase of 2 Peter 2:22, "The dog is turned to his own vomit again; and the sow that was washed to her wallowing in the mire."*

79 want *be lacking (for other stars).*

DOLPHIN   Me well, which is the prescript Praise and          50
    Perfection of a good and particular Mistress.

CONSTABLE   Nay, for methought yesterday your
    Mistress shrewdly shook your Back.

DOLPHIN   So perhaps did yours.

CONSTABLE   Mine was not bridled.                              55

DOLPHIN   O then belike she was old and gentle, and
    you rode like a Kern of Ireland, your French Hose
    off, and in your strait Strossers.

CONSTABLE   You have good Judgment in Horsemanship.

DOLPHIN   Be warn'd by me then: they that ride so,           60
    and ride not warily, fall into foul Bogs: I had
    rather have my Horse to my Mistress.

CONSTABLE   I had as live have my Mistress a Jade.

DOLPHIN   I tell thee, Constable, my Mistress wears
    his own Hair.                                         65

CONSTABLE   I could make as true a Boast as that if
    I had a Sow to my Mistress.

DOLPHIN   *Le chien est retourne a son propre*
    *vomissement, et la truie lavee au bourbier.*
    Thou mak'st use of any thing.                         70

CONSTABLE   Yet do I not use my Horse for my
    Mistress, or any such Proverb so little kin to
    the Purpose.

RAMBURES   My Lord Constable, the Armor that I saw
    in your Tent tonight, are those Stars or Suns         75
    upon it?

CONSTABLE   Stars, my Lord.

DOLPHIN   Some of them will fall tomorrow, I hope.

CONSTABLE   And yet my Sky shall not want.

DOLPHIN   That may be, for you bear a many               80

421

81    superfluously    *The Dolphin's implication is that the Dolphin bears more stars (honors) than he is really entitled to.*

86–87  with his Desert    *with as much weight as he deserves.*

91    fac'd out of my Way    *both (a) impeded in my movements by all the faces in the pathway, and (b) "faced down" (intimidated or outfought).*

92    fain    *gladly, eagerly.*

94    go to Hazard with me    *roll the dice with me.*

96    go your self to Hazard    *put yourself at risk (demonstrate your own valor). The Constable's point is that the Dolphin's first task is to obtain twenty prisoners to stake in a wager.*

104–5  tread out    *dance or walk on contemptuously.*

108–9  he will still be Doing    *he will always be about to do what he boasts of.* Doing *had sexual implications in Shakespeare's time. The Constable may be saying that the only kind of manly "Activity" the Dolphin is capable of is that which pertains to a "Mistress" (presumably one other than his horse). But in keeping with his other comments in this scene, he seems more likely to be implying that the Dolphin is capable of just as much "Harm" (line 110) sexually as militarily.*

superfluously, and 'twere more Honor some were
away.

CONSTABLE   Ev'n as your Horse bears your Praises,
who would trot as well were some of your Brags
dismounted.                                                      85

DOLPHIN   Would I were able to load him with his
Desert! Will it never be Day? I will trot
tomorrow a Mile, and my Way shall be paved
with English Faces.

CONSTABLE   I will not say so, for fear I should be        90
fac'd out of my Way; but I would it were
Morning, for I would fain be about the Ears of
the English.

RAMBURES   Who will go to Hazard with me for twenty
Prisoners?                                                       95

CONSTABLE   You must first go your self to Hazard
ere you have them.

DOLPHIN   'Tis Midnight, I'll go arm my self.    *Exit.*

ORLEANCE   The Dolphin longs for Morning.

RAMBURES   He longs to eat the English.                     100

CONSTABLE   I think he will eat all he kills.

ORLEANCE   By the white Hand of my Lady, he's a
gallant Prince.

CONSTABLE   Swear by her Foot, that she may tread
out the Oath.                                                    105

ORLEANCE   He is simply the most active Gentleman
of France.

CONSTABLE   Doing is Activity, and he will still be
Doing.

ORLEANCE   He never did Harm that I heard of.               110

CONSTABLE   Nor will do none tomorrow: he will keep

423

116     What's he?    *Who's that?*

121–
22
    never . . . Lackey    *The Constable implies that the only one who has ever been the victim of the Dolphin's "Valor" is his page.*

122–
23
    'Tis . . . bate.    *The Constable compares the Dolphin's valor to a hawk, which was kept hooded until it was ready to be released to pursue its prey; an eager hawk would bate (flap) its wings in anticipation of the hunt. The Constable's point is that the Dolphin's hooded (concealed) valor will not so much bate as 'bate (abate, dwindle) when it is given an opportunity to show its mettle. The Constable is talking about more than one kind of "hooded Valor," and that implication is continued in the references to "Will," "Devil," "your Friend," "Eye" [I], and "Fool" in the lines that follow.*

127     take up that    *meet that challenge, as in picking up an opponent's gage (pledge to engage in single combat).*

130     Have at the very Eye    *hit the eye of the target.*

133     Bolt    *arrow, but with a play on "semen."*

134     shot over    *shot above the target.*

135–
36
    over-shot    *bested.*

139     Who hath measur'd the Ground?    *The Constable's question probably has less to do with the accuracy of the measurement than with his skepticism that anyone was brave enough to take it. No doubt he assumes that this information has been provided by the Dolphin. When he learns that it was the Lord Grandpre (line 140), his tone changes completely.*

424

that Good Name still.

ORLEANCE   I know him to be Valiant.

CONSTABLE   I was told that, by one that knows him
better than you.                                                          115

ORLEANCE   What's he?

CONSTABLE   Marry he told me so himself, and he said
he car'd not who knew it.

ORLEANCE   He needs not, it is no hidden Virtue in
him.                                                                          120

CONSTABLE   By my faith, Sir, but it is: never any
body saw it but his Lackey. 'Tis a hooded
Valor, and when it appears, it will bate.

ORLEANCE   "Ill Will never said well."

CONSTABLE   I will cap that Proverb with "There is        125
Flattery in Friendship."

ORLEANCE   And I will take up that with "Give the
Devil his due."

CONSTABLE   Well-plac'd: there stands your Friend
for the Devil. Have at the very Eye of that              130
Proverb with "A Pox of the Devil."

ORLEANCE   You are the better at Proverbs by how
much "A Fool's Bolt is soon shot."

CONSTABLE   You have shot over.

ORLEANCE   'Tis not the first time you were over-          135
shot.

*Enter a Messenger.*

MESSENGER   My Lord High Constable, the English lie
within fifteen hundred Paces of your Tents.

CONSTABLE   Who hath measur'd the Ground?

425

144    peevish   *foolish.*

146    so far out of his Knowledge   *both (a) so far from familiar territory (where he knows what he is doing), and (b) so far from where ordinary prudence would take him.*

147    Apprehension   *ability to recognize the danger they are in.*

153    Mastiffs   *dogs used in bull and bear baiting; proverbial for ferocity.*

155    winking   *with their eyes closed. In lines 155–57 Orleance is comparing the English to their mastiffs and attributing to them the heedless fury that results from a blindness to common sense.*

160    Just, just   *precisely, even so.*

160–   sympathize with   *resemble; literally, share feelings with.*
61

161    robustious and rough   *reckless and beast-like.*

166    shrowdly   *shrewdly; sharply, painfully.*

169    Stomachs   *The stomach was the seat of both appetite and valor.*

MESSENGER   The Lord Grandpre.                          140

CONSTABLE   A valiant and most expert Gentleman.
   Would it were Day! Alas poor Harry of England:
   he longs not for the Dawning as we do.

ORLEANCE   What a wretched and peevish Fellow is
   this King of England, to mope with his fat-        145
   brain'd Followers so far out of his Knowledge!

CONSTABLE   If the English had any Apprehension,
   they would run away.

ORLEANCE   That they lack: for if their Heads had
   any intellectual Armor, they could never wear       150
   such heavy Head-pieces.

RAMBURES   That Island of England breeds very valiant
   Creatures: their Mastiffs are of unmatchable
   courage.

ORLEANCE   Foolish Curs, that run winking into the     155
   Mouth of a Russian Bear, and have their Heads
   crush'd like rotten Apples! You may as well
   say that's a valiant Flea that dare eat his
   Breakfast on the Lip of a Lion.

CONSTABLE   Just, just: and the Men do sympathize      160
   with the Mastiffs in robustious and rough
   coming on, leaving their Wits with their Wives.
   And then give them great Meals of Beef and
   Iron and Steel; they will eat like Wolves and
   fight like Devils.                                  165

ORLEANCE   Ay, but these English are shrowdly out
   of Beef.

CONSTABLE   Then shall we find tomorrow they have
   only Stomachs to eat, and none to fight. Now


427

171   a'  *o' (of the)*.

172   **We shall . . . Englishmen**  *This comment makes it clear that on the eve of the battle of Agincourt, all the French (not just the Dolphin) are completely confident of a lopsided victory.*

is it time to arm. Come, shall we about it?

ORLEANCE   It is now two a' Clock: but let me see,
　　by ten
We shall have each a hundred Englishmen.

*Exeunt.*

IV. Chorus    *The Chorus now prepares us for the climactic battle between the English and the French at Agincourt.*

1        entertain Conjecture of   *open your minds to imagine.*

3        wide Vessel    *the half-sphere of the Heavens now shielded from the Sun's rays.*

5        stilly    *both (a) quietly, and (b) incessantly.*

6        That    *so that.*
         fix'd Sentinels    *sentinels in their places.*

8        Fire answers Fire    *for every fire in one camp there is a corresponding fire in the other camp.*
         paly    *pale.*

9        Battail    *army, battalion.*
         umber'd    *shadowed, brownish yellow.*

# Act Four

CHORUS    Now entertain Conjecture of a Time
When creeping Murmur and the poring Dark
Fills the wide Vessel of the Universe.
From Camp to Camp, through the foul Womb
   of Night,
The Hum of either Army stilly sounds,                              5
That the fix'd Sentinels almost receive
The secret Whispers of each other's Watch.
Fire answers Fire, and through their paly
   Flames
Each Battail sees the other's umber'd Face.
Steed threatens Steed, in high and boastful
   Neighs                                                          10
Piercing the Night's dull Ear; and from the
   Tents

43¹

12     accomplishing    *equipping, outfitting.*

14     dreadful Note    *frightening sounds.*

17     Proud of their Numbers    *confident because they are so numerous.*
       secure in Soul    *filled with a sense of security.*

18     lusty    *jovial.*

19     play at Dice    *wager over (as in III.vii.94–95).*

20     creeple    *creeping along like a cripple.*

23     Sacrifices    *animals about to be offered as sacrifices.*
       watchful    *unsleeping.*

24     inly ruminate    *inwardly contemplate.*

25     sad    *serious, solemn.*

27     Presented them    *presented themselves, appeared.*

28     So    *like so.*

29     ruin'd    *wasted away, like architectural ruins.*

35     Note    *sign.*

36     dread    *intimidating.*
       enrounded    *surrounded.*

37     iot    *jot, iota.*

39     over-bears Attaint    *conquers any sign (taint) of weakness.*

The Armorers accomplishing the Knights,
With busy Hammers closing Rivets up,
Give dreadful Note of Preparation.
The Country Cocks do crow, the Clocks do toll;     15
And, the third hour of drowsy Morning nam'd,
Proud of their Numbers and secure in Soul,
The confident and over-lusty French
Do the low-rated English play at Dice,
And chide the creeple tardy-gaited Night,          20
Who, like a foul and ugly Witch, doth limp
So tediously away. The poor condemned English,
Like Sacrifices, by their watchful Fires
Sit patiently, and inly ruminate
The Morning's Danger; and, their Gesture sad       25
Investing lank-lean Cheeks and War-worn Coats,
Presented them unto the gazing Moon
So many horrid Ghosts. O now who will behold
The Royal Captain of this ruin'd Band
Walking from Watch to Watch, from Tent to Tent,    30
Let him cry "Praise and Glory on his Head!"
For forth he goes, and visits all his Host,
Bids them good morrow with a modest Smile,
And calls them Brothers, Friends, and
     Countrymen.
Upon his Royal Face there is no Note               35
How dread an Army hath enrounded him,
Nor doth he dedicate one iot of Color
Unto the weary and all-watched Night,
But freshly looks, and over-bears Attaint
With Cheerful Semblance and Sweet Majesty,         40
That ev'ry Wretch, pining and pale before,

433

43    Largess   *bounty; here pronounced "lár-jess."*

44    lib'ral   *generous.*

45    Mean and Gentle   *common men and gentlemen.*

46    as may Unworthiness define   *as far as one so unworthy (namely, the Chorus) may describe it.*

50    Foils   *blunted swords for use in fencing. There may also be a hint of "Foils" in another sense: dull backgrounds used to grace (set off by contrast) a lustrous gem. If so, however, the Chorus is introducing the notion only to encourage the audience to reject it as inappropriate for a dramatic presentation too crude to do anything more than "disgrace" (line 49) the noble object it seeks to display.*

51    Right ill dispos'd   *most inadequately deployed.*

53    Minding . . . be   *being put in mind of the real things by those inadequate "Mock'ries" (imitations) that seek to represent them.*

IV.i   *This scene takes place in the English camp at Agincourt.*

3    God morrow   *It is not clear whether this is a greeting to Bedford, or an oath similar to "God give good e'en" and parallel to "God Almighty." Modern editions normally emend "God" to "Good."*

5    distill it out   *extract it, draw it out.*

7    good Husbandry   *good management of one's affairs.*

Beholding him, plucks Comfort from his Looks.
A Largess Universal, like the Sun,
His lib'ral Eye doth give to ev'ry one,
Thawing cold Fear, that Mean and Gentle all                45
Behold, as may Unworthiness define,
A little touch of Harry in the Night.
And so our Scene must to the Battle fly,
Where, O for pity, we shall much disgrace
With four or five most vile and ragged Foils              50
(Right ill dispos'd, in Brawl ridiculous)
The Name of Agincourt. Yet sit and see,
Minding things True by what their Mock'ries be.

*Exit.*

# Scene 1

*Enter the King, Bedford, and Gloucester.*

KING   Gloucester, 'tis true that we are in great
      Danger;
   The greater therefore should our Courage be.
   —God morrow, Brother Bedford: God Almighty,
   There is some Soul of Goodness in things Evil,
   Would Men observingly distill it out,                   5
   For our bad Neighbor makes us early Stirrers,
   Which is both Healthful and good Husbandry.
   Besides, they are our outward Consciences,

10     **dress us fairly for our End**   *prepare ourselves for death.*

12     **make . . . himself**   *derive moral instruction from the Devil himself.*

15     **Were**   *would be.*
        **churlish**   *surly, unfriendly.*

16     **likes**   *pleases.*

19     **Upon Example**   *by making them examples to illustrate moral and spiritual truths.*
        **eased**   *rested, comforted.*

20     **quick'ned**   *enlivened, rejuvenated.*

21     **defunct**   *moribund, no longer functioning.*

22     **Break . . . Grave**   *break out of the grave in which they have been sleeping.*

23     **With casted Slough**   *having cast away the skin they have sloughed off (like snakes).*
        **Legerity**   *nimbleness.*

S.D.    **Exeunt Gloucester and Bedford.**   *This stage direction is not to be found in the First Folio, which provides only a general* Exeunt *following line 34. It may be that Gloucester and Bedford only begin their exit at this point and linger briefly for Erpingham.*

29     **attend**   *stay with, be of service to.*

32     **then**   *therefore.*

436

And Preachers to us all: admonishing
That we should dress us fairly for our End.                    10
Thus may we gather Honey from the Weed,
And make a Moral of the Div'l himself.

*Enter Erpingham.*

—Good morrow, old Sir Thomas Erpingham:
A good soft Pillow for that good white Head
Were better than a churlish Turf of France.                    15
ERPINGHAM    Not so, my Liege: this Lodging likes me
    better,
Since I may say, now lie I like a King.
KING    'Tis good for Men to love their present Pains
Upon Example: so the Spirit is eased;
And when the Mind is quick'ned, out of doubt                   20
The Organs, though defunct and dead before,
Break up their drowsy Grave and newly move
With casted Slough and fresh Legerity.
Lend me thy Cloak, Sir Thomas. —Brothers both,
Commend me to the Princes in our Camp;                         25
Do my good morrow to them, and anon
Desire them all to my Pavilion.
GLOUCESTER    We shall, my Liege.
                     *Exeunt Gloucester and Bedford.*
ERPINGHAM    Shall I attend your Grace?
KING                                    No, my good Knight.
Go with my Brothers to my Lords of England:                    30
I and my Bosom must debate a while,
And then I would no other Company.

34     'a   *have.*
        cheerfully   *in a manner that heartens me. If the Folio* Exeunt
        *before this line is an accurate indication of stage practice, the
        King speaks this line about rather than to Erpingham. It
        would seem to make equally good stage sense, however, to treat
        it as a reply to Erpingham's farewell.*

35     Che vous la?   *Who are you there?*

38     base, comm'n, and popular   *Pistol's inimitable way of say-
        ing "a commoner."*

40     Trail'st . . . Pike?   *Do you carry a pike? Pistol's question is
        an indirect way of asking "Are you a member of the infantry?"*

42     Then . . . King.   *The King is drawing a distinction be-
        tween himself and a monarch who has more than one kingdom
        under his rule.*

43     Bawcock   *good fellow (from the French* beau coq).

44     Imp   *child.*

46     Bully   *a term of endearment, like "chap."*

47     le Roy   *French for "the King."*

51     Saint Davy's Day   *March 1, the day set aside to honor the
        sixth-century Saint David.*

ERPINGHAM    The Lord in Heaven bless thee, Noble
    Harry.
KING    God 'a mercy, old Heart, thou speak'st
    cheerfully.                                    *Exit Erpingham.*

                    *Enter Pistol.*

PISTOL    *Che vous la?*                                          35
KING    A Friend.
PISTOL    Discuss unto me, art thou Officer,
    Or art thou base, comm'n, and popular?
KING    I am a Gentl'man of a Company.
PISTOL    Trail'st thou the puissant Pike?
KING                          Ev'n so; what are you?          40
PISTOL    As good a Gentl'man as the Emperor.
KING    Then you are a better than the King.
PISTOL    The King's a Bawcock, and a Heart of Gold,
    A Lad of Life, an Imp of Fame, of Parents good,
    Of Fist most valiant: I kiss his dirty Shoe,              45
    And from my Heart-string I love the lovely Bully.
    What is thy Name?
KING                          Harry le Roy.
PISTOL                          Le Roy?
    A Cornish Name: art thou of Cornish Crew?
KING    No, I am a Welchman.
PISTOL                          Know'st thou Fluellen?
KING                                              Yes.
PISTOL    Tell him I'll knock his Leek about his Pate      50
    Upon Saint Davy's Day.
KING                          Do not you wear
    Your Dagger in your Cap that day, lest he

    439

54      **Figo**   *an obscene gesture. Pistol has directed it against Fluellen in III.vi.60.*

S.D.      **Manet**   *remain.*

59      **fewer**   *Fluellen means "lower," more quietly.*
        **Admiration**   *Fluellen means "scandal."*

60      **aunchient**   *ancient.*

61      **Prerogatifes**   *prerogatives, principles.*

63      **Pompey the Great**   *a Roman general and statesman (106–48 B.C.), who was a member of the First Triumvirate. Pompey was defeated by Julius Caesar at Pharsalia and murdered shortly thereafter.*

64–65      **Tiddle-tadle, Pibble-bable**   *Both expressions refer to idle chatter. As it happens, Fluellen's example is ill-chosen: "Pompey's Camp" (line 65) was noted for its lack of discipline and sobriety, and that probably led to Pompey's downfall.*

73      **prating Coxcomb**   *strutting rooster. In this instance, Fluellen is on target.*

75      **in your own Conscience**   *to your own way of thinking. Fluellen's expression is a reminder that in Shakespeare's time "Conscience" was a word that also included what we now mean by "consciousness."*

Knock that about yours.

PISTOL                    Art thou his Friend?

KING   And 's Kinsman too.

PISTOL                         The Figo for thee then.

KING   I thank you: God be with you.

PISTOL                         My name is Pistol call'd.   55

KING   It sorts well with your Fierceness.

*Exit Pistol. Manet King, stepping to one side.*

*Enter Fluellen and Gower.*

GOWER   Captain Fluellen.

FLUELLEN   'So, in the Name of Iesu Christ, speak
     fewer. It is the greatest Admiration in the
     Universal World, when the true and aunchient     60
     Prerogatifes and Laws of the Wars is not kept.
     If you would take the pains but to examine the
     Wars of Pompey the Great, you shall find, I
     warrant you, that there is no Tiddle-tadle
     nor Pibble-bable in Pompey's Camp; I warrant     65
     you, you shall find the Ceremonies of the Wars,
     and the Cares of it, and the Forms of it, and
     the Sobriety of it, and the Modesty of it, to
     be otherwise.

GOWER   Why the Enemy is loud, you hear him all       70
     Night.

FLUELLEN   If the Enemy is an Ass and a Fool, and a
     prating Coxcomb, is it meet, think you, that
     we should also, look you, be an Ass and a Fool,
     and a prating Coxcomb, in your own Conscience    75
     now?

441

80 Though . . . Fashion  *though it wears somewhat quaint apparel.*

81 Care  *conscientiousness.*

91 Under Sir Thomas Erpingham.  *The King is telling the truth: he is "under" Erpingham's cloak (line 24).*

95 wrack'd upon a Sand  *shipwrecked upon a sandbar.*

98 meet  *fitting.*

101 the Element shows to him  *the sky looks to him.*

102-3 Humane Conditions  *human qualities.*

103 His Ceremonies laid by  *the trappings of monarchy set aside.*

GOWER   I will speak lower.

FLUELLEN   I pray you, and beseech you, that you
will.                              *Exeunt Fluellen and Gower.*

KING   Though it appear a little out of Fashion,                    80
There is much Care and Valor in this Welchman.

*Enter three Soldiers, John Bates, Alexander Court,
and Michael Williams.*

COURT   Brother John Bates, is not that the Morning
which breaks yonder?

BATES   I think it be: but we have no great cause to
desire the approach of Day.                                        85

WILLIAMS   We see yonder the Beginning of the Day,
but I think we shall never see the End of it.
—Who goes there?

KING   A Friend.

WILLIAMS   Under what Captain serve you?                           90

KING   Under Sir Thomas Erpingham.

WILLIAMS   A good old Commander, and a most kind
Gentleman. I pray you, what thinks he of our
Estate?

KING   Even as Men wrack'd upon a Sand, that look                  95
to be wash'd off the next Tide.

BATES   He hath not told his Thought to the King?

KING   No: nor it is not meet he should. For though
I speak it to you, I think the King is but a
Man as I am. The Violet smells to him as it                        100
doth to me; the Element shows to him as it
doth to me; all his Senses have but Humane
Conditions. His Ceremonies laid by, in his

443

105　Affections　*desires and feelings.*
　　　higher mounted　*placed in a more exalted social position.*

107　Reason of Fears　*reasons to be afraid.*

108　out of doubt　*without doubt.*

109　relish　*taste, flavor.*

110　possess him　*take possession of him, instill in him (the King).*

111　he　*the King.*

113　show　*reveal, display.*

116–　at all adventures　*under any circumstances, however hazard-*
17　　*ous.*

117　so we were quit here　*so long as we were removed from here.*

118–　I will . . . King　*I will speak my thoughts about the King.*
19　　*But of course the King's words here are spoken with dramatic*
　　　*irony: what he also means is "I will speak my thoughts of the*
　　　*King" in the sense "I will speak the King's thoughts (because*
　　　*my thoughts are his thoughts)."*

128　his Quarrel　*his dispute, reason for entering into conflict.*

131　seek after　*seek to know.*

Nakedness he appears but a Man, and though his
Affections are higher mounted than ours, yet          105
when they stoop, they stoop with the like
Wing. Therefore, when he sees Reason of Fears,
as we do, his Fears, out of doubt, be of the
same relish as ours are; yet in Reason, no man
should possess him with any Appearance of Fear,      110
lest he, by showing it, should dishearten his
Army.

BATES   He may show what outward Courage he will;
but I believe, as cold a Night as 'tis, he
could wish himself in Thames up to the Neck;          115
and so I would he were, and I by him, at all
adventures, so we were quit here.

KING   By my troth, I will speak my Conscience of
the King: I think he would not wish himself
any where but where he is.                            120

BATES   Then I would he were here alone; so should
he be sure to be ransomed, and a many poor
men's Lives saved.

KING   I dare say you love him not so ill to wish
him here alone, howsoever you speak this to           125
feel other men's Minds. Methinks I could not
die any where so contented as in the King's
company, his Cause being just and his Quarrel
honorable.

WILLIAMS   That's more than we know.                  130

BATES   Ay, or more than we should seek after: for
we know enough if we know we are the King's
Subjects. If his Cause be wrong, our Obedience
to the King wipes the Crime of it out of us.

445

136    heavy Reckoning to make    *serious responsibility to bear.*

138–    at the Latter Day    *on the day of the Last Judgment.*
39

140    Surgeon    *physician.*

141    upon    *with. So also in the phrases that follow.*

143    rawly left    *abruptly left (without farewells and without proper provisions being made for their welfare).*

145    charitably dispose of any thing    *make provision for anything in the context of Christian love.*

146    Blood is their Argument    *killing is their only concern right now.*

149    against all proportion of Subjection    *in violation of the very relationship between a subject and his ruler.*

150–    sent about Marchandise    *sent out as a merchant (trader).*
51

151    sinfully miscarry    *die in a state of sinfulness.*

152    imputation of    *responsibility for.*

157    irreconcil'd Iniquities    *sins not confessed, repented, and forgiven.*

158    Author of    *agent or cause of.*

160    bound    *committed, required, responsible.*

165    never    *Modern usage would call for "ever" here.*

WILLIAMS    But if the Cause be not good, the King    135
    himself hath a heavy Reckoning to make, when
    all those Legs and Arms and Heads chopp'd off
    in a Battle shall join together at the Latter
    Day and cry all, "We died at such a place,
    some swearing, some crying for a Surgeon, some    140
    upon their Wives left poor behind them, some
    upon the Debts they owe, some upon their
    Children rawly left." I am afear'd there are
    few die well that die in a Battle: for how can
    they charitably dispose of any thing when    145
    Blood is their Argument? Now, if these Men do
    not die well, it will be a Black Matter for
    the King that led them to it; who to disobey
    were against all proportion of Subjection.

KING    So, if a Son that is by his Father sent about    150
    Marchandise do sinfully miscarry upon the Sea,
    the imputation of his Wickedness, by your rule,
    should be imposed upon his Father that sent
    him. Or if a Servant, under his Master's
    Command transporting a sum of Money, be    155
    assailed by Robbers and die in many
    irreconcil'd Iniquities, you may call the
    Business of the Master the Author of the
    Servant's Damnation. But this is not so. The
    King is not bound to answer the particular    160
    Endings of his Soldiers, the Father of his Son,
    nor the Master of his Servant: for they
    purpose not their Death when they purpose
    their Services. Besides, there is no King, be
    his Cause never so spotless, if it come to the    165

447

166    arbitrement of Swords    *judgment determined by the outcome of battle.*

167    peradventure    *perhaps.*

168    contrived    *plotted.*

169    beguiling    *deceiving, cheating.*

170    broken Seals of Perjury    *pledges made but not kept.*

171    Bulwark    *shield, protection, pretext.*

174    outrun Native Punishment    *evaded punishment in their native land.*

176    Beadle    *an officer who punished criminals, usually by whipping them.*

177–
78    for before-Breach . . . Quarrel    *for their earlier crimes against the King's laws [while fighting] in the King's current war.*

179    the Death    *execution.*

181    die unprovided    *die without having prepared their souls for the Day of Judgment.*

184    visited    *punished.*

188    Moth    *mote, speck; an allusion to Matthew 7:3 and Luke 6:41.*

189    Advantage    *benefit (because his soul is prepared for Heaven).*

194    see    *behold, experience.*
       His Greatness    *his grace (loving mercy).*

448

arbitrement of Swords, can try it out with all
unspotted Soldiers. Some, peradventure, have
on them the Guilt of premeditated and contrived
Murther; some, of beguiling Virgins with the
broken Seals of Perjury; some, making the Wars          170
their Bulwark, that have before gored the
gentle Bosom of Peace with Pillage and Robbery.
Now, if these Men have defeated the Law, and
outrun Native Punishment, though they can out-
strip Men, they have no Wings to fly from God.         175
War is His Beadle, War is His Vengeance: so
that here Men are punish'd for before-Breach
of the King's Laws in now the King's Quarrel.
Where they feared the Death, they have borne
Life away; and where they would be safe, they          180
perish. Then if they die unprovided, no more
is the King guilty of their Damnation than he
was before guilty of those Impieties for the
which they are now visited. Every Subject's
Duty is the King's, but every Subject's Soul            185
is his Own. Therefore should every Soldier in
the Wars do as every Sick Man in his Bed: wash
every Moth out of his Conscience. And dying so,
Death is to him Advantage; or not dying, the
Time was blessedly lost wherein such                    190
Preparation was gained. And in him that
escapes, it were not Sin to think that, making
God so free an Offer, He let him outlive that
Day to see His Greatness and to teach others
how they should prepare.                                195
WILLIAMS    'Tis certain, every Man that dies ill,

449

198    answer it    *answer for it (bear responsibility for it).*

200    lustily    *vigorously, wholeheartedly.*

208–   You . . . Monarch.    *Williams is saying "You pay him back*
10     *then." He says that for a private citizen to challenge his*
       *monarch would be just as foolhardy ("perilous") as to go into*
       *battle armed with nothing more than a popgun made out of*
       *hollowed elder wood.*

212    Peacock's Feather    *the feather of a bird proverbial for vanity.*

215    is something too round    *goes too far, is somewhat too sweep-*
       *ing.*

215–   I should . . . convenient.    *I would challenge you to single*
16     *combat if this were the time and place for the settling of private*
       *grievances.*

221    Gage    *pledge of honor.*

222    Bonnet    *cap.*

the Ill upon his own Head; the King is not to
answer it.

BATES   I do not desire he should answer for me, and
yet I determine to fight lustily for him.                          200

KING   I my self heard the King say he would not be
ransom'd.

WILLIAMS   Ay, he said so, to make us fight
cheerfully: but when our Throats are cut, he
may be ransom'd, and we ne'er the wiser.                           205

KING   If I live to see it, I will never trust his Word
after.

WILLIAMS   You pay him then: that's a perilous Shot
out of an Elder-gun that a poor and a private
Displeasure can do against a Monarch. You may                      210
as well go about to turn the Sun to Ice with
fanning in his Face with a Peacock's Feather.
You'll never trust his Word after: come, 'tis
a foolish Saying!

KING   Your Reproof is something too round; I should     215
be angry with you if the Time were convenient.

WILLIAMS   Let it be a Quarrel between us, if you
live.

KING   I embrace it.

WILLIAMS   How shall I know thee again?                   220

KING   Give me any Gage of thine, and I will wear it
in my Bonnet; then if ever thou dar'st
acknowledge it, I will make it my Quarrel.

WILLIAMS   Here's my Glove: give me another of thine.

KING   There.                                            225

WILLIAMS   This will I also wear in my Cap: if ever
thou come to me and say, after tomorrow, "This

48¹

228    take thee    *give you.*

235    Be Friends    *quit quarreling.*

236    enow    *enough.*

237    reckon    *count.*

239–    for they . . . Shoulders    *The "Crowns" the French bear*
40    *on their shoulders are their heads. The King implies that the*
*French outnumber the English twenty to one: hence the odds in*
*"French Crowns" (coins), lines 238–39.*

240–    but . . . Clipper    *The King continues the puns on coins and*
42    *heads. Cutting or clipping English crowns (coins worth five*
*shillings) was illegal, but of course in England that prohibi-*
*tion did not apply to the currency of other countries.*

245    We    *Here the King means "I."*

249    neglect    *forgo, surrender, deny themselves.*

251    Ceremony    *all the honors, regalia, pomp, and privileges that*
*attend the institution of monarchy.*

253–    What kind of God . . . Worshippers?    *The King is*
55    *pointing out that monarchs are even lower than their subjects*
*in terms of life's comforts and pleasures. This would seem to*
*suggest that kingship has nothing to do with divinity. But of*
*course the kind of "God" the King describes here sounds very*
*much like the real God who, through His Incarnation in*
*Christ, suffered "more of mortal Griefs" than do His "Wor-*
*shippers."*

is my Glove," by this Hand I will take thee a
Box on the Ear.

KING   If ever I live to see it, I will challenge it.                    230

WILLIAMS   Thou dar'st as well be hang'd.

KING   Well, I will do it, though I take thee in the
King's company.

WILLIAMS   Keep thy Word: fare thee well.

BATES   Be Friends, you English Fools, be Friends;            235
we have French Quarrels enow, if you could
tell how to reckon.

KING   Indeed the French may lay twenty French
Crowns to one they will beat us, for they
bear them on their Shoulders; but it is no            240
English Treason to cut French Crowns, and
tomorrow the King himself will be a Clipper.

*Exeunt Soldiers.*

Upon the King. Let us our Lives, our Souls,
Our Debts, our careful Wives, our Children,
and
Our Sins lay on the King: We must bear all.            245
O hard Condition, Twin-born with Greatness,
Subject to the Breath of ev'ry Fool
Whose Sense no more can feel but his own
Wringing.
What infinite Heart's-ease must Kings neglect
That Private Men enjoy! And what have Kings            250
That Privates have not too, save Ceremony,
Save gen'ral Ceremony? And what art thou,
Thou Idol Ceremony? What kind of God
Art thou, that suffer'st more of mortal Griefs
Than do thy Worshippers? Where are thy Rents?            255

453

256     Comings-in    *revenues, income.*

258     Of    *composed of, made of nothing more than.*
        ought    *anything.*

259     Place    *exalted position. The King puns on this sense in line 267.*

262     in stead of    *in the place of.*

267     Will . . . Bending?    *Will it be cured by curtsies and obeisance?*

269     Command the Health of it    *maintain or restore its health. For similar sentiments, see the comments of Henry V's father and grandfather in I.iii.212–14 and 224–31 of* Richard II.

270     King's Repose    *The King's remarks on sleep recall those of his father at the beginning of III.i in* 2 Henry IV.

271     find thee    *find thee out, expose thee.*

274     inter-tissu'd    *interwoven.*

275     farsed    *farced, stuffed.*

276     Pomp    *magnificence, glory.*

280     Slave    *serf, bondman.*

281     vacant    *empty.*

What are thy Comings-in? O Ceremony,
Show me but thy Worth. What, is thy Soul
Of Adoration? Art thou ought else
But Place, Degree, and Form, creating Awe
And Fear in other Men, wherein thou art                    260
Less happy, being fear'd, than they in fearing?
What drink'st thou oft, in stead of Homage
   sweet,
But poison'd Flatt'ry? O be Sick, great
   Greatness,
And bid thy Ceremony give thee Cure!
Thinks thou the fiery Fever will go out                    265
With Titles blown from Adulation?
Will it give place to Flexure and low Bending?
Canst thou, when thou command'st the Beggar's
   Knee,
Command the Health of it? No, thou proud Dream
That play'st so subtly with a King's Repose,               270
I am a King that find thee: and I know
'Tis not the Balm, the Scepter, and the Ball,
The Sword, the Mace, the Crown Imperial,
The inter-tissu'd Robe of Gold and Pearl,
The farsed Title running 'fore the King,                   275
The Throne he sits on, nor the Tide of Pomp,
That beats upon the high Shore of this World.
No, not all these, thrice-gorgeous Ceremony,
Not all these, laid in Bed Majestical,
Can sleep so soundly as the wretched Slave                 280
Who, with a Body fill'd and vacant Mind,
Gets him to rest, cramm'd with distressful
   Bread;

455

283   horrid Night   *the dark night of the souls of those whose burdens will not allow them restful sleep.*

284   like a Lackey   *like a footman who runs alongside his master's coach.*
      from the Rise to Set   *from dawn to dusk.*

285   Phoebus   *one of the names of the Sun God; here, as in line 287, the Sun itself.*

286   Elysium   *the Elysian Fields of classical mythology, more or less equivalent to the Heaven of Christian tradition.*

287   Hyperion   *another name for the Sun God. Technically, Hyperion was the father of Helios; both were associated with the Sun, as was Phoebus.*

288   so   *thus.*

289   profitable Labor   *productive work; work that contributes to the well-being of the commonwealth.*

292   Forehand and Vantage   *both terms mean "advantage" here.*

294   gross   *unrefined, coarse.*
      wots   *knows, realizes.*

296   Whose   *the King's.*
      the Peasant best advantages   *bring more benefits to the peasant than to the King.*

297   jealous of   *fearful because of.*

303   Reck'ning . . . Numbers   *counting up the numbers of the enemy.*

456

Never sees horrid Night, the Child of Hell,
But like a Lackey, from the Rise to Set,
Sweats in the Eye of Phoebus, and all Night          285
Sleeps in Elysium; next day after Dawn
Doth rise and help Hyperion to his Horse
And follows so the ever-running Year
With profitable Labor to his Grave.
And but for Ceremony, such a Wretch,                 290
Winding up Days with Toil and Nights with
    Sleep,
Had the Forehand and Vantage of a King.
The Slave, a Member of the Country's Peace,
Enjoys it, but in gross Brain little wots
What Watch the King keeps to maintain the Peace,    295
Whose Hours the Peasant best advantages.

*Enter Erpingham.*

ERPINGHAM   My Lord, your Nobles, jealous of your
      Absence,
    Seek through your Camp to find you.
KING                           Good old Knight,
    Collect them all together at my Tent.
    I'll be before thee.
ERPINGHAM           I shall do 't, my Lord.   *Exit.*   300
KING   O God of Battles, steel my Soldiers's Hearts,
    Possess them not with Fear! Take from them now
    The sense of Reck'ning of th' opposed Numbers:
    Pluck their Hearts from them. Not today, O
      Lord,
    O not today, think not upon the Fault          305

457

306  compassing   *taking possession of, encompassing.*

313  Chauntries   *chapels where special prayers and masses were chanted for the souls of the dead.*

316  after all   *after the deposition and murder of an anointed king have already occurred.*

320  stay   *wait.*

My Father made in compassing the Crown.
I Richard's Body have interred new,
And on it have bestow'd more contrite Tears
Than from it issu'd forced Drops of Blood.
Five hundred Poor I have in yearly Pay,                    310
Who twice a Day their wither'd Hands hold up
Toward Heav'n to pardon Blood; and I have built
Two Chauntries, where the sad and solemn
   Priests
Sing still for Richard's Soul. More will I do,
Though all that I can do is Nothing worth,                 315
Since that my Penitence comes after all,
Imploring Pardon.

*Enter Gloucester.*

GLOUCESTER   My Liege.
KING        —My Brother Gloucester's Voice. —Ay,
  I know thy Errand, I will go with thee.
  The Day, my Friends, and all things stay for
    me.                     *Exeunt.*  320

IV.ii     *The scene shifts back to the French camp at Agincourt.*

1     gild    *coat with gold.*

2     Monte Cheval!    *Mount Horse!*
       Verlot Lacquay    *varlet (valet) lackey.*

3     Via . . . Terre!    *Away, Waters and Earth!*

4     Rien . . . Feu?    *Nothing more? [Not] Air and Fire [too]?*
       Cieux    *the Heavens themselves.*

6     Heark    *note, observe. Also spelled "Hark."*
       present    *immediate.*

8     spin    *spray.*

9     doubt    *intimidate, frighten (a sense preserved in "redoubt-
         able"). Modern editions normally emend to* dout, *"do out,"
         extinguish. No doubt Shakespeare intends to combine the two
         senses.*
       with superfluous Courage    *with our overabundance of
         courage.*

460

# Scene 2

*Enter the Dolphin, Orleance, Rambures,*
*and Beaumont.*

ORLEANCE   The Sun doth gild our Armor: up, my
    Lords!
DOLPHIN   *Monte Cheval!* My Horse, *Verlot Lacquay!*
    Ha!
ORLEANCE   O brave Spirit!
DOLPHIN                    *Via, les Eaux et Terre!*
ORLEANCE   *Rien puis? L'Air et Feu?*
DOLPHIN                          *Cieux,*
    Cousin Orleance!

*Enter Constable.*

        —Now, my Lord Constable?                    5
CONSTABLE   Heark how our Steeds, for present
    Service, neigh.
DOLPHIN   Mount them, and make incision in their
    Hides
    That their hot Blood may spin in English Eyes
    And doubt them with superfluous Courage. Ha!
RAMBURES   What, will you have them weep our
    Horses' Blood?                                    10
    How shall we then behold their nat'ral Tears?

461

12 embattail'd *drawn up in battalions in preparation for battle.*

15 Fair Show *impressive appearance.*

16 Shales *shells.*

19 Curtle-axe *cutlass.*

20 That *so that.*

22 The Vapor of our Valor *The Constable's words will take on an ironic cast in the light of subsequent events. Here the V sounds evoke another word,* vanity *(which literally means vapor or bubbles), that aptly epitomizes the hubris of the French.*

23 positive *certain.*

24 Lacquies *lackeys. The spelling probably indicates that the word is to be spoken with a French accent, as in line 2.*

26 Squares of Battail *squared formations.*
  enow *enough.*

27 hilding *worthless.*

28 Mountain's Basis *foothill, base of a mountain.*
  by *nearby. In lines 28–29 the Constable echoes what we have heard earlier about how Edward III stood on a mountain and smiled while his son led an English army to victory over the French. See I.ii.103–14 and II.iv.53–62.*

33 Tucket Sonance *trumpet call.*

34 dare *terrify.*

*Enter a Messenger.*

MESSENGER   The English are embattail'd, you French
    Peers.
CONSTABLE   To Horse, you gallant Princes, straight
    to Horse!
Do but behold yond poor and starved Band,
And your Fair Show shall suck away their Souls,      15
Leaving them but the Shales and Husks of Men.
There is not Work enough for all our Hands,
Scarce Blood enough in all their sickly Veins
To give each naked Curtle-axe a Stain,
That our French Gallants shall today draw out      20
And sheathe for lack of Sport. Let us but blow
    on them,
The Vapor of our Valor will o'erturn them.
'Tis positive 'gainst all exceptions, Lords,
That our superfluous Lacquies and our Peasants,
Who in unnecessary Action swarm      25
About our Squares of Battail, were enow
To purge this Field of such a hilding Foe,
Though we upon this Mountain's Basis by
Took stand for idle Speculation;
But that our Honors must not. What's to say?      30
A very little Little let us do
And all is done. Then let the Trumpets sound
The Tucket Sonance, and the Note to mount:
For our Approach shall so much dare the Field
That England shall couch down in Fear and      35
    yield.

37   Yond . . . Bones   *Grandpre describes the famished English soldiers as if they were little more than walking corpses.*

38   Ill-favor'dly become   *are too ugly for.*

39   Curtains   *banners.*

41   Big Mars   *the threatening God of War.*
banqu'rout   *bankrout (bankrupt). The Folio spelling suggests an attempt to render a French accent.*

42   Beaver   *visor.*

44   Torch-staves   *lances resembling the candlesticks on ornamental candelabra.*

45   Lob down   *droop.*

46   down roping   *trickling down in rope-like streams.*

47   gimmal'd   *jointed.*

48   Chaw'd   *chewed.*

49   Executors   *those who dispose of the dead and their possessions.*

52   Battail   *army, battalion.*

53   liveless   *lifeless.*

54   stay for   *await.*

GRANDPRE    Why do you stay so long, my Lords of
      France?
    Yond Island Carrions, desp'rate of their Bones,
    Ill-favor'dly become the Morning Field:
    Their ragged Curtains poorly are let loose,
    And our Air shakes them passing scornfully.                    40
    Big Mars seems banqu'rout in their beggar'd
      Host,
    And faintly through a rusty Beaver peeps.
    The Horsemen sit like fixed Candlesticks,
    With Torch-staves in their Hand; and their
      poor Jades
    Lob down their Heads, dropping the Hides and
      Hips;                                                        45
    The Gum down roping from their pale-dead Eyes,
    And in their pale dull Mouths the gimmal'd Bit
    Lies foul with Chaw'd-grass, still and motionless;
    And their Executors, the knavish Crows,
    Fly o'er them all, impatient for their Hour.                   50
    Description cannot suit itself in Words
    To demonstrate the Life of such a Battail,
    In Life so liveless as it shows itself.
CONSTABLE    They have said their Prayers, and they
      stay for Death.
DOLPHIN    Shall we go send them Dinners, and fresh
      Suits,                                                       55
    And give their fasting Horses Provender,
    And after fight with them?

IV.iii   *The scene shifts back to the English camp at Agincourt.*

5   a fearful Odds   *a terrifying disadvantage.*

6   bu'y   *be with.*

CONSTABLE   I stay but for my Guard. On to the Field!
    I will the Banner from a Trumpet take,
    And use it for my Haste. Come, come away;    60
    The Sun is high, and we out-wear the Day.    *Exeunt.*


# Scene 3

*Enter Gloucester, Bedford, Exeter, Erpingham with all
his Host, Salisbury, and Westmerland.*

GLOUCESTER   Where is the King?
BEDFORD   The King himself is rode to view their
    Battail.
WESTMERLAND   Of Fighting Men they have full
    threescore thousand.
EXETER   That's five to one; besides they are all
    fresh.
SALISBURY   God's Arm strike with us: 'tis a fearful
    Odds!    5
    God bu'y you, Princes all: I'll to my Charge.
    If we no more meet till we meet in Heaven,
    Then joyfully, my noble Lord of Bedford,
    My dear Lord Gloucester, and my good Lord
    Exeter,
    And my kind Kinsman, Warriors all, adieu.    10
BEDFORD   Farewell, good Salisbury, and good luck
    go with thee.

467

13    mind   *put in mind, remind.*

14    fram'd   *composed.*

20    enow   *enough.*

25    upon my Cost   *at my expense.*

26    yearns   *grieves, troubles.*

32    share from me   *take from my share.*

33    the best Hope I have   *that which I most aspire to. The King's sentiments resemble those of Hotspur in I.iii.199–205 of* 1 Henry IV. *But they lack the rhetorical excess of Hotspur's remarks, and they place personal honor firmly in the context of a patriotic cause. After the battle, moreover, the King's tone changes completely.*

34    Host   *army.*

EXETER   Farewell, kind Lord; fight valiantly today.
And yet I do thee wrong to mind thee of it,
For thou art fram'd of the firm truth of Valor.

*Exit Salisbury.*

BEDFORD   He is as full of Valor as of Kindness,                15
Princely in both.

*Enter the King.*

WESTMERLAND        O that we now had here
But one ten thousand of those Men in England
That do no Work today!
KING                        What's he that wishes so?
My Cousin Westmerland. No, my fair Cousin,
If we are mark'd to die, we are enow                            20
To do our Country loss; and if to live,
The fewer Men, the greater Share of Honor.
God's Will, I pray thee wish not one Man more!
By Jove, I am not covetous for Gold,
Nor care I who doth feed upon my Cost;                         25
It yearns me not if Men my Garments wear;
Such outward things dwell not in my Desires.
But if it be a Sin to covet Honor,
I am the most offending Soul alive.
No 'faith, my Coz, wish not a Man from England:               30
God's Peace, I would not lose so great an Honor
As one Man more methinks would share from me
For the best Hope I have! O do not wish one
   more.
Rath'r proclaim it, Westmerland, through my Host,

469

35      Stomach to   *both (a) appetite for, and (b) guts for.*

37      Convoy   *transport.*

40      This Day . . . Crispian   *October 25 was the day when the Church celebrated two saints, Crispinus and Crispianus, brothers who fled Rome and were martyred in A.D. 287. Because of their trade, they became the patron saints of shoemakers.*

42      a'   *on.*

44      live   *live to.*

45      Vigil   *religious commemoration of the occasion.*

48      had   *obtained.*

49      forget   *are forgetful.*

50      with Advantages   *with embellishments.*

63      gentle his Condition   *turn him from a commoner into a gentleman.*

That he which hath no Stomach to this Fight,                    35
Let him depart; his Passport shall be made,
And Crowns for Convoy put into his Purse.
We would not die in that Man's Company
That fears his Fellowship to die with us.
This Day is call'd the Feast of Crispian:                        40
He that outlives this Day and comes safe Home
Will stand a' tiptoe when this Day is nam'd
And rouse him at the Name of Crispian.
He that shall see this Day and live Old Age
Will yearly on the Vigil feast his Neighbors                     45
And say "Tomorrow is Saint Crispian."
Then will he strip his Sleeve and show his Scars
And say "These Wounds I had on Crispin's Day."
Old Men forget; yet all shall be forgot,
But he'll remember, with Advantages,                             50
What Feats he did that Day. Then shall our
    Names,
Familiar in his Mouth as Household Words,
Harry the King, Bedford and Exeter,
Warwick and Talbot, Salisbury and Gloucester,
Be in their flowing Cups freshly remember'd.                     55
This Story shall the Good Man teach his Son;
And Crispin Crispian shall ne'er go by,
From this Day to the Ending of the World,
But we in it shall be remembered:
We Few, we Happy Few, we Band of Brothers                        60
(For he today that sheds his Blood with me
Shall be my Brother: be he ne'er so vile,
This Day shall gentle his Condition).

68     bestow  *prepare.*

70     expedience  *speed.*

72     backward  *reluctant, hesitant.*

77     likes  *pleases.*

S.D.    Tucket  *trumpet call.*

80     compound  *agree, settle.*

And Gentlemen in England now a-bed
Shall think themselves accurst they were not
    here,                                      65
And hold their Manhoods cheap whiles any speaks
That fought with us upon Saint Crispin's Day.

*Enter Salisbury.*

SALISBURY   My Sov'reign Lord, bestow your self with
    speed:
    The French are bravely in their Battails set,
    And will with all expedience charge on us.    70
KING   All things are ready if our Minds be so.
WESTMERLAND   Perish the Man whose Mind is
    backward now.
KING   Thou dost not wish more help from England,
    Coz?
WESTMERLAND   God's Will, my Liege, would you
    and I alone,
    Without more help, could fight this Royal Battail!    75
KING   Why now thou hast unwish'd five thousand Men,
    Which likes me better than to wish us one.
    You know your Places: God be with you all.

*Tucket. Enter Montjoy.*

MONTJOY   Once more I come to know of thee, King
    Harry,
    If for thy Ransom thou wilt now compound    80
    Before thy most assured Overthrow:

82      Gulf    *maelstrom.*

83      englutted    *drowned, swallowed.*

84      mind    *put in mind.*

86      Retire    *departure, withdrawal.*

91      achieve me    *win me, take possession of me.*

93–94   The Man . . . him.    *The King alludes to one of Aesop's fables; he changes the animal in the story from a bear to a lion, a traditional symbol of royalty.*

95      A many    *a number.*

97      live in Brass    *be preserved in permanent form.*

101     reeking    *in vapors (like their spirits).*

For certainly thou art so near the Gulf
Thou must needs be englutted. Besides, in
  mercy
The Constable desires thee thou wilt mind
Thy Foll'wers of Repentance, that their Souls     85
May make a peaceful and a sweet Retire
From off these Fields where, Wretches, their
  poor Bodies
Must lie and fester.
KING                          Who hath sent thee now?
MONTJOY   The Constable of France.
KING   I pray thee bear my former Answer back:     90
Bid them achieve me, and then sell my Bones.
Good God, why should they mock poor Fellows
  thus?
The Man that once did sell the Lion's Skin
While the Beast liv'd was kill'd with hunting
  him.
A many of our Bodies shall no doubt          95
Find Native Graves, upon the which, I trust,
Shall witness live in Brass of this Day's Work.
And those that leave their valiant Bones in
  France,
Dying like Men, though buri'd in your Dunghills,
They shall be fam'd: for there the Sun shall
  greet them,                                  100
And draw their Honors reeking up to Heaven,
Leaving their Earthly Parts to choke your Clime,
The Smell whereof shall breed a Plague in
  France.

475

104      abounding    *both (a) abundant, and (b) rebounding.*

105      crasing    *ricocheting.*

107      in relapse of Mortality    *in resurrection from Death, rebounding from the grave.*

109      Warriors for the Working-day    *workaday warriors.*

115      in the Trim    *in their best array.*

117      in fresher Robes    *in the robes they will wear in Heaven.*

117–19      they will pluck . . . Service    *Having removed the French soldiers' livery, the English soldiers will remove the French soldiers themselves from military service. The King may be echoing the French crowns image from IV.i.238–40. If so, his implication is that, like coins that are no longer current (either because they are out of date or because they are damaged), the French soldiers will be taken out of circulation.*

121      levi'd    *demanded, collected.*

Mark then abounding Valor in our English:
That, being dead, like to the Bullets' crasing,                    105
Break out into a second course of Mischief,
Killing in relapse of Mortality.
Let me speak proudly. Tell the Constable
We are but Warriors for the Working-day:
Our Gayness and our Gilt are all besmirch'd                       110
With rainy Marching in the painful Field;
There's not a piece of Feather in our Host
(Good Argument, I hope, we will not fly),
And Time hath worn us into Slovenry.
But by the Mass, our Hearts are in the Trim,                      115
And my poor Soldiers tell me, yet ere Night
They'll be in fresher Robes or they will pluck
The gay new Coats o'er the French Soldiers'
   Heads
And turn them out of Service. If they do this
(As, if God please, they shall), my Ransom then                  120
Will soon be levi'd. Herald, save thou thy
   Labor:
Come thou no more for Ransom, gentle Herald.
They shall have none, I fear, but these my
   Joints,
Which, if they have as I will leave 'em them,
Shall yield them little, tell the Constable.                      125
MONTJOY   I shall, King Harry. And so fare thee well:
   Thou never shalt hear Herald any more.          *Exit.*
KING   I fear thou wilt once more come again for a
   Ransom.

130    **Vaward**  *vanguard.*

IV.iv    *This scene takes place on the battlefield at Agincourt.*

S.D.    **Excursions**  *sorties, charges into combat.*

2–3    **Je pense . . . qualite.**  *"I think that you are a gentleman of good quality (family)."*

4    **Qualitie . . . me!**  *Pistol, who appears to understand no French, picks up the word "qualite" and then adds a phrase of his own, possibly one that echoes the refrain of a Irish song.*

6    **Seigneur Dieu**  *Lord God. Pistol's response in the next speech indicates that he believes that the soldier has identified himself as "Lord Dew."*

8    **Perpend**  *listen to, ponder.*

9    **Fox**  *sword. The name apparently derives from the trademark on a special kind of swordblade.*

11    **Egregious**  *huge.*

12    **O prenes . . . moy!**  *"O have mercy! Take pity on me!"*

13    **Moy**  *Pistol assumes that "moy" is an amount of money.*

14    **Rim**  *diaphragm.*

*Enter York.*

YORK   My Lord, most humbly on my Knee I beg
    The leading of the Vaward.                                     130
KING   Take it, brave York. —Now, Soldiers, march
    away.
    —And how thou pleasest, God, dispose the Day!
                                    *Exeunt.*

# Scene 4

*Alarum. Excursions. Enter Pistol, French Soldier, Boy.*

PISTOL   Yield, Cur!
SOLDIER   *Je pense que vous estes le Gentilhomme de
    bonne qualite.*
PISTOL   Qualitie calmie custure me! Art thou a
    Gentleman? What is thy Name? Discuss.                    5
SOLDIER   *O Seigneur Dieu!*
PISTOL   O Signieur Dew should be a Gentleman.
    Perpend my words, O Signieur Dew, and mark:
    O Signieur Dew, thou diest on point of Fox,
    Except, O Signeur, thou do give to me                    10
    Egregious Ransom.
SOLDIER   *O prenes misericorde! Aye pitie de moy!*
PISTOL   Moy shall not serve: I will have forty Moys:
    For I will fetch thy Rim out at thy Throat

479

16–17　Est . . . Bras?　*"Is it impossible to escape the force of your arm?" Pistol's reply in the next line indicates that the "s" in* Bras *was pronounced on the Elizabethan stage.*

19　luxurious　*lecherous.*

20　perdonne moy　*"pardon me."*

24　Escoute . . . appele?　*"Listen: what is your name?"*

26–27　I'll fer . . . him　*Pistol plays menacingly on the sound of the soldier's name. Though Pistol doesn't know it,* Fer *probably means either "iron" or "sword" in this context. Pistol's word* firk *probably means "whip" or "strike" (though the word was also a euphemism for another four-letter word); and* ferret *means "harass, worry" (in the manner of a ferret).*

32　Que dit il　*"what does he say?"*

33–35　Il me . . . Gorge.　*"He commands me to tell you that you must prepare yourself; for this soldier is disposed at this very moment to cut your throat."*

36　Owy . . . permafoy　*Pistol's mangled French for "Yes, cut [his] throat, by my faith."*

39–42　O je vous . . . Escus.　*"O I beg you, for the love of God, to pardon me! I am a gentleman of a good house (family); preserve my life, and I will give you two hundred crowns."*

In Drops of crimson Blood.                                          15

SOLDIER  *Est il impossible d'eschapper la force de*
    *ton Bras?*

PISTOL  Brass, Cur?
    Thou damned and luxurious Mountain-goat,
    Offer'st me Brass?

SOLDIER              *O perdonne moy!*                              20

PISTOL  Say'st thou me so? Is that a Ton of Moys?
    —Come hither, Boy, ask me this Slave in French
    What is his Name.

BOY  *Escoute: comment estes vous appele?*

SOLDIER  *Monsieur le Fer.*

BOY              He says his Name is Monsieur Fer.                  25

PISTOL  Monsieur Fer: I'll fer him, and firk him,
    and ferret him: discuss the same in French
    unto him.

BOY  I do not know the French for "fer," and
    "ferret," and "firk."                                          30

PISTOL  Bid him prepare, for I will cut his Throat.

SOLDIER  *Que dit il, Monsieur?*

BOY  *Il me commande a vous dire que vous faites*
    *vous prest; car ce Soldat ici est dispose tout*
    *a cette heure de couper vostre Gorge.*                        35

PISTOL  Owy, cupple Gorge, permafoy,
    Peasant, unless thou give me Crowns, grave
        Crowns;
    Or mangled shalt thou be by this my Sword.

SOLDIER  *O je vous supplie, pour l'amour de Dieu,*
    *me pardonner! Je suis le Gentilhomme de bonne*                40
    *Maison; garde ma Vie, et je vous donneray*
    *deux cents Escus.*

49    Petit . . . il?   *"Little Master, what did he say?"*

50–53  Encore . . . Francisement.   *"Once more, that it is con-
      trary to his oath to pardon any prisoner; nevertheless, for the
      crowns that you promise him, he is content to give you liberty,
      freedom."*

54–58  Sur . . . Angleterre.   *"Upon my knees I give you a thou-
      sand thanks; and I esteem myself happy that I have fallen into
      the hands of a knight, I think, the most brave, valiant, and
      greatly distinguished lord of England."*

67    Suive . . . Captaine.   *"Follow the great captain."*

72    this Roaring . . . Play   *The Boy compares Pistol to one of
      the conventional character-types in the morality plays of the
      fifteenth and sixteenth centuries.*

72–73  that . . . Dagger   *In some of the morality plays the Vice
      apparently taunted the Devil with a threat to use his lath
      sword to trim the Devil's long nails.*

PISTOL  What are his words?

BOY  He prays you to save his Life: he is a
Gentleman of a good House, and for his Ransom          45
he will give you two hundred Crowns.

PISTOL  Tell him my Fury shall abate, and I
The Crowns will take.

SOLDIER  *Petit Mounsieur, que dit il?*

BOY  *Encore qu'il est contre son Jurement de*          50
*pardonner auncun Prisonnier; neant-moyns, pour*
*les Escus que vous lui promettes, il est content*
*a vous donner la Liberte, le Franchisement.*

SOLDIER  *Sur mes Genoux je vous donne mille*
*Remerciments; et je m'estime heureux que je*          55
*tombe entre les mains d'un Chevalier, je pense,*
*le plus brave, valiant, et tres distingue*
*Seigneur d'Angleterre.*

PISTOL  Expound unto me, Boy.

BOY  He gives you upon his Knees a thousand Thanks,    60
and he esteems himself happy that he hath
fall'n into the Hands of one, as he thinks,
the most brave, valorous, and thrice-worthy
Signeur of England.

PISTOL  As I suck Blood, I will some Mercy show.       65
—Follow me.

BOY  *Suive vous le grand Capitaine.*

*Exeunt Pistol and French Soldier.*

—I did never know so full a Voice issue from
so empty a Heart. But the Saying is true: "The
empty Vessel makes the greatest Sound."                70
Bardolph and Nym had ten times more Valor than
this Roaring Divel i' th' Old Play, that every

483

74      they are both hang'd   *In this offhand reference we learn the fate of Nym.*

76      Luggage   *supplies.*

IV.v    *We now move to the French part of the battlefield.*

1       Diable!   *the Devil!*

2       O Seigneur . . . perdu!   *"O Lord, the day is lost, all is lost!"*

3       Mort Dieu, my Vie!   *"Death of God, my life!"*

5       Plumes   *The Dolphin probably refers to the ornamental feathers the French wore on their helmets. King Henry has referred mockingly to them in IV.iii.112–13.*

6       mechante   *wicked, malicious.*

8       perdurable   *perpetual.*

one may pare his Nails with a Wooden Dagger,
and they are both hang'd, and so would this be
if he durst steal any thing adventurously. I          75
must stay with the Lackeys with the Luggage of
our Camp: the French might have a good prey of
us if he knew of it, for there is none to guard
it but Boys.                                    *Exit.*

# Scene 5

*Enter the Constable, Orleance, Bourbon,*
*the Dolphin, and Rambures.*

CONSTABLE   *O Diable!*

ORLEANCE   *O Seigneur, le Jour est perdu, tout est*
  *perdu!*

DOLPHIN   *Mort Dieu, ma Vie!* All is confounded, all!
  Reproach and everlasting Shame
  Sits mocking in our Plumes.          *A short Alarum.*   5
  *O mechante Fortune,* do not run away!

CONSTABLE   Why all our Ranks are broke!

DOLPHIN   O perdurable Shame: let's stab our selves!
  Be these the Wretches that we play'd at Dice for?

ORLEANCE   Is this the King we sent to for his
  Ransom?                                               10

12    In   *into the fray. So also with* Back.

14    with his Cap in Hand   *in the posture of a beggar or servant.*

15    Pander   *pimp.*

18    spoil'd   *ruined, defeated.*

20    enow   *enough.*

22    Order   *both (a) plan, and (b) command.*

IV.vi    *The scene continues at Agincourt. We now shift back to the English camp.*

2    yet . . . Field   *the French are still on the field of battle.*

BOURBON   Shame and eternal Shame, nothing but
     Shame!
     Let us die! In once more! Back again,
     And he that will not follow Bourbon now,
     Let him go hence and, with his Cap in Hand
     Like a base Pander, hold the Chamber Door          15
     Whilst by a Slave no gentler than my Dog
     His fairest Daughter is contaminated.
CONSTABLE   Disorder, that hath spoil'd us, friend
     us now:
     Let us on Heaps go offer up our Lives.
ORLEANCE   We are enow yet living in the Field          20
     To smother up the English in our Throngs
     If any Order might be thought upon.
BOURBON   The Div'l take Order now: I'll to the
     Throng;
     Let Life be short, else Shame will be too long.

                                        *Exeunt.*

# Scene 6

*Alarum. Enter the King and his Train, with Prisoners.*

KING   Well have we done, thrice-valiant
     Countrymen!
     But all's not done; yet keep the French the
     Field.

3  commends him *sends his respects.*

7  Array *blood-soaked apparel.*

8  Larding *enriching.*

9  Yoke-fellow *inseparable companion.*
   owing *owning. Here the context gives the word the sense of "earning."*

11  haggled over *hacked up.*

12  Gore *blood.*
   insteep'd *saturated.*

17  then fly abreast *then let our souls fly side by side.*

19  Chivalry *deeds of valor.*

21  raught *reached.*

22  gripe *grip, grasp.*

26  espous'd to Death *both (a) married to Death, and (b) married (to Suffolk) till Death. Exeter's phrasing echoes "till death us depart" in the marriage ceremony of the Elizabethan Book of Common Prayer.*

31  all my Mother *all the feminine tenderness I inherited from my mother.*

EXETER  The Duke of York commends him to your
     Majesty.
KING  Lives he, good Uncle? Thrice within this Hour
     I saw him down, thrice up again and fighting;                5
     From Helmet to the Spur all Blood he was.
EXETER  In which Array, brave Soldier, doth he lie,
     Larding the Plain; and by his bloody side,
     Yoke-fellow to his Honor-owing Wounds,
     The noble Earl of Suffolk also lies.                         10
     Suffolk first died; and York, all haggled over,
     Comes to him where in Gore he lay insteep'd,
     And takes him by the Beard, kisses the Gashes
     That bloodily did yawn upon his Face.
     He cries aloud, "Tarry, my Cousin Suffolk,                   15
     My Soul shall thine keep company to Heaven;
     Tarry, sweet Soul, for mine, then fly abreast,
     As in this glorious and well-foughten Field
     We kept together in our Chivalry."
     Upon these Words I came, and cheer'd him up.                 20
     He smil'd me in the Face, raught me his Hand,
     And with a feeble gripe says "Dear my Lord,
     Commend my Service to my Sovereign."
     So did he turn, and over Suffolk's Neck
     He threw his wounded Arm and kiss'd his Lips;                25
     And, so espous'd to Death, with Blood he seal'd
     A Testament of Noble-ending Love.
     The pretty and sweet manner of it forc'd
     Those Waters from me which I would have stopp'd
     But I had not so much of Man in me,                          30
     And all my Mother came into mine Eyes

489

33–34   I must . . . too   *I am forced to negotiate an agreement with my misty eyes or they will issue tears too. Here* mixtful *means both (a) misted over, and (b) full of moisture.*

36   reinforc'd   *reconstituted as a fighting force.*

37   Then   *therefore. The King's order in line 37, though seemingly savage, is dictated by a prudent concern that the prisoners might revolt and join their rejuvenated French companions on the attack.*

IV.vii   *The scene continues at Agincourt.*

1   Luggage   *Fluellen probably means the lackeys left to guard the chests and caskets filled with clothing and supplies. But he may be referring to the luggage itself, which has been "killed" in the sense expressed in lines 8–10.*

3   arrant   *audacious.*

6   not a Boy left alive   *We learn here that the Boy who had been Falstaff's page was one of the casualties of the French raid on the luggage. Shakespeare has given us a premonition of this slaughter in IV.iv.75–79.*

10–12   wherefore . . . Throat   *Gower's comment here makes it clear that what precipitated the "Alarum" at the end of the previous scene was the raid on the English camp.*

13   he was porn at Monmouth   *Fluellen is proud of the fact that such a "gallant King" was born in his native Wales.*

490

And gave me up to Tears.

KING                              I blame you not;
For hearing this, I must perforce compound
With mixtful Eyes or they will issue too.          *Alarum.*
But heark, what new Alarum is this same?                        35
The French have reinforc'd their scatter'd Men.
Then ev'ry Soldier kill his Prisoners;
Give the Word through.                             *Exeunt.*


# Scene 7

*Enter Fluellen and Gower.*

FLUELLEN   Kill the Poys and the Luggage! 'Tis
    expressly against the Law of Arms; 'tis as
    arrant a piece of Knavery, mark you now, as
    can be offer't in your Conscience now, is it
    not?                                                         5
GOWER   'Tis certain, there's not a Boy left alive,
    and the Cowardly Rascals that ran from the
    Battle ha' done this Slaughter. Besides they
    have burned and carried away all that was in
    the King's Tent, wherefore the King most                     10
    worthily hath caus'd every Soldier to cut his
    Prisoner's Throat. O 'tis a gallant King!
FLUELLEN   Ay, he was porn at Monmouth, Captain
    Gower. What call you the Town's Name where

15    Pig   *What Fluellen means, of course, is "Big."*

28    Situations   *topographies, sites.*

32–33  all one   *all the same.*

36    indifferent well   *reasonably well, with little or no difference.*

37    Figures   *symbolic relationships. Here as elsewhere in his discourse, Fluellen manifests a relish for rhetorical flourishes.*

38–40  in his Rages . . . Indignations   *Here Fluellen's "variations" are, as he would say, "all one." They exemplify a rhetorical device whereby one amplified a topic by saying the same thing in a number of essentially synonymous ways.*

41    Intoxicates   *intoxicated.*

43    Clytus   *Cleitus, a friend killed by Alexander the Great at a banquet in 328 B.C.; both were drunk at the time.*

Alexander the Pig was born?                                    15

GOWER   Alexander the Great.

FLUELLEN   Why I pray you, is not "Pig" Great? The
   Pig, or the Great, or the Mighty, or the Huge,
   or the Magnanimous, are all one Reckonings,
   save the Phrase is a little variations.                      20

GOWER   I think Alexander the Great was born in
   Macedon; his Father was called Philip of
   Macedon, as I take it.

FLUELLEN   I think it is in Macedon where Alexander
   is porn. I tell you, Captain, if you look in the Maps  25
   of the 'Orld, I warrant you sall find, in the
   Comparisons between Macedon and Monmouth,
   that the Situations, look you, is both alike.
   There is a River in Macedon, and there is also
   moreover a River at Monmouth: it is call'd Wye    30
   at Monmouth, but it is out of my Prains what
   is the Name of the other River. But 'tis all
   one; 'tis alike as my Fingers is to my Fingers,
   and there is Salmons in both. If you mark
   Alexander's Life well, Harry of Monmouth's Life    35
   is come after it indifferent well: for there is
   Figures in all things. Alexander, God knows,
   and you know, in his Rages, and his Furies,
   and his Wraths, and his Cholers, and his Moods,
   and his Displeasures, and his Indignations,         40
   and also being a little Intoxicates in his
   Prains, did in his Ales and his Angers, look
   you, kill his best Friend Clytus.

GOWER   Our King is not like him in that; he never
   kill'd any of his Friends.                                  45

493

53     **great-belly Doublet**   *Fluellen refers to a doublet (a man's close-fitting jacket) with two thicknesses. Fittingly, Fluellen associates Falstaff with a "great" (stuffed) rather than a "thin" doublet. Fluellen's comparisons are, of course, ludicrous. But despite the dissimilarities that constitute the basis for his parallels between Alexander-Cleitus and Hal-Falstaff, his remarks provide the audience with yet another reminder of the human costs involved in Harry of Monmouth's progress from the "Madcap Prince of Wales" in* 1 Henry IV *to "the Mirror of all Christian Kings" in* Henry V.

54     **Gipes**   *gibes, taunts.*

64     **Or void**   *or otherwise leave.*

66     **skirr**   *scurry.*
        **swift**   *speedily.*

67     **Slings**   *slingshots.*

FLUELLEN  It is not well done, mark you now, to
    take the Tales out of my Mouth ere it is made
    and finished. I speak but in the Figures and
    Comparisons of it. As Alexander kill'd his
    Friend Clytus, being in his Ales and his Cups,    50
    so also Harry Monmouth, being in his right
    Wits and his good Judgments, turn'd away the
    fat Knight with the great-belly Doublet: he
    was full of Jests, and Gipes, and Knaveries,
    and Mocks; I have forgot his Name.    55
GOWER  Sir John Falstaff.
FLUELLEN  That is he: I'll tell you, there is good
    Men porn at Monmouth.
GOWER  Here comes his Majesty.

*Alarum. Enter King Harry and his Train and Bourbon
    with Prisoners. Flourish.*

KING  I was not angry since I came to France    60
    Until this Instant. —Take a Trumpet, Herald,
    Ride thou unto the Horsemen on yond Hill:
    If they will fight with us, bid them come down,
    Or void the Field; they do offend our Sight.
    If they'll do neither, we will come to them    65
    And make them skirr away as swift as Stones
    Enforced from the old Assyrian Slings;
    Besides, we'll cut the Throats of those we
        have,
    And not a Man of them that we shall take
    Shall taste our Mercy. Go and tell them so.    70
                                    *Exit Herald.*

495

74    fin'd   *reserved (confined), staked.*

76    charitable License   *kind permission, authorization.*

78    book   *list.*

81    mercenary Blood   *the blood of soldiers who fight for pay rather than volunteer their services (as was normally the case with noblemen and gentlemen).*

82    Vulgar   *common men.*

84    Fret   *chafe.*

85    Yerk out   *jerk out, kick.*
       armed   *spiked.*

86    leave   *permission.*

88    truly   *honestly.*

89    if the Day be ours   *if you have conceded victory to us.*

*Enter Montjoy.*

EXETER    Here comes the Herald of the French, my
    Liege.
GLOUCESTER    His Eyes are humbler than they us'd
    to be.
KING    How now, what means this, Herald? Know'st
    thou not
        That I have fin'd these Bones of mine for
        Ransom?
        Com'st thou again for Ransom?
MONTJOY                    No, great King:    75
        I come to thee for charitable License,
        That we may wander o'er this Bloody Field
        To book our Dead and then to bury them;
        To sort our Nobles from our Common Men.
        For many of our Princes (woe the while!)    80
        Lie drown'd and soak'd in mercenary Blood;
        So do our Vulgar drench their Peasant Limbs
        In Blood of Princes; and the wounded Steeds
        Fret Fetlock-deep in Gore, and with wild Rage
        Yerk out their armed Heels at their dead
            Masters,    85
        Killing them twice. O give us leave, great
            King,
        To view the Field in safety and dispose
        Of their dead Bodies.
KING                    I tell thee truly, Herald,
        I know not if the Day be ours or no;
        For yet a many of your Horsemen peer    90
        And gallop o'er the Field.

497

93     hard by   *adjacent to the field.*

98     an 't   *if it.*

105–6   did good Service . . . Caps   *This detail seems to have originated with Fluellen. He refers to the battle of Crécy (1346). But the wearing of the leek on Saint David's Day is usually thought to have derived from a Welsh victory over the Saxons on March 1 in* A.D. *540. "Monmouth Caps" were round-shaped and brimless.*

109    takes no scorn to wear   *has no objection to wearing.*

119    Ieshu   *Jesus.*

HERALD The Day is yours.

KING Praised be God, and not our Strength, for it.
What is this Castle call'd that stands hard by?

HERALD They call it Agincourt.

KING Then call we this the Field of Agincourt, 95
Fought on the Day of Crispin Crispianus.

FLUELLEN Your Grandfather of famous Memory,
an 't please your Majesty, and your great-Uncle
Edward the Plack Prince of Wales, as I have
read in the Chronicles, fought a most prave 100
Pattle here in France.

KING They did, Fluellen.

FLUELLEN Your Majesty says very true. If your
Majesties is rememb'red of it, the Welchmen
did good Service in a Garden where Leeks did 105
grow, wearing Leeks in their Monmouth Caps,
which your Majesty know to this Hour is an
honorable Badge of the Service. And I do
believe your Majesty takes no scorn to wear
the Leek upon Saint Tavy's Day. 110

KING I wear it for a memorable Honor,
For I am Welch, you know, good Countryman.

FLUELLEN All the Water in Wye cannot wash your
Majesty's Welsh Plood out of your Pody, I can
tell you that: God pless it, and preserve it 115
as long as it pleases His Grace, and his
Majesty too!

KING Thanks, good my Countryman.

FLUELLEN By Ieshu, I am your Majesty's Countryman,
I care not who know it. I will confess it to 120
all the 'Orld; I need not to be ashamed of

499

124    him    *Montjoy.*

125    just Notice of    *precise information about.*

131    Gage    *pledge.*
       withal    *with.*

135    swagger'd with me    *talked and acted boastfully to me.*

137    take    *give, strike.*

143    Craven    *lying coward.*

145–   of great sort    *of high rank.*
46

146    quite from the Answer of his Degree    *altogether above
       having to make answer to a man so low-ranking as a common
       soldier. The King's point is that a nobleman or a gentleman
       could not, without dishonor, accept a challenge from someone
       so far below him in station.*

147    Ientleman    *The Folio's unusual spelling probably indicates
       Fluellen's pronunciation of this word. It also reminds us that
       many other syllables that are now spelled and pronounced with
       a " j " (normally rendered with an " i " in Shakespeare's time)
       would have had a more vowel-like sound in Elizabethan Eng-
       lish.*

your Majesty, praised be God, so long as your
Majesty is an honest Man.

KING  God keep me so.

*Enter Williams.*

                —Our Heralds go with him.
Bring me just Notice of the Numbers dead                    125
On both our parts. —Call yonder Fellow hither.
                          *Exeunt Heralds with Montjoy.*

EXETER  Soldier, you must come to the King.

KING  Soldier, why wear'st thou that Glove in thy
  Cap?

WILLIAMS  And 't please your Majesty, 'tis the           130
  Gage of one that I should fight withal, if he be
  alive.

KING  An Englishman?

WILLIAMS  And 't please your Majesty, a Rascal that
  swagger'd with me last Night: who, if alive          135
  and ever dare to challenge this Glove, I have
  sworn to take him a Box a' th' Ear; or if I
  can see my Glove in his Cap, which he swore,
  as he was a Soldier, he would wear if alive, I
  will strike it out soundly.                          140

KING  What think you, Captain Fluellen: is it fit
  this Soldier keep his Oath?

FLUELLEN  He is a Craven and a Villain else, and 't
  please your Majesty in my Conscience.

KING  It may be his Enemy is a Gentleman of great     145
  sort quite from the Answer of his Degree.

FLUELLEN  Though he be as good a Ientleman as the

501

148     Lucifer    *the name given Satan in Isaiah 14:12. It means "light-bearer."*

          Belzebub    *Beelzebub, described as "the prince of the devils" in Matthew 12:24.*

152     Jack-sauce    *saucy (cheeky) fellow.*

154     Conscience    *Here as elsewhere, Fluellen uses this word to mean something like "consciousness." In this instance it refers primarily to judgment.*

164     Favor    *token of esteem.*

165     Alanson    *the Duke of Alençon.*

167     Helm    *helmet.*

170     thou dost me love    *you perform an act that demonstrates your love to me.*

173     fain    *like to; gladly, eagerly.*

174     aggrief'd    *aggrieved, offended.*

178     and    *if it.*

Divel is, as Lucifer and Belzebub himself, it
is necessary, look your Grace, that he keep
his Vow and his Oath. If he be perjur'd, see          150
you now, his Reputation is as arrant a Villain
and a Jack-sauce as ever his black Shoe trod
upon God's Ground, and his Earth, in my
Conscience, la!

KING   Then keep thy Vow, Sirrah, when thou meet'st   155
the Fellow.

WILLIAMS   So I will, my Liege, as I live.

KING   Who serv'st thou under?

WILLIAMS   Under Captain Gower, my Liege.

FLUELLEN   Gower is a good Captain, and is good      160
knowledge and literatured in the Wars.

KING   Call him hither to me, Soldier.

WILLIAMS   I will, my Liege.                  *Exit.*

KING   Here, Fluellen, wear thou this Favor for me,
and stick it in thy Cap. When Alanson and my      165
self were down together, I pluck'd this Glove
from his Helm. If any Man challenge this, he
is a Friend to Alanson, and an Enemy to our
Person. If thou encounter any such, apprehend
him, and thou dost me love.                  170

FLUELLEN   Your Grace doo's me as great Honors as
can be desir'd in the Hearts of his Subjects. I
would fain see the Man that has but two Legs
that shall find himself aggrief'd at this Glove,
that is all. But I would fain see it once, and      175
please God of his Grace that I might see.

KING   Know'st thou Gower?

FLUELLEN   He is my dear Friend, and please you.

503

185    haply   *by chance.*

192    Choler   *anger. Choler was one of the humours, one that was thought to be the result of an excess of yellow bile (fire) in the system.*

193    return   *requite, retaliate for.*

IV.viii    *The scene continues in a different part of the English camp at Agincourt.*

1    warrant   *wager, assure you.*

KING    Pray thee go seek him, and bring him to my
          Tent.                                                    180
FLUELLEN    I will fetch him.                          *Exit.*
KING    My Lord of Warwick, and my Brother Gloucester,
          Follow Fluellen closely at the heels.
          The Glove which I have giv'n him for a Favor
          May haply purchase him a Box a' th' Ear.                 185
          It is the Soldier's: I by bargain should
          Wear it my self. Follow, good Cousin Warwick.
          If that the Soldier strike him, as I judge
          By his blunt bearing he will keep his Word,
          Some sudden Mischief may arise of it:                    190
          For I do know Fluellen valiant
          And, touch'd with Choler, hot as Gunpowder,
          And quickly will return an Injury.
          Follow and see there be no harm between them.
          —Go you with me, Uncle of Exeter.         *Exeunt.*  195


# Scene 8

*Enter Gower and Williams.*

WILLIAMS    I warrant it is to knight you, Captain.

*Enter Fluellen.*

FLUELLEN    God's will and His pleasure, Captain, I

505

3      apace   *with haste.*

10     'Sblud   *an abbreviation for "God's blood," an oath referring to the Crucifixion.*

13     be forsworn   *fail to keep my word.*

15     Plows   *blows.*

22     contagious   *Fluellen probably means "outrageous"; but it is not inconceivable that he also considers treason a disease and is anxious to prevent its spread.*

beseech you now, come apace to the King: there
is more good toward you, peradventure, than is
in your Knowledge to dream of.                                    5

WILLIAMS   Sir, know you this Glove?
FLUELLEN   Know the Glove? I know the Glove is a
   Glove.
WILLIAMS   I know this, and thus I challenge it.
                                            *He strikes him.*
FLUELLEN   'Sblud, an arrant Traitor as any's in the        10
   Universal World, or in France, or in England!
GOWER   How now, Sir? You Villain!
WILLIAMS   Do you think I'll be forsworn?
FLUELLEN   Stand away, Captain Gower: I will give
   Treason his Payment into Plows, I warrant you.        15
WILLIAMS   I am no Traitor.
FLUELLEN   That's a Lie in thy Throat. —I charge
   you in his Majesty's Name, apprehend him: he's
   a Friend of the Duke Alanson's.

            *Enter Warwick and Gloucester.*

WARWICK   How now, how now, what's the matter?        20
FLUELLEN   My Lord of Warwick, here is, praised be
   God for it, a most contagious Treason come to
   light, look you, as you shall desire in a
   Summer's Day. Here is his Majesty.

            *Enter King and Exeter.*

KING   How now, what's the matter?                            25
FLUELLEN   My Liege, here is a Villain, and a

   507

31    Fellow    *mate.*

32    change    *exchange.*

38    lousy    *lice-infested.*

39    is pear    *will bear.*

40    will Avouchment    *will vouch; will stand up for me.*

Traitor that, look your Grace, has strook the
Glove which your Majesty is take out of the
Helmet of Alanson.

WILLIAMS   My Liege, this was my Glove; here is         30
    the Fellow of it. And he that I gave it to in
    change promis'd to wear it in his Cap; I
    promis'd to strike him if he did. I met this
    Man with my Glove in his Cap, and I have
    been as good as my Word.                            35

FLUELLEN   Your Majesty, hear now, saving your
    Majesty's Manhood, what an arrant, rascally,
    beggarly, lousy Knave it is. I hope your
    Majesty is pear me Testimony and Witness,
    and will Avouchment, that this is the Glove of      40
    Alanson that your Majesty is give me, in your
    Conscience now.

KING   —Give me thy Glove, Soldier.
    Look, here is the Fellow of it.
    'Twas I indeed thou promisedst to strike,           45
    And thou hast given me most bitter Terms.

FLUELLEN   And please your Majesty, let his Neck
    answer for it, if there is any Martial Law in
    the World.

KING   —How canst thou make me Satisfaction?           50

WILLIAMS   All Offenses, my Lord, come from the
    Heart. Never came any from mine that might
    offend your Majesty.

KING   It was our Self thou didst abuse.

WILLIAMS   Your Majesty came not like your Self. You    55
    appear'd to me but as a Common Man: witness the
    Night, your Garments, your Lowliness. And what

509

58    under that Shape    *in that disguise and situation.*

66    Crowns    *coins worth five shillings each.*

72    Prabbles    *brabbles, conflicts.*

74    will    *will have.*

77    wherefore . . . Pashful?    *why should you be so reluctant?*

78    Silling    *shilling.*

79    change it    *exchange it (give you another in its place).*

80    numb'red    *counted.*

82    of Good Sort    *of high rank.*

your Highness suffer'd under that Shape, I
beseech you take it for your own Fault, and not
mine. For had you been as I took you for, I                    60
made no Offense. Therefore I beseech your
Highness pardon me.

KING  Here, Uncle Ex'ter, fill this Glove with
     Crowns
     And give it to this Fellow. —Keep it, Fellow,
     And wear it for an Honor in thy Cap            65
     Till I do challenge it. —Give him the Crowns.
     —And Captain, you must needs be Friends with
     him.

FLUELLEN  By this Day, and this Light, the Fellow
     has Mettle enough in his Belly. —Hold, there
     is Twelvepence for you, and I pray you to       70
     serve God, and keep you out of Prawls and
     Prabbles, and Quarrels and Dissensions, and I
     warrant you it is the better for you.

WILLIAMS  I will none of your Money.

FLUELLEN  It is with a Good Will: I can tell you it   75
     will serve you to mend your Shoes. Come,
     wherefore should you be so Pashful? Your Shoes
     is not so good; 'tis a good Silling, I warrant
     you, or I will change it.

*Enter Herald.*

KING  Now, Herald, are the Dead numb'red?            80

HERALD  Here is the Number of the slaught'red
     French.                    *He hands the King a Document.*

KING  What Prisoners of Good Sort are taken, Uncle?

5¹¹

89    bearing Banners   *carrying banners with their coats of arms on them.*

95    Mercenaries   *paid soldiers.*

105   lusty   *vigorous, spirited.*

EXETER    Charles, Duke of Orleance, Nephew to the
        King;
      John, Duke of Bourbon, and Lord Bouciqualt;
      Of other Lords and Barons, Knights and Squires,        85
      Full fifteen hundred, besides Common Men.
KING    This Note doth tell me of ten thousand French
      That in the Field lie slain: of Princes in
        this Number,
      And Nobles bearing Banners, there lie dead
      One hundred twenty-six; added to these,                90
      Of Knights, Esquires, and gallant Gentlemen,
      Eight thousand and four hundred, of the which
      Five hundred were but yesterday dubb'd Knights.
      So that in these ten thousand they have lost
      There are but sixteen hundred Mercenaries;            95
      The rest are Princes, Barons, Lords, Knights,
        Squires,
      And Gentlemen of Blood and Quality.
      The Names of those their Nobles that lie dead:
      Charles Delabreth, High Constable of France;
      Jaques of Chatilion, Admiral of France;              100
      The Master of the Cross-bows, Lord Rambures;
      Great Mast'r of France, the brave Sir Guichard
        Dolphin;
      John, Duke of Alanson; Anthony, Duke of Brabant,
      The Brother to the Duke of Burgundy;
      And Edward, Duke of Barr. Of lusty Earls,            105
      Grandpre and Roussi, Faulconbridge and Foyes,
      Beaumont and Marle, Vaudemont and Lestrale.
      Here was a Royal Fellowship of Death!
      Where is the Number of our English Dead?


513

115    **Ascribe we all**  *do we give the credit.*
        **Stratagem**  *intrigues, tricks (such as ambushes).*

116    **plain Shock**  *direct combat.*
        **even Play of Battail**  *fair matching of armed forces.*

119    **wonderful**  *to be wondered (marveled) at.*

124    **and**  *and it (if it).*

130    **Non Nobis**  *"Not to Us," the opening phrase of a hymn based on Psalm 115: "Not unto us, O Lord, not unto us, but unto thy name give glory."*
        **Te Deum**  *another well-known hymn, beginning "We praise thee, O God."*

131    **with Charity enclos'd in Clay**  *given Christian burial rites.*

132    **Callice**  *Calais, a French town on the English Channel.*

133    **more Happy**  *happier.*

*The Herald hands him another Document.*

Edward, the Duke of York; the Earl of Suffolk;                110
Sir Richard Ketly; Davy Gam, Esquire;
None else of Name; and of all other Men,
But five and twenty. —O God, Thy Arm was here:
And not to us, but to Thy Arm alone,
Ascribe we all. When, without Stratagem,                       115
But in plain Shock and even Play of Battail,
Was ever known so great and little Loss
On one part and on th' other? Take it, God,
For it is none but Thine.

EXETER                              'Tis wonderful!

KING   Come, go we in procession to the Village.              120
And be it Death proclaimed through our Host
To boast of this, or take that Praise from God
Which is His only.

FLUELLEN   Is it not lawful, and please your Majesty,
to tell how many is kill'd?                                    125

KING   Yes, Captain; but with this Acknowledgment,
That God fought for us.

FLUELLEN   Yes, my Conscience, He did us great good.

KING   Do we all holy Rites:
Let there be sung *Non Nobis* and *Te Deum*,                   130
The Dead with Charity enclos'd in Clay;
And then to Callice, and to England then,
Where ne'er from France arriv'd more Happy Men.

                                                   *Exeunt.*

V. Chorus     *The Chorus transports us to a time five years following the English victory at Agincourt.*

1     Vouchsafe    *be kind enough to grant.*

2     prompt    *remind.*

3     admit    *allow.*

5     in their huge and proper Life    *in all the details pertaining to their vast time, number, and individual episodes.*

7     Grant him there    *allow us to take him there in your imaginations.*

9     Athwart    *crossing (opposing the waves).*

10     Pales in the Flood    *walls in the water.*

12     Whiffler    *an officer designated to keep the way clear for a procession. In lines 9–13 the Chorus compares the sea to a whiffler, holding the crowd at a distance to allow the King's ships to reach the shore without impediments.*

# Act Five

*Enter Chorus.*

CHORUS  Vouchsafe to those that have not read the
    Story
That I may prompt them; and of such as have,
I humbly pray them to admit th' Excuse
Of Time, of Numbers, and due Course of things,
Which cannot in their huge and proper Life          5
Be here presented. Now we bear the King
Toward Callice. Grant him there, there seen,
Heave him away upon your winged Thoughts
Athwart the Sea. Behold the English Beach
Pales in the Flood with Men, Wives, and Boys,       10
Whose Shouts and Claps out-voice the
    deep-mouth'd Sea,
Which, like a mighty Whiffler 'fore the King,
Seems to prepare his way. So let him land,

14    solemnly   *ceremoniously.*

16    Black-heath   *an open plain to the southeast of London.*

17    Where that   *where.*
      desire   *request, urge.*

18    bruised   *battered.*

21    Trophy   *token of victory.*
      Signal   *sign.*
      Ostent   *display.*

22    Quite from himself   *completely away from himself.*

23    quick Forge and Working-house   *living blacksmith's shop,
         a metaphor for the brain or the mind.*

25    in best Sort   *of highest rank and in their finest apparel.*

29    a lower . . . Likelihood   *a less elevated but well-loved sim-
         ilarity.*

30    the Gen'ral . . . Empress   *a reference to the Duke of Es-
         sex, whom the Queen had sent to Ireland on March 27, 1599,
         to put down a rebellion. Well before Essex arrived back in
         September, it was known that he would not be returning
         victoriously; so this reference helps us date* Henry V.

32    broached   *impaled.*

33    quit   *leave.*

38    The Emp'ror's . . . France   *In May 1416 the Holy Ro-
         man Emperor, Sigismund, visited England to help negotiate a
         truce.*

And solemnly see him set on to London.
So swift a pace hath Thought that even now          15
You may imagine him upon Black-heath,
Where that his Lords desire him to have borne
His bruised Helmet and his bended Sword
Before him through the City: he forbids it,
Being free from Vainness and Self-glorious
   Pride,                                            20
Giving full Trophy, Signal, and Ostent
Quite from himself to God. But now behold,
In the quick Forge and Working-house of
   Thought,
How London doth pour out her Citizens!
The May'r and all his Brethren in best Sort,        25
Like to the Senators of th' antique Rome,
With the Plebeians swarming at their Heels,
Go forth and fetch their Conqu'ring Caesar in,
As by a lower but by loving Likelihood
Were now the Gen'ral of our Gracious Empress,       30
As in good time he may, from Ireland coming,
Bringing Rebellion broached on his Sword,
How many would the peaceful City quit
To welcome him. Much more, and much more Cause,
Did they this Harry. Now in London place him:       35
As yet the Lamentation of the French
Invites the King of England's stay at home,
The Emp'ror's coming in behalf of France
To order Peace between them. And omit
All the Occurrences, what ever chanc'd,             40
Till Harry's Back-return again to France.

42 play'd *performed (as an actor).*

43 rememb'ring *reminding.*

44 brook Abridgment *tolerate an abbreviated account (of five years' history).*

45 After *following.*

V.i *This scene takes place at the English camp in France. It is now 1420, and the English have just begun their third invasion of France (a second having been made in 1417, two years after the English victory at Agincourt).*

1 Nay, that's right *Gower refers to something that has been said just before the audience begins eavesdropping on the conversation.*

2 Saint Davy's . . . past. *As we learn in line 10, March 1 was yesterday.*

4 asse *as.*

5 scald *scabby, diseased.*

12 breed *initiate.*

my Leek, or I will peat his Pate four days.
—Bite, I pray you; it is good for your green                45
Wound, and your ploody Coxcomb.

PISTOL   Must I bite?

FLUELLEN   Yes certainly, and out of Doubt, and out
of Question too, and Ambiguities.

PISTOL   By this Leek, I will most horribly revenge—      50
I eat and eat! I swear—

FLUELLEN   Eat, I pray you. Will you have some more
Sauce to your Leek? There is not enough Leek
to swear by.

PISTOL   Quiet thy Cudgel: thou dost see I eat!             55

FLUELLEN   Much good do you, scald Knave, heartily.
Nay, pray you throw none away; the Skin is
good for your broken Coxcomb. When you take
occasions to see Leeks hereafter, I pray you
mock at 'em, that is all.                                              60

PISTOL   Good.

FLUELLEN   Ay, Leeks is good: hold you, there is a
Groat to heal your Pate.

PISTOL   Me a Groat?

FLUELLEN   Yes verily, and in truth you shall take         65
it, or I have another Leek in my Pocket, which
you shall eat.

PISTOL   I take thy Groat in earnest of Revenge.

FLUELLEN   If I owe you any thing, I will pay you in
Cudgels; you shall be a Woodmonger, and buy    70
nothing of me but Cudgels. God bu'y you, and
keep you, and heal your Pate.                      *Exit.*

PISTOL   All Hell shall stir for this!

GOWER   Go, go, you are a counterfeit cowardly Knave.

525

75     began    *begun.*

76     upon an honorable Respect    *out of respect for an honorable occasion.*

77     predeceased Valor    *the valor of those who died long before we were born.*

78     avouch    *maintain, stand up for.*

79     gleeking and galling    *mocking and insulting.*

85     Condition    *disposition, mode of behavior.*

86     play the Huswife with me    *betray me, treat me contemptuously, the way a shrewish hussy does her craven man.*

87     my Doll    *Why Pistol refers to "my Doll" rather than "my Nell" (the name of Mistress Quickly, to whom he is married) is unclear. One possibility is that "Doll" is simply a term of endearment for Quickly. Another is that this is just another of Shakespeare's minor oversights. A third is that a scribe or compositor misread the name in the manuscript.*
         Spittle    *'spital, an abbreviated form of "hospital."*

88     Malady of France    *probably syphilis or another venereal disease.*

89     My Rendezvous    *my place of resort.*

92     And . . . Hand    *and incline toward being a quick-fingered pickpocket.*

95     Gallia Wars    *wars in France.*

Will you mock at an ancient Tradition, began                    75
upon an honorable Respect, and worn as a
memorable Trophy of predeceased Valor, and
dare not avouch in your Deeds any of your
Words? I have seen you gleeking and galling
at this Gentleman twice or thrice. You thought,              80
because he could not speak English in the
Native Garb, he could not therefore handle an
English Cudgel. You find it otherwise, and
henceforth let a Welsh Correction teach you a
good English Condition. Fare ye well.          *Exit.*       85

PISTOL    Doth Fortune play the Huswife with me now?
News have I that my Doll is dead i' th' Spittle
Of a Malady of France, and there
My Rendezvous is quite cut off.
Old do I wax, and from my weary Limbs                       90
Honor is cudgel'd. Well, Bawd I'll turn,
And something lean to Cutpurse of quick Hand.
To England will I steal, and there I'll steal.
And Patches will I get unto these Cudgell'd Scars
And swear I got them in the Gallia Wars.       *Exit.*      95

**V.ii**  *This final scene takes place in the palace of the King of France.*

1  **Peace to this Meeting**  *The King's benediction is appropriate, for the purpose of the gathering is to negotiate a peace.*
 **wherefore**  *for which.*

2  **Brother France**  *King Charles VI.*
 **our Sister**  *the Queen of France.*

5  **Royalty**  *royal family.*

12  **Issue**  *outcome. But in view of what will be negotiated, another kind of "issue" will also result.*
 **England**  *King Henry V. The Folio prints "Ireland," perhaps as a misreading of "Ingland" in the manuscript.*

# Scene 2

*Enter, at one Door, King Henry, Exeter, Bedford,*
*Gloucester, Warwick, Westmerland, and other Lords;*
*at another, Queen Isabel, the King of France,*
*the Duke of Bourgogne, Katherine, Alice,*
*and other French.*

KING   Peace to this Meeting, wherefore we are met!
   Unto our Brother France, and to our Sister,
   Health and fair time of Day. —Joy and good
      Wishes
   To our most fair and Princely Cousin Katherine.
   —And as a Branch and Member of this Royalty,          5
   By whom this great Assembly is contriv'd,
   We do salute you, Duke of Bourgogne.
   —And Princes French and Peers, Health to you
      all.
FRANCE   Right joyous are we to behold your Face,
   Most worthy Brother England, fairly met!              10
   —So are you, Princes English, every one.
QUEEN   So happy be the Issue, Brother England,
   Of this good Day, and of this gracious Meeting,
   As we are now glad to behold your Eyes:
   Your Eyes, which hitherto have borne                  15

17     The fatal Balls of murth'ring Basilisks   *The Queen's image recalls the tennis balls the Dolphin presented to King Henry in I.ii. She refers to deadly ("fatal") balls shot from a type of cannon known as the basilisk—so named because it was thought to resemble a mythical serpent whose eyes struck dead anyone who looked into them.*

19     Quality   *power, nature.*

20     Griefs   *both (a) grievances, and (b) sorrows.*

23     on equal Love   *Bourgogne means that he bears equal love to both the parties he has worked so hard to bring together.*

27     Bar   *This may refer to an actual bar separating the representatives from one another, as in a courtroom. It also completes a circle initiated by reference to various "Bars" in I.ii. 35–42.*

31     congreeted   *exchanged friendly greetings.*

33     Rub   *any obstacle or surface irregularity that interfered with the course of a rolling ball in the game of bowls.*

36     best Garden of the World   *Bourgogne's long description of an unweeded France recalls John of Gaunt's paean to the "demi-Paradise" across the English Channel in II.i of* Richard II, *near the beginning of an epic cycle that Shakespeare is now drawing to a close in* Henry V.

39     her Husbandry   *the results of her labor.*
           on   *in.*

40     it   *its.*

41     Vine   *grapevine (for the making of wine).*

In them against the French that met them in
  their Bent
The fatal Balls of murth'ring Basilisks.
The Venom of such Looks we fairly hope
Have lost their Quality, and that this Day
Shall change all Griefs and Quarrels into Love.          20
KING    To cry Amen to that, thus we appear.
QUEEN    You English Princes all, I do salute you.
BOURGOGNE    My Duty to you both, on equal Love.
  Great Kings of France and England: that I have
    labor'd
With all my Wits, my Pains, and strong
    Endeavors,                                             25
To bring your most Imperial Majesties
Unto this Bar and Royal Interview,
Your Mightiness on both parts best can witness.
Since then my Office hath so far prevail'd
That Face to Face, and Royal Eye to Eye,                  30
You have congreeted, let it not disgrace me
If I demand before this Royal View
What Rub or what Impediment there is
Why that the naked, poor, and mangled Peace,
Dear Nurse of Arts, Plenties, and joyful Births,         35
Should not in this best Garden of the World,
Our fertile France, put up her lovely Visage?
Alas, she hath from France too long been
    chas'd,
And all her Husbandry doth lie on Heaps
Corrupting in it own Fertility.                           40
Her Vine, the merry Cheerer of the Heart,

42      even-pleach'd   *smoothly layered.*

44      fallow Leas   *uncultivated fields.*

45      Darnel, Hemlock, Femetary   *three weeds that grow profusely on land that has been ploughed but left unplanted.*

46      Coulter   *blade.*

47      deracinate such Savag'ry   *root out such a return to wildness.*

48      Mead   *meadow.*
        erst   *earlier, at one time.*

49      Burnet   *a plant used for cattle fodder.*

50      Wanting   *lacking (but needing).*
        withal unc'rrected   *and thus untrimmed.*
        rank   *overgrown.*

51      Conceives by Idleness   *bears the fruits of neglect.*
        nothing teems   *gives birth to nothing.*

52      Docks, Thistles, Kecksies, Burs   *another assortment of weeds.*

58      Sciences   *learning and skills.*

61      defus'd   *unkempt, disordered.*

65      Let   *hindrance.*

66      Inconveniences   *things that are unfitting or unnatural.*

Unpruned dies; her Hedges even-pleach'd,
Like Pris'ners wildly overgrown with Hair,
Put forth disorder'd Twigs; her fallow Leas
The Darnel, Hemlock, and rank Femetary                    45
Doth root upon, while that the Coulter rusts
That should deracinate such Savag'ry;
The even Mead, that erst brought sweetly forth
The freckled Cowslip, Burnet, and green Clover,
Wanting the Scythe, withal unc'rrected, rank,             50
Conceives by Idleness, and nothing teems
But hateful Docks, rough Thistles, Kecksies,
    Burs,
Losing both Beauty and Utility;
And all the Vineyards, Fallows, Meads, and
    Hedges,
Defective in their Natures, grow to Wildness.            55
Ev'n so our Houses, and our selves and
    Children,
Have lost, or do not learn for want of Time,
The Sciences that should become our Country,
But grow like Savages (as Soldiers will
That nothing do but meditate on Blood)                   60
To Swearing and stern Looks, defus'd Attire,
And ev'ry thing that seems unnatural.
Which to reduce into our former Favor,
You are assembled; and my Speech entreats
That I may know the Let why gentle Peace                 65
Should not expel these Inconveniences
And bless us with her former qualities.
KING    If, Duke of Burgony, you would the Peace,
    Whose Want gives growth to th' Imperfections

533

71    Accord   *agreement.*

72    Tenures   *tenors, general principles.*
particular Effects   *special provisions.*

73    You . . . Hands   *you will find outlined in the document you are holding.*

77    curselary   *cursory, quick-scanning. This word is not recorded elsewhere, and may be a Shakespearean coinage. Most editors substitute either "cursitory" or "cursorary."*

78    Pleaseth   *if it would please.*

81–82    we will . . . Answer   *we will quickly give you a decisive response.*

88    advantageable . . . Dignity   *to the advantage of the English monarchy.*

90    consign thereto   *agree to it.*

94    When Articles . . . on   *when provisions too nitpickingly demanded are inflexibly insisted upon.*

96    Capital   *principal (literally, head).*

Which you have cited, you must buy that Peace　　　70
With full Accord to all our just Demands,
Whose Tenures and particular Effects
You have enschedul'd briefly in your Hands.

BOURGOGNE　The King hath heard them: to the
　　which as yet
There is no Answer made.

KING　　　　　　　　　　Well then: the Peace　　75
　　Which you before so urg'd lies in his Answer.

FRANCE　I have but with a curselary Eye
　　O'er-glanc'd the Articles. Pleaseth your Grace
　　T' appoint some of your Council presently
　　To sit with us once more, with better Heed　　80
　　To re-survey them, we will suddenly
　　Pass our accept and peremptory Answer.

KING　Brother, we shall. —Go, Uncle Exeter,
　　And Brother Clar'nce, and you, Broth'rs
　　　Gloucester,
　　Warwick, and Huntington: go with the King,　　85
　　And take with you free pow'r to ratify,
　　Augment, or alter as your Wisdoms best
　　Shall see advantageable for our Dignity,
　　Any thing in or out of our Demands,
　　And we'll consign thereto. —Will you, fair
　　　Sister,　　　　　　　　　　　　　　　90
　　Go with the Princes, or stay here with us?

QUEEN　Our gracious Brother, I will go with them:
　　Happily a Woman's Voice may do some good,
　　When Articles too nicely urg'd be stood on.

KING　Yet leave our Cousin Kath'rine here with us.　　95
　　She is our Capital Demand, compris'd

98    Fair Kath'rine   *Members of Shakespeare's audience would probably have been reminded of another wooing scene in which a plain-spoken suitor insists on being left alone with the Katherine he wishes to marry. There, of course, the "Kate" is "Katherine the Curst," and the play is an early comedy,* The Taming of the Shrew.

99    vouchsafe   *condescend.*

103    your England   *Katherine means "your English," of course.*

106    brokenly   *in fragments. The King contrasts "brokenly" with "soundly" (line 104); one of the meanings of* sound *is "whole."*

108–9    Pardonne . . . me."   *"Pardon me, I do not know what 'like me' means." The King takes her words at face value ("what is like me") in his reply.*

112–13    Que . . . Anges?   *"What does he say? That I am like the angels?"*

114–15    Ouy . . . il.   *"Yes, truly, save your Grace, so he says."*

118–19    O bon Dieu . . . Tromperies.   *"O good God, the tongues of men are full of deceits."*

124    The Princess . . . Englishwoman.   *The King means that Katherine's suspicion of flattery is a virtue that makes her seem like a wise Englishwoman already.*

125    fit for   *suited to.*

Within the Fore-rank of our Articles.

QUEEN   She hath good leave.

*Exeunt all but King Henry, Katherine, and Alice.*

KING                              Fair Kath'rine, and most fair,
Will you vouchsafe to teach a Soldier Terms
Such as will enter at a Lady's Ear                              100
And plead his Love-suit to her gentle Heart?

KATHERINE   Your Majesty shall mock at me: I cannot
speak your England.

KING   O fair Katherine, if you will love me soundly
with your French Heart, I will be glad to hear         105
you confess it brokenly with your English
Tongue. Do you like me, Kate?

KATHERINE   *Pardonne moy,* I cannot tell wat is
"like me."

KING   An Angel is like you, Kate, and you are like      110
an Angel.

KATHERINE   —*Que dit il? Que je suis semblable a les
Anges?*

ALICE   *Ouy, verayment, sauf vostre Grace, ainsi dit
il.*                                                                                  115

KING   I said so, dear Katherine, and I must not
blush to affirm it.

KATHERINE   —*O bon Dieu, les langues des Hommes sont
pleines de Tromperies.*

KING   —What says she, fair one? That the Tongues      120
of Men are full of Deceits?

ALICE   *Ouy,* dat the Tongues of de Mans is be full
of Deceits: dat is de Princess.

KING   The Princess is the better Englishwoman.
—I' faith, Kate, my Wooing is fit for thy              125

537

128–  thou . . . Crown   *The King means that he would appear to*
30     *Katherine to be an unsophisticated rustic.*

130    mince it   *speak with Courtier-like indirection and delicacy*
       *(serving up refined and "pre-chewed" mince-meat rather than*
       *plain beef).*

133    wear out my Suit   *exhaust what I have to say (with a pun on*
       *wearing out one's suit of clothes).*

134    Clap Hands . . . Bargain   *clasp hands to seal an agree-*
       *ment.*

136    Sauf vostre honneur   *"Save your honor."*

138    you undid me   *you would undo me (defeat me).*

141    Measure   *both (a) poetic meters, and (b) dance measures.*

143    Vauting   *vaulting.*

144    under the correction of   *at the risk of being reproved for.*

145    leap into a Wife   *Many of the King's images are sexually*
       *suggestive.*

146    Buffet   *box, fight with my fists.*

146–  Bound my Horse   *make my horse jump.*
47

148    Jack-an-Apes   *monkey or ape.*

149–  Look greenly   *look like a bashful, moonstruck lover.*
50

151–  downright Oaths   *blunt, manly swearing. Here the King's*
52     *words echo those that Hotspur spoke to his Kate near the end*
       *of III.i in* 1 Henry IV.

Understanding. I am glad thou canst speak no
better English; for if thou couldst, thou
wouldst find me such a plain King that thou
wouldst think I had sold my Farm to buy my
Crown. I know no ways to mince it in Love, but          130
directly to say "I love you." Then if you urge
me farther than to say "Do you in faith?" I
wear out my Suit. Give me your Answer, i' faith
do, and so Clap Hands and a Bargain. How say
you, Lady?                                             135

KATHERINE   *Sauf vostre honneur,* me understand well.

KING   Marry, if you would put me to Verses, or to
Dance for your sake, Kate, why you undid me.
For the one I have neither Words nor Measure;
and for the other, I have no strength in           140
Measure, yet a reasonable measure in Strength.
If I could win a Lady at Leap-frog, or by
Vauting into my Saddle with my Armor on my
Back, under the correction of Bragging be it
spoken, I should quickly leap into a Wife. Or       145
if I might Buffet for my Love, or Bound my
Horse for her Favors, I could lay on like a
Butcher, and sit like a Jack-an-Apes, never
off. But before God, Kate, I cannot Look
greenly, nor gasp out my Eloquence, nor I have      150
no cunning in Protestation; only downright
Oaths, which I never use till urg'd, nor
never break for urging. If thou canst love a
Fellow of this Temper, Kate, whose Face is not
worth Sun-burning, that never looks in his          155
Glass for love of any thing he sees there, let

539

157–  I speak to thee plain Soldier   *both (a) I speak to thee as an*
58        *unvarnished soldier, and (b) I speak to thee in the unadorned*
          *language of a blunt soldier.*

162   uncoin'd   *uncounterfeited, unfeigned.*

163   Constancy   *fidelity and reliability.*

168   Prater   *idle talker.*

169   fall   *fail, grow old and ineffective.*

171   curl'd Pate   *head of curly hair.*

172   wax hollow   *grow vacant and expressionless.*

175   truly   *reliably, consistently.*

179   fairly   *agreeably.*

184   Friend of France   *The King cleverly takes Katherine's mean-*
          *ing and turns it to his own advantage; as the conqueror of*
          *France, he will no longer be "the Enemy of France" but its*
          *master.*

thine Eye be thy Cook. I speak to thee plain
Soldier. If thou canst love me for this, take
me. If not, to say to thee that I shall die is
true; but for thy Love, by the Lord, no. Yet I      160
love thee too. And while thou liv'st, dear
Kate, take a Fellow of plain and uncoin'd
Constancy, for he perforce must do thee right,
because he hath not the gift to woo in other
places. For these Fellows of infinite Tongue,      165
that can rime themselves into Ladies' Favors,
they do always reason themselves out again.
What, a Speaker is but a Prater, a Rime is but
a Ballad; a good Leg will fall, a straight Back
will stoop, a black Beard will turn white, a      170
curl'd Pate will grow bald, a fair Face will
wither, a full Eye will wax hollow; but a good
Heart, Kate, is the Sun and the Moon, or rather
the Sun and not the Moon, for it shines bright
and never changes, but keeps his Course truly.      175
If thou would have such a one, take me; and
take me, take a Soldier; take a Soldier, take
a King. And what say'st thou then to my Love?
Speak, my Fair, and fairly, I pray thee.

KATHERINE   Is it possible dat I sould love de      180
Enemy of Fraunce?

KING   No, it is not possible you should love the
Enemy of France, Kate; but in loving me, you
should love the Friend of France. For I love
France so well that I will not part with a      185
Village of it; I will have it all mine. And
Kate, when France is mine, and I am yours,

193–   Je . . . mienne.  *The King says, in halting French, essen-*
97     *tially what he has said in English: "I, when in possession of*
       *France, and when you have possession of me . . . then thou*
       *art France, and you are mine."*

195    Saint Dennis   *Saint Denis, the patron saint of France.*

196    speed   *help.*

201–3  Sauf . . . parle.   *"Save your honor, the French that you*
       *speak, it is better than the English that I speak."*

205    most truly falsely   *most genuinely and honestly when most*
       *false to the niceties of grammar and usage (of a language not*
       *our own).*

206    at one   *This phrase epitomizes the resolution the King seeks*
       *and wins, and it places the final scene of* Henry V *in some-*
       *thing analogous to the mood that prevails in the conclusions to*
       *Shakespeare's festive comedies. There "at-onement" is all,*
       *and the resulting marriages signify a momentary achievement*
       *of concord that approximates cosmic harmony.*

212    Closet   *private chamber.*

217    cruelly   *The King wittily plays on "mercifully" in line 216.*
       *What he means by "I love thee cruelly" is that he himself is the*
       *victim of Love's lack of mercy.*

218    saving Faith   *a faith that keeps me from surrendering to de-*
       *spair (and thus dying damned).*

then yours is France, and you are mine.

KATHERINE  I cannot tell wat is dat.

KING  No, Kate? I will tell thee in French, which 190
I am sure will hang upon my Tongue like a new-
married Wife about her Husband's Neck, hardly
to be shook off. *Je, quand sur le possession de
Fraunce, et quand vous aves le possession de
moy* (Let me see, what then? Saint Dennis be 195
my speed!), *donc vostre est Fraunce, et vous
estes mienne.* It is as easy for me, Kate, to
conquer the Kingdom as to speak so much more
French. I shall never move thee in French,
unless it be to laugh at me. 200

KATHERINE  *Sauf vostre honneur, le Francois que
vous parleis, il et meilleur que l'Anglois le quel je
parle.*

KING  No faith it's not, Kate: but thy speaking of
my Tongue, and I thine, most truly falsely, 205
must needs be granted to be much at one. But
Kate, doo'st thou understand thus much English?
Canst thou love me?

KATHERINE  I cannot tell.

KING  Can any of your Neighbors tell, Kate? I'll 210
ask them. Come, I know thou lovest me; and at
Night, when you come into your Closet, you'll
question this Gentlewoman about me; and I know,
Kate, you will to her dispraise those parts in
me that you love with your Heart. But good Kate, 215
mock me mercifully, the rather, gentle Princess,
because I love thee cruelly. If ever thou beest
mine, Kate, as I have a saving Faith within me

543

| | |
|---|---|
| 219 | skambling   *scrambling, struggling.* |
| 222 | Saint George   *the patron saint of England.* |
| | compound   *literally, put together.* |
| 223– | that . . . Beard   *Audiences who had watched Shakespeare's* |
| 24 | *three earlier plays about the troubled reign of the weak and* |
| | *ineffectual King Henry VI would find these lines grimly ironic.* |
| 225– | Flower-de-Luce   *fleur-de-lis (lily), the national emblem of* |
| 26 | *France.* |
| 231 | moi'ty   *moiety, half.* |
| 232– | la plus belle . . . Deese   *"the most beautiful Katherine in* |
| 33 | *the world, my very dear and divine Goddess."* |
| 234 | ave fause   *"have false."* |
| 235 | Demoiselle   *maiden.* |
| 240 | Blood   *intuition, feelings.* |
| 241 | untempering   *unpersuasive (literally, "unsoftening").* |
| 242 | beshrew   *curse.* |
| 243 | he was thinking . . . me   *his mind was preoccupied with* |
| | *civil wars when he conceived me.* |
| 244 | stubborn Outside   *rugged exterior.* |
| 249 | do no more Spoil   *both (a) exact no further losses, and (b)* |
| | *ruin no more.* |

tells me thou shalt, I get thee with skambling,
and thou must therefore needs prove a good                         220
Soldier-breeder. Shall not thou and I, between
Saint Dennis and Saint George, compound a Boy,
half French, half English, that shall go to
Constantinople and take the Turk by the Beard?
Shall we not? What say'st thou, my fair Flower-                    225
de-Luce?

KATHERINE    I do not know dat.

KING    No: 'tis hereafter to know, but now to promise.
Do but now promise, Kate, you will endeavor for
your French part of such a Boy; and for my                        230
English moi'ty, take the Word of a King and a
Bachelor. How answer you, *la plus belle Katherine
du Monde, mon tres cher et devin Deese?*

KATHERINE    Your Majesty ave fause French enough
to deceive de most sage Demoiselle dat is en                      235
Fraunce.

KING    Now fie upon my false French! By mine Honor
in true English, I love thee, Kate; by which
Honor I dare not swear thou lovest me, yet my
Blood begins to flatter me that thou doo'st,                      240
notwithstanding the poor and untempering effect
of my Visage. Now beshrew my Father's Ambition:
he was thinking of Civil Wars when he got me,
therefore was I created with a stubborn Outside,
with an aspect of Iron, that when I come to                       245
woo Ladies I fright them. But in faith, Kate,
the elder I wax, the better I shall appear. My
Comfort is that Old Age, that ill layer-up of
Beauty, can do no more Spoil upon my Face.

545

254    avouch  *acknowledge.*

258    withal  *with.*

262    Fellow with  *equal to.*

264    broken Music  *music divided into parts for playing or singing.*

268    de Roy mon Pere  *"de King my father."*

274–
78    Laisse . . . Seigneur.  *"Don't, my Lord; leave off, stop! My faith, I do not wish that you should abase your dignity in kissing the hand of (our Lord!) an unworthy servant. Excuse me, I beg you, my very mighty Lord."*

280–
82    Les Dames . . . Fraunce.  *"The ladies and maids to be kissed before their wedding, it is not the custom in France."*

Thou hast me, if thou hast me, at the worst; 250
and thou shalt wear me, if thou wear me, better
and better. And therefore tell me, most fair
Katherine, will you have me? Put off your
Maiden Blushes, avouch the Thoughts of your
Heart with the Looks of an Empress, take me by 255
the Hand, and say "Harry of England, I am
thine"; which Word thou shalt no sooner bless
mine Ear withal but I will tell thee aloud
"England is thine, Ireland is thine, France is
thine, and Henry Plantagenet is thine"; who, 260
though I speak it before his Face, if he be
not Fellow with the best King, thou shalt find
the best King of good Fellows. Come, your
Answer in broken Music: for thy Voice is Music,
and thy English broken. Therefore Queen of all, 265
Katherine, break thy Mind to me in broken
English: wilt thou have me?

KATHERINE    Dat is as it shall please *de Roy mon Pere.*

KING    Nay, it will please him well, Kate; it shall
please him, Kate. 270

KATHERINE    Den it sall also content me.

KING    Upon that I kiss your Hand, and I call you my
Queen.

KATHERINE    *Laisse, mon Seigneur, laisse, laisse!*
*Ma foy, je ne veux point que vous abaisse* 275
*vostre grandeur en baisant la main d'une (nostre*
*Seigneur!) indigne Serviteur. Excuse moy, je*
*vous supplie, mon tres puissant Seigneur.*

KING    Then I will kiss your Lips, Kate.

KATHERINE    *Les Dames et Demoiselles pour estre baisee* 280

547

287    entendre bettre que moy   *"understands better than me."*

290    Ouy verayment.   *"Yes, truly."*

291    nice   *quaint, petty, precisely correct.*

293    List   *barrier (such as the confined area, known as the lists, where jousts took place).*

295    that follows our Places   *that follows from (is a consequence of) our positions in society.*

302    they   *Katherine's lips.*

*devant leur nopscese, il n'est pas la costume de*
*Fraunce.*

KING   Madame my Interpreter, what says she?

ALICE   Dat it is not be de Fashion pour le Ladies of
France—I cannot tell wat is *baiser* en Anglish.         285

KING   To kiss.

ALICE   Your Majesty *entendre* bettre *que moy.*

KING   It is not a fashion for the Maids in Fraunce
to kiss before they are married, would she say?

ALICE   *Ouy verayment.*         290

KING   O Kate, nice Customs cur'sy to great Kings.
Dear Kate, you and I cannot be confin'd within
the weak List of a Country's Fashion. We are
the Makers of Manners, Kate; and the Liberty
that follows our Places stops the Mouth of all         295
Fault-finds, as I will do yours, for upholding
the nice Fashion of your Country in denying me
a Kiss. Therefore patiently, and yielding—

*He kisses her.*

You have Witchcraft in your Lips, Kate. There
is more Eloquence in a Sugar-touch of them         300
than in the Tongue of the French Council; and
they should sooner persuade Harry of England
than a general Petition of Monarchs. Here comes
your Father.

*Enter the French Power, and the English Lords.*

BOURGOGNE   God save your Majesty! My Royal         305
Cousin, teach you our Princess English?

KING   I would have her learn, my fair Cousin, how

549

309    apt    *quick to learn.*

310    Condition    *disposition, manner.*

317    Circle    *Bourgogne plays on the sexual sense of this word. Mercutio indulges in a similar conjuring game with a "Mistress' Circle" as the object in II.i.24 of* Romeo and Juliet.

318–19    Love . . . blind    *The Cupid that Bourgogne would "conjure up" (line 317) is a "hard Condition" (line 323) that maiden "Modesty" (line 321) is not permitted to see.*

324    consign    *agree, consent.*

325    wink    *close their eyes.*

330    consent winking    *either (a) consent with her eyes closed, or (b) consent to closing her eyes.*

331    wink on her to consent    *either (a) close my eyes while looking on her, so that she will feel free to consent, or (b) wink at her knowingly, to encourage her to consent.*

334    Flies at Bartholomew-tide    *Bourgogne refers to Saint Bartholomew's Day, August 24, when flies become sluggish and tame.*

334–35    Blind, though they have their Eyes    *Bourgogne probably means "consenting though they can 'see' what they are doing." But he is probably also playing on "Eyes" (female "circles") and "I's" (upright letters that are "true likenesses" of "a naked blind Boy").*

336–37    abide looking on    *endure being looked at (let alone touched).*

perfectly I love her, and that is good English.

BOURGOGNE   Is she not apt?

KING   Our Tongue is rough, Coz, and my Condition 310
is not smooth: so that having neither the Voice
nor the Heart of Flattery about me, I cannot
so conjure up the Spirit of Love in her that
he will appear in his true Likeness.

BOURGOGNE   Pardon the Frankness of my Mirth if I 315
answer you for that. If you would conjure in
her, you must make a Circle: if conjure up
Love in her in his true Likeness, he must
appear naked and blind. Can you blame her then,
being a Maid yet ros'd over with the Virgin 320
Crimson of Modesty, if she deny the appearance
of a naked blind Boy in her naked seeing Self?
It were, my Lord, a hard Condition for a Maid
to consign to.

KING   Yet they do wink and yield, as Love is blind 325
and enforces.

BOURGOGNE   They are then excus'd, my Lord, when
they see not what they do.

KING   Then, good my Lord, teach your Cousin to
consent winking. 330

BOURGOGNE   I will wink on her to consent, my Lord,
if you will teach her to know my Meaning. For
Maids well summer'd and warm kept are like
Flies at Bartholomew-tide—Blind, though they
have their Eyes—and then they will endure 335
handling which before would not abide looking
on.

KING   This Moral ties me over to Time and a hot

551

340 in the latter End *The King plays on at least three senses of this phrase: (a) seasonal (at the end of a "hot Summer"), (b) anatomical (in the "tail"), and (c) sexual (at the end of a "Time" of wooing).*

347 perspectively *The French King refers to "perspectives," paintings in which one saw one image (here "the Cities") while looking at the canvas straight on, and another ("a Maid") while viewing it from an angle (here symbolizing the individual perspective, as opposed to the general, public one).*

349 Maiden Walls *both (a) the unbreached walls of French cities that have never been invaded, and (b) the unbroken hymen of a virgin maid.*

354–56 so the Maid . . . my Will *thus the maiden who was a potential impediment to my getting my wish (because of my condition that she be granted to me along with the French crown) will now be the "Way" (means) to my getting my "Will" (France as well as she). In view of the previous sexual wordplay, the King is undoubtedly punning on "Will" here as a word not only for sexual desire but also for the genitalia of both genders. Shakespeare plays on the various meanings of "Will" in Sonnets 135 and 136.*

361 According . . . Natures *in accordance with the strict terms proposed. It is conceivable that even this phrase involves a phallic play on* firm.

366–70 Nostre . . . Franciae *The French and Latin phrases both mean "Our very dear son, Henry, King of England, Heir of France."*

Summer; and so I shall catch the Fly, your
Cousin, in the latter End, and she must be                    340
Blind too.

BOURGOGNE   As Love is, my Lord, before it loves.

KING   It is so; and you may, some of you, thank
Love for my Blindness, who cannot see many a
fair French City for one fair French Maid that    345
stands in my Way.

FRANCE   Yes, my Lord, you see them perspectively:
the Cities turn'd into a Maid. For they are
all girdled with Maiden Walls, that War hath
never ent'red.                                                             350

KING   Shall Kate be my Wife?

FRANCE   So please you.

KING   I am content, so the Maiden Cities you talk
of may wait on her: so the Maid that stood in
the Way for my Wish shall show me the Way to   355
my Will.

FRANCE   We have consented to all Terms of Reason.

KING   Is't so, my Lords of England?

WESTMERLAND   The King hath granted ev'ry Article:
His Daughter first; and in sequel All,                         360
According to their firm proposed Natures.

EXETER   Only he hath not yet subscribed this: where
your Majesty demands "That the King of France,
having any occasion to write for matter of
Grant, shall name your Highness in this Form,    365
and with this Addition, in French, *Nostre tres
cher Fils Henry Roy d'Angleterre, Heritiere de
Fraunce;* and thus in Latin, *Praeclarissimus
filius noster Henricus, Rex Angliae et Heres*

553

372    **your Request . . . pass** *What the King of France means, of course, is that King Henry's marriage to Princess Katherine will make such a declaration unnecessary. The English King will be his real son-in-law rather than his legal "son" in terms of the negotiated treaty. One effect of the marriage is to strengthen the legitimacy of the lines of succession in both countries.*

376–77    **from her Blood raise up / Issue** *both (a) from her bloodline conceive offspring, and (b) from her ardor "raise up" the male "Issue" (seed) that will effect that consummation so devoutly to be wished.*

380    **Conjunction** *union; literally, coming together.*

381    **Neighborhood** *neighborliness, loving fellowship.*

389    **being two, are one in Love** *This formulation derives ultimately from Genesis 2:24, "There shall a man leave his father and his mother, and shall cleave unto his wife: and they shall be one flesh."*

391    **ill Office** *wrongdoing, dereliction of duty.*
        **Jealousy** *suspicion, mistrust.*

393    **Pation** *paction; compact, agreement.*

394    **their incorp'rate League** *their physical alliance. Here "incorp'rate" is used both literally (to describe a union of two bodies into "one flesh") and symbolically (to describe a union of two kingdoms and two peoples). The King's "two bodies" (one his individual, physical body; the other his symbolic, collective identity as the embodiment of his kingdom) become merged as "England" marries "France."*

554

*Franciae.*

FRANCE   Nor this I have not, Brother, so denied,
But your Request shall make me let it pass.

KING   I pray you then, in Love and dear Alliance,
Let that one Article rank with the rest,
And thereupon give me your Daughter.       375

FRANCE   Take her, fair Son, and from her Blood
   raise up
Issue to me, that the contending Kingdoms
Of France and England, whose very Shores look
   pale
With envy of each other's Happiness,
May cease their Hatred; and this dear
   Conjunction       380
Plant Neighborhood and Christian-like Accord
In their sweet Bosoms; that never War advance
His bleeding Sword 'twixt England and fair
   France.

LORDS   Amen.

KING   Now welcome, Kate. —And bear me witness all,   385
That here I kiss her as my Sov'reign Queen.
                       *Flourish.*

QUEEN   God, the best Maker of all Marriages,
Combine your Hearts in one, your Realms in one:
As Man and Wife, being two, are one in Love,
So be there 'twixt your Kingdoms such a
   Spousal,       390
That never may ill Office, or fell Jealousy,
Which troubles oft the Bed of blessed Marriage,
Thrust in between the Pation of these Kingdoms
To make divorce of their incorp'rate League:

397 Amen! *So be it.*

399– we'll . . . Leagues *To ensure the solidity of the alliance,*
400 *the King will have all the French nobility, beginning with*
 *Burgundy (the usual English spelling and pronunciation of*
 *Bourgogne), take an oath of fealty to him and his new Queen.*

S.D. Sennet *a trumpet fanfare.*

That English may as French, French Englishmen,          395
Receive each other. God speak this Amen!

ALL   Amen!

KING   Prepare we for our Marriage: on which Day,
My Lord of Burgundy, we'll take your Oath
And all the Peers', for surety of our Leagues.          400
Then shall I swear to Kate, and you to me,
And may our Oaths well kept and prosp'rous be.

*Sennet. Exeunt.*

EPILOGUE   *The Chorus puts in a final appearance to draw the story to a fitting close. Given its theme, it is appropriate that the Epilogue is in the form of a Shakespearean sonnet. Shakespeare had employed this device earlier in the Choruses of* Romeo and Juliet.

1   rough and all-unable   *crude and inadequate.*

2   bending   *This word probably has at least three meanings in this context: (a) bending over his writing-desk with his pen, (b) stooping under the weight of the play's mighty subject matter, and (c) humbly bowing in hope of receiving the audience's approval.*

3   In little Room   *There are probably at least three relevant implications here: (a) in the author's study (and in the mind there confined), (b) in a brief dramatic vehicle (the play we have just seen or read), and (c) in a small theatre space (the "Wooden O" referred to in the Prologue).*

4   Mangling by Starts   *breaking up into a series of brief starts and stops (episodes, scenes) a complex period of uninterrupted history.*

9   Sixt   *sixth. Similarly "fift" is the normal spelling in the Folio printing of* The Life of Henry the Fift.
    in Infant Bands   *while still in swaddling clothes.*

13   Which oft our Stage hath shown   *a reference to Shakespeare's three earlier plays on* Henry VI.
    for their sake   *probably "for the sake of the earlier plays."*

14   let . . . take   *accept this play (and perhaps this epilogue).*

# Epilogue

*Enter Chorus.*

CHORUS    Thus far with rough and all-unable Pen,
Our bending Author hath pursu'd the Story,
In little Room confining mighty Men,
Mangling by Starts the full Course of their Glory.
Small Time, but in that Small most greatly liv'd    5
This Star of England. Fortune made his Sword,
By which the World's best Garden he achieved,
And of it left his Son Imperial Lord.
Henry the Sixt, in Infant Bands crown'd King
Of France and England, did this King succeed,    10
Whose State so many had the Managing
That they lost France, and made his England bleed,
Which oft our Stage hath shown; and for their
    sake,
In your fair Minds let this Acceptance take.    *Exit.*

FINIS

559